Relating through Prayer

EARLY CHRISTIANITY IN THE CONTEXT OF ANTIQUITY

Edited by Anders-Christian Jacobsen,
Christine Shepardson and Jörg Ulrich

Volume 21

Zu Qualitätssicherung und Peer Review der vorliegenden Publikation

Die Qualität der in dieser Reihe erscheinenden Arbeiten wird vor der Publikation durch die Herausgeber der Reihe sowie durch Mitglieder des Wissenschaftlichen Beirates geprüft.

Notes on the quality assurance and peer review of this publication

Prior to publication, the quality of the work published in this series is reviewed by the editors of the series and by members of the academic advisory board.

Maria Louise Munkholt Christensen

Relating through Prayer

Identity Formation in Early Christianity

PETER LANG

Bibliographic Information published by the Deutsche Nationalbibliothek
The Deutsche Nationalbibliothek lists this publication in the Deutsche National-
bibliografie; detailed bibliographic data is available in the internet at
http://dnb.d-nb.de.

Library of Congress Cataloging-in-Publication Data
A CIP catalog record for this book has been applied for at the Library
of Congress.

ISSN 1862-197X
ISBN 978-3-631-67093-4 (Print)
E-ISBN 978-3-653-06345-5 (E-PDF)
E-ISBN 978-3-631-71055-5 (EPUB)
E-ISBN 978-3-631-71056-2 (MOBI)
DOI 10.3726/978-3-653-06345-5

© Peter Lang GmbH
Internationaler Verlag der Wissenschaften
Berlin 2019
All rights reserved.

Peter Lang – Berlin · Bern · Bruxelles · New York ·
Oxford · Warszawa · Wien

This publication has been peer reviewed.

www.peterlang.com

Foreword and Acknowledgments

This book is a slightly revised version of my PhD Dissertation which I defended at Aarhus University on 28 August 2015. The defence was the culmination of my theological education at Aarhus University. I am grateful to many people who have patiently supported me in the process of writing and publishing my doctoral dissertation: I am very grateful to my PhD supervisor Prof. Dr. Anders-Christian Jacobsen for his help and support throughout my PhD studies. I thank the members of my assessment committee at the PhD defence, Associate Prof. Dr. Jakob Engberg, Associate Prof. Dr. Brouria Bitton-Ashkelony and Prof. Dr. Lorenzo Perrone. Moreover, I thank my current employer, Prof. Dr. Peter Gemeinhardt, at the Georg-August-Universität Göttingen, for his support, and I thank his skilful assistant Johanna Jürgens who has helped me finish editing parts of the manuscript. Remaining mistakes are my responsibility.

I also wish to show my gratitude towards many good colleagues and friends who made my time as a PhD student in Aarhus particularly enriching. I thank Sasja E. Mathiasen Stopa, Lone Slot Nielsen, Uffe Holmsgaard Eriksen, Erin Wright, Søren S. Jensen, Nicholas Marshall, Lea Wierød Borčak, Anne Linde Førgaard, Karen Olsen, Monica Louise E. Jensen, Sophie-Lønne R. Hundebøll, Nanna Munk Petersen and Laura Munk Petersen. I thank my colleagues and friends in Göttingen and the new friends that I have met in the ecumenical movement. Many more have deserved to be mentioned. In particular, I wish to thank my parents, my mother Kirsten Munkholt and my father Agner Christensen, for all their love, help and faith in me. I regret that my father will not see the published book, but I am thankful that he got to read the dissertation. I thank my brother, Jakob Munkholt Christensen, for all his precious help and support. I dedicate this work to my brother as a small token of gratitude.

The idea to study the theme of prayer originally derived from an interest in prayer in the modern world and a perplexity about prayer. Prayer is a phenomenon so immensely human and Christian, but still so difficult to grasp or study. The poet Leonard Cohen commented on his poetical collection of prayers, *Book of Mercy*, and expressed an ambiguity about prayer: "Now I find it's the toughest book to talk about. Because it is prayer. One feels a little shy about the whole thing. We're such a hip age. Nobody wants to affirm those realities. [...] Sophistication is the current style. We're growing rich. Our cities are getting big. Our kids are going to university. It's appropriate for the times. But the practice of religion, the gathering of people to articulate the burden of their predicament, those things are important, too."[1]

Göttingen, August 2018.

---

1   A. Twigg, *Strong Voices: Conversations with Fifty Canadian Authors*, Madeira Park 1988, 291.

Contents

Part II: Textual Analysis

3 The relationship established with God in prayer 115

Part III: Final Conclusion, Considerations and Perspectives

Introduction

Prayer was ubiquitous in antiquity, and it is hard to find an early Christian text with no reference to prayer at all. Christian ideas of prayer developed under heavy influence from Judaism and Greco-Roman religion and philosophy. This study examines how prayer was understood in early Christian theology, and what function prayer had in the life of the early Christian congregations. The aim is to shed light on the effect of prayer on Christian identity formation in ante-Nicene Christianity and point to prayer as a multifaceted phenomenon that aligned and linked individual and collective Christian identity. Concrete prayer practice is allusive, but the link made between prayer and Christian life is available to us in early Christian texts.

In some studies on early Christianity, prayer is mentioned as a feature that had an important and formative effect on Christians and their communities. This is often taken as something more or less self-evident, for instance when Karen King, in a discussion of Gnostic ethics, notes *en passant* that prayer was one of the means by which people of antiquity tried to reach freedom from passions and demonic influences, as well as to achieve spiritual development.[2] The present study sets out to investigate this link between prayer and being Christian. It investigates the historical effects of the Christian theology and instructions of prayer. The primary sources from which conclusions will be deferred are instructive, normative and theological in character. It is the four earliest treatises on prayer in Christian history, written by Clement of Alexandria, Origen, Tertullian and Cyprian, respectively, in the beginning of the third century. Three of these commentaries centre on the Lord's Prayer which frequently and unsurprisingly is held up as the quintessential Christian prayer.

---

2   K. L. King, *What is Gnosticism?* Cambridge 2005, 208. See also M.C. Kiley (ed.), *Prayer from Alexander to Constantine. A Critical Anthology*, London 1997, 251: "'Prayer is a primary means of socializing oneself into and participating in such an order of existence'. Hence, in the development of early Christianity, prayer language was an especially powerful tool for the maintenance of a developing Christian self-identity."

This study on prayer in the early church is a historical study of Christian theology and piety. It arose from a range of questions of both a theological and historical nature and from an interest in learning how Christian piety and practice contributed to attracting people to Christianity. My hypothesis is that the Christian instructions regarding prayer and the theology of prayer was a fundamental part of Christian piety and practice and a decisive factor in the spread of Christianity. I aim at unfolding the theologies of prayer carefully, because I agree with John Behr that a study on Christianity in antiquity that does not take an interest in theology is "a map drawn without regard for the real topography."[3] Moreover, I make use of modern sociological theory and thereby follow a trend that has manifested itself in studies on early Christianity – a shift away from purely theological perspectives on the ancient material towards sociological, textual and historical approaches.[4] Since the subject of this study is prayer, I find it justifiable to combine theological, historical and sociological approaches, because prayer, even personal prayer, was a social activity in the early church. The relational character of prayer is expressed by the numerous prepositions used in relation with prayer in the sources under consideration: It matters whom the Christians prayed "to," "through," "in," "for," "with" and "in the name of."[5] The sociological considerations are used to clarifying the reciprocal relationship that appears to have existed in the early Christian communities – between theology and practice and between the congregation and the individual. Still, of course, as already the late antique Neoplatonic philosopher Iamblicus expressed in regard to prayer: "In fact, it is a worthy

---

3   J. Behr, *Asceticism and Anthropology in Irenaeus and Clement*, Oxford 2000, 14. However, back in 1986 A. Cameron noted: "It seems to be more acceptable at the moment for an ancient historian to appeal to social or economic factors than to the realm of ideas" (A. Cameron, *Redrawing the Map. Early Christian Territory after Foucault*, in: JRS 76 (1986), 266).

4   E. Iricinschi/H.M. Zellentin (eds.), *Heresy and Identity in Late Antiquity*, TSAJ, Tübingen 2008, 7.

5   I am aware that not all of these are prepositional phrases in the original languages; "in the Spirit" is for instance expressed with an instrumental dative, πνεύματι, in Or. or. e.g 2,5 (Koetschau); and with an instrumental ablative "spiritu" in Tert. Or., e.g. 28 (Schleyer).

subject of study in itself"[6], and the three fundamental chapters of the current volume, *Chapters 3 to 5*, are an analysis of the sources on prayer.

A remark of caution needs to be made from the outset since the study takes up the theme of identity. The current focus on identity in historical research is to some extent spurred by a contemporary interest in and search for identity as such in the post-modern period. The modern focus on events and phenomena forming identity in the past merge with a contemporary need for a clearly outlined identity in the present. The historian must be careful not to carve out the historical remnants so that they fit into his or her own identity building. However, humans of course need the past to navigate in the present, and as Michel Foucault wrote: "It is good to have nostalgia towards some periods on the condition that it's a way to have a thoughtful and positive relation to your own present."[7] Consequently, in this study I have been open to the possibilities that a new perspective on history provides, and I have tried to avoid the pitfall of using history for the purpose of modern identity politics. I am not a sociologist, and I do not claim that my use of the theories on identity and self is original. However, the application of these modern ideas on historical material on prayer is part of a novel discourse.[8]

The dissertation is divided into three main parts. Part I draws the theoretical and historical frame around the study and consists of two chapters: *Chapter 1* presents explorations of identity theories and provides literary surveys of scholarship on relevant themes: prayer, self and identity in antiquity. *Chapter 2* sets the historical stage, as it contains a context analysis and a presentation of the authors under investigation, as well as of prayers in their works, and of the treatises to be investigated. Part II is the textual analysis of the four treatises under investigation. This part is divided into three chapters, each of which deals with an aspect of the socializing character of Christian prayer. *Chapter 3* focuses on how prayer established a relationship between the individual and God. *Chapter 4* deals with other social relations that were reinforced by prayer in direct and indirect ways.

---

6   Iamblic. Myst. V. 26. (Clarke/Dillon/Hershbell).
7   M. Foucault, *Technologies of the Self*, in: L.H. Martin et al. (eds.), *Technologies of the Self. A Seminar with Michel Foucault*, Amherst 1988, 12.
8   For a literary survey, see below paragraph 1.6.

Finally, *Chapter 5* examines how the individual Christian was expected to connect with his/her own "self" in prayer.[9] The final Part III of this study consists of final considerations, conclusions and perspectives. Here the textual analyses are summed up, and a conclusion is drawn about the influence of prayer on the establishment and rise of Christianity within the Roman Empire. We shall see that, among Christians in different parts of the Roman Empire, prayer was envisioned as a life-transforming activity, and as such it was relevant for, what we nowadays term, Christian identity.

---

9   The structure of the work thus reflects the main kinds of connections established in prayer, cf. K.L. Ladd/B. Spilka, *Inward, Outward, and Upward: Cognitive Aspects of Prayer* in: JSSR 41, 3 (2002), 475-484.

Part I: Setting the Stage

1 Theory, method and previous scholarship

This chapter presents the identity theories and theories on the formation of self which constitute the frame of the present study. Many of the theoretical assumptions that will be used are drawn from a certain vein of sociological/philosophical studies called "Symbolic Interactionism" or from the French philosopher Michel Foucault. This delimitation is made in order not to be carried away by the huge amount of writings on self and identity, and also because "symbolic interactionism" is especially relevant when the theme is prayer, since prayer is a symbol used in the social world. In order to clarify what is meant by "prayer," "self," "identity" and "identity formation" in the present study, the immediately following paragraphs are dedicated to definitions and theories.

1.1 "Prayer" – avoiding a rigid definition

It makes sense to open a study on prayer with a definition of prayer. This is, however, difficult because it is impossible to deduce just one definition of prayer from the source material under investigation. Prayer is a "Sammelgattung,"[10] and also among Christian thinkers in the early church, prayer was comprehended in a very broad fashion. Origen's treatise, *Perì Euchês,* testifies to such a multifaceted perception of prayer since in this text alone, one finds several ideas of what prayer is: Origen envisions prayer in a concrete and verbal sense in accord with Paul as consisting of "supplication, intercession, pleas and thanksgivings" (1 Tim 2:1);[11] furthermore, Origen understands prayer as something purely internal that has to do with paying complete attention to God;[12] and moreover, Origen also defines prayer broadly as life itself when lived in a certain way.[13] In

---

10 Klaus Berger's reflection, quoted in Ostmeyer, *Kommunikation mit Gott und Christus: Sprache und Theologie des Gebetes im Neuen Testament,* Tübingen 2006, 13. For more on the varied meanings of prayer, see E. Severus, *Gebet I,* in: T. Klauser (ed.), RAC 8, Stuttgart 1972.
11 Or. or. 14.2. (Koetschau; tr. Stewart-Sykes).
12 Id. 20.2.
13 E.g. Or. or. 12.2; 22.5. (Koetschau; tr. Stewart-Sykes).

Origen's treatise, we also find prayer understood as contemplation and conversation, as he writes that, ideally, the one who is praying "contemplate (ἐννοεῖν) God alone, and hold modest and solemn converse (ὁμιλεῖν) with the one who hears them."[14] The idea of prayer as conversation with God is an essential aspect of the Christian idea of prayer. We find prayer directly referred to as "conversation" or "converse" (ὁμιλία) in some Christian writings, and the idea is indirectly present in even more.[15] Clement of Alexandria, who precedes Origen, writes in *Stromateis* 7,39: "Prayer, then, to speak somewhat boldly, is converse with God (ὁμιλία πρὸς τὸν θεὸν ἡ εὐχή·)." As we shall see, according to the early Christian theologians, "prayer" also occasionally referred to a mental ascension (ἀνάβασις) to God or "prayer" could be almost synonymous with contemplation (θεωρία) of God. These ideas are mostly developed in the Greek theological tradition, but also in the Western tradition, we find a broad understanding of what prayer is and does.[16] Often, it is not obvious whether the authors who wrote about prayer promoted individual or collective prayer. At one point, Cyprian refers to Christian prayer (*oratio*) as "common" (*publica*) and "collective" (*communis*) and express that the content of Christian prayer should be focused on the needs of others.[17] There is a tendency that collective and liturgical prayers are seen as most beneficial[18] among the

---

14 Or. or. 9.2. See also Clem. Strom. 7.7.35 (Hort/Mayor) for the consideration that praying to God is like talking to a wise man (cf. Or. or. 8.2 (Koetschau; tr. Stewart-Sykes), treated below in paragraph "3.1.1.3. God as Father and Friend").

15 Clem. Strom. 7.7.39 (Hort/Mayor); Evag. *On Prayer* 3 (Migne; tr. Sinckewicz): "Prayer is a communion of the mind with God (Η προσευχὴ, ὁμιλία ἐστὶ νοῦ πρὸς Θεόν)"; Gr.Nyss. or. dom. 1 (Oehler): "prayer is a conversation (ὁμιλία) with God and a contemplation (θεωρία) of invisibility realities."; the term is also used by Max.Tyr. in Dissertationes 5.8 (Trapp): "But you believe the philosopher's prayer to be a request for what he does not have, whereas in my opinion it is a conversation (ὁμιλίαν) or discussion (διάλεκτον) with the gods about what he does have, and a demonstration of his virtue."

16 Méhat focuses on ὁμιλία and ἀνάβασις as understandings of prayer in the Christian Greek tradition (Méhat, *Sur deux définitions de la prière*, in G. Dorival/A. Le Boulluec (eds.), *Origeniana Sexta, Louvain* 1995, 115–120).

17 Cypr. Dom. orat. 8 (Réveillaud; tr. Stewart-Sykes).

18 Regarding collective prayer, see below paragraph 4.3.1.

early Christian authors investigated in the following, but that does not take away the responsibility of each individual Christian to pray at appointed times and "always."[19] "Prayer" is thus both an individual and collective address to God related to manifold reflections regarding the appropriate content of praise, thanksgiving, confession and petition. A sharp distinction between individual and collective or liturgical prayer is not made in the treatises; we shall return to this blurring of the lines between individual and collective prayer when dealing with the French sociologist M. Mauss' understanding of private prayer as a social act. Exactly in the blurring of the lines between what is reckoned as individual and collective lies a potential for identity formation of a comprehensive kind.

Modern studies are aware of the difficulty in narrowing down the subject of prayer without losing its essence. In *Encyclopedia of Religion*, Sam Gill describes "prayer" as text, act and subject,[20] and he defines the act of praying poetically by stating that "prayer is one means by which [the] gap of createdness is overcome, if but momentarily."[21] Another broad definition is given by Friedrich Heiler:

> "Das Gebet ist ... eine lebendige Beziehung des Menschen zu Gott, ein Fühlungnehmen, eine Zuflucht, eine unmittelbare Berührung, ein innerer Kontakt, ein persönliches Verhältnis, ein wechselseitiger Austausch, eine Zwiesprache, ein Umgang, ein Verkehr, eine Gemeinschaft, eine Vereinigung zwischen einem Ich und Du."[22]

In the contemporary publication *Early Christian Prayer and Identity formation* a working definition of prayer is as follows:

> "Prayer is a verbal and nonverbal communication with God, proceeding from a relationship of trust. This act of communication usually has a purpose, either in seeking divine assistance, guidance, or some kind of intervention. Since this act

---

19 Regarding ceaseless prayer and times of prayer, see below paragraphs 3.2.3. and 3.2.5.3.

20 S. Gill, *Prayer*, in: L. Jones (ed.), *Encyclopedia of Religion*, Detroit 2005, 7367–72.

21 Id.

22 F. Heiler, *Das Gebet. Eine religionsgeschichtliche und religionspsychologische Untersuchung*, München 1920, 490.

of communication is integrated in a relationship, prayer includes gratitude, adoration and praises as well."[23]

In *Theologische Realenzyklopädie*, Carl Heinz Ratschow writes that prayer
is a personal and dialogical approach: "die vornehmlich "personhafte",
dialogische Zuwendung eines Menschen zu Gott."[24] This latter definition
fits the ancient idea of prayer as "conversation" with God.

Since the definition of prayer needs to be broad to encompass the com-
plexities of the early Christian sources, this study sets out with an understanding of prayer as "conversation" or "communing" with God. This
definition deliberately gives rise to several associations, such as "communicating with," "being in touch with" and "feeling close to."[25] This communication can be more or less formalized, and it can be undertaken by an
individual alone, as well as collectively by a group; in an unformal setting
as well as part of formal liturgical actions. Although, prayer thus can refer
to quite different phenomena and acts, the basic idea of communing with
God holds the different aspects of prayer together within an early Christian
mind-set.

Also within "symbolic interactionism," the sociological stream of
thought to which I shall shortly make recourse, prayer is understood in a
rather broad fashion. In *The Handbook of Symbolic Interactionism*, prayer
is described as "a transcendent symbol"[26], because prayer points beyond
itself to a transcendent "reality." One could argue that prayer is a symbol
on more levels than one since both the physical gestures connected to prayer
and the wording of prayer are symbolic and point beyond their apparent
meaning. Symbolic interactionism stresses the importance of symbols in
human interaction, and prayer can be seen as one such symbol that affects
human life on more levels: Prayer is a way of communicating with both

---

23 R. Hvalvik/K.O. Sandnes (eds.), *Early Christian Prayer and Identity Formation*,
    Tübingen 2014, 4.
24 C.H. Ratschow, *Gebet I. Religionsgeschichtlich*, in: TRE 12 (1984), 32.
25 In her study on prayer in the works of Philo, Leonhardt defines prayer broadly
    as "communication with God" (J. Leonhardt, *Jewish Worship in Philo of
    Alexandria*, Tübingen 2001, 101).
26 L.T.Reynolds/N.J. Herman-Kinney (eds.), *Handbook of Symbolic Interactionism*,
    Walnut Creek, CA 2003, 626.

God, with other human beings and with oneself. Thus, prayer can be understood as part of human interaction with God, but also as communication among human beings or even as communication internally in the individual human being who engages in the act of praying. It is these different aspects of prayer that are dealt with in the following.

1.2 Identifying identity in general[27] – it's all "the same"

The word identity is derived from the Latin pronoun *idem*, meaning "the same." The word, identity, began to be used in learned Latin in the renaissance period, and it found its way into English language only in the late sixteenth century. In the beginning, the word was used in logic, as is illustrated by G.W. Leibniz' logical principle from the seventeenth century: *principium identitatis indiscernibilium*,[28] i.e. the principle of the identity of the indiscernible. Leibniz' principle entails that if the same qualities are attached to given entities, then these entities are, in fact, the same (if x = y, then y = x). This idea of "sameness" is also a constituting element in the much later psychological and sociological identity theories, because identity inherently has to do with the fact that people and groups, although constantly developing, are perceived and perceive themselves as being (more or less) "the same" over a span of time. In fact, human beings are dependent on a degree of continuity and stableness, both regarding themselves and the world around them. The sociologist Anthony Giddens conceptualizes this basic need for stability when he talks about "ontological security" that comes with stable relations and a stable self-identity.[29] The very "courage to be," that is known from the theology of Paul Tillich, arises, according to Giddens, from this "ontological security."[30] "Identity" is thus no mere detail – in theology or life.

---

27 The title of this paragraph is inspired by: P. Gleason, *Identifying Identity. A Semantic History*, in: The Journal of American History, 69/4 (1983).

28 "Princippet om identiske størrelsers uskelnelighed," *Filosofisk Leksikon*, identitet (K. Michelsen et al., *Filosofisk Leksikon*, København 2008).

29 A. Giddens, *Modernity and Self-Identity. Self and Society in the Late Modern Age*, Stanford 1991, 38.

30 Id.

For a long time, the concept of identity did not take on psychological or sociological connotations. In antiquity and medieval times, the idea that every human being has an individual character was more likely explained by reference to an individual's "soul," "spirit" or "character." The fact is that "our current notion of 'identity' is historically fairly recent. Identity is a modern concept and not something that people have eternally needed or sought as such. If they were trying to establish, defend, or protect their identities, they thought about what they were doing in different terms."[31] Not until modernity, did the empiricist philosophers start to question the idea of an integrated self or a soul detached from the body. That happened in the 17th century, when for instance John Locke wrote his *Essay concerning Human Understanding.* According to Locke, the identity of a human being consists in its rational consciousness – the rationality is the only stable feature in the individual.[32] Thus the soul started losing conceptual terrain from the early modern period, and this eventually left room for another way to talk about how humans, whether acting alone or collectively, come into being and constitute themselves.

In the 1940s, the American developmental psychologist, Erik H. Erikson, introduced the term identity into the social sciences. Erikson employed the term identity to describe the outcome of the personal development that takes place during childhood and adolescence. From Erikson's perspective, identity is something like a personal "kernel" developed during the first decades of life. However, according to the identity studies of the social sciences that were developed in the following decades, not even a "kernel" of identity is considered stable in human life.[33] The main characteristic of

---

31 E.A. Clark, *History, Theory, Text. Historians and the Linguistic Turn,* Cambridge 2004, 10.

32 "For since consciousness always accompanies thinking and it is that, that makes everyone to be, what he calls self; and thereby distinguishes himself from all other thinking things, in this alone consists personal Identity i.e. the sameness of rational being." (P. Phemister (ed.), *John Locke. An Essay Concerning Human Understanding* 1690, Oxford 2008).

33 P. Stachel, *Identität. Genese, Inflation und Probleme eines für die zeitgenös- sischen Sozial- und Kulturwissenschaften zentralen Begriffs,* in: AKuG 87/2 (2005), 404.

the modern scientific usage of "identity" is that it is something changeable, processual and socially constructed. Identity is something that constantly evolves and is affected by the social circumstances that a person encounters.[34] Human beings constantly adjust their identity, and identity formation is a never-ending process.

Identity is not only affected by the individual, but also by the social context of the individual and the groups to which he/she belongs. For this reason, identity theories distinguish between personal identity, role identity, social identity, collective identity and group-identity.[35] Social identity and collective identity have to do with the overall categories to which an individual belongs, e.g. religious affiliation, whereas the personal identity is more distinct and refers to how the individual thinks of and defines him-/herself. However, the social and personal aspects of identity are interdependent. Many theories have been proposed about identity formation, and the following presentation will predominantly deal with identity as understood within the way of thought of "symbolic interactionism."[36]

---

34 E.g. F. Barth, *Ethnic Groups and Boundaries. The Social Organization of Cultural Difference*, London 1969; R. Jenkins, *Rethinking Ethnicity, Arguments and Explorations*. Thousand Oaks 1997.

35 Burke and Stets, *Identity Theory and Social Identity Theory*, Social Psychology Quarterly
63/3 (2000), 224–237.

36 In the theological field of practical theology, the identity concept that was developed by Erik H. Erikson and in the wake of George Herbert Mead has been criticized for the inherent assumption that human "identity" progressively develops. The German theologian Henning Luther has pointed to the danger of a misunderstanding concerning identity when the identity formation is seen as something that potentially can lead to a harmonious goal. Henning Luther criticizes the idea of a perfect, integrated or constant identity. Instead, he suggests that one should rather perceive human life and identity as fragmentary. Even if Henning Luther admits himself that his critique is mostly directed at a popular misunderstanding of the two mentioned streams of thought, his comments are helpful in pointing to and underlining the fragmentary character of identity (H. Luther, "Identität und Fragment," *Religion und Alltag*, Stuttgart 1992, 160-182).

1.3 Self and identity[37]

1.3.1 Selves and symbols

Symbolic interactionism evolved in the United States in the first decades of the 20th century. Its founding father was George Herbert Mead (1863–1931) who primarily taught philosophy, but made big contributions to the social sciences as well. He is considered as a founding father of social psychology and as a forerunner of "social constructivism." Mead held positions first at University of Michigan and later at University of Chicago where he worked together with other scholars that shaped symbolic interactionism, e.g. the sociologist Herbert Blumer who coined the term *symbolic interactionism*. As noted in the previous section, the concept "identity" first came into use in the social sciences well into the 20th century. In accordance with this, Mead did not use the term "identity" himself, but his younger followers easily introduced the concept of "identity" into the framework of "symbolic interactionism."

Mead advanced the theory that society is constantly evolving through *interaction*. Mead's theory is that human beings are born without selves, but selves develop as people interact. The self is developed through an inner dialogue between the "I" and the "me," where the "me" reflects the inter-nalized "voice" of the social groups in which the individual is involved. Mead called this internalized "voice" of "the social group" "the generalized other," and he held that it utters within us the values, attitudes, and beliefs of society. According to Mead, human beings are able to see themselves through the eyes of "the generalized other." This entails that we as human beings can become objects to ourselves, revaluate our understandings and act accordingly.[38] Mead phrases it:

---

37 J.D. Baldwin, *George Herbert Mead. A Unifying Theory for Sociology*, New York 1986; J.M. Charon, *Symbolic Interactionism*, London 2007; G.H. Mead, *Mind, Self & Society. From a standpoint of a social behaviorist*, C.W. Morris (ed.), Chicago 1967; Reynolds/Herman-Kinney, 2003; S. Stryker, *From Mead to a Structural Symbolic Interactionism and Beyond*, in: Annual Review of Sociology 34 (2008).

38 Mead's emphasis on the reflexivity of the "self" resembles Søren Kierkegaard's utterance (by the pseudonym Anti-Climacus): "But what is the self? The self is a relation which relates itself to its own self, or it is that in the relation [which accounts for it] that the relation relates itself to its own self; the self is not the

"The self is something which has a development: it is not initially there at birth but arises in the process of social experience and activity, that is, develops in the given individual as a result of his relations to that process as a whole and to other individuals within that process."[39]

Although Mead in his career only sketched the development of the "self," he also offered the dictum that "self mirrors society."[40] This idea entails that "intrapersonal, interpersonal, and intergroup relations share many essential common structural and processual features."[41] Because of this we can approach not only individuals, but also groups, such as the early Christian congregations from a symbolic interactionist approach. This fits with a conclusion by two other influential sociologists, Peter Bergman and Thomas Luckmann, who hold that: "Identity is a phenomenon that emerges from the dialectic between individual and society."[42] If this holds true, also Christian identity emerges from the encounter between the individual Christian, who is historically most often unknown to us, and the congregation and further society.

1.3.2 Identity within symbolic interactionism

A single coherent definition of identity does not exist, not even within symbolic interactionism.[43] Contrary, several theories of identity have been developed, e.g. by Sheldon Stryker, George J. McCall, J.L. Simmons and Peter Burke.[44] However, a consensus seems to exist that identity is used not directly as a synonym for "self"; but as a term that denotes: "self-concept"

---

relation but [consists in the fact] that the relation relates itself to its own self." (S. Kierkegaard (ed.), *The Sickness unto Death*, Princeton 1849/1943). For a comparison between Mead and Kierkegaard, see S. Willert, *George Herbert Mead and Sören Kierkegaard as theorists of the self. Paper presented at SAAP*, Annual Conference (Society for the Advancement of American Philosophy), Spokane 2011.

39 Mead, 1967, 135.
40 Stryker, 2008, 19.
41 Reynolds/Herman-Kinney, 2003, 375.
42 Quoted from Hvalvik/Sandnes, 2014, 15.
43 Reynolds/Herman-Kinney, 2003, 367.
44 J.H. Turner, *Contemporary Sociological Theory*, Thousand Oakes, CA 2013, 331-55; Chapter 16: "Symbolic Interactionist Theories of Identity." Broadly speaking, there are two ways of understanding identity, either as primarily arising in certain situations, termed "situational identity", or as dominated

or "part of the self."[45] In social interaction, each individual activates certain aspects of his or her self in accordance with the context, and such
representations of the self are what we refer to as identities.[46] G.P. Stone
has characterized identity as follows:

> "Almost all writers using the term imply that identity establishes what and where
> the person is in social terms. It is not a substitute word for "self." Instead, when
> one has identity, he is situated – that is, cast in the shape of a social object by the
> acknowledgement of his participation or membership in social relations. One's
> identity is established when others place him as a social object by assigning him
> the same words of identity that he appropriates for himself or announces. It is
> in the coincidence of placements and announcements that identity becomes a
> meaning of the self (…)." [47]

J.M. Charon explains further:

> "Social interaction shapes our identities. It is not others who create who we are…
> Instead, identity results from a negotiation process that arises in social interac-
> tion. We label others in interaction; we present our identities in interaction; we
> tell others who we think they are in interaction. Through it all we come [to] think
> of our self as something; an identity is formed, and our action is now influenced
> by who in the world we think we are." [48]

Thus, our personal identity at any given moment is an amalgam of our own
and others' understanding of whom we are. In the same way, the identity
of a group is defined by both insiders and outsiders.

Furthermore, an important part of the symbolic interactionist identity
theory is that "identities" are hierarchically structured. People have multiple
identities and draw on various identities in various situations. The different
identities/aspects of our self-concept, however, do not have the same value,

---

by outward structures in society, hence the label "*structural* symbolic interactionism" (Reynolds/Herman-Kinney, 2003, 368 ff.).
45 M.R. Leary, *Handbook of Self and Identity*, New York 2003, 128–152: "A
Sociological Approach to Self and Identity." M.B. Brewer points out that this is
the "American" way of conceptualizing identity, whereas Europeans are more
inclined to think beyond the level of the individual (M.B. Brewer, *The Social
Self. On Being the Same and Different at the Same Time*, in: *Personality and
Social Psychology Bulletin*. 17/5 (1991), 34).
46 Leary, 2003, 132.
47 Reynolds/Herman-Kinney, 2003, 367.
48 Charon, 2007, 153.

some features of a person's identity are normally more important than others. In other words, one identity is more salient to the individual or the group and is therefore more frequently activated. S. Stryker explains "identity salience" in the following way: "Identities are ordered in a salience hierarchy, defined as the likelihood that an identity will be invoked in a variety of situations."[49] The fact that people have more identities and can switch between them is a characteristic feature of liberal postmodern societies, where people are not bound in a specific role all the time, as people more often were in premodern societies.[50] However, the terminology of "identity salience" helps verbalize also elements of antique society. For instance, one can assume that "Christian identity" had a high salience for converts during the first centuries, when becoming Christian was a choice with possible extreme consequences. As an idealized example of the Christian identity as a salient identity, we can look at Perpetuas' account in *The Martyrdom of Saints Perpetua and Felicitas*, where Perpetua refuses to renounce her Christian faith, and says to her father:

> "Father," said I, "do you see this vase here, for example, or waterpot or whatever?" "Yes, I do," said he. And I told him: "Could it be called by any other name than what it is?" And he said: "No." "Well, so too I cannot be called anything other than what I am, a Christian."[51]

In this idealized account, Perpetua is holding her Christian identity so salient that she breaks her family ties because of it. She shows that she is committed to her Christian identity and acts accordingly. Obviously, Perpetua's reaction is literarily styled, but this proves to us that the Christian ideal was complete identification with one's Christian identity, and Christians of the period must have been aware of this claim, although we cannot know with which degree of consequence they acted in relation to their Christian identity.

---

49 Stryker, 2008, 20.
50 We must distinguish between premodernity, modernity and postmodernity. For more information on what characterizes postmodern identity, see: A. Elliot/P. du Gay (eds.), *Identity in Question*, London 2009. They label the postmodern self as fluid, fragmented, discontinuous, decentred, dispersed, culturally eclectic, hybrid-like (p. xii).
51 *m.Perp.* 3 (Musurillo).

In his book, *Christians and their Many Identities in Late Antiquity. North Africa, 200–400 CE*, Éric Rebillard proposes that Christian identity was not a salient identity for most Christians – at least only intermittently, rather Christianness was thought of as one identity among several. Éric Rebillard points to an "internal plurality of the individual" that made it possible for Christians to understand "Christianness" as just one kind of identity out of many, e.g. the identity of being a Roman citizen. Rebillard argues that most Christians organized their identities laterally rather than hierarchically; consequently he proposes that "Christian identity" was just one among several identities that people of Late Antiquity could activate. Bishops and other religious leaders wanted their followers to organize their identities hierarchically, with "Christian" being the overriding one, but people did generally not do this.[52] Thus Rebillard assumes that Christians took part in non-Christian groups and activities as well as Christian groups with relative ease. Although I am of course not suggesting that Christians lived in a Christian vacuum, my argumentation is the opposite of the one forwarded by Rebillard, because my perspective is different, and I look at the ideal of prayer. The present study builds on the hypothesis that even though Christians were not completely aligned with the ambitious ideals of their leaders, Christians *were* (made) aware of their particular Christian identity and its exclusivity. One of the most important elements of Christian identity was exactly its excluding nature. I claim that this ideal Christian identity was strengthened by several means, for instance by liturgy, close relations in the congregation and prayer with a certain inherent theology.

The strength of a group has to do with the group member's sense of belonging, and it seems to me unrealistic that the Christian groups could exist and expand as rapidly as it happened if their members completely disregarded the Christian demand for exclusivity. According to S. Stryker, salient identities depend on the degree to which a person feels committed to the people/group in which his/her identity is constituted: "To the degree that one's relationships to a set of others depend on being a particular kind of person and playing out particular roles, one is committed to being

---

52 É. Rebillard, *Christians and Their Many Identities in Late Antiquity, North Africa, 200–450 CE*, New York 2012, 92 ff.

that kind of person."[53] It seems probable that in the first centuries CE, the Christian identity became the prevailing, and being Christian was an identity that secured certain important relationships within the congregation and with the Christian God.

According to the prevailing assumption in modern identity theories, neither an individual nor a group is completely in command when it comes to their identity, since identity also has to do with the social world in which the individual or the group is embedded. Therefore, "[c]ompared to self and self-concept, identity is an even more social conception as it indicates a specific location within some form of social structure."[54] For this reason, one cannot study personal identities without acknowledging social identities. To understand the individual, one must understand the whole social world in which he/she is embedded.

1.3.3 Identity formation – a double-sided process

As indicated above, identity has to do with the way people perceive themselves and are being perceived by others. Identity is the result of *who you are* and correspondingly of *who you are not;* and at the same time, identity is influenced by how other people classify you. As such identity formation has to do with both a "positive" and a "negative" categorization. The positive categorization consists in the qualities or attributes that we prescribe to ourselves or to our own group; the negative categorization has to do with how we perceive other people or groups in contrast to ourselves. In fact, as Lorenzo Perrone writes: "one may infer that 'identity' generally has to do with the perception of the 'self' in relation to the 'other', thus implying a dialectic of similarity and difference."[55]

It is obvious from history and experience that people tend to categorize one another, and that these categorizations are frequently negative. Categorization is simply a human mode of comprehension. One sees an example of the tendency to negative categorization of others in the fact

---

53 Stryker, 2008, 20.
54 Reynolds/Herman-Kinney, 2003, 368.
55 L. Perrone, *Prayer and the Construction of Religious Identity in Early Christianity*, in: POC 53 (2003), 262.

that Christianity in the first centuries often were referred to as something negative: a "superstition."[56] Because identity formation has to do with being in opposition to certain "others" and avoiding to be identical with these others, it is enlightening to study how individuals and groups draw boundaries around themselves by using identity markers and literary strategies to avoid the "others." M. Kahlos has pointed to one such boundary in the Christian social world, upheld by certain literary genres: "One of the frontiers demarcated and constantly rectified in the Christian polemical and apologetic literature was the one between Christians and pagans. Christian opinion leaders implanted and then polarized the Christian–pagan dichotomy in order to strengthen the Christian *Selbstverständnis*."[57] There is, however, more to identity formation than this process of "othering."[58]

It is obvious that people assert positively how they understand themselves, and they make positive self-affirmations. Therefore, when studying identity, it is interesting not only to look for negative categorizations, overt identity markers and boundaries, but also to look into the content of belief and practice to understand how a certain identity is formed from an insider's perspective. Sometimes the content is fatally neglected in the assumption that content really only matters as means of differentiation between groups. This was for instance the case when the Norwegian anthropologist Frederik Barth in 1969 investigated ethnic groups and wrote that: "The critical focus of investigation from this point of view becomes the ethnic *boundary* that defines the group, not the cultural stuff that it encloses."[59] The present study points to the importance of "cultural stuff" in the process of upholding a stable identity, both personally and collectively. As such the present study is influenced by the cultural turn as analytical shift, and for this reason, theology and prayer are taken very seriously as symbols that express and meanwhile form social life and identity.

---

56 Suet. Nero 16 (Warmington).
57 M. Kahlos, *Debate and Dialogue. Christian and Pagan Cultures c. 360-430*, Farnham 2007, 2.
58 Hvalvik/Sandnes, 2014, 17.
59 Barth, 1969, 15.

1.3.4 Michel Foucault on selves

Although the symbolic interactionist approach to identity primarily will constitute the frame around the present study, recourse will also be made to Michel Foucault and his thought-provoking studies on the history of the self. Michel Foucault (1926–84), the French philosopher and cultural historian, studied, among other things, the development of the self in antiquity. In Chapter 5, we shall return to his views; therefore, the introduction here will be rather short. Foucault, like Mead, pointed to the conclusion that the self is not a substance, but a form that varies in different contexts. In the 1980s, Michel Foucault analysed Greco-Roman philosophy and late antique Christian monastic spirituality.[60] Foucault was interested in the development of the modern self, but he reckoned that both Christian asceticism and ancient philosophy had influenced the current idea of self, although in different ways.[61] Foucault held that among Greco-Roman philosophers, care of the self was a matter of self-mastery, of doing certain actions and being virtuous, whereas the care of the self among Christian monks primarily was a matter of becoming aware of, confessing and mastering one's thoughts. The monks were supposed to scrutinize their thoughts and turn them to God.[62]

In his writings on the subject, Foucault focused on "technologies of the self." He held that different technologies "permit individuals to effect by their own means or with the help of others a certain number of operations

---

60 Foucault investigated the development of the self in antiquity in volume 2 and 3 of his *History of the Self*. Volume 2 is *The Use of Pleasure (Histoire de la sexualité, II: l'usage des plaisirs)* and volume 3: *The Care of the Self (Histoire de la sexualité, III: le souci de soi)*, both volumes were published in 1984. I will not go into detail with these works. Foucault died before he could finish a fourth volume, *Les Aveux de la Chair*, in which he intended to focus specifically on the influence of Christianity on the self (this volume has recently been published posthumously: M. Foucault, *Histoire de la sexualité 4. Les aveux de la chair (Confessions of the Flesh)*, ed. by Frédéric Gros, Paris 2018.). However, Foucault also treated this subject in a lecture series that has been published (M. Foucault, *The Hermeneutics of the Subject. Lectures at the Collège de France 1981-82*, ed. by Frédéric Gros, New York 2001).

61 Foucault, 1988, 21.

62 Id. 45.

on their own bodies and soul, thoughts, conduct, and way of being, so as to transform themselves in order to attain a certain state of happiness, purity, wisdom, perfection or immortality."[63] Foucault asserted that Christianity emphasized "self-knowledge" as a technique to form the selves. Christians were ideally supposed to detect and denounce their own selves. This proposed method of inwardly scrutiny, in itself, created a certain kind of introspective self within Christian culture. Foucault's studies lack some accuracy due to their untimely ending and what seems to be a preconceived idea of ancient Christianity. However, the orthodox scholar, John Behr, has found Foucault's approach to subjectivity promising, while Behr has also criticized Foucault for being caught up in his own ideas about the relationship between power and knowledge, and for showing too little interest in the vertical and eschatological perspective of Christians in Late Antiquity.[64] Nonetheless Foucault's theories point to very interesting patterns of self-formation and to the profound historical role of Christianity. In the last decades, more scholars of early Christianity have used Foucault's theories as frame work when dealing with the development of Christian selves; we shall get back to these studies below and to the idea of prayer as a "technology of the self."

1.3.5 Prayer as social act

About a hundred years ago, the French sociologist M. Mauss proposed some theories concerning prayer and wrote a thesis, *La prière et les rites oraux*, that was never completed. One of the ideas to which he wanted to draw attention in his thesis is that prayer has "a social content – it is a social act."[65] In other words, prayer has an effect on the social world and is itself affected by it. Thus, no praying man is an island, but receives the impetus to pray in a certain way from his religious community and its way of believing, acting and praying. M. Mauss wrote:

> "Even when prayer is individual and free, even when the worshippers choose freely the time and mode of expression, what they say always uses hallowed

---

63 Id. 18.
64 Behr, 2000, 14-15.
65 W.S.F. Pickering (ed.), *Marcel Mauss. La Prière. 1909*, New York 2003, 12.

language and deals with hallowed things, that is, ones endorsed by social tradition. Even in mental prayer where, according to the formula, Christians abandon
themselves to the Spirit ... this spirit which controls them is the spirit of the
Church. The ideas that they generate are those of the teaching of their own sect
and the sentiments which they speculate on are in accord with the moral doctrine
of their denomination. ... Prayer is social not only in content but also in form."[66]

Consequently, in M. Mauss' view, even the secret prayer links the praying
individual to a social group, because the same idea of God and the same
idea of perfection, morality and world are present in the individual's consciousness as well as in the social consciousness. According to M. Mauss,
the phenomenon of prayer cannot be limited only to the uttered (or unuttered) words, but also encompasses the cluster of ideas that lies behind,
i.e. the worldview, moral codex and dogma. Agreeing with M. Mauss on
this, I argue that the act of praying is an act of acceptance and wrestling
with the ideas of the social world. The English literate Joseph Sterrett states
something similar when he writes: "Just as easily as prayer can be recog-
nition of common belief, practice and religious identity, it can be a form
of opposition."[67]

When thought of in this way, it seems likely that the act of praying has
an influence on both personal identity and group identity because prayer
is a heavily loaded symbol of what the church stands for, and in the act of
praying the individual and the church influence each other. The notion that
the church constrains the individual in the act of praying has been illustra-
tively expressed by A. G. Hamman: "A Christian, even in the midst of his
most intimate prayer, existentially carries the Church within himself in the
same manner as the turtle carries its shell."[68]

1.3.6 Identity studies as frame

Identity is constantly formed in the meeting between any individual and the
social world. In the current study, the fleeting concept of Christian identity
will be investigated in relation to prayer. Notwithstanding the differences in

---

66 Id. 31.
67 J.W. Sterrett, *Re-reading early modern prayer as social act. Examples from
    Shakespeare*, in: Literature Compass 10/6 (2013), 502.
68 Quoted from Perrone, 2003, 264.

interpreting "identity," certain points can be emphasized as characteristic for a general symbolic interactionist approach to identity:

- Identity formation is a social process;
- Identity comes into being where an individual or a group of people with a certain self-perception meets the social perception that others have of him/her/them;
- Identity thus has to do with relations and is formed in interaction.
- Actions and other gestures and symbols influence and express identity.
- Identities are ordered hierarchically according to commitment to social groups.

Relating these insights to the theme of prayer in the early church, questions arise, such as: How could prayer position an individual socially in the third century AD? Which effects did prayer have in the social world? How could a person's self-conception be influenced by prayer? Was prayer used to contribute to form a Christian group identity? These questions will be guiding principles in the analysis. Chapter 4 will look at the relations established to God the Father in prayer and look into how prayer was expected to be understood and practised; Chapter 5 will deal with ethics in combination with prayer, and with relations established to other social agents by way of prayer; and Chapter 6 will investigate how prayer was supposed to influence the individual. The focus will be interchangeably on personal and collective Christian identity.

1.4 A theological theory on prayer and life

The present study sets out with the hypothesis that a reciprocal relationship existed between Christian prayer, Christian identity, Christian doctrines and the social settings in which Christianity evolved. Already the fifth century Augustine-disciple, Prosper of Aquitaine, wrote what has come to be famously summarized as: *lex orandi, lex credendi,* "the rule of prayer is the rule of believing."[69] Thereby Prosper of Aquitaine pointed to

---

69 He actually wrote: *"... ut legem credendi ex statuat supplicandi."* ("... so that the rule for interceding/prayer should establish the rule for believing."). G.W. Lathrop, *Holy People. A Liturgical Ecclesiology,* Minneapolis 2006, 103.

the linkage between (liturgical) prayer and theology. He did so to combat Semi-pelagianism and point to God's grace as originator of both prayer and theology.[70] The twentieth century theologian Karl Barth embraced the axiom *lex orandi, lex credendi* and hailed it as "one of the most profound descriptions of the theological method."[71] According to Barth, the very essence of theology lies in the liturgical action of adoration, thanksgiving and petition, and it is prayer that enhances ethics and faith.[72] The statement, *lex orandi, lex credendi*, can of course be contested – sometimes worship and theology seem far apart, but in the early church, the two were held together as we shall see below. Theological reflection, liturgy, private prayer and behaviour were all expressions of Christian piety.

The French theologian Adalbert G. Hamman studied prayer in the twentieth century and found reason to extend the axiom, *lex orandi, lex credendi,* with a third joint: *lex vivendi.*[73] With this addition, the statement expresses that a person's way of praying does not only influence his way of believing, and vice-versa, but also influences the life that he/she leads. In other words, the way people live is – *or should be* – in accordance with the way they believe and the way they pray. An alternative formulation that stresses the interpersonal dimension of life is: *lex orandi, lex credendi, lex convivendi.*[74] This means that the way people pray and believe influences and even determines how they live *together*. Finally, a third alternative adds *lex agendi* (a rule of action or behaviour) or *lex bene operandi* (law of good working).[75] These theological reflections are by no means an exhaustive

---

70 M.E. Johnson, *Praying and Believing in Early Christianity. The Interplay between Christian Worship and Doctrine*, Collegeville 2013, 23.

71 K. Barth, *The Humanity of God*, Loisville 1960, 90.

72 Id.

73 A. G. Hamman, *La prière chrétienne et prière païenne, formes et différences*, in: W. Haase (ed.), *Aufstieg und Niedergang der römischen Welt: Geschichte und Kultur Roms im Spiegel der neueren Forschung*, Berlin 1980, 1238: "Et ce caractère existentiel de la prière contraste puissamment avec le formalisme païen et meme avec l'initiation mystérique qui n'est jamais une μετάνοια. La *lex orandi*, pour le chrétien est une *lex credendi*, et ajoutonds, une *lex vivendi.*"

74 D. Smit, *Worship – and civil Society? Perspectives from a Reformed Tradition in South Africa*, in: W.F. Storrar et al. (eds.), *A World for All? Global Civil Society in Political Theory and Trinitarian Theology*, Grand Rapids 2011, 256.

75 Johnson, 2013, 95 ff. Johnson quotes Nathan Mitchell for adding *lex agendi*.

treatment of the scholarly work in the field, but are mentioned here, in order to show that it is not a new idea to see prayer as intermingled with faith and life and even social relations.

1.5 Methodology: Turning to historical criticism and moving beyond

Roughly speaking, this study will move between a historical-critical approach, an analytical and comparative approach, and an application of the introduced identity theory to the results of the analysis. This examination thus manoeuvre on both an *emic* and an *etic* level, because it investigates what the texts convey about prayer (emically) and tries to systematize the results by using the modern categories of "self" and "identity" (etically).

When dealing with a theory on social relations, one should avoid the "sociological fallacy"[76] of applying modern theories to ancient material without due caution. For this reason the sources are not only studied in their historical context, it is also taken for granted that texts written for an (early Christian) audience try to impose certain interpretations on their readers/hearers and form them. What one can study on the basis of treatises on prayer is thus in particular their theological and edifying content which came from certain powerful theologians which, time has shown, came to have an impact on Christian discourse. When Friedrich Heiler, in his classical work on prayer, *Das Gebet*, accounts for the sources that scholars have at their disposal, when studying prayer, he only attaches secondary significance to the theological treatises that shall be investigated here.[77] Heiler clarifies this by pointing out that the treatises are often determined

---

76 This fallacy is mentioned by M. Thellbe, *Prayer and Identity*, in: R. Hvalvik/ K.O. Sandnes (eds.), *Early Christian Prayer and Identity Formation*, Tübingen 2014, 115–136.

77 Heiler, 1920, 36.
The texts that will be investigated in the following are not prayers *per se*, they are what Sam Gill terms "metaprayer," "the communications in religious traditions about prayer" (Gill, 2005, 7370). Armin Geertz calls such communications/texts "meta-reflections" and "social reproduction" in the form of philosophy, theology and tradition maintenance (A. Geertz, *Comparing Prayer*, in: W. Braun/R.T. McCutcheon (eds.), *Guide to the Study of Religion*, London 2000, 123).

by an underlying philosophical agenda, and the naïve religious experience of
prayer is superseded by ethical and rational considerations. In other words,
according to Heiler, in treatises we are dealing with secondary reflections
rather than with the "actual" phenomenon of prayer.[78] If Heiler is right
in evaluating the source material like this, it would mean that the theological treatises are not suited as sources for a historical study of prayer
because they are normative texts. However, I dismiss Heiler's reservation
for the following reasons: We do find substantial historical information on
prayer and its role when reading the treatises, because 1) when we read
the sources "against the grain," they indirectly give us historical information. 2) Moreover, there is information about set hours for prayer as well
as postures and rules, which must reflect some historical reality even if
heavily idealized. Most importantly, 3) when it comes to identity formation, historical facts are not necessarily as important as the way in which
they are presented. The Italian scholar Lorenzo Perrone points to this,
when he writes: "... religious identities always rely on elements of personal
and social consciousness more than on the facts alone. Therefore the early
Christian discourse on prayer can help us to guess its weight in the perception of a distinctive religious identity."[79] In other words, the treatises on
prayer are actually relevant when studying early Christian identity formation, because they give an impression of what one could term the "social
consciousness" in the Christian communities - that is the shared ideas in
their groups and the symbols that they found had special importance. In
these treatises, prayer receives a lot of attention and weight in Christian
life; even if we cannot know how and when people in fact prayed, we
can say something about the importance attached to prayer and the ideas
surrounding prayers. When taking into consideration that some of these
treatises were produced to educate lay people on prayer, it seems the more

---

78 Recently, Joseph Sterrett, a scholar of English literature, has dealt with prayer
   as a phenomenon with social consequences, and he points to a common mistake
   of distinguishing "real, valid" prayers from "unreal, unvalid" prayers based
   on their sincerity and interiority (Sterrett, 2013, 496); "the process of making
   these distinctions and applying such definitions is something that rests fully on
   a social act that gives prayer its meaning in the first place" (Id.).
79 Perrone, 2003, 266.

reasonable that the treatises show us part of basic Christian *education* and hence were shaping what we here label "Christian identity."

In many studies that deal with identity formation in early Christianity, it is taken for granted that antiquity was a period where "social identity" dominated. This is for example the case in Greg Woolf's study that I shall quote below.[80] Thus scholars of antiquity often choose to deal explicitly with collective identity and social identity because of "the Mediterranean collective culture"[81], and because the literature from antiquity is often judged to be more relevant for studying larger structures than personal identity.[82] That the more individual-oriented "symbolic interactionisme" and Foucaultian theory are chosen as frame in this study could therefore be questioned, because these streams of thought are focused on the self and microstructures. However, because the sources that will be analysed here present prayer as a form of communication, and because they focus much attention on the individual's heart, mind, spirit etc., I have judged it reasonable to look at prayer as influencing both individuals and groups, and thus having repercussions both for personal and social identities.

1.6 Previous scholarship

The following paragraphs will present previous scholarship relevant for the present study. As the present study entails different themes, namely both prayer, self and identity, and the combination of the three, the previous scholarly work is presented under three headlines: "Literature on Christian prayer in Antiquity," "Literature on 'self' and 'identity' in Antiquity" and "Literature on Christian prayer, self and identity in Antiquity." I shall introduce several relevant titles and go into more detail with selected works that will set the stage for the current study.

---

80 G.D. Woolf, *Ritual and the Individual in Roman Religion*, in: J. Rüpke (ed.), *The Individual in the Religions of the Ancient Mediterranean*, Oxford 2013, 136. See below, paragraph 1.6.2.1.

81 Hvalvik/Sandnes, 2014, 17.

82 P.A. Harland, *Dynamics of Identity in the World of the Early Christians*, New York 2009, 8.

1.6.1 Literature on Christian prayer in antiquity

1.6.1.1 Works from the twentieth century

With the introduction of the historical critical method in the modern period, prayer became an object of scrutiny in its own right in the discipline of church history and later also in the emerging study of religion.[83] The historical-critical paradigm that demands accuracy and descriptive investigations has lasted well into the twentieth century and has resulted in an illuminating series of studies on prayer in the early church, such as Eduard von der Goltz' *Das Gebet in der ältesten Christenheit, eine geschichtliche Untersuchung* (1901), Otto Dibelius' *Vaterunser* (1903),[84] A. G. Hamman's *La Prière. Les Trois Premiers Siècles* (1963) and a wealth of studies on the development of liturgical prayers.[85] In general, the collective and liturgical prayers of the early church have received much more scholarly attention than personal prayer.[86] Other studies have compared Christian treatises on

---

83 In premodernity, theological reflections were often combined with prayer as method in a way that is still lauded by some systematical theologians to the present day. In his *Einführung in die Evangelische Theologie* (1962), Karl Barth writes that prayer is the first and fundamental act when doing theology (Barth, 1962, 176). In the course of theological history, several works have taken the form of prayer, most prominently Augustine's *Confessiones* and Anselm of Canterbury's *Proslogion*.

   Andrew Louth has stated that most "Orthodox are critical of the development of theology in the West, in particularly the way theology had developed as an academic discipline, remote from the life of prayer (a complaint already heard in the West from the fourteenth century onwards)" (Louth in his Foreword to J. Behr, *The Way to Nicaea*, New York 2001, ix).

84 About the scientific study of prayer, Pickering notes: "Around the turn of the [twentieth] century there was indeed a rich stream of studies by theologians, philosophers of religion and church historians who were attempting to apply objective, 'scientific' approaches to religious phenomena in which prayer was seen as a significant component. They used the approaches of critical history, original languages, psychology, and comparative studies." (Pickering, 2003, 6).

85 For an overview of liturgical studies, see Bradshaw, 2002.

86 C. Stewart, *Prayer*, in: S.A. Harvey/D.G. Hunter (eds.), *The Oxford Handbook of Early Christian Studies*, Oxford 2008, 744-763, 745. One reason for this is that there are more sources testifying to liturgical prayers than personal prayers, but still it is remarkable how little attention personal prayer have received, even in studies on early Christian asceticism.

prayer,[87] while Maria-Barbara von Stritzky compared early Christian treatises on prayer with philosophical works of their time.[88]

A Protestant scholar as von der Goltz went about his historical job by describing different prayers and theological treatises carefully and briefly evaluating their content. Concerning the four writers under investigation in this thesis, von der Goltz' evaluation is as follows: He criticizes Clement of Alexandria for being too aristocratic and philosophical in his treatment of prayer, but compliments him for his belief that prayer is communication of the heart with God.[89] Furthermore, von der Goltz recognizes Origen's spiritualization of prayer as a means of making Christians like to God, but also criticizes him for his philosophical bias.[90] When it comes to the Latin authors, von der Goltz characterizes the euchological treatises of Tertullian and Cyprian as practical in character, "praktisch durch und durch," and lauds them for addressing ordinary Christians as opposed to the elitism that one encounters in the Alexandrian tradition.[91] In comparing the texts by the Alexandrian and Latin authors, von der Goltz points to "der wesentlichste Unterschied morgenländischen und abendländishen Christentum," which he believes is the philosophical emphasis of the Alexandrian writers as opposed to the moral discipline of the Latin authors. In general, this difference between East and West is a point frequently raised in scholarship.[92] However, the difference can be emphasized too strongly, because each of the traditions point to both practice and spirituality in relation with prayer.

In the beginning of the 20th century, the study of religion was on its rise, and prayer quickly became a theme of interest. Marcel Mauss, the nephew of Émile Durkheim, wrote the already mentioned thesis, *La prière*

---

87 R.I. Simpson, *The Interpretation of Prayer in the Early Church*, London 1965; K.B. Schnurr, *Hören und Handeln. Lateinische Auslegungen des Vaterunsers in der Alten Kirche bis zum 5. Jahrhundert*, Freiburg 1985.

88 M.B. von Stritzky, *Studien zur Überlieferung und Interpretation des Vaterunsers in der frühchristlichen Literatur*, Münster 1989.

89 E.F. von der Goltz, *Das Gebet in der ältesten Christenheit. Eine Geschichtliche Untersuchung*, Leipzig 1901, 266.

90 Id. 278.

91 Id. 279.

92 E.g. M.J. Brown, *The Lord's Prayer through North African Eyes. A Window into Early Christianity*, New York 2004.

et les rites oraux, that was printed privately in 1909, but somewhat forgotten for decades thereafter. Later, Friedrich Heiler published a famous work, *Das Gebet. Eine religionsgeschichtliche und religionspsychologische Untersuchung* (1919). The book, which is still a *classic*, has a broad scope, and Heiler refers to much ancient material of both Christian and non-Christian provenance. In general, Heiler tends to favour Protestant ideals, and he concludes that "prophetic-biblical prayer" is the highest form of prayer, characterized by its individual character, the underlying personal relationship with God and the opportunity to pray without any restrictions or limitations. Heiler states that "Luthers Gebet ist echtes prophetisches Gebet..."[93]

During the twentieth century the theological climate changed in different confessions, which is evident from e.g. the Second Vatican Council. The change made it possible for new themes and authors to be studied. Catholic scholars, such as Adalbert G. Hamman, began to focus their attention on early Christian prayer, also in the works of Clement and Origen.[94] Since then more theologians have used the euchological treatises to unfold patristic theology.[95] Of the four euchological treatises studied here, it is Origen's *Perì Euchês* that has received most scholarly attention. A comprehensive survey of literature on *Perì Euchês* is given by Lorenzo Perrone.[96]

By the end of the 20th-century, a large corpus of scholarship on prayer in the New Testament, the early church and its context had been produced. One can find comprehensive bibliographies in: *Bibliographie analytique de*

---

93 Heiler, 1920, 245.

94 E.g. A. G. Hamman, *La prière. Les trois premiers siècles*, Tournai 1962.

95 Wilhelm Gessel, Walther Völker, André Mehat, Allain le Boulluec, etc.

96 L. Perrone, *Origenes' Rede vom Gebet zwischen Frömmigkeit und Theologie. Zur Rezeption von Peri euchēs in der modernen Forschung*, in: A. Fürst (ed.), *Origenes und sein Erbe im Orient und Okzident*, Adamantiana: Texte und Studien zu Origenes in seinem Erbe 1, Münster 2011. For more or less systematic overviews of studies on the three other texts, see for Clem. Strom. 7 the bibliography by Annewies van den Hoek, in: M. Havrda/V. Hušek/J. Plátova (eds.), *The Seventh Book of the Stromateis. Proceedings of the Colloquium on Clement of Alexandria*, Leiden 2012, 14-36; for a list of literature on Tert. Or. see *The Tertullian Project*'s website; for a few titles on Cypr. Dom. orat. see Schnurr, 1985.

la prière grecque et romaine. Deuxième édition complétée et augmentée (1898–2003)[97] and in *The Lord's Prayer and Other Prayer Texts from the Greco-Roman Era* (1994). In the latter no less than 1999 titles are listed under different headings.[98] A decade after this publication, in 2001, J. H. Neyrey called the bibliography "a major contribution."[99] However, he found it "fair to say that in terms of methods of interpreting prayer, even this latest effort ... brings little new to the table." He lamented that mostly there is just one perspective on prayer: "the perspective of form criticism and history-of-religions examination of background, but not necessarily from the perspective of interpretation."[100] J. K. Coyle makes the same observation in his article "What Was "*Prayer*" for Early Christians?" from 1999. He points to the fact that the tendency among scholars has been "towards the descriptive, rather than the analytical."[101] The present study aims to strike a balance between the old and new perspectives.

1.6.1.2 *Recent studies on prayer in the early church*

When looking at the recent studies on prayer in the early church, there are fine contribution from scholars studying prayer in the early church both historically and with an interest in theological developments. To this category belongs the Italian classicist Lorenzo Perrone. His major opus, *La preghiera secondo Origene* (2011), is rather classic in objective and method. Perrone explicitly states that in this work it is not historical or identity-issues that

---

97 G. Freyburger/L. Pernot/F. Chapot/B. Laurot (eds.), *Bibliographie analytique de la prière grecque et romaine. Deuxième édition complétée et augmentée (1898-2003)*, Turnhout 2008.

98 Also since this bibliography was published, prayer has been dealt with in more studies, e.g. R. Hammerling (ed.), *A History of Prayer. The First to the Fifteenth Century*, Leiden 2008 and several studies mentioned below; for more titles, especially on prayer in the New Testament and its surroundings, see also Ostmeyer, 2006, 1-28; Hvalvik/Sandnes, 2014, 1 n1.

99 J.H. Neyrey, *Prayer, In Other Words. A Social Science Model for Interpreting Prayers*, in: J.J. Pilch (ed.), *Social Scientific Models for Interpreting the Bible: Essays by the Context Group in Honor of Bruce J. Malina*, Leiden 2001, 350.

100 Id.

101 J.K. Coyle, *What Was "Prayer" for Early Christians?*, in: P. Allen/W. Mayer/L. Cross (eds.), *Prayer and Spirituality in the Early Church* 2, Sydney 1999, 25.

are his concern, but the intellectual and dogmatical history of prayer.[102] The voluminous book is primarily devoted to Origen's treatise *On Prayer*, which is analysed thoroughly. Perrone shows how prayer, according to Origen, is an "impossible gift" which can only be in the possession of humans by the grace of God and the work of the Holy Spirit. Perrone dedicates chapter 9, *La costruzione di un modello*, to the survey of different patristic models of theologies of prayer from the third to the fifth century. Perrone notes how much the early authors have in common and concludes that it is due to the Biblical texts that they share.[103]

Also Joseph Brown has recently written a book on ancient theology of prayer, *The Lord's Prayer through North African Eyes* (2004). Brown focuses on two Christian authors, Clement of Alexandria and Tertullian, which he presents as products of their respective Greco-Roman milieus. Brown notes how these authors have frequently been studied "myopically" (shortsightedly), when in fact they should be studied "hyperopically" (farsightedly), namely in their Greco-Roman context. Brown is interested in inferring a "cultic *didachē*" from the works of the two Christian authors; he wants to recover their "critical reflection upon cultic practices."[104]

Worth mentioning in this context is also Maria-Barbara von Stritzky's article "Gebet und Tat im christlichen Alltag. Gedanken früher Kirchenväter."[105] In her article, von Stritzky is looking for the interdependence of theology and ethical practice in connection with the early interpretations of prayer. The present study derives inspiration from these works and tries to strike an accord between reading the sources as theological texts and seeing them hyperopically in their Greco-Roman contexts.

---

102 L. Perrone, *La preghiera secondo Origene. L'impossibilità donata*, Letteratura Cristiana Antica. Nuova Serie 24, Brescia 2011, 512.

103 See the Bibliography below.

104 Brown, 2004, 132; "cultic *didachē*" is a word that Brown has taken over from Hans Dieter Betz.

105 M.B. von Stritzky, *Gebet und Tat im christlichen Alltag. Gedanken früher Kirchenväter*, in: H. Grieser/A. Merkt (eds.), *Volksglaube im antiken Christentum*, Darmstadt 2009.

1.6.2 Literature on self and identity in antiquity

As Lorenzo Perrone mentions in his article "Die Zukunft der Patristik"[106], there has been a "wissenschaftsoziologische Veränderung" in patristics, and in this transformation of patristic studies "identity" has become a popular concept, a *Modewort*.[107] To illustrate the popularity of identity within the last decades, I can refer to titles such as: Judith Lieu's *Christian Identity in the Jewish and Greco-Roman World* (2004) and Philip A. Harland's *Dynamics of Identity in the World of the Early Christians. Associations, Judeans, and Cultural Minorities* (2009).[108] In the following, I shall treat self and identity together, since identity, as we have seen, reflects a part of the self.

1.6.2.1 Foucault, Brakke, Shulman, Stroumsa, Rüpke, etc.

In the anthology, *Religion and the self in Antiquity* (2005), published by David Brakke et al., it is noted that historians have begun to follow the trend from anthropology and from Michel Foucault in understanding the self as a "cultural construction fashioned through discursive practice."[109] Furthermore, it is mentioned that: "In an ancient context, the self was a religious concept: for some, it was an entity separable from the body and yearning for contact with the divine, while for others it constituted an expression of the divine in its own right."[110] These two hypotheses also underlie the present study: (1) the self is developed in discourses, and (2) for people of antiquity what we term "self" had to do with the divine. In Patricia Cox Miller's contribution to the book, "Shifting Selves in Late Antiquity," she detects a transformation in the way in which the self is

---

106 L. Perrone, *Die Zukunft der Patristik. Überlegungen und Hoffnungen aus Vergangenheit und Gegenwart,* in: FZPhTh 60 (2013), 5-19.
107 Id. 14.
108 More titles could be mentioned, as well as research groups, e.g. "Det kristne menneske - konstruksjon av ny identitet i antikken" (1997–2001); see H. Moxnes, *Det kristne menneske. Konstruksjon av ny identitet i antikken,* in: Norsk Teologisk Tidsskrift 1 (2003), 3-7.
109 D. Brakke,/M. Satlow/S. Weitzman (eds.), *Religion and the self in Antiquity,* Bloomington 2005, 1; 5-6; 222 ff.
110 Id. 2.

represented. The transformation takes place in the third to fifth century. It is a transformation from the idea that the self's divine core could be realized more or less directly by an individual, to the later idea that the individual needs mediators to reach the divine, for example by use of theurgy.

Guy G. Stroumsa has made several contributions to the general study of ancient self-formation. In 1999, he and Jan Assmann published, *Transformations of the Inner Self in Ancient Religions*; in 2002, David Schulman and Stroumsa published another anthology, *Self and Self-Transformation in the History of Religions*: and in 2009, Stroumsa published *The End of Sacrifice,* in which he also touches upon the transformation of selves in antiquity. Stroumsa presents interesting considerations, but in general the books are rather theoretical and less historical specific. The book by Schulman and Stroumsa has a very wide scope because its frame is the theory of the *Achsenzeit* which is the idea that "a dramatic change of paradigm" occurred in various archaic cultures in about 500 B.C.E.[111] Schulman and Stroumsa assert that with this change of paradigm came a new reflexivity of the self. It is noteworthy for our purpose that in Stroumsa's and Schulman's book from 2002, it is emphasized that: "Ritual is perhaps the creative mode of religious life par excellence - the arena in which the person is created along with his or her universe."[112] In other words, the subject has the possibility of transformation in the religious ritual which includes prayer. The authors ponder: "What happens to the self in the course of daily prayer, or in the course of sacrifice, or when taking the Eucharist? In all such cases, we should probably assume a dynamic, restless quality to 'selfness.'"[113]

In the volume *The Individual in the Religions of the Ancient Mediterranean* (2013), edited by Jörg Rüpke, Greg Woolf also considers the effects of ritual on identity. Woolf notes that "ritual mediates between individual and group"[114], and "Naturally the two dimensions

---

111 G. Stroumsa and D. Schulman (eds.), *Self and Self-Transformation in the History of Religions*, Oxford 2002, 7.
112 Id., 6.
113 Id.
114 G.D. Woolf, *Ritual and the Individual in Roman Religion*, in: J. Rüpke (ed.), *The Individual in the Religions of the Ancient Mediterranean,* Oxford 2013, 136.

of identity – the sense of self and social identity – are not wholly independent of one another, although it is common enough for them to be in
tension."[115] Furthermore, Woolf asserts that in antiquity, social identity
was more important than personal identity. He notes that "most recent
discussion of the concept [of individuality] are quite sceptical about the
emergence in the Roman period of quasi-modern subjectivities centred on
self-conscious and internalized individuality."[116] Woolf finds that in antiquity there is "no real sign of an ethic of individualism... nor is there a sense
that one's internal self is in some sense the real, essential, and defining
core in one's being. Seneca, Pliny the Younger, and Epictetus all devote a
good deal of attention to the production of the self, but always viewed as
a being in action, a person defined relationally."[117] Subsequently, Woolf
states that there was not personalized religion in antiquity comparable
to the personalized religiosity of today, simply because the individual in
antiquity was more of a relational, socio-centred person than an autonomous self. "A great gulf separated ancient forms of individualization from
those of the early modern and modern world."[118] This notion of selves in
antiquity is worth bearing in mind as a critical reminder that we cannot
simply assume that identity and self in antiquity and (post-)modernity
are easily comparable. Nonetheless, I am less sceptical than Woolf is,
and I shall argue that Christian piety was a part of the development of
"quasi-modern subjectivities centred on self-conscious and internalized
individuality." A recent collective volume edited by Éric Rebillard and
Jörg Rüpke, *Group Identity and Religious Individuality in Late Antiquity*,
also sheds light on the dialectics between group identity and religious
individuality, and brings the individual into focus.[119] Likewise, the ECR-
project "Lived Ancient Religion," led by Jörg Rüpke, has drawn attention

---

115 Id. 149.
116 Id. 153-154.
117 Id. 154. This is very similar to the thoughts of Foucault, cf. below paragraph
      5.1.2.
118 Id.
119 É. Rebillard/J. Rüpke, *Group Identity and Religious Individuality in Late
      Antiquity*, Washington 2015.

to the orant, the praying agent, and thus to the individual performing ritual and prayer.[120]

1.6.2.2 *J.B. Rives: A historian's view on Roman identity*

The present study is informed by the historian J.B. Rives' conclusions in *Religion and Authority in Roman Carthage from Augustus to Constantine* (1995) and in his article "Religion in the Roman empire" (1999).[121] J.B. Rives accentuates that religion was an important aspect of Roman identity.[122] He thereby agrees with the previously mentioned book by Stroumsa which holds that "Identity, which in the Hellenistic world had been defined, first of all, in cultural and linguistic terms, became essential religious in the Roman Empire. This change amounted to nothing less than a revolution in the criteria of identity."[123] Rives describes how people in the Roman Empire had freedom to construct their own specific religious identity, "in so far as in their private lives they were not obliged to worship any particular set of deities or adhere to any particular doctrine."[124] There was no single religion in the Roman Empire, and locally the civic cult took different shapes. However, the public cult was seen as a very important matter, and it was the place where civic and ethnic identity was shaped: "Identification with and participation in the public cults of Rome created a sense of community with one's fellow citizens and reinforced one's own sense of being Roman."[125] This was the case in Rome itself and in the empire in general. "Roman culture thus involved a crucial nexus between religion, Roman identity and public power."[126] Rives holds that especially the imperial cult conveyed a

---

120 J. Albrecht et al., *Religion in the making: the Lived Ancient Religion approach,* in: *Religion* 48, 4 (2018), 568-593 and M. Patzelt, *Über das Beten der Römer. Gebete im spätrepublikanischen und frühkaiserzeitlichen Rom als Ausdruck gelebter Religion,* Berlin/Boston 2018.

121 J.B. Rives, *Religion in the Roman empire,* in: J. Huskinson (ed.), *Experiencing Rome. Culture, Identity and Power in the Roman Empire,* Oxford 1999, 245-276.

122 Id. 257.

123 Stroumsa in: D. Brakke/M. Satlow/S. Weitzman (eds.), *Religion and the self in Antiquity,* Bloomington 2005, 184.

124 Rives, 1999, 257.

125 Id.

126 Id. 258.

feeling of Roman identity; it connected the dispersed locale elites with each other and with Rome;[127] and furthermore, the "basic cult practices of sacrifice and prayer articulated the relationship between the emperor and his subjects."[128] Thus the individual Roman citizen, wherever he was located in the empire, stood in direct relation to the genius of the emperor.[129]

1.6.3 Literature on Christian prayer, self and identity in antiquity

When it comes to the subject of the combination of prayer, self and identity in early Christianity, there have been a few and quite recent predecessors to the present work. Studies dealing explicitly with the topic prayer and identity can be narrowed down to the German anthology: *Identität durch Gebet. Zur Gemeinschaftsbildenden Funktion institutionalisierten Betens in Judentum und Christentum* (2003), an article by Lorenzo Perrone: "Prayer and the Construction of Religious Identity in Early Christianity" (2003), an article by the Danish Jesper Hyldahl: "I Guds varetægt. Bønnens betydning for kristen identitet i den tidlige kirke" ("In God's care. The meaning of Prayer for Christian Identity in the Early Church," 2009) and the recent *Early Christian Prayer and Identity Formation* (2014). When including works on the "self," it is also worth mentioning chapters and articles such as Esther Menn's "Prayer of the Queen: Esther's Religious Self in the Septuagint," Michael L. Satlow's "Giving for a Return: Jewish Votive

---

127 Id. 264.

128 Id. 266.

129 George Herbert Mead, father of symbolic interactionism, made the exact same observation in the beginning of the twentieth century: "It is interesting to see how this situation appeared in the Roman Empire. There the relationship of the emperor to the subjects as such was one of absolute power, but it was defined in legal terms which carried over the definitions that belonged to Roman law into the relationship between the emperor and his subjects. This, however, constituted too abstract a relationship to meet the demands of the community, and the deification of the emperor under these conditions was the expression of the necessity of setting up some sort of more personal relation. When the Roman member of the community offered his sacrifice to the emperor he was putting himself into personal relationship with him, and because of that he could feel his connection with all the members of the community." (Mead, 1967, 312).

Offerings in Late Antiquity,"[130] Brouria Bitton-Ashkelony's " 'More Interior than the Lips and the Tongue': John of Apamea and Silent Prayer in Late Antiquity," as well as Bitton-Ashkelony and Aryeh Kofsky's "Spiritual Exercises: the Continuous Conversation of the Mind with God"[131] and Derek Krueger's book *Liturgical Subjects* (2014).

The German essay collection, *Identität durch Gebet*, was made as a part of a project on Jewish-Christian relations. Therefore, it naturally tends to focus on Christian prayer and identity in relation/opposition to Jewish prayer and Jewish identity. Paul Bradshaw shows that methodological issues make a direct comparison of Christian and Jewish prayer texts difficult.[132] There are not many theoretical concerns in the book, but much information about Christian history and liturgy. From this book, it becomes evident that Christian liturgical prayer and identity owe a lot to Judaism. For the purpose of the present study, especially Harald Buchinger's article "Gebet und Identität bei Origenes. Das Vaterunser im Horizont der Auseinandersetzung im Liturgie und Exegese" on Origen's exegetically oriented identity is interesting. In this article, Buchinger shows that for the exegete Origen, it was not the Lord's Prayer in itself that formed his identity, but the "spiritual meaning" of the Lord's Prayer.[133] Thus prayer can point beyond its wording, as the Lord's Prayer did for Origen.

Lorenzo Perrone's article: "Prayer and the Construction of Religious Identity in Early Christianity" is a point of departure for this present thesis, because the article brings together thoughts on identity and antique texts on

---

130 M.L. Satlow, *Giving for a Return. Jewish Votive Offerings in Late Antiquity*, in D. Brakke/M. Satlow/S. Weitzman (eds.): *Religion and the self in Antiquity*, Bloomington 2005, 91-108.

131 B. Bitton-Ashkelony/A. Kofsky, *The Monastic School of Gaza*, Leiden 2006, 157-182.

132 P. Bradshaw, *Parallels between Early Jewish and Christian Prayers. Some Methodological Issues*, in: A. Gerhards/A. Doeker/P. Ebenbauer (eds.), *Identität durch Gebet. Zur gemeinschaftsbildenden Funktion institutionalisierten Betens in Judentum und Christentum*, Paderborn 2003, 21-36, 21.

133 H. Buchinger, *Gebet und Identität bei Origenes. Das Vaterunser im Horizont der Auseinandersetzung um Liturgie und Exergese*, in: A. Gerhards/A. Doeker/P. Ebenbauer (eds.), *Identität durch Gebet. Zur gemeinschaftsbildenden Funktion institutionalisierten Betens in Judentum und Christentum*, Paderborn 2003, 307-354, 329.

prayer. In a way the present work is an expansion of the intent of Perrone's article. Perrone understands identity as having "to do with the perception of the 'self' in relation to the 'other'."[134] He comments on the plasticity of prayer that makes it an essential component of every religion,[135] and he rightly remarks that prayer involves so many aspects that it is best to work with a somewhat flexible category and not a narrow definition.[136] In the euchological treatises from the second and third century, Perrone sees "the creation of a new semantics of prayer"[137] that is strongly influenced by the cultural "others."[138]

The recent anthology, *Early Christian Prayer and Identity Formation*, published in the fall of 2014 is very similar to the present study concerning its intent to show that "Christian identity finds one of its most distinct expressions in Christian prayer, and also, conversely, that this identity was shaped and gradually formed by prayer."[139] However, the book primarily deals with the New Testament period, although Karl Olav Sandnes also investigates the interpretation of the Lord's Prayer in the treatises of Tertullian and Cyprian. Sandnes points to the connection between baptism and the Lord's Prayer, and to the fact that the privilege of addressing God as Father is given to the baptized. This link between ritual and prayer is important, as Sandnes notes, because "rituals are means of both expressing and strengthening the identity of a group."[140] The book entails fine theoretical considerations, especially in Mikael Tellbe's contribution "Prayer and Identity." Thellbe chooses to focus on "social identity" theories because he is interested in the antique "Mediterranean collective culture."[141] Among different themes, Thellbe dwells on the close connection between identity and ritual: "Rituals are typical examples of identity forming behaviour

---

134 L. Perrone, *Prayer and the Construction of Religious Identity in Early Christianity*, in: POC 53 (2003), 261.
135 Id. 263.
136 Id. 263.
137 Id. 277.
138 Id. 287.
139 Hvalvik/Sandnes, 2014, 1.
140 Id. 228.
141 Thellbe, 2014, 17.

and action."[142] To prove the point, he refers to Roy A. Rappaport and other theorists. Thellbe also mentions narratives and beliefs as important for identity formation: "a common history and narrative could provide a rationale and character to group existence."[143]

In another volume, Esther Menn's article, "Prayer of the Queen: Esther's Religious Self in the Septuagint,"[144] calls attention to prayer as a means for the individual to position himself/herself in relation to the divine. Esther's prayer "identifies her as fundamentally a relational self, although the self's relationality is not dependent on the immediate presence of human community or individual."[145] The relational quality of prayer is thus partly presented. But as Michael L. Satlow shows in another contribution "Giving for a Return: Jewish Votive Offerings in Late Antiquity,"[146] the vertical relation between the praying person and the deity is but one relation established in prayer. Satlow shows how inscriptions about votive offerings express a relation between human and divine, but also address other human beings. The inscriptions are meant for display and thereby introduce a vertical dimension in the prayer endeavour. These observations by Menn and Satlow make us aware that prayer works in different "dimensions," horizontally and vertically, and prayer is thus a very relational and social thing, a fact to which we shall shortly return.

In her article " 'More Interior than the Lips and the Tongue': John of Apamea and Silent Prayer in Late Antiquity" (2012), Brouria Bitton-Ashkelony points to the function of silent prayers as parttaking in shaping selves in antique ascetic milieus: "These prayers were, in fact, new spiritual exercises or new technologies of the self in the Foucaultian sense of the term, serving as a tool for orienting the self toward the divine, and they profoundly affected mystical techniques and language in eastern

---

142 Id. 18.
143 Id. 23.
144 E. Menn, *Prayer of the Queen: Esther's Religious Self in the Septuagint*, in: D. Brakke/M. Satlow/S. Weitzman (eds.), *Religion and the self in Antiquity*, Bloomington 2005, 70-90.
145 Ead. 72.
146 Satlow, 2005, 91-108.

Christianity."[147] This point is similar to a point that will be proposed in this study. Chronologically, Bitton-Ashkelony's prime interest is the period from the fourth century and thus begins where the present study ends.

In Derek Krueger's book *Liturgical Subjects* (2014), he investigates "how Byzantine Christians came to see themselves through the liturgy."[148] Krueger shows persuasively that Byzantine Christians "gained access to themselves through penitential rhetoric."[149] He reckons that the Byzantine Christians developed an introspective conscience and a "negative self-image" mediated in ritual practice by means of hymnography and prayer.[150] The liturgy was thus a matrix for the self. Krueger finds that this self was penitential in essence and grounded in a pattern of sin and redemption. The Byzantine Christians used self-blame and penance to fight sin, and they saw themselves as minor characters in dialogue, face-to-face, with Christ.[151] There are several similarities between my own project here and Krueger's investigation, although there is no overlap in text material, and there is a shift in focus from "self" to "identity" which however can be said to be different sides of the same coin. Similarly, I want to show that prayer as repetitive action took part in forming a certain self and identity.

---

147 B. Bitton-Ashkelony, *"More Interior than the Lips and Tongue"*. *John of Apamea and Silent Prayer in Late Antiquity*, in: JECS 20/2 (2012), 304.

148 D. Krueger, *Liturgical Subjects. Christian Ritual, Biblical Narrative, and the Formation of the Self in Byzantium*, Philadelphia 2014, 3.

149 Id. 221.

150 Id. 219.

151 Id. 218.

2 Contexts and authors

The purpose of this chapter is to draw a historical frame around the present study and introduce the Christian euchological treatises from the third century. The context is important because identity has to do with the social world in which the individual is embedded: "Compared to self and self-concept, identity is an even more social conception as it indicates a specific location within some form of social structure."[152] Identity studies force us to recognize that self-categorizations and social identities are "relative, varying, context-dependent properties."[153] In other words, contexts are important for identity.

The task of analysing the context and presenting the sources will be carried out in the following manner: Firstly, the contexts of the four authors will be depicted. Secondly, the philosophical ideas of prayer from the period will be outlined. Thirdly, a summary of Christian prayer in the first three centuries will be presented, together with a treatment of its relation to Jewish prayer. Fourthly, the Christian authors, as well as their way of constructing prayer and the structure of their euchological treatises will be dealt with. Finally, the concrete use and audience of the four treatises will be investigated.

2.1 A tale of three cities: Alexandria, Carthage and Caesarea Maritima

2.1.1 General considerations

E.R. Dodds dubbed late antiquity "an age of anxiety," but even more than this it was an age of spirituality, piety and prayer.[154] Just by taking into

---

152 Reynolds/Herman-Kinney, 2003, 368.
153 Turner et al., "Self and collective: Cognition and social context." *Personality and Social Psychology Bulletin*, 20(5), 1994, 454-463, 456.
154 In *Pagan and Christian in an age of anxiety: some aspects of religious experience from Marcus Aurelius to Constantine*, Dodds suggests that: "the entire century, pagan as well as Christian, was moving into a phase in which religion was to be coexistive with life, and the quest for God was to cast its shadow over all other human activities" (E.R. Dodds, *Pagan and Christian in an age*

consideration all the sarcophagi and mural paintings with figures standing in *Orans* (a posture where the arms are raised in prayer), it seems clear that people of late antiquity tried to communicate with the divine – or at least, wished to be represented on their grave monuments as having been prayerful and pious.[155]

In antiquity, there were primarily two ways of approaching the gods and set things straight: by sacrifice and prayer, θυσίαι καί εὐχαί.[156] These were the two principal modes of Greco-Roman religion which in general had a quasi-legal and very technical character, also when it came to prayer.[157] Traditionally, it has been pointed out that in the Roman world, the efficacy of prayer was thought to depend on the exact pronunciation of a text, and the use of precise and traditional language was seen as very important when praying in the Roman cult.[158] The world of Greco-Roman antiquity was

---

of anxiety, Cambridge 1965, 101). Dodds might be right, and it might be related to the spiritual growth of the same age, cf. "Age of Spirituality" (K. Weitzmann (ed.), *Age of Spirituality. Late Antique and Early Christian Art, Third to Seventh Century*, New York 1980). However, Weitzmann argues that there is a large degree of continuity from classical antiquity to late and "Christian" antiquity regarding spirituality expressed in art.

155 On the frequent image of a woman standing in prayer, Birk notes: "The popularity of the *Orans* illustrates a shift toward the spiritual, though she is not, by definition, Christian... She is a symbolic expression of a new form of virtue (i.e. piety in relation to Christian belief) combined with the traditional cultural understanding of how to express ideas through iconographic language... The figure of the *Orans* combined elements from representations of the Muses, the learned woman and *Pietas*." (S. Birk, *Using Images for Self-Representation on Roman Sarcophagi*, in: S. Birk/T. Myrup Kristensen/B. Poulsen (eds.), *Using Images in Late Antiquity*, Oxford 2014, 33-47, 43-44).

156 A. Dihle, *Das Gebet der Philosophen*, in: E. Campi/L. Grane/A.M. Ritter (eds.), *Oratio. Das Gebet in patristischer und reformatorischer Sicht Festschrift zum 65. Geburtstag von Alfred Schindler*, Göttingen 1999, 23.

157 In the most recent research another emphasis has been made; it is pointed out that Roman prayer was a more varied and engaging activity than has been assumed in earlier scholarship; see M. Patzelt, *The Rhetoric of Roman Prayer. A Proposal for a Lived Religion Approach*, in: RRE 4 (2018), 162-86 and M. Patzelt, *Über das Beten der Römer*, 2018.

158 Quintilian mentions that the ancient carmina of the Salii were unintelligible to his contemporaries, including the priest (Inst. 1.6.40). To avoid mistakes, prayers were written in books and dictated to the chief magistrate beforehand

very serious when it came to religion, and piety was an ideal, because piety in relation to the cult was understood as safeguarding order and prosperity for life in general.[159] Ungodliness and malpractice of the cult posed a major threat in the mind-set of people in antiquity, even philosophers guarded the cult.[160] Roger S. Bagnall explains it thus: "In paganism, what is central is action, the cult. The religion is the sum of the dedications, the sacrifices, the rituals: the interaction of human and divine."[161] This, however, does not mean that Greco-Roman religion was a uniform phenomenon. Contrary, as J.B. Rives has shown: "The deities to whom people prayed and made offerings varied a great deal. Some were gods with public cults, while others were deities of an individual's own choosing."[162] Furthermore, since there was no dogma, people could pursue their own ideas of God to a vide degree without restrictions.[163]

The good life according to a mainstream Greco-Roman mentality thus presupposed piety, εὐσέβεια or *pietas*, on part of human beings. But two dangers always lurked: either that people would be overly religious/superstitious (δεισιδαιμονία) or not religious enough/"atheists" (ἀθεότης). Plato defined atheism as all of the following: (1) not believing in the existence of the gods, (2) not believing that the gods care about human beings, (3) believing that the gods can be bribed with sacrifices and prayers.[164] The latter attitude was designated as impiety, ἀσέβεια. Later philosophers of late antiquity had similar thoughts, also directly in relation with prayer. In his commentary on Plato's *Timaeus*, the Neoplatonic philosopher Porphyry resumed how there are three ways of denying the usefulness of prayer: by

---

(Cic. nat. 2.4.10-11; Plin. n.h. 28.3.11). See: S.I. Johnston (ed.), *Religions of the Ancient World. A Guide*, Cambridge 2004, 366.

159 On the term piety, Dodds wrote: "The Greeks were apt to think of piety as a contractual relation rather than a state of mind." (E.R. Dodds (ed.), *Plato. Gorgias*, Oxford 1959, 336).

160 Dihle, 1999, 24. J. Engberg, *Impulsore Chresto. Opposition to Christianity in the Roman Empire c. 50-250*, Frankfurt 2007.

161 R.S. Bagnall, *Egypt in Late Antiquity*, Princeton 1993, 261.

162 J.B. Rives, *Religion and Authority in Roman Carthage from Augustus to Constantine*, Oxford 1995, 186.

163 Rives, 1995, 191.

164 Pl. Lg. 885b-910d (Burnet).

denying the existence of gods; by denying the involvement of the gods in human affairs; or by claiming that gods are involved in human life, but everything happens by necessity. These objections were also known by the Christian authors who also reacted to them. In his work *Stromateis*, Clement mentions this: "At this point I am reminded of the opinions which are being secretly propagated by certain heterodox persons, belonging to the heresy of Prodicus, against the use of prayer."[165] For Origen, this so-called problem of prayer prompted him to deal with the theme in his treatise *On Prayer*. Before returning to the philosophical considerations on prayer in late antiquity, the following passages will focus on the general religious context in which the authors under investigation formed their theological thoughts. In order to delimit this context, the focus will be on the three cities Alexandria, Carthage and Caesarea Maritima where the four Christian authors lived and worked for parts of their lives, viz. Clement and Origen lived in Alexandria, and Tertullian and Cyprian in Carthage. Actually, both Clement and Origen fled Alexandria, presumably just before they wrote their respective texts on prayer. They might both have travelled to Palestine, and Origen certainly settled in Caesarea Maritima. However, both authors are fundamentally "Alexandrian," and the Alexandrian culture is where they developed their basic theological assumptions.

Alexandria and Carthage were two vibrant centres in the late antique Roman Empire in regard to religion, philosophy, commerce and politics. Alexandria was second only to Rome, and Carthage challenged its position. Also Caesarea entailed a rich and diverse cultural life. The three cities were located in three different Roman provinces: Alexandria in the province of *Aegyptus*, Carthage in *Africa Proconsularis* and Caesarea Maritima in the province of *Provincia Syria Palaestina*. By the third century, they were all provincial capitals led by a proconsul. The three cities have another feature in common to which they owe their prominence – they had harbours that facilitated the flow of ideas and cargo. Also, all the three cities were affected by the empirical crisis of the third century which was caused by civil war, plague and economic depression.[166]

---

165 Clem. Strom. 7.7.41 (Hort/Mayor).
166 P. Brown, *The World of Late Antiquity. From Marcus Aurelius to Muhammad*, London 1971, 22.

2.1.2 Alexandria ad Aegyptum

Alexandria was the intellectual capital of the Greco-Roman world, a huge and diverse city. In the first century AD, Dion Chrysostom made the following observation: "I behold among you Alexandrians not merely Greeks and Italians and people from neighboring Syria, Libya, Cilicia, nor yet Ethiopians and Arabs from more distant regions, but even Bactrians and Scythians and Persians and a few Indians."[167] Such a quotation testifies to Alexandria's character as a dynamic, cosmopolitan melting pot with heterogeneous groups of citizens. The coexistence of such a varied multiethnic population was not unproblematic. For instance, the Jews were harassed and revolted, causing unrest in 38–41, 66 and 115–117. At the latter occurrence, the Jewish community was wiped out in Alexandria,[168] and the Jews did not return as a notable group in the city before the fourth century. Until 117 the Alexandrian Jews had their own quarter in the city, it constituted a *politeuma* (an independent community within the city under its own laws and government)[169] and had several synagogues.[170] The most notable of these synagogues was the so-called Great Synagogue, a beautiful, big building. It was "so immense that the hazzan had to wave a brightly colored scarf so that the huge congregation, some too distant to hear, could respond with the Amen after a benediction."[171] The Great Synagogue was demolished during the unrest in 115–17.[172] Despite of differences, the Jews were obviously in dialogue with the Greco-Roman intellectual elite and left its mark on it. For instance, Philo's writings from the first century and his allegorical reading of the Holy Scriptures came to inspire both Clement and Origen. The forced removal of the Jews and Jewish Christians from Alexandria probably is part of the explanation of the distinct Hellenic

---

167 Dion Chrys. *Orationes* 32.40 (Cohoon/Crosby).
168 K. Shillington, *Encyclopedia of African History*, Abingdon 2005.
169 Rives, 1995, 222. De Lange points to the flimsy evidence of Judaism in Alexandria between 117 and the Jewish revival in the fourth century (N. De Lange, *Origen and the Jews*. Cambridge 1976, 9).
170 C. Haas, *Alexandria in Late Antiquity. Topography and Social Conflict*, Baltimore 1997, 96-97. See Phil. Spec. 2.15.62.
171 Haas, 1997, 97, referring to Babylonian Talmud Sukkah 51b.
172 Eus. chron. 2.223 (see Haas, 1997, 102 n. 33). Brown, 2004, 98.

character of the Christianity that we find in the works of Clement and Origen.

Besides the Jews and eventually the Christians, the majority of the Alexandrians worshipped Greco-Roman and Egyptian gods. M. J. Brown notes how, according to some scholars, paganism and Alexandrian identity were intimately intertwined in the ancient mind.[173] A true Alexandrian was thus a pagan that worshipped pagan deities. J. Ferguson mentions a selection of the deities worshipped in Alexandria: The Egyptian gods and goddesses, Isis and Osiris and Harpocrates, Hathor and Cnephis, Ra and Ptah, the Greek deities, Zeus and Poseidon, Demeter and Kore, Apollo and Hermes, Hera and Aphrodite, Pan and Nemesis and Tyche. Foreign cults existed as well. Apart from the god of the Jews, we find Adonis, the Thracian Bendis, the Persian Mithras. Besides all these divinities was the ruler-cult, in which Roman emperors were worshipped, some even in their own lifetime.[174] Also, the syncretistic Egyptian-Hellenistic god Serapis/Sarapis was worshipped in the Alexandrian Serapeum. The Serapeum attracted suppliants that were willing to pay for cultic services, e.g. incubation.[175] In a letter preserved from the third century, a male, Aurelios Demareus, wrote to his sister or wife, that he had made a prayer (ἡ εὐχὴ) to "the great god Serapis" in the Serapeum of Alexandria for himself, his family and for the "great hopes of mankind."[176] Apparently, the supplicant had prayed for his family before, but now that he had prayed in the Serapeum, he believed that his prayer would be more efficient. In the letter, he calls his prayer: "now an even greater act of worship (ἔτιμεῖζον προσκυνεῖ) in the great Sarapeum (ἐν τῷ μεγάλῳ Σαραπείῳ)." He thereby testifies to the emphasis on physical location in relation to Greco-Roman pagan cults. In the Roman society, worship most often took place near an altar or holy place, either privately or publicly.[177] Although the Notitia Urbis Alexandrinae enumerates 2478

173 Brown, 2004, 106.
174 E. Ferguson (ed.), *Clement of Alexandria. Stromateis, Books 1–3*, The Fathers of the Church, Volume 85, Washington 1991, 6.
175 Brown, 2004, 104.
176 *A prayer to Sarapis* in P. Oxy. 1070, translation in M.C. Kiley (ed.), *Prayer from Alexander to Constantine. A Critical Anthology*, London 1997, 181-184.
177 K.J. Dover writes about this and states that: "it is doubtful whether anyone was prepared to assert explicitly that there were limits to the range of divine

temples and shrines in Alexandria about the third century,[178] according to Roger S. Bagnall, the traditional Greco-Roman cults were in decline in Alexandria, which was probably because of the general crisis of the empire.[179] Bagnall further hypothesizes that this must have been devastating to the sense of community in Egypt at large; "[the] cult as an organizing principle in society was lost. It may be that this vacuum helped make the spread of Christianity in Egypt so explosive in the fourth century: it replaced the lost structure of life."[180]

Christianity was found in multiple forms during the first centuries in Alexandria, "there was a strong strain of heterodoxy, or at least of diversity, there until the early third century."[181] The variations of "Christianity" are evidenced by the *Nag Hammadi*-texts that testify to the presence of Gnosticism in Egypt. In the *Nag Hammadi Library* one can find Gnostic prayers, e.g. *Prayer from the Apostle Paul*.[182] This prayer is thought to come from Valentinian Gnosticism and dates to the second or third century. It resembles an utterance from the canonical Pauline corpus (1 Cor 2:9), but in this Gnostic version it is combined with typical Gnostic concepts such as "angel-eyes" and "archon-ears."

During the third century, Alexandria experienced some unrest in the form of plague, civil war and foreign occupation (Palmyrene occupation in 270–72). In 215 the Emperor Caracalla slaughtered a number of people in Alexandria as response to criticism of his reign, and several times the Christians were persecuted, e.g. in 201 on the order from Septimius Severus.

---

hearing; the point of taking an oath at an altar or in a sanctuary was to enhance its solemnity and leave no room for doubt that the taker was acting deliberately and in full consciousness of what he was doing" (K.J. Dover, *Greek Popular Morality in the Time of Plato and Aristotle*, Oxford 1974, 257).

178 M. bar Elias, *Chronicle* 5.3, in: M. Fraser, *A Syriac Notitia Urbis Alexandrinae*, JEA 37 (1951), 103-108, probably based on a 4th -5th century Greek original. See A.S. Atiya (ed.), *The Coptic Encyclopedia*, New York 1990, 95b-103a.

179 Bagnall, 1993, 267

180 Bagnall, 1993, 268. Other scholars, however, do not see the crisis and decline of Pagan religion as the immediate reason for the rise of Christianity.

181 R. Heine, "The Alexandrians" in F. Young et al. (eds.), *The Cambridge History of Early Christian Literature*, Cambridge 2004, 113-130, 117.

182 Kiley, 1997, 291. C. Markschies, *Gnosis. An Introduction*, London 2003, 121.

However, Alexandria "retained its place as one of the preeminent cities of the Mediterranean."[183]

2.1.3 Carthage

In comparison with Alexandria, Carthage was not so deeply Hellenized.[184] Of course the entire Mediterranean area was more or less influenced by Greek *paideia*, but "North Africa's experience of Hellenization remained only sporadic and regionally determined."[185] Carthage was dominated by the Romans, and as M.J. Brown notes, if the Greeks had philosophy as an emblem of their intellectual life, "for the Romans it was law."[186] It surely holds true that the mentality of both Tertullian and Cyprian was forensic.

A historical overview of Carthage's dramatic history includes mentioning of the three Punic wars (246–146 B.C.E.) that resulted in Rome's conquest of the city in 146 B.C.E. The city was symbolically crushed when the Romans under the command of General Scipio flattened its citadel, the Byrsa hill.[187] According to the later Roman writer Macrobius, before the conquest, general Scipio conducted a Roman ritual, a *devotio*, in which he dedicated the soon-to-be conquered city to Dis Pater, saying:

> "Father Dis, Veiovis, Manes, or by whatever other name it is right to call you (*sive vos quo alio nomine fas est nominare*): ... In place of myself (*vicarios pro me*), my duty, and my office, I dedicate (*devoveo*) and curse [Carthage and its people] in place of the Roman people, our armies and legions... I call on you, mother Earth, and you, Jupiter, as witnesses."[188]

Scipio's prayer is an example of how different types of Roman officials, such as generals, magistrates and priests offered prayers before war, before sacrifice and at important state occasions. Scipio's devotion had the desired effect in the ancient mindset, because the Romans won the battle. Undoubtedly the

---

183 F. Young et al. (eds.), *The Cambridge History of Early Christian Literature*, Cambridge 2004, 117.
184 K.B. Stern, *Inscribing Devotion and Death. Archaelogical Evidence for Jewish Populations of North Africa*, Leiden 2007, 52.
185 Id.
186 Brown, 2004, 179.
187 Rives, 1995, 41.
188 Macr. Sat. 3,9,10 ff. (Kaster), written in the fifth century.

defeat left a mark on the Carthaginian consciousness, and 350 years later
Tertullian could still address the "Men of Carthage" and expect their immediate remembrance of Scipio and the conquest.[189] In fact, in *Apologeticum*,
Tertullian not only refers to the Roman conquest of Carthage, he also uses
it to illustrate the weakness of the gods of Carthage since they let the city be
defeated by the Romans. Contrary, Tertullian hails the Christian God as the
real God to whom one ought to pray in order to benefit the welfare of the
empire.[190] Returning to Scipio's prayer, it is worth noting that it was carefully addressed to a named deity with the assurance "or by whatever other
name it is right to call you." Because the Romans were afraid to summon
the wrong or no deity, they were careful in formulating their invocations.
In both Greek and Roman traditions, the exact address of a prayer was
vital in order for a specific god to feel obliged to help. Therefore addresses
in Greco-Roman prayers were frequently more elaborate and could include
"whether god or goddess" (*Si Deus, si Dea*), when the gender of a god was
unknown,[191] or "by whatever name" (*quocumque nomine*).

After the conquest of Carthage in 146 B.C.E., it would last about a cen-
tury before the Roman rulers took interest in the area. Caesar reconstituted
Carthage as a Roman colony under the name *Colonia Concordia Iulia
Karthago*.[192] At some point in the first century B.C.E. several Roman areas in
Africa were united as one province under the name *Africa Proconsularis*.[193]
Roman law, language and cult were introduced there, and an act of *inter-
pretatio romana* took place.

Along with the Roman restoration and construction of harbours, fora,
temples, etc. in Carthage, traders and immigrants arrived and settled in the
flourishing city, thus creating the multifaceted culture and society in which
Tertullian and Cyprian lived. By the third century, Carthage was once again
a flourishing and large metropolis with a hinterland of agricultural farm-
land. In order to give an example of a prayer from the area, I shall mention
a prayer from a small town outside of Carthage:

---

189 Tert. Apol. 25,8 (Becker) and Pall. 1 (Hunink).
190 Tert. Apol. 26,1 ff. (Becker).
191 E.g. Cato agr. 139 (in Kiley, 1997, 130).
192 Rives, 1995, 21-22. Brown, 2004, 168.
193 Rives, 1995, 22.

"Oreobazagra, Oreobazagra, Abrasax, Makhar, Semeseilam, Stenakhta, Lorsakthe, Koriaukhe, Adonaie, lord gods, hinder and turn away from this estate and from the crops growing in it ... hail, rust, the fury of Typhonian winds and the swarm of evil-doing locusts, so that none of these forces may fasten upon this estate or any of the crops in it..."[194]

This prayer shows different things about the religious culture of pagan Carthage: Firstly, the religious life was varied, and this prayer was probably written down by a sort of magician. The dedication is not usual. Furthermore, a prayer like this testifies to the ease with which people called upon gods for help with mundane undertakings. Prayers have been found that expressed wishes of attracting business, winning sexual partners and doing harm to one's enemies.[195]

As it was the case in Alexandria, in Carthage the population was also varied – a mix of Romans, Jews, Greeks, Numidians, Phoenicians, Libyans, etc. – and they worshipped many different deities. In Carthage one finds for instance the cult of the Capitoline Triad, i.e. Jupiter, Juno and Minerva;[196] J.B. Rives notes that "The cult of the Capitoline Triad, perhaps more than any other, was central to the collective religious identity of Roman citizens."[197] Also Venus was worshipped in Carthage, although she was not one of the most traditional deities in the Roman pantheon, probably Concordia too, Ceres who was an innovation in comparison to the Roman cult, Mars, Apollo, Roma (the divinized city), Dea Caelestis, Saturn, Mercury, Pluto, Hercules, Neptun, Sol Invictus, impersonal deities such as Victoria, Securitas, and deities from mystical cults such as Mithras and the Magna Mater, as well as the Greco-Egyptian Sarapis, etc.[198] Moreover, there was the imperial cult where emperors were believed to be divine and now functioned as key mediators between the human and the divine.[199] According to J.B. Rives, the imperial cult played a key role in creating a collective

---

194 Quoted from Rives, 1995, 193.
195 Id. 194.
196 Both indicated by archeological evidence and mentioned in the Urso charter (Rives, 1995, 40).
197 Id. 39.
198 Id. 44 ff. & 248. Brown, 2004, 188-192.
199 Rives, 1995, 51. An expression of this is an honorific prayer offered to the Emperor Augustus' divine essence on an altar from the first-century Gaul.

religious identity for the empire, and he argues that the persecutions of Christians were caused by a reality with too many different religious identities that threatened the homogeneity of the Roman society. In this situation, Christians were singled out and accused, although in reality the different cults of Carthage did not have that much in common.[200]

Whether or not there was a notable number of Jews in Carthage is a debated question, as well as the questions about what characterized the Carthagian Jews, and what kind of interaction there was between Jews and Christians. J.B. Rives finds that "a variety of evidence points to a relatively significant [Jewish] community developing in the second century CE at the latest."[201] Probably this community was predominately Greco-Romanized in character as other diaspora communities.[202] J.B. Rives and P.A. Harland suggest that in the Carthaginian context, the Jews probably resembled a Roman collegium, because they formed private associations that met on a regular basis.[203] Tertullian probably had very little contact with actual Jews, and when he wrote *Adversus Judaeos*, his sources were likely predominantly a "hermeneutical Jew,"[204] i.e. a constructed Jew developed from the accounts in the Scriptures, created as a contrast to the Christian self-definition.[205]

Concerning the Christians in Carthage, it is quite telling that the first evidence we have is a martyr story from 180, *The Passion of the Scillitan Martyrs*. Christian life was probably not particularly easy in this metropolis, and occasionally it was life-threatening. The clash of Pagans and the Christians is spelled out in the story of the Scillitan martyrs. Herein we are told that the proconsul Saturninus tried to make some Christians deny their faith and return to worshipping the Roman emperor. "Saturninus the proconsul said: We too are religious, and our religion is simple, and we swear by the genius of our lord the Emperor, and pray for his welfare (*et*

200 Id. 249.
201 Id. 215 ff. Babylonian Talmud RHSh 26a.
202 Id. 218 f.
203 Id. 222.
204 J. Cohen, *Living Letters of the Law. Ideas of the Jew in Medieval Christianity*, Oakland 1999, 3.
205 G.D. Dunn, *Tertullian's Aduersus Iudaeos. A Rhetorical Analysis*, Washington 2008, 15 ff.

pro salute eius supplicamus), as you also ought to do."[206] In this account, it is noticeable that prayer is used as a sign of religious identity among the Roman officials. The accused Christians, however, cannot pray to the emperor, and they end up confessing their monotheistic Christian faith by the final prayer-formula "Thanks be to God (*Deo gratias*)."[207]

About thirty years after the events recorded in the *The Passion of the Scillitan Martyrs*, Tertullian wrote that if all the Christians in Carthage were killed, the city would be more or less depopulated.[208] Although exaggerating, he thereby testifies to a large community of Christians in Carthage. Also in Carthage, Christianity was internally a varied phenomenon, and Tertullian lashed out against Marcion and Valentinus. Eventually, Tertullian himself was attracted to the new prophecy Montanism that arrived from Asia. The Montanists' emphasis on the free movement of the Holy Spirit must be seen historically as a counter-reaction towards the developing institutionalization of the church. About fifty years later, Cyprian came to embrace and affirm the institutionalization.

2.1.4 Caesarea Maritima, caput Judaea

Caesarea Maritima was the city to which Origen fled twice: in 216 when Emperor Caracalla persecuted the philosophers in Alexandria and again at about 231 due to a conflict with bishop Demetrios of Alexandria. It was presumably in Caesarea that Origen wrote his treatise on the Lord's Prayer, and I will therefore briefly mention Caesarea here. Caesarea had a Greco-Roman and a Jewish-Palestinian heritage, "a dual heritage" that continuously characterized the city and probably made Origen feel at home there, intellectually. Caesarea had an extremely good location, as it was placed conveniently on the land route from Alexandria to Antioch. The city centre of Caesarea was a temple for Augustus. According to Josephus, here one could find a statue of Roma and a statue of Augustus shaped according to the image of Zeus.[209] Evidence of reverence for other pagan

---

206 Acta scill. 3 (Musurillo).
207 Id.
208 Tert. Scap. 5.2. (tr. Thelwall).
209 H. Bietenhard, *Caesarea, Origenes und die Juden*, Stuttgart 1974, 7; Josephus b.j. 1.414.

deities in Caesarea is attested by coins bearing pictures of "the triad Tyche-Astarte, Dionysus and Demeter, as well as representations of Sarapis, in addition to Zeus, Poseidon, Apollo, Ares, Helios, Heracles and Nike."[210] Communication with the deities were sought and is attested, e.g. by curse tablets found in the prefects' palace, the latest probably from the fourth century.[211] Among several other attempts of communication with the divine in Caesarea is also a magical gem from the third or fourth century with the wording "Iao Sabaoth. Adonai Michael... victory of Iamou." The address is ΙΑΩΣΑΒΑΟΘ, that is Ιαω(θ) Σαβαω(θ) and is an attempt to invoke the God in a Jewish fashion, as it means "Lord of hosts," יְהוָה צְבָאוֹת, in Hebrew.[212] The content of the prayer seems to be the victory of the otherwise unknown Iamou.

During the Great Jewish Revolt in 66–70 Caesarea was a Roman stronghold, and afterwards in 71 or 72, Vespasian made Caesarea a Roman colony in the Province of Judaea. Later, after the Bar Kokhba revolt in 132–35, Hadrian merged the provinces of Judea and Syria into the *Province of Syria Palaestina*.[213] Although there was conflict between the Jews and the pagans in Caesarea on several occasions, and the Jews suffered severe blows – the city at one point being "completely emptied of Jews"[214] – the Jewish tradition was, according to H. Bientenhard, continuously in existence in Caesarea, and already by the third century, the Jews had regained some independence in the city.[215] Also for the rabbis Caesarea was a centre, although the Jewish patriarch resided in Sefforis and Tiberia. "The rabbis of Caesarea" is a frequent expression in the Palestinian Talmud.[216] Furthermore regarding the Jews in Caesarea, it has been claimed that part

210 T.L. Donaldson, *Religious Rivalries and the Struggle for Success in Caesarea Maritima*, Waterloo 2000, 138.
211 Bishop Eusebius of Caesarea preached against curse tablets (Eus. l. C. 13.4 (Heikel)).
212 W. Ameling et al. (eds.), *Caesarea and the Middle Coast: 1121-2160*, Berlin 2011, 585.
213 A. Lewin, *The archaeology of Ancient Judea and Palestine*, Los Angeles 2005, 33.
214 Josephus b.j. 2.457, quoted in Donaldson 2000.
215 Bietenhard, 1974, 11.
216 Id. 9.

of the *Mishnah* was compiled in Caesarea.[217] In the second half of the third
century, the rabbi Abbahu worked there. One tradition on prayer tells us
that this Rabbi Abbahu and a Jewish pantomimist, Pantokakus (literally
"five sins"), once met in Caesarea. It was during a time of drought, and
Rabbi Abbahu sought a man to pray for rain. He asks Pantokakus about
his occupation, and Pantokakus says that he made five sins every day when
performing in the theatre and doing other work.

> **He [i.e. R. Abbahu] said to him:** 'And what good deed have you done?'
>
> **He [i.e. Pantokakus] said to him:** 'One day I was decorating the theatre, and
> a woman came and stood behind a column and cried. I said to her: What
> troubles you? And she said: My husband is imprisoned and I wanted to see
> what I can do to free him.' So I sold my bedstead and the cover of my bed-
> stead, and I gave her their proceeds. And I said to her: 'This is yours, free your
> husband, but do not sin.'
>
> **R. Abbahu said to him:** 'You are entitled to pray and to be answered (by God).' "[218]

Lieberman explains that "in addition to the regular services in the Synagogue,
prayers were offered in the streets on special occasions such as droughts;
during these the scholars sometimes turned to the pious man among the
common folk to intervene before God on their behalf."[219] Origen must
have been influenced by the Jewish environment in Caesarea. Occasionally
Origen refers to "the Hebrews,"[220] but their identity is unknown.[221] At
one point in his writings, Origen seems to be directly inspired by the
aggadic interpretation, i.e. when he comments on the image of the ox (or
calf in Greek) licking up the grass of the field in Numbers 32.4, Origen
writes: "Just as the calf (tears up) the greenery with its mouth, so too the
holy people, making war with its lips, has its weapons in its mouth, because
of its prayers."[222] In comparison the Rabbinic interpretation is: "Just as an
ox's strength is in his mouth, so too [Israel's] strength is in their mouth... as
an ox gores with his horns, so they gore with their prayers."[223] Moreover,

---

217 De Lange, 1976, 8.
218 Donaldson, 2000, section 7.5 quotes y. Taan. 1.4, 64a.
219 S. Lieberman, *Greek in Jewish Palestine*, New York 1942, 30.
220 De Lange, 1976, 30 f.
221 Id. 132.
222 Or. hom. I-28 in Num. 13.22.5. quoted from De Lange, 1976, 131.
223 See Num. R. XX.4 in De Lange, 1976, 207, n. 96.

an example of resemblance between Origen and the rabbinic tradition is the use of the prayer of Hannah as a model for the correct manner of praying by both Origen[224] and the Rabbis.[225] Thus, it would seem that Origen is inspired by the Jewish milieu of his time.

2.1.5 Prayer and identity in the metropoles of the Roman Empire

The foregoing historically oriented contextual analysis has shown that prayer, understood as human contact with the deities, was ubiquitous in the ancient world. Prayer was a widespread phenomenon, and as we have seen Greco-Roman identity was marked by reverence for many different deities. The widespread cults of, e.g. Serapis and Augustus created coherence and community in the far-flung Roman Empire, and these cults thereby created some sense of a collective Roman identity. As J.B. Rives has shown, this was the case on an official level, but in the civic community, religious identities varied a lot, and that was a problem for the authorities.

The Christians stood out because their worship, prayer included, from the outset excluded all pagan deities and therefore the official identity of the Greco-Roman world. The Pagan Lucian of Samosata said it directly in the mid-first century:

> "[Jesus] that first lawgiver of theirs persuaded them that they are all brothers the moment they transgress and deny the Greek gods and begin worshipping (προσκυνῶσιν) that crucified sophist and living by his laws."[226]

The Christian community and identity were constituted by this exclusion of the pagan pantheon, which came to the fore in prayer. This exclusiveness made the Christians incompatible with the Greco-Roman cult, and thereby, as J.B. Rives has shown, they were not only in opposition to the Greco-Roman cults, but to the salient identity of the Romans.

---

224 Or. or. 2.5, 4.1, 16.3 (Koetschau).
225 R. Hamnuna, B. *Ber.* 31[ab] in De Lange, 1976, 196, n.50.
226 Lucian of Samosata Peregr. 18, quoted in Van Voorst, *Jesus Outside the New Testament*, Grand Rapids 2000, 59.

2.2 Non-Christian philosophies on prayer

In antiquity, prayer in various forms was an essential part of life and was a theme that pagan intellectuals had to deal with, just as the Christians and Jews did.[227] If we turn to late antique philosophy, we find treatises on prayer that are more or less comparable with the treatises on prayer formulated by Christians; among these philosophical treatises are:[228] the Stoic Epictetus's *Discourses* and the abbreviated version thereof, *Handbook* (first century); the Stoic Marc Aurel's *Meditations* (ca. 180); the Middle-Platonist Maximus of Tyre's *Fifth Oration on Prayer* (second century); the Neo-Platonist Plotinus' *Enneads* (mid-third century); the Neo-Platonist Porphyry's *Letter to his wife Marcella* (late third century).

Also within Hellenistic Judaism, one finds written reflections on prayer, e.g. by the Hellenistic Jew Philo of Alexandria who was himself Hellenized and influenced by the contemporary Platonic philosophers. When reading the philosophical texts, their eclectic character becomes clear. The ideas, even though ascribed to different philosophical "schools," can be difficult to keep apart from one another. In regard to prayer, a number of assumptions are recurrent in the Stoic and Neo-Platonic traditions of late antiquity, as well as in Hellenistic Judaism and Christianity. One common theme is the so-called problem of prayer, which refers to the question whether prayer, and petitionary prayer in particular, is relevant. This issue is closely related to the themes of providence and petition. In the following, I shall paint a broad and generalizing picture of the philosophical traditions by describing their understanding of prayer and providence, petition, sacrifice and virtue.

---

227 Already Plato and Aristotle wrote on the subject. "There are many isolated references in Plato's dialogues... Aristotle wrote a [Peri Euches], of which only a single fragment survives" (M B Trapp, *Maximus of Tyre, The Philosophical Orations*, Oxford 1997, 41). J.M. Rist summarizes Plato's view: "All goods can be achieved without it [prayer], though, if properly indulged, prayer can certainly do no harm and might be supposed to induce the proper attitudes in the citizens." (J.M. Rist, *Plotinus. Road to Reality*, Cambridge 1967, 200; cf. lg. 801A (Burnet)).

228 D.T. Runia, *The Pre-Christian Origin of Early Christian Spirituality*, in: P. Allen/W. Mayer/L. Cross (eds.), *Prayer and Spirituality in the Early Church II*, Brisbane 1999, 13.

2.2.1 Prayer and providence (πρόνοια)

Questions concerning God's providence and determinism were raised time and again in intellectual circles of late antiquity, also by Origen in *Perì Euchês* as we shall see below. While all philosophers, except for the ever-doubting Sceptics, seemed to agree that there is one or more gods, they differed when it came to the question whether these gods have determined everything beforehand. This question was important in relation to prayer, because *if* the Gods have ordained everything beforehand, do prayers then have a purpose? The Stoics believed in determinism; they believed in destiny, εἱμαρμένη, as a determined causal nexus. However, according to the Stoic philosophers, one thing has not been determined, and that is our attitude. Our attitude and choice is still "up to us" (ἐφ' ἡμῖν).[229] The Stoic philosopher Epictetus gives an example of a prayer in *Handbook* 53 which expresses the desire to follow the divine ordering by choice:

"In every thing (circumstance) we should hold these maxims ready to hand: "Lead me, O Zeus, and thou O Destiny, the way that I am bid by you to go: to follow I am ready. If I choose not, I make myself a wretch, and still must follow."[230]

Despite of this belief in determinism, both Epictetus and Marc Aurel thought that prayer *was* a meaningful endeavour. Epictetus argued that prayer and worship were pre-determined – like everything else – and therefore it had to take place. It was, however, important for Epictetus that no one prayed for that which they ought to take care of themselves. Therefore, Epictetus urged action instead of prayer, when it came to concrete ordeals:

"We cannot help but be in fear, we cannot help but be in anxiety. And then we say, 'O Lord God, how may I escape anxiety?' Fool, have you not hands? Did not God make them for you? Sit down now and pray forsooth that the mucus in your nose may not run! Nay, rather wipe your nose and do not blame God! What then? Has he given you nothing that helps in the present case? Has he not given you endurance, has he not given you magnanimity, has he not given you courage?"[231]

---

229 Epict. Ench. 1.1. (Schenkl; tr. Long).
230 Epict. Ench. 53 (Schenkl; tr. Long).
231 Epict. Diatr. 2.16.11 (Henderson; tr. Oldfather).

Marc Aurel was of the opinion that prayer in itself is a way to come to terms with the already-fixed realities. According to Marc Aurel, prayer is an exercise that strengthens the mind. If you want to pray for something that you desire, you should rather pray not to care about it in the first place. If you are attracted to a woman, you should therefore not pray to have her, but not to lust after her.[232]

Determinism was also thought of as a reality by the Neo-Platonists who saw it as impossible to turn God from his purpose by doing or thinking something particular or crying or making supplications and sacrifices.[233] Nevertheless, Porphyry writes that: "To pray to god is not evil, but failure to give thanks is most wicked."[234] Furthermore, "The prayer... accompanying good deeds is pure as well as quite acceptable."[235] With such expressions, also Porphyry shows that he accepted certain prayers as meaningful.

Characteristic for Stoicism is that God is inside cosmos, and inside all humans; the same rationality, *logos,* fills both the individual and the entire cosmos. Everything is co-dependent, and there is sympathy between the elements in cosmos, also between human beings and the heavenly bodies that were widely believed to possess divine rational souls.[236] This Stoic idea of co-dependence was taken over by the Neo-Platonists, who believed that because of this cosmic sympathy, prayers are responded to in a causal fashion. A prayer is an act, to which the universe reacts, "like a musical string which, plucked at one end, vibrates at the other also."[237] A prayer is thus part of "one melodic system (μία ἁρμονία)," Plotinus says.[238] However, according to Plotinus, the response that such a prayer causes is not thought of as deriving from a conscious or wilful decision. Both magical incantations and philosophical petitions resonate and have an effect:

> "Similarly with regard to prayers; there is no question of a will that grants; the powers that answer to incantations do not act by will... In other words, some

---

232 Marc Aurel, *Meditationes* 9,40 (Haines; tr. Staniforth).
233 Porph. Marc. 19 (Wicker).
234 Id. 23.
235 Id. 24.
236 J.M. Rist, 1967, 203.
237 Plot. Enn. 4.4.41 (Henry/Schwyzer; tr. MacKenna/Page).
238 Id.

influence falls from the being addressed upon the petitioner - or upon someone else - but that being itself, sun or star, perceives nothing of it all."[239]

According to Plotinus' view of prayers, there are prayers in the form of petitions and magical enchanting that resonate in the universe, but they are not received by "a will that grants."[240] There exists a higher form of prayer, according to Plotinus, a contemplation that links the individual's intellect with the intelligible realm. I shall return to this below and here draw the conclusion that these philosophical interpretations of prayer do not entail a personal God in a classical Jewish or Christian sense.

2.2.2 Petitionary prayers

In general, the philosophers leave no room for petitionary prayers. Maximus of Tyre is a famous example of a philosopher who dismisses petitions and reckoned such prayers only as "misguided prayers of foolish men."[241] If petitions seem to have a happy outcome, this should not be attributed to gods, but to chance:

> "When by deceit or force men obtain what they pray for, but not what they truly desire, they attribute the gifts to the gods, even though it was not from the gods that they received it. God does not distribute evils; they are rather the gift of chance coming blindly from their unreasoning source like the cheery greetings of drunkards."[242]

According to the philosophers, legitimate prayer is frequently thought of as either a conversation with God or an elevation of the mind to God, but definitely not as requests.[243] Furthermore, legitimate prayer has to do with deeds, because: "It is not the tongue of the wise man that is worthy of

---

239 Plot. Enn. 4.4.40 (Henry/Schwyzer; tr. MacKenna/Page).
240 J. Dillon, *The Platonic Philosopher at Prayer*, in: J. Dillon/A. Timotin (eds.), *Platonic Theories of Prayer*, Boston 2016, 13
241 Max.Tyr. Fifth Oration 5.1. (tr. Trapp).
242 Id. 5.1.19-24.
243 Id. 8.
    Prayers that expressed human desires or mundane wishes were a taboo for philosophers, although Marc Aurel for a moment nostalgically lauds a simple request to Zeus: "The Athenians pray, "Rain, rain, dear Zeus, upon the fields and plains of Athens. Prayers should either not be offered at all, or else be offered as simple and ingenuous as this." (*Meditations* 5,7 (Haines; tr. Staniforth).

honour in God's eyes, but rather his deeds. For a wise man in his silence
honors God, but the foolish man, even when he is praying and offering
sacrifices, defiles the divine. Therefore the wise man alone is a priest; he
alone is God-beloved; he alone knows how to pray."[244]

The Alexandrian Jew Philo, although influenced by contemporary philosophy, did not exclude petitionary prayers in general, but maintained
that "a prayer is a request for good things,"[245] which suits Plato's conviction that prayers should be made only for good, beautiful and righteous
things.[246] An example of a worthy request is made by Philo himself: "I
for my part would pray that if I ever have thought up to do a wrong, the
wrongdoing should fail."[247] Moreover, according to Philo, it is legitimate to
pray for (1) God's presence within one's conscience,[248] (2) for a life without
excesses,[249] (3) for a happy old age, (4) a happy death[250] and (5) virtue.[251]
According to Philo, the intention is important, and if the supplicant is dear
to God, he/she will be heard.[252] In the end, however, the ultimate effect of
prayer lies, also for Philo, "in opening the way to Him through virtue, not
necessarily in granting individual prayers."[253] Within intellectual circles of
late antiquity, there was not much room left for petitionary prayers, and
in general any attempt of receiving material and concrete gains from the
divine was looked upon with suspicion.

2.2.3 Prayer, sacrifice (θυσία) and further practice (Ἔργα ... πράγματα)

Prayer and sacrifice were the main links between gods and humans in late
antique cult practice, although some ambiguity surrounded the practice

---

244 Porph. Marc. 16 (Wicker).
245 Philo, *De agricultura* 99 (Leonhardt, 2001, 111).
246 Pl. lg. 687d-e (Burnet); see Leonhardt, 2001, 111-114.
247 Philo, *De posteritate Caini* 81 (Leonhardt, 2001, 111).
248 Philo, *De fuga et inventione* 118 (Leonhardt, 2001, 112).
249 Philo, *Quod Deus immutabilis sit* 164 (Leonhardt, 2001, 112).
250 Philo, *De sacrificiis Abelis et Caini* 99 (Leonhardt, 2001, 112).
251 Philo, *De agricultura* 168. *De ebrietate* 224. *De somniis* 2,101. Leonhardt
     points out how praying for virtue resembles "the well-known Jewish prayer
     for wisdom" (Leonhardt, 2001, 114).
252 Philo, *Quod Deus immutabilis sit* 156 (Leonhardt, 2001, 114).
253 Leonhardt, 2001, 139.

of sacrifice. Prayer and sacrifice were bound together in the cult, but the question posed by the philosophers was if the cult actions made any sense. Porphyry was of the opinion that "God's altars, if they are consecrated, do not harm us; if they are neglected, they do not help us."[254] Marc Aurel expressed an equally sceptic opinion: "Many grains of incense fall on the same altar: one sooner, one later – it makes no difference (διαφέρει δ' οὐδέν)."[255] Even if sacrifices were common and thought of as vitally important for the success of the Roman Empire, philosophers remained sceptic or indifferent in relation to the phenomenon. It was, however, also a dominating idea that gods deserved veneration, but that this praise might as well consist of prayer and praise or even of a virtuous life, and that this could substitute material sacrifices. Such reinterpretations of sacrifice were expressions of a spiritualization of the cult that took place in both Pagan philosophy, Judaism[256] and Christianity.[257] Also the classic cult-critique was upheld. According to this critique, the sacrificial institution should be upheld but harshly criticized because of the possible absence of ethical behaviour among its participants.[258]

If the philosophers had been able to decide, prayer would probably have become a highly mental endeavour by the third century and would not have been used as an accessory to sacrifice, but this was obviously not the case. People, disregarding the philosophic criticism, did not really stop praying for whatever they wanted, and only slowly did they cease to sacrifice. Still in the fourth century, the Roman official Sallustius expressed the following opinion: "Prayers without sacrifice are mere words, whereas if sacrifice is

---

254 Porph. Marc. 18 (Wicker).
255 Marc Aurel, *Meditationes* 4,15 (Haines; tr. Staniforth).
256 Kiley, 1997, 90: "Reflecting biblical and Greek philosophical traditions, Philo is fully persuaded that the only rightful response of people to the providential care bestowed on them by God is the activity of prayer and praise. No other 'gift' will suffice since all things are God's." Kiley mentions the following references as argumentation: Philo, *De Plantatione* 130; spec. 1.271; cf. Psalm 50:12-13; Acts 17:24-5: Seneca [citing Plato], Epistles, 65.8.
257 Just. apol. I.13 (Minns/Parvis); Tert. Or. 28 (Schleyer); Clem. Strom. 7.6.31.7 (Hort/Mayor).
258 Such critique is classical in the sense that it is known from the Hebrew Bible and classic philosophers, e.g. Amos 5:21-24 and Theophrastus.

added, the words gain life, the word giving power to the life and the life animating the word."[259]

2.2.4 Prayer, virtue (ἀρετή) and salvation (σωτηρία)

Not all forms of prayer were looked upon as unjustified in philosophical discourse. The philosopher's prayer was held at high regard. In order to understand how the effects of prayer were understood among philosophers of late antiquity, it is essential to understand their belief in a divine part within human beings. They imagined that humans have a spark of divinity within themselves, a *logos*, which constitute the rational part of the soul.[260] Stoics held that this *logos* quite literally is a fragment of God, ἀπόσπασμα τοῦ Θεοῦ,[261] "and that the rationality which we possess is a fragment of God's rationality."[262] Marcus Aurel put it like this:

> "To live with the gods is to show them at all times a soul contended with their awards, and wholly fulfilling the will of the inward divinity, that particle of himself, which Zeus has given to every man for ruler and guide – the mind and the reason."[263]

It was this divine centre of the individual that was thought to make the endeavour of praying possible; since it was a point of reference between humans and god. The effect of prayer was understood as a further approximation between the individual and the divine, namely as a refinement of rationality or virtue. If such prayers are petitionary, it is in the sense that God is asked to confer goods of a moral, intellectual or spiritual character.[264]

In contrast to the Stoics, the Neo-Platonists imagined God as being outside the visible world, but the Neo-Platonist also believed in the existence

---

259 Sal., *Concerning the Gods and the Universe* xvi (Nock).
260 "Alle in der Kaiserzeit massgebenden Philosophien betrachteten den Wesenskern des Menschen als göttlich… Die Gottheit… war darum dem eigenen Inneren verwandt. Hier liegt die wichtigste Voraussetzung für die philosophische Lehre vom Gebet als Kommunikation mit der Gottheit." (Dihle, 1999, 29).
261 Epict. diatr. 2.8.11 (Schenkl, tr. Long).
262 K. Seddon, *Epictetus' Handbook and the Tablet of Cebes. Guides to Stoic Living*, Oxford 2006, 21.
263 Marc Aurel, *Meditationes* 5,27 (Haines; tr. Staniforth); cf. 12.1.
264 K. Algra, "Epictetus and Stoic theology" in T. Scaltsas and A.S. Mason (eds.) *The Philosophy of Epictetus*, Oxford 2007, 32-55.

of a divine spark within human beings; "Reason says: the divine is entirey present everywhere; Its temple among men has been firmly established only in the thought of the wise man,"[265] Porphyry writes. Because of this divine spark, the individual is capable of communicating with God through prayer or contemplation. The very contact with the divine is to be understood as a sort of prayer, "an aspiration to be present to the divine, an aspiration that moves the soul to awaken from its outer preoccupations so as to turn toward and receive what is always present."[266] Prayer is a way for the lower levels in cosmos to perceive a higher reality, by the soul stretching towards God. Plotinus writes:

> "we first invoke God himself not in loud words, but in that way of prayer which is always within our power, leaning in our soul towards him by aspiration, alone towards the Alone (μονος πρὸς μόνον)"[267]

For both Stoics and Neo-Platonists, the ideal is for the soul to return, ἐπιστροφή, to God and have union, συναφή, with God and the intelligible world. This could happen through philosophical contemplation during which the individual would achieve likeness with the divine by an act of imitation. Porphyry writes that "the wise man both makes himself acceptable to God and becomes divine by the similarity of his own disposition to the immortal blessedness..."[268] The Platonists formulated the ideal as "becoming like to God," ὁμοίωσις Θεῷ; the Stoics also phrased the goal as "to follow God" (ἀκολουθεῖν τῷ Θεῷ) or imperative "follow God!" (ἕπου Θεῷ). Marc Aurel was not modest concerning human capability, he claimed that: "It is perfectly possible to be godlike, even though unrecognized as such."[269] Becoming like to God meant being virtuous as God is virtuous and developing a pure mind.[270] Plotinus suggests that after having been likened

---

265 Porph. Marc. 11 (Wicker).
266 Wakoff, *Awaiting the Sun: A Plotinian Form of Contemplative Prayer*, in: J. Dillon/A. Timotin (eds.), *Platonic Theories of Prayer*, Boston 2016, 75.
267 Plot. Enn. 5.1.6.9 (Henry/Schwyzer; tr. MacKenna/Page).
268 Porph. Marc. 17 (Wicker).
269 Marc Aurel, *Meditationes* 7.67 (Haines; tr. Staniforth).
270 Porph. Marc. 16 (Wicker).

to God, one can "call on God, maker of the sphere whose image you now hold, and pray Him to enter."[271]

Philosophical contemplation was supposed to lead to virtue and thus to perfection, and the philosopher's prayer was an auxiliary to approach the divine.[272] It remained, however, a task of the individual to approach the divine. It does not make sense to pray for a virtuous soul; you have to bring it about yourself, but you can pray and thereby be in conversation with the divine.[273] The *pura mens* is developed when the individual knows God and subsequently aligns himself/herself with God, as Porphyry writes:

> "For God, as being the father of all, has indeed no lack of anything; but it is well for us when we adore him by means of justice, chastity, and other virtues, making our life itself a prayer to him and seeking to know him. For seeking to know him purifies us, while imitation of him deifies us by bringing our disposition in line with his."[274]

Philosophy, prayer and virtue (ἀρετή) were thus entwined, and their utmost consequence was salvation (σωτηρία). That human beings are always responsible for their own spiritual growth and salvation is poignantly formulated by Plotinus when he wrote that prayers do not win battles, but trained men win battles.[275] From a Neo-Platonic perspective, the Christian reliance on salvation by faith without endeavour could only be regarded as "intellectual

---

271 Plot. Enn. 5.8.9 (Henry/Schwyzer; tr. MacKenna/Page). For a discussion of the address of this prayer and the distinction between "nous" and "the World Soul"/"the One," see Rist, 1967, 210.
    Here Plotinus seems to value prayer. However, at other times he seems to disregard prayer, see e.g. Porph. Plot. 10 (tr. Mackenna): "Amelius was scrupulous in observing the day of the New-Moon and other holy-days and once asked Plotinus to join in some such celebration; Plotinus refused: 'It is for those Beings to come to me, not for me to go to them'."

272 Plot. Enn. 5.1.6 (Henry/Schwyzer; tr. MacKenna/Page). See also Max.Tyr. Fifth Oration 8 (tr. Trapp).

273 See also Max.Tyr. Fifth Oration 5,8 (tr. Trapp).

274 Augustine quotes this from Porph. Philosophy from Oracles, in Aug. civ. 19.23 (Dombart/Kalb).

275 "[T]he law decrees that to come safe out of battle is for fighting men, not for those that pray. The harvest comes home not for praying but for tilling; healthy days are not for those that neglect their health: we have no right to complain of the ignoble getting the richer harvest if they are the only workers in the fields, or the best." (Plot. Enn. 3.2.8 (Henry/Schwyzer; tr. MacKenna/Page)).

laziness."[276] The philosophers strived to progress and believed that they were able to do so because of the divine within themselves. Maria-Barbara von Stritzky refers to this kind of salvation as: "... die σωτηρία... für die der Mensch selbst sorgen muss und die er aufgrund der nie verlorenen Verbindung, ja sogar der Identität mit dem Seinsgrund, aus eigener Kraft erreichen kann."[277]

Philosophical prayer is a part of the development and a means of reaching a certain state of mind where the philosopher is unified with the divine and develops a corresponding attitude. According to the philosophers, not everyone is capable of philosophical prayer and contemplation leading to virtue. Some – in fact, most people – are philosophical amateurs, ἀμαθεῖς. Such amateurs could, according to Porphyry, look to theurgy and through rituals of theurgy come a bit further in his/her spiritual progress.[278]

In Hellenistic Judaism, as we find it in the works of Philo of Alexandria, there is a similar idea of knowledge as salvific, although for Philo the salvific knowledge was not awareness of the divine within, "but rather of recognizing one's status over against God."[279] For Philo therefore, the knowledge of God was not aimed at union with God as much as an awareness of one's relationship with God, "a dialogic relation between two wholly unequal partners."[280] Actually for Philo, knowledge of God is impossible, and even Moses' prayer to see God's face was not granted.[281] However, also Philo had the idea that God can enter into the individual as response to prayer, and thereby exalt the mind of that person.[282]

---

276 H. Wittaker, *The Purpose of Porphyry's Letter to Marcella*, in: SO 76/1 (2010), 151.

277 Stritzky, 1989, 94.

278 Id. 96. See B.A. Pearson, *Theurgic Tendencies in Gnosticism and Iamblichus's Conception of Theurgy*, 253-75, in: R.T. Wallis/J. Bregman, *Neoplatonism and Gnosticism*, Albany 1992, 260.

279 P. Allen/W. Mayer/L. Cross (eds.), *Prayer and Spirituality in the Early Church II*, Brisbane 1999, 18. Cf. Rabbi Eliezer: "When you pray, know before whom you stand" (Gemara Berakhot 28).

280 Allen, 1999, 18.

281 Leonhardt, 2001, 112, cf. Philo, *De fuga et inventione* 164-165: "For, says God, "thou shalt see my back parts, but my face thou shalt not Behold."

282 Philo, *De sobrietate* 64 (Colson/Whitaker).

The virtuous prayer of the philosopher was held as an ideal, "… it is a prayer made within the context of correct moral and theological understanding."[283] The philosopher who has the ability to pray in this way serves also as a messenger and representative for the divine.[284] When dealing with prayer, it is noteworthy that Philo thinks of Israel as holding the position of the high priest, the intercessor for the whole human race.[285] Jutta Leonhardt interprets Philo's view on prayer in such a way that "Jewish prayer [is] the prayer of the philosopher nation to the one true God, which corresponds to the idea common in late antiquity that only the philosopher can pray in truth."[286] In the next chapter, we shall see how Christians placed primarily Jesus Christ in the role of the high priest and believed him to be the way to God, but also developed ideas about how each individual Christian can pray correctly and be in contact with God.

2.2.5 Non-Christian prayer and identity

According to the Stoic and Neo-Platonic philosophers, prayer had the ultimate purpose of connecting the individual to God; "Prayer is a means of uniting the One in ourselves with the One in itself."[287] By way of prayer, the individual could achieve an approximation to the divine and affect union with God. Being like to God meant becoming virtuous – and herein lay salvation. J.M. Rist describes the philosophers' prayers as "unspoken prayers, prayers which arise from a soul whose passions are stilled and silent and which will attain its vision in that silence which for Plotinus is a clear note of the presence of the One."[288] As such, philosophical prayer was essentially a "self-centred" act.

Since the union with God was thought only to be obtainable for a certain kind of wise people, i.e. the philosophers, the philosophical systems were dominated by spiritual elitism.[289] The philosophers' prayer was expected to

---

283 O'Brien, *Prayer in Maximus of Tyre*, in: J. Dillon/A. Timotin (eds.), *Platonic Theories of Prayer*, Boston 2016, 65.
284 Id., 67.
285 Phil. spec. 1.97 (Leonhardt, 2001, 128).
286 Leonhardt, 2001, 141.
287 Rist, 1967, 212.
288 Id. 211.
289 P. Allen et al. Brisbane 1999, 15.

lead to virtue and hence to a distinctive behaviour and feature from which other people could also benefit. Nevertheless, prayer in the philosophical tradition was an endeavour that had to do with the praying person's own self. As D.T. Runia notes "… philosophy was the concern of the individual for his or her self."[290] D.T. Runia calls the philosophical spirituality a reflective spirituality, because it forces the individual to reflect on the prayer and oneself.[291] We shall see that the same to some degree was the case in Christianity, where Christians were ordered to scrutinize their own will and sinfulness. However, in Christianity, the community played a very important role in regard to prayer in contrast to the situation for the philosophers.

Looking at the philosophical texts from the perspective of identity theory, we see that the philosophers were in the midst of identity formation when praying. In contemplative prayer, they created an idea of who they were and should be, and how they should act in society – in other words, they created a potential identity that corresponded to the world around them as they perceived it. The philosophers, according to their texts, were aware that they were doing something special and refined, exactly because of their ability to become united with God and activate the divinity within. Their ability to higher contemplation set them apart, and it all began with praying and contemplation – *a philosopher's prayer*. Philosophical prayer was the mark of a collective, but highly exclusive identity. Although a certain form of contact with the divine was idealized in philosophical milieus, an unease with the phenomenon of prayer remained in the philosophical treatises. Praying if it meant asking God for anything was a provocation for the philosophers, this "problem of prayer" thus remained to be dealt with by Christian authors such as Origen.

2.3 Christian prayer in the first three centuries A.D. – a summary

The Christian treatises that will be explored in this book contain some of the earliest extant reflections on Christian prayer that have been preserved from antiquity. Clement's treatise is referred to as "the oldest Christian

---

290 Runia, 1999, 15.
291 Id. 13.

theological statement on the subject"[292], although Tertullian's treatise might be even older. Therefore, we cannot compare the treatises with any earlier Christian material of the same sort. However, these treatises of course did not develop *ex nihilo*, but built on and depart from traditions of how Christian and also Pagan and Jewish prayer was understood and practised in and around early Christian congregations. The following paragraphs give a summary of Christian prayer during the first three centuries A.D., from the mid-first to the late third century. I deal with this time frame, as I believe E.F. von Goltz was correct when he pointed to a development in Christian prayer and a kind of tipping point at the end of the third century.[293] By that time, the liturgical material becomes vast, and standardization takes place within the evermore organized Church and in the monastic milieus. The first three centuries thus constitute a first phase of development regarding Christian prayer, characterized by variety.[294]

2.3.1 The interdependence of Christianity and Rabbinic Judaism

Next to the Hebrew Bible and early Christian Scriptures, the Jewish synagogue has traditionally been understood as another major influence on early Christian prayer. In earlier scholarship, from Gregory Dix onwards, it was the habit to look for Jewish precedents for almost every early Christian prayer.[295] However, as Bradshaw has pointed out, "the extent to which very early Christian prayers were influenced by Jewish models can be overestimated."[296] In fact, the relationship between the worship of Rabbinic Judaism, on the one hand, and the early Christian worship, on the other,

---

292 Simpson, 1965, 36.
293 Goltz refers to the change by stating that: "Das Beten der Christen ist etwas anderes geworden und die Geschichte des Gebets, soweit sie für uns überhaupt erkennbar ist, wird ein Stück der komplizierten Geschichte des christlichen Kultus." (Goltz, 1901, X).
294 On the development of liturgy, see P. Bradshaw, *Daily Prayer in the Early Church. A Study of the Origin and Early Development of the Divine Office*, London 1981 and Bradshaw 2002.
295 D.G. Dix, *The Shape of the Liturgy*, London 1945; Bradshaw, 2002, 122-126.
296 A. Gerhards/A. Doeker/P. Ebenbauer (eds.), *Identität durch Gebet. Zur gemeinschaftsbildenden Funktion institutionalisierten Betens in Judentum und Christentum*. Paderborn 2003, 29.

was probably dominated by reciprocity – Christianity and Rabbinic Judaism developed as if they were "twins."[297] The simultaneous development makes it difficult to say which ideas about and patterns of prayer were profoundly Christian. Both Christianity and Judaism were in a formative phase in the first centuries; this was the case for Judaism because it had lost its temple in Jerusalem and had to create new forms of worship that did not centre on this concrete sanctuary.[298] There is no clear answer to the question when Christianity and Judaism had formed contrasting self-identities and thus stopped developing concurrently.[299]

Rabbinic Judaism produced a tractate on public worship and private prayer, *Mishnah Berakoth,* part of the *First Mishnah* and probably compiled in the beginning of the third century; later, the *Tosefta Berakoth* was added, but the redaction history of the two texts is obscure, and it seems that Judaism entailed huge regional differences.[300] Prayer was as all-pervading a phenomenon in Judaism as in Christianity. This can be seen in the fact that a synagogue could also be designated as a "house of prayer," προσ ευχή.[301] To some degree the worship of Christianity and Judaism conflated, but of course the ways had to part because of the Christological focus of the Christians that meant that their prayers were spoken to Jesus, "in the name of" or "through Jesus"[302] and in the eschatological expectation of His *parousia.*[303] "It was, therefore, imperative that the Christian community

---

297 Gerhards/Doeker/Ebenbauer, 2004, 41. On the interdependence, see also: Katzoff, 2009.

298 G. Stroumsa, *The End of Sacrifice. Religious Transformations in Late Antiquity,* Chicago 2009. See below, "3.2.2.3. Prayer as spiritual sacrifice."

299 Some scholars believe it to have been already in the first centuries, others like Boyarin, believe the so-called parting of the ways to have taken place much later in the fourth century. See Katzoff, 2009, 315.

300 Leonhardt, 2001, 1.

301 I. Levinskaya, *A Jewish or Gentile Prayer House? The meaning of* ΠΡΟΣΕΥΧΗ, in: TynB 41/1 (1990), 155.

302 John 14:13-14; 15:16; 16:23 ff.; Rom 1:8; 7:25; Col 3:17; 1 Pet 2.5; Did. 9.4; 1 Clem. 61.3. See L. Hurtado, *The Place of Jesus in Earliest Christian Prayer and its Import for Early Christian Identity,* in: R. Hvalvik/K.O. Sandness (eds.), *Early Christian Prayer and Identity Formation,* Tübingen 2014, 35-56.

303 Eph 6:18. Cf. Jesus' command to his disciples to "watch and pray" (Mark 14:32-42; Matt 26:36-46; cf. Luke 22:40-46.).

should form itself as a clearly defined entity distinct from the Jewish community. It had become the Church perhaps even before it had realized that this had happened."[304]

2.3.2 The earliest Christian prayer practice

The New Testament and the Hebrew Bible form an essential inspiration for the euchological treatises of Tertullian, Cyprian, Origen and Clement. In particular the Lord's Prayer, Paul's admonitions to pray always and recourses to the psalms occur frequently in the Christian treatises on prayer. There is, however, a peculiar lack of references to many other New Testament prayer-like texts, such as the Lucan canticles of Mary, Zachariah and Simeon,[305] the disciple's prayer for boldness[306] and "The song of the lamb."[307] The lack of New Testament prayer patterns is a general observation when studying early Christian texts, and it therefore seems questionable that the New Testament prayers were in widespread use in early Christianity.[308] Even the Lord's Prayer is rather seldom in sources from the first three centuries,[309] but it probably did work as an important identity

---

304 Rordorf, quoted from Bradshaw, 1981, 24.

305 Luke 1:46-55; 1:68-79; 2:29-32.

306 Acts 4:24-30.

307 Rev 5:9-13.

308 P. Bradshaw, *Parallels between Early Jewish and Christian Prayers. Some Methodological Issues*, in: A. Gerhards/A. Doeker/P. Ebenbauer (eds.), *Identität durch Gebet. Zur gemeinschaftsbildenden Funktion institutionalisierten Betens in Judentum und Christentum*, Paderborn 2003, 30.

309 The references to the Lord's Prayer in early Christianity give an ambiguous picture of its use. On the one hand, the Lord's Prayer had already by the third century become a Christian prayer par excellence which we see for instance in the treatises that shall be studied in the following. Apart from the euchological treatises of Tertullian, Cyprian and Origen, we find the extant version of the Lord's Prayer in three sources from the first three centuries: in two Gospels, Luke 11:2c-4 and Matt 6:9b-13 (from the last half of the first century), in the church order Did. 8,2-3 (from the first half of the second century) and in The Acts of Thomas 143 (144), (from the early third century). Furthermore, there are many allusions to the Lord's Prayer in early Christian literature (Stritzky 1989, 7-19). However, the use of the Lord's Prayer should not be overestimated. As D. Y. Hadidian has noted, in the period between Didache (100-159 A.D.) and Bishop Sarapion's Prayer Book (c. 350 A.D.), only two

marker.[310] In both *Didachē* and in *The Acts of Thomas*, the Lord's Prayer is connected to either baptism or the Eucharist, and it has been proposed that the Lord's Prayer was a standard component after baptism and in the Eucharist from an early point.[311] Taking the scarcity of evidence for concrete liturgical use into consideration, it seems that the Lord's Prayer was especially used for didactic purposes in the catechetical training, as we see in the treatises under investigation.[312]

---

liturgical sources quote the Lord's Prayer *in toto*, namely Didachē and the Apostolic Constitutions (D.Y. Hadidian, *The Lord's Prayer and the Sacraments of Baptism and of the Lord's Supper in the Early Church*, in: StLi 15 (1982/83), 137. There is no direct reference to the Lord's Prayer in the *Apostolic Tradition*, and B.S. Easton's suggestion that the allusion to the "white stone" given by the bishops to the newly baptized in chapter 23,14 is a reference to the Lord's Prayer seems unnecessarily speculative (B.S. Easton, *The Apostolic Tradition of Hippolytus*, Cambridge 1934, 95-96). From Augustine, we know that in fourth-century Hippo the catechumens were taught the Lord's Prayer at the very end of their catechumenate, in a ceremony that took place one week before the Easter vigil. In the fourth century, the Lord's Prayer as well as the creed and the shape of the sacraments were kept secret from non-Christians (*disciplina arcani*). The Lord's Prayer was "given to" the cathecumens at the *traditio orationis*. The formal explanations of the Lord's Prayer in the treatises of Origen, Tertullian and Cyprian could indicate that the Lord's Prayer was explained to the catechumens in a like manner, but we cannot know when and where. Alistair Stewart-Sykes suggests that Cyprian's treatise was used in the evening before the Easter vigil, but this cannot be confirmed either (A. Stewart-Sykes, *On the Lord's Prayer. Tertullian, Cyprian, Origen*, Yonkers 2004, 93 n. 25). On the liturgical use of prayer in relation with baptism, see also: Aug. serm. 58. See W. Rordorf, *The Lord's Prayer in the Light of Its Liturgical Use in the Early Church*, in: StLi 14 (1980/81), 1-19; M.D. Boulet, *Le Notre Père dans la liturgie*, in: La Maison-Dieu 85 (1966), 75-91.

310 K.O. Sandnes, *The First Prayer. Pater Noster in the Early Church*, in: R. Hvalvik/K.O. Sandnes (eds.), *Early Christian Prayer and Identity Formation*, Tübingen 2014, 209-232, 223.

311 S.J. Kistemaker, *The Lord's Prayer in the First Century*, in: JETS (1978), 23-28; Sandnes, 2014, 209-32. The first direct example of the use of the Lord's Prayer in the eucharist is from the fourth century in Cyril of Jerusalem in his Fifth mystagogical homily.

312 This also seems to be the case in the fourth century, since the Lord's Prayer by then is still notably absent in the extant liturgies but mentioned more frequently in catechetical sermons (e.g. Aug. serm. 56-59; CyrH. catech. 19-23; Chromat. Sermo 40; Ambr. sacram.; Thdr.Mops. *Eleventh Catechetical Homily*). See

In general we are dealing with a very limited material when study-ing actual prayer texts from the early church. The liturgical scholar Paul Bradshaw disappointingly concludes: "The few texts that might seem to qualify as genuine liturgical material, such as those in the *Didache* and probably some of those in the so-called *Apostolic Tradition* [...], are so small in number that their ability to tell us how early Christians prayed is extremely limited."[313] A lack of material is thus one obstacle when studying the wording of early Christian prayers. Another reason why the study is challenging is that prayers, in general, were probably free among both Christians and Jews in the first centuries.[314] Private prayers as well as liturgical prayers seem to have been free,[315] and even the Lord's Prayer might have been understood as a perfect template or pattern for Christian prayer, and not as a prayer bound by its specific wording.[316] Nevertheless, Tertullian and Cyprian focus on the wording of the Lord's Prayer and prob-ably wanted it to be used in its given form, because they believed it to be perfect. That prayer was rather free is reflected in the different formulations that have been rendered to us – for instance, Christian prayers could be directed to God,[317] our (holy) Father,[318] Our Lord,[319] Master (Almighty),[320]

Hammerling, 2008, 167 ff.; K.B. Schnurr, *Hören und Handeln. Lateinische Auslegungen des Vaterunsers in der Alten Kirche bis zum 5. Jahrhundert*, Freiburg 1985.

313 Gerhards/Doeker/Ebenbauer, 2003, 32.

314 Bradshaw, 1981, 17-18; Bradshaw, 2002, 141-42; on free prayers in Judaism, see J. Heinemann, *The Fixed and the Fluid in Jewish Prayer*, in: G.H. Cohn/H. Fisch (eds.), *Prayer in Judaism. Continuity and Change*, Lanham, MD 1996, 45-52.

315 Apostolic Tradition 10.4-5 (Botte): "It is not necessary for the bishop to use the exact words given above... Let each pray as his talent permits." See also Tert. Apol. 30 (Becker; tr. Souter): "We pray... without a promter, for our prayers are from the heart."

316 G.J. Bahr, *The Use of the Lord's Prayer in the Primitive Church*, in: JBL 85/2 (1965), 154. W. Webber, *Early Christian Views of the Lord's Prayer*, in: T.J. Marinello/H.H.D. Williams (eds.), *My Brother's Keeper. Essays in Honor of Ellis R. Brotzman*, Eugene 2010, 61-77, 64.

317 E.g. Acta Cypriani 4,3 (Musurillo).

318 E.g. Did. 10.1 (Rordorf/Tuilier); Matt 26:39.42.44.

319 E.g. m.Pion. 21,8-9 (Musurillo).

320 E.g. 1 Clem. 59.4; 60.3. Did. 10.3 (Rordorf/Tuilier).

Jesus (Christ),[321] (name of the) cross,[322] the blood of Christ,[323] heavenly King,[324] Holy Spirit,[325] Maranatha,[326] etc.

Regarding the concrete practice of prayer among the early Christians, we only have scattered information. Thus *Didachē*, for instance, prescribes that the Lord's Prayer should be prayed three times daily, which was probably the same threefold prayer pattern that the Jews practised at the time.[327] Besides such statutory prayers, prayer occurs in a lot of different situations in Christian texts, obviously in connection with baptism,[328] Eucharist and other meals,[329] martyrdom,[330] casting lot,[331] healings,[332] forgiveness of sins,[333] worship per se,[334] funerals[335] and so on. Prayer was together with fasting and almsgiving an essential aspect of a pious life within both Judaism and early Christianity, as we can see in the context of the Lord's Prayer in Matthew.[336] Prayer was thus an integral aspect of a pious life.

The prayers of the Pauline letter corpus show us how thanksgiving and petition were ideally related in Christian prayer, e.g. in the Letter to the Philippians Paul writes: "Do not be anxious about anything, but in everything *by prayer and supplication with thanksgiving* let your requests be

---

321 E.g Acts 7:59-60; M.Carp. 4, 6 (Musurillo); Or. hom. I-9 in Is. 5,2 (Baehrens).
322 A.Petr. 37 (Vouaux): "O, name of the cross".
323 *Adoratio sanguinis Christi* (Wessely in: Hamman 1989, 136).
324 E.g. 1 Clem 61,2 (Bihlmeyer/Schneemelcher).
325 Or. hom. in Lev. 1,5 (Baehrens).
326 1 Cor 16:22; Did. 10.6 (Rordorf/Tuilier). Maranatha is an Aramaic expression meaning either "Our Lord has come" or "come, our Lord!"
327 Did. 8.3 (Rordorf/Tuilier). See also Bradshaw, 1981, 1-3; 25-26 and below paragraph 3.2.5.
328 E.g. Just. apol. 1.65 (Minns/Parvis).
329 E.g. Did. 9-10 (Rordorf/Tuilier); Tert. Apol. 39 (Becker; tr. Souter). Other meals: 1 Tim 4:4 ff.
330 m.Polyc. 14 (Musurillo); Acts 7:59-60.
331 Acts 1:24-25.
332 Acts 3:2-9.
333 1 John 5:16.
334 1 Cor 14:15, Tert. Apol. 39 (Becker; tr. Souter); Hipp. trad.ap. 35 (tr. Dix/Chadwick).
335 Gr. Naz. or. 7.24 (PG 35, quoted in Hamman 1989, 188-89).
336 Matt 6:1-18.

made known to God."[337] In general, thanksgiving is an important element in early Christian prayers, and thanksgiving is also one of the "types" of prayer that is listed as recommendable in 1 Timothy 2:1. Here, the author of 1 Timothy calls for expressions of thanks (εὐχαριστίας), along with petitions (δεήσεις), prayers (προσευχάς) and intercessions (ἐντεύξεις). The reason why people should direct these types of prayer to God is simply that: "This is good, and it is pleasing in the sight of God our Savior."[338] The fact that thanksgiving should accompany any Christian prayer illustrates the centrality of thanksgiving. It is not obvious that this should be the case, since in the surrounding world, praise was often the response to the gods, instead of thanks. P. Stengel has noted that in Homer and later also, prayers of gratitude are scarce,[339] and Claus Westermann has noted how praise ("Lob") was what Jews gave to God in prayer.[340]

The centrality of thanksgiving is also visible in the way that the Christians adopted a certain Jewish prayer form, namely opening a prayer with hodayah/todah ("thanks to"). The Jewish way of beginning a prayer was either with bᵉrākāh ("blessed be") or hodayah/todah ("thanks to").[341] The Greek-speaking Christians used the word εὐλογῶ instead of bᵉrākāh, and εὐχαριστῶ instead of hodayah. The Christians preferred the "Thanks to"-formula (hodayah), whereas the rabbis of Rabbinic Judaism favoured the "Blessed be"-formula (bᵉrākāh).[342] The different wording can very well be seen as part of the marked differentiation of their religious identities. The same might be the case in another choice of word. The Christians preferred to call prayer προσευχή, as preferred in the Septuaginte, instead of the usual and Pagan εὐχή (meaning prayer, supplication or vow).[343] It seems that the Christians thereby marked themselves as different from the Pagans;

---

337 Phil 4:6; see also 1 Thess 5:16-18; Rom 1:8-9.
338 1 Tim 2:3.
339 P. Stengel, *Die griechischen Kultusaltertümer*, München 1898, 71. See also H.S. Versnel (ed.), *Faith, Hope and Worship. Aspects of Religious Mentality in the Ancient World*, Leiden 1981, 43.
340 C. Westermann, *Lob und Klage in den Psalmen*, Göttingen 1983, 20-25.
341 J. Betz, *The Eucharist in the Didache*, in: J.A. Draper (ed.), *The Didache in Modern Research*, Leiden 1996, 244-75, 258.
342 Bradshaw, 1981, 12-16; 33. Bradshaw, 2002, 43-44.
343 H. Greeven, TDNT 2, 775-784.

"Il semble donc que le christianism d'entrée de jeu, *a voulu se démarquer,* jusque dans le vocabulaire choisi, par rapport à l'usage profane et païen, en lui préférant l'usage des Septante."[344]

2.3.3 Popular religion and Christian prayer

While the Christians were praying in accord with the Holy Scriptures, they were also praying in ways that were not aligned with the developing "orthodox" theology. In order to give a true picture of Christian prayer in the first centuries, it is also necessary to look at examples of prayers of a more mundane and popular character, expressions of what have been termed popular religion or "Volksfrömmigkeit." Such prayers are often characterized by having a magical effect, i.e. an immediate, external and beneficial effect for the one praying. To this category of prayers are also requests driven by outspoken egoistic motives (*Gebetsegoismus*) and prayers wishing for something ethically dubious. These ideas and practices existed among Christians and surrounded the authors of the euchological treatises.

As examples of prayers that seem egoistic, ethically dubious and magical in nature, I will call attention to two prayers in the *Apocryphal Acts of Peter* from the second century. These are prayers embedded in a narrative, but interesting since they are strikingly unorthodox. At one instance in the text, a Christian by name of Marcellus places himself in a prayer posture by raising his hands and confessing his faith in Jesus Christ. Then he addresses the "Lord" in order to have a sign that he shall live and not be punished by Caesar. Marcellus himself suggests that the sign could be the immediate restoration of a broken statue in front of him. This request is granted as "the statue became whole."[345] Thereafter, Marcellus believes "with his whole heart in the name of Jesus Christ... by whom all things impossible become possible."[346] Although, faith is the product of this prayer, it represents a pitfall of testing God and seeking signs. This is not the only "marvel" as effect of prayer in the *Acts of Peter*. Later Peter himself needs to invoke the Lord when Simon the Magician "astonished the people by his flying." In

---

344 Hamman, 1980, 1194. Emphasis added.
345 A.Petr. 11 (Vouaux; tr. Ehrman).
346 Id.

order for people not to be led astray by this magician, Peter cried unto the Lord: "Make haste, O Lord, show your mercy and let him fall down and become crippled but not die; let him be disabled and break his leg in three places." And so it happened.[347]

Another use of prayer that was not lauded in theological treatises is the use of prayer texts as amulets. A number of papyri with prayers on them have been found, especially in Egypt, and these findings have given rise to the hypothesis that such leaves were used as amulets and charms with apotropaic power to protect their owners.[348] Such papyri could of course also have been used as memory aids, but the fact that the texts on the papyri are sometimes rendered incorrectly suggest that it was not the wording of the prayers that were important, but the artefact itself. Thus the papyrus *P.Princ 2.107*, stemming from the fourth to sixth century, reads πατηρ υμων εν της ουρανης αγιασθητω τω θελημα σου τον αρτον υμων των επιουσιων, which means something like: "Your Father who is in heaven, hallowed be your will; your daily bread."[349] Since this formulation is not rendering the Lord's Prayer correctly, it seems improbable that such a text was created for reading. It is a hypothesis that this papyrus was in the possession of an illiterate who understood it as protective. The most frequently quoted passages on such leaves are psalms, especially Psalm 90, and the Lord's Prayer.[350] The Lord's Prayer and the psalms were probably understood as particularly effective, being at the same time a prayer and an oracle from God.[351] Still in the fourth century, the amulets posed a problem for the church and were forbidden at the Synod of Laodicea.[352]

---

347 Id. 32.
348 T.J. Kraus has collected and discussed papyri, parchment and wooden/clay tablet containing the Lord's Prayer (T.J. Kraus, *Manuscripts with the Lord's Prayer. They are More than Simply Witnesses to that Text Itself*, in: T.J. Kraus/T. Nicklas (eds.), *New Testament Manuscripts*, Leiden 2006, 227-266.). See also Webber, 2010, 70.
349 B. Nongbri, *The Lord's Prayer and XMГ. Two Christian Papyrus Amulets*, in: Harvard Theological Review 104 (2011), 61-62, n. 5.
350 D.G. Martinez, *The Papyri and Early Christianity*, in: R.S. Bagnall (ed.), *The Oxford Handbook of Papyrology*, Oxford 2009, 591.
351 Id. 593.
352 Canon 36: "They who are of the priesthood, or of the clergy, shall not be magicians, enchanters, mathematicians, or astrologers; nor shall they make

Yet another way of communicating with God is found in an oracle question to Christ that has been preserved from the fifth/sixth century. The question posed is basic: "Is it your will that I travel to Chiut?"[353] and it reminds of the pagan oracle tradition.[354]

These examples of popular religion show that there were some differences between the ideals of the religious elite and popular practices and ideas. "Popular Christianity, to the extent that we are able to trace it, bears witness to a religious syncretism that suggests that the fine theological definitions of orthodoxy, preached by bishops such as Cyprian, were exhortations to what ought to be rather than reflections of what is."[355] This, however, does not mean that there was no commensurability between theology and lay piety. In his article "Hohe Theologie und schlichte Frömmigkeit? Eine Beobachtungen zum Verhältnis von Theologie und Frömmigkeit in der Antike," Christoph Markschies points to the fact that theology and lay piety were connected, and as an example of this he mentions the prayers frequently found in Origen's homilies.[356]

2.3.4 Christian identity through prayer

A sketch of early Christian prayer like the one given in the preceding paragraphs shows that Christian prayer was a multifaceted, free and

what are called amulets, which are chains for their own souls. And those who wear such, we command to be cast out of the Church." (tr. Percival).

353 Papyrus Oxy. 926, quoted in C. Markschies, *Zwischen den Welten wandern. Strukturen des antiken Christentums*, Frankfurt am Main 1997, 111. See also (J. Černý: "Egyptian Oracles" in R.A. Parker (ed.), *A Saite Oracle Papyrus from Thebes in the Brooklyn Museum*, Providence 1962, 35-48,47; C. Riggs (ed.), *The Oxford Handbook of Roman Egypt*, Oxford 2012, 413): "O God almighty; if thou dost instruct me, thy servant Paulos, to go to Antinoo[polis], give me order through this label!" (from a Christian papyrus from seventh- or eight-century Oxyrhynchus).

354 R.L. Fox, *Pagans and Christians in the Mediterranean world from the second century AD to the conversion of Constantine*, London 1988.

355 A. Brent, *Cyprian and Roman Carthage*, Cambridge 2010, 229.

356 C. Markschies, *Hohe Theologie und schlichte Frömmigkeit? Einige Beobachtungen zum Verhältnis von Theologie und Frömmigkeit in der Antike*, in: H. Grieser/A. Merkt (eds.), *Volksglaube im antiken Christentum*, Darmstadt 2009, 456-471, 464 ff.

flexible endeavour in antiquity. Therefore, it is not a simple task to outline the earliest development of Christian prayer. It seems that the definition and use of prayer depended on the context and circumstances of
the ones praying, and the only common feature of the various prayers is
the wish to invoke and communicate with God. It varies how the communication with God takes place, and which words are used. Although
varying, the words used to pray and to describe prayer show how different identities find their expression by a certain vocabulary. The Jews
and Christians thus began to favour different words when praying, and
Christians and Pagans tended to use different words about "prayer."
However, at this early point of development, the dividing lines between
the different groups were still not clear. The Christian treatises that will be
analysed below create some order in the various ideas, expectations and
practices related to prayer, and they try to outline how Christians should
pray; thus, I will argue they tried to strengthen the developing Christian
identity.

2.4 Four Christian authors and their prayers

In the following paragraphs, the Christian authors, Clement, Origen,
Tertullian and Cyprian, will be introduced and the extant prayers that one
finds in their writings. I mention these prayers in order to show how the
authors prayed and encouraged prayer, before looking to the euchological
treatises where they give interpretations of and recommendations on prayer.
The reason for this is to get a fuller picture of the said authors' ideas of
prayer.[357]

---

357 Daniel Scheerin mentions that it is not possible to get the full image of Origen's
theology of prayer, if one only reads *Perì Euchês* and not his homilies (D.
Sheerin, "The Role of Prayer in Origen's Homilies," in: C. Kannengiesser/W.L.
Petersen (eds.), *Origen of Alexandria. His World and his Legacy*, Notre Dame
1988, 201 n. 4). L. Perrone is of the same opinion, whereas W. Gessel chooses
to focus on just or. (Perrone, *preghiera*, 2011, 42).

2.4.1 Clement of Alexandria

Titus Flavius Clemens lived in the second half of the second century, c. 150–215.[358] He might have come from Athens before settling in Alexandria.[359] Both of these settings place him firmly in a context where pagan philosophy thrived, and he had huge insight into pagan religion and philosophy.[360] Clement's world view has rightly been described as "the common blend of Platonist metaphysics and Stoic ethics together with Aristotelian logic and terminology."[361] Clement himself defines philosophy broadly: "... philosophy -- I do not mean the Stoic, or the Platonic, or the Epicurean, or the Aristotelian, but whatever has been well said by each of those sects, which teach righteousness along with a science pervaded by piety, -- this eclectic whole I call philosophy."[362] Having this "eclectic whole" as backdrop, Clement viewed Christ as the fulfilment of all foregone cultural ambitions. According to Clement, philosophy was to the Greek world what the Law was to the Hebrews: a preparatory process leading to Christ, who was the perfect revelation of God.[363] Clement had high expectations to his Christian audience whom he exhorted to "exhibit [them]selves as a bright pattern of virtue, such as we ourselves have in Christ."[364]

From Clement's own works, we know that he converted to Christianity in Alexandria, and he then became head of a catechetical school in the city, where he perhaps taught Origen.[365] In 202–3 the persecution by Septimius

---

358 His time of birth is unknown; from a letter we know that by 215 he was already dead (Eus. h.e. 6.11; 6.14.8 (Bardy)).
359 Epiph. panar. 1.6 (Holl).
360 Jerome, *De viris illustribus* 38 (Barthold).
361 H. Chadwick, *Early Christian thought and the classical tradition. Studies in Justin, Clement and Origen*, Oxford 1966, 40 f.
362 Clem. Strom. 1.7 (Früchtel/Stählin/Treu).
363 Id. 1.28.3; 7.2.11.
364 Clem. paed. 2.10.4 (SC 158; tr. Wilson).
365 Eus. h.e. 6.6 (Bardy). Today scholars agree that in the second century, it was probably not so much a formalized catechetical school in Alexandria as a Christian group under the influence of Clement... Moreover, it is debated whether Origen really was a pupil of Clement, because Origen never refers to Clement (A.C. Itter, *Esoteric Teaching in the Stromateis of Clement of Alexandria*, Leiden 2009, 8 ff.).

Severus raged against Christians and made Clement leave Alexandria, possibly for Cappadocia.[366] Clement died in this exile, sometime before 215.

2.4.1.1 Prayers of Clement

Clement ends his writing *Paedagogus* with a prayer and a poetic hymn,[367] the latter is also occasionally labelled as a poem or a prayer.[368] These texts are highly formalized, but still give us an insight into Clement's style as a Christian author and worshipper and thereby also possibly into the Christian congregation in Alexandria. We have no sources to the Alexandrian liturgy at this early time, but "the use of the plural [we] at the end of the hymn indicates that Clement had the community in mind while writing it."[369]

In the prayer, called *Prayer to the Paidagogus*, Clement addresses "the Instructor," παιδαγωγέ, with the epithets "Father, Charioteer of Israel, Son and Father, both in one, O Lord." With this address, Clement identifies both the Old Testament God with the New Testament God and the Father with the Son. The expression used to describe the oneness of Father and Son is ἓν ἄμφω, literally "in both," which testifies to a slightly monarchical Christology where Father and Son exit as "modes" of the divine.[370] God is furthermore described as a "good and not a harsh judge" and as the "All-good, All-lovely, All-wise, All-just One," who is invoked to "be gracious," ἵλαθι. According to the prayer, grace is needed for human beings to become perfect and to come to know God. These two strands, being perfect and knowing, is exactly what leads to salvation within Clement's universe.[371] *Prayer to the Paidagogus* is also a prayer for the Holy Spirit to come and create peaceful circumstances for the individual who has avoided sin and has been changed. Clement parallels this change with becoming a citizen (πολιτευομένους) in the community of God (ἐν τῇ σῇ μετατιθεμένους πόλει).

---

366 Clem. Strom. 1–3 (Früchtel/Stählin/Treu).
367 Clem. paed. III 12, 101,1-4 (SC 158). "[A]mong the first examples of Christian poetry that is not based on models from the Psalms (Kiley, 1997, 296).
368 Kiley, 1997, 296.
369 Id. 300.
370 A. G. Hamman, *Das Gebet in der Alte Kirche*, Bern, Berlin, Frankfurt, New York, Paris, Wien 1989, 47.
371 Clem. Strom. 7.7.47 (Hort/Mayor).

Being a Christian thus consists in a change effected by God through the Holy Spirit, but it also depends on the individual accomplishing a God-like nature and rejecting a sinful existence. For the possibility of such an existence until the "perfect day" (εἰς τὴν τελείαν ἡμέραν), Clement wants to thank and praise "the Alone Father and Son, Son and Father, the Son, Instructor and Teacher, with the Holy Spirit." In this prayer, Clement expresses petition, thanksgiving and concludes with a doxology. A hymn follows immediately after the prayer, *Hymn of the Holy Clement to Christ the Saviour*. The hymn is addressed to "Saviour Jesus." The content of the hymn deals with and is a prayer for virtue and the salvific effect of Jesus, e.g. "You pull the pure fish out of the hostile storm you draw them to the life of blessedness."

2.4.2 Origen

Origen's life spans the period from 185[372] to 253/54[373]. He seems to have been an Alexandrian by birth, a child of Christian parents, and from his childhood educated both in the Holy Scriptures and in classical studies. These two strands are visible throughout Origen's work, and made Porphyry think that Origen betrayed philosophy by mixing it with Christianity.[374] "But what for Porphyry stood as a fault was for Origen the glory of the Christian philosophy: that divine revelation as given in the sacred texts should be harmonized with philosophical searching through the medium of spiritualizing exegesis."[375] Origen's philosophical striving, however, did not interfere with his steadfast Christocentric and soteriological focus,[376] and his method was the allegorical reading by which he deferred spiritual (*pneumatic, noetic*) meaning from the Holy Scriptures. After the martyrdom of his father, Origen worked as grammaticus and as catechist in the Alexandrian church.[377] Later he

---

372 Eus. h.e. 6.2.12 (Bardy).
373 Id. 7.1.
374 Id. 6.19.
375 J.A. McGuckin, *The Westminster Handbook to Origen*, Louisville 2004, 18. This can of course be discussed, for some Origen's theology was too philosophical.
376 McGuckin, 1989, 19.
377 Eus. h.e. 6.3.3 (Bardy).

supported himself humbly by receiving money from wealthy patrons. Among these benefactors was Ambrose, a former adherent to Valentinian Gnostic Christianity,[378] who requested Origen to write *Perì Euchês*. Another of Origen's patrons was a woman who let him study in her house together with another theologian that she sponsored, Paul of Antioch. Paul was a gnostic, and Eusebius in his *Church History* feels the need to emphasize that although Origen studied in the same house as this gnostic theologian, he never once "prayed in common" with a gnostic,[379] thus indicating that prayer involves a certain level of unity that was not fitting between Origen and the heretic.

In 216, Origen fled Alexandria when the troops of Emperor Caracalla raged in the city because of a political mockery of the emperor.[380] At this occasion, Origen travelled to Caesarea in Palestine, as he did again in c. 232 due to a conflict with bishop Demetrius of Alexandria. In Palestine, Origen was ordained as presbyter, and this – probably along with other issues of divergence between the two – made Bishop Demetrius of Alexandria raise quite a controversy against him.[381] In his job as presbyter in Caesarea Maritima, Origen had more pastoral-oriented assignments than earlier, such as preaching and leading gatherings in prayer.[382] It was probably here that he wrote his treatise *Perì Euchês*[383] in which one recognizes a pastoral concern. About 235, when the persecution by Maximinus broke out, Origen had to stay in hiding and perhaps flee from Caesarea Maritima. After Maximinus' reign, Origen could again take up his duties, but this had an abrupt ending when Decius became emperor and began persecuting Christians in 250. Origen was arrested and tortured, and after the persecution had ended, Origen died as a confessor.[384]

---

378 Id. 7,18.
379 Id. 6.2.13-14.
380 Cass. Dio, *Historia Romana* 78,22-23 (Cary/Foster).
381 Eus. h.e. 6.23.4 (Bardy).
382 Eus. h.e. 6.22 (Bardy).
383 R.E. Heine, *Commentary on the Gospel According to John, Books 13-32*, in: FaCh 89 (1993), 4-5.
384 Origen's teaching was condemned by the fifth ecumenical council in 553.

2.4.2.1 Prayers of Origen

It is easy pickings to find prayers in Origen's writings. In his homilies and commentaries, one particular petition is frequent: a prayer that God by his grace and Logos may make the true meaning of the Scriptures understandable. For instance, in his *Homily on Jeremiah*, Origen writes: "… I pray that I discover something true in regard to the passage (εὔχομαι εὑρίσκειν τι εἰς τὸν τόπον ἀληθές)."[385] There are many more examples like this.[386] This kind of prayer has to do with the allegorical method with which Origen interprets the Holy Scriptures. Origen's petition is a prayer with a hermeneutical aim of opening the deeper meanings of the Scriptures. Without the Spirit and the "mind of the Logos," Scripture is locked, and the proper understanding is only obtainable with the enlightenment of the Logos.[387] In his *Letter to Gregory*, Origen points explicitly to the importance of prayer for understanding:

> "And do not be content with knocking and seeking, for *what is most necessary for understanding divine things is prayer* (ἀναγκαιοτάτη γὰρ καὶ ἡ περὶ τοῦ νοεῖν τὰ θεῖα εὐχή), and in urging us to this the Saviour says not only, 'Knock, and it shall be opened to you,' and 'Seek, and you shall find,' but also 'Ask, and it shall be given you.'"[388]

In *Commentary on the Song of Songs*, the prayer for understanding has a twist, because here Origen not only prays that he must understand the Scripture, but also that he must be able to communicate its meaning to others. Origen prays: "let us pray the Father of the almighty word and bridegroom, that He Himself will open to us the gates of this mystery, whereby we may be enlightened not only for the understanding of these things, but also for the propagation of them…"[389]

---

385 Or. Hom. Ier. 20,1 (Nautin; tr. Smith).
386 "Let us pray God to grant us grace to open the Scriptures…" (Or. hom. I-2 in Cant. 2.11) etc.
For more examples and a treatment of Origen's prayers in his homilies, see: D. Sheerin, *The Role of Prayer in Origen's Homilies*, in: C. Kannengiesser/W.L. Petersen (eds.), *Origen of Alexandria. His World and his Legacy*, Notre Dame 1988.
387 Buchinger, 2003, 313.
388 Or. ep. 4.12 (Koetschau; tr. Crombie). Emphasis added.
389 Or. Cant. 2,8 (tr. Lawson).

Furthermore, in his homilies Origen prays for progress in understanding and virtue. With such prayers, Origen resembles the pagan philosophers in that he also believes the individual to be able to progress in understanding and consequently in virtue; however, according to Origen this is only possible by the help of the Logos. As Karen Jo Torjesen has noted, it is the Logos that enables progression.[390] In one instance in his *Homilies on Luke*, Origen prays to behold Christ, and he addresses "Almighty God" and "Jesus himself, the little child."[391] The importance of the Logos is also brought to the fore in other prayers by Origen, for instance when he prays that Christ may "put to death 'sin reigning over our bodies' and reign alone in us."[392] This prayer shows how Origen prays for the defeat of sin, and how life with Christ is characterized by a certain conduct and an awareness of one's sinful nature. This is also a major theme in his euchological treatise, and when he enumerates the elements, τόποι, that ought to constitute a prayer, confession (of sin) is also a part (ἐξομολόγησιν).[393] Daniel Sheerin has pointed to two main aspects about prayers in Origen's homilies: They are either about opening Scripture or have a paradigmatic character, meaning that the prayers themselves are reflections on the correct attitude worth praying for. Sheerin sees that for Origen, "meditation on the Law of the Lord and prayer are inextricably linked."[394]

2.4.3 Tertullian

Quintus Septimus Florens Tertullianus is the first Latin Christian author who can be identified and located more or less precisely. Tertullian was born in Carthage, he lived c. 155–230,[395] he was married and he was probably a convert to Christianity.[396] As a Christian, Tertullian came to sympathize

---

390 K.J. Torjesen, *Hermeneutical Procedure and Theological Method in Origen's Exegesis*, Berlin 1985, 137.
391 Or. hom. I-39 in Lc. 15.5 (Migne; tr. Lienhard).
392 Id. 30,4.
393 Or. or. 33 (Koetschau; tr. Stewart-Sykes).
394 Sheerin, 1988, 207.
395 T.D. Barnes, *Tertullian. A Historical and Literary Study*, Oxford 1971, 1 ff.
396 E.g. Tert. Paen. 1 (ed. Borleffs) and Apol. 18.4 (Becker, tr. Souter): "We too once laughed at this: we sprang from your ranks; Christians are made Christians, and not born such."

with the Montanists and their strict moralism. Several of the traditionally held facts about Tertullian are debated, such as Tertullian being a son of a Roman official, a lawyer by trade and a presbyter in Carthage. Also the earlier consensus that Tertullian broke with the Catholic Church in the early third century is questioned. The prevailing assumption is nowadays that Tertullian's increasing attachment to Montanism is not to be understood as a break with the Catholic Church – since the church in Carthage at that time was not a defined entity.

Tertullian was reluctant to combine philosophy and Christianity,[397] although he could not help doing it in the intellectual milieu of late antiquity. Tertullian believed in the materiality of God and the soul, as did the Stoics. Tertullian designated the Scriptures *divinas*;[398] and he saw the New Testament as the fruit of the seed of the Old Testament.[399] He held that the Scriptures could only correctly be interpreted with awareness of tradition,[400] and that it must be read in accordance with the rule of the church.[401] Although he primarily understood the Scriptures literally; he held that the Scriptures were also supposed to be interpreted figuratively.[402]

Finally worth mentioning about Tertullian is his harsh eschatological thoughts. He feared eternal punishment and meant that one ought to fear God – that is the backdrop of his writings. The fear is not necessarily a negative thing according to Tertullian, since it will spur attention and concentration on what is important, e.g. prayer and brotherly-kindness and love.[403]

2.4.3.1 Prayers of Tertullian

In a short article, O. W. Holmes enumerates more than 200 references to prayer that can be found in Tertullian's works.[404] O.W. Holmes notes that Tertullian uses about 17 different Latin words about prayer, e.g.: *orare,*

---

397 Tert. Praescr. 7.11 (Refoulé; tr. Bindley): e.g. "Away with those who bring forward a Stoic or Platonic or dialectic Christianity!"
398 Tert. Apol. 20 (Becker).
399 Tert. Marc. 4.11 (Evans).
400 Tert. Praescr. 15 ff. (Refoulé; tr. Bindley).
401 Tert. Val. 4.1 (Riley).
402 Tert. Marc. 4.9 (Evans).
403 Tert. Fug. 1.7 (Bulhart).
404 O.W. Holmes, *Tertullian on Prayer,* in: TynB 6-5 (1960), 27-32.

oratio, adorare, exorare, postulare and *loqui,* and he consequently concludes that "Tertullian is clearly attracted to the idea of prayer as the natural
fellowship of friend with Friend. He employs *loqui,* the easy talk of one with
another..."[405] I do not find this to be the case, since Tertullian does generally
not present God as a "friend" and the communication between God and
human beings are not presented as particularly friendly in the works of
Tertullian. Furthermore, O.W. Holmes correctly notes that mystic and med-
itative prayer is not frequently found in Tertullian's work.[406] To Holmes'
enumeration, I can add that, as far as I know, there are not extant prayers
in Tertullian's works, but there are several mentions of how the Christians
prayed according to Tertullian, and of how they ought to pray. Two tendencies are noticeable regarding Tertullian's mentioning of prayer: One
has to do with his apologetic agenda that makes Tertullian focus on how
the entire Roman Empire benefits from Christian prayer. Thus he states in
Apologeticum that: "We pray always for all the emperors, that they may
have a long life, a safe rule, a family free from danger, courageous armies, a
faithful senate, loyal subjects, a peaceful world, all that a man and a Caesar
pray for."[407] Related to this idea of the importance of the Christians' intercession is Tertullian's belief that it is, in fact, the prayers of the Christians
that are delaying judgement day. "We pray, too, for the emperors, for their
ministers and for all in authority, for the welfare of the world, for the prev-
alence of peace, for the delay of the final consummation."[408] Elsewhere,
Tertullian also writes: "We have no desire, then, to be overtaken by these
dire events; and in praying that their coming may be delayed, we are lending
our aid to Rome's duration."[409] One should however note that the complete opposite approach is taken by Tertullian in *De Oratione* 5, where
he states that the Christians should pray for the consummation: "... how
could anyone ask for an extension of this world, when the Kingdom of
God, for whose coming we pray, is directed toward the consummation of
this world." Such contrasting utterances point to the difficulty in judging

---

405 Id. 30.
406 Id. 29.
407 Tert. Apol. 30 (Becker, tr. Souter).
408 Id. 39.
409 Id. 32.

how the Christians then actually prayed and what they hoped for. However, the idea that the fate of the entire world is in the hands of the Christians are prevalent in Tertullian's writings, whether he dwells on their ability to delay or precipitate the end.

The other tendency in regard to Tertullian's focus when mentioning prayer has to do with his pastoral concern about sin and intercessory prayer as a condition for forgiveness. I find that a telling utterance is the very last phrase in *De Baptismo*: "Only I pray, that when you ask, you would also remember me, Tertullian a sinner."[410] This is a request from Tertullian to his congregation that they may intercede for him. A prayer like this shows Tertullian's emphasis on the importance of intercession. Tertullian deals with the problem of penitence and forgiveness of sins at several occasions. In *De Paenitentia* from before 206, and in *De Pudicitia* from 210/11,[411] Tertullian comments further on this, and a development is noticeable between these two writings. In the early text, *De Paenitentia*, Tertullian expresses the opinion that sinners can be forgiven by intercessory and penitential prayers, but it is important "to maintain prayers and fasts, to groan, to weep and make outcries unto the Lord your God; to bow before the feet of the presbyters, and kneel to God's altar; to enjoin on all the brethren to be ambassadors to bear his supplication (before God)."[412] Contrary, in the later treatise, *De Pudicitia*, Tertullian expresses the opinion that there are sins so severe that they cannot be forgiven at all by the church.[413] However, even in such cases, it is better for the penitent to pray for forgiveness, because in the end it is Jesus Christ who dispenses forgiveness and not the church. In case of severe sins like homicide and adultery, the church can offer "compassion," but not communion;[414] "it is only Our Lord that forgives sins, and especially sins unto death, [penitence] is not in vain. For if [the penitent] is praying to God and so lying on [his/her] knees before Him, [the penitent] will in this manner do much more to gain forgiveness, while [he/she] is invoking the help of God alone…"[415] It

---

410 Tert. Bapt. 20 (Evans).
411 Barnes, 1971, 55.
412 Tert. Paen. 9.4 (ed. Borleffs).
413 Tert. Pud. 2 (Micaelli/Munier; tr. Claesson), quoting 1 John 5:16.
414 Id. 3.4.
415 Id. 3.3-4.

is evident that Tertullian has the theme of penitence and sin very much at heart. In his writings, there is therefore an emphasis on prayer as a medium for forgiveness of sins. This emphasis is not absent in the Greek treatises, but much less accentuated by Clement and Origen.

2.4.4 Cyprian

Thascius Caecilius Cyprianus was born in 200/10 to pagan parents. He was a *rhetor* before he converted to Christianity in 246. Already two years after his conversion in 248/49, he was elected bishop of Carthage. During his episcopate, Cyprian summoned up to 85 bishops of Latin Africa to several synods where he presided. According to the strongly panegyric *Vita Cypriani,* he lived on a country estate in Carthage until he sold it and gave the money to the poor Christians.[416] It is probable that Cyprian was in contact with the common people, and that Cyprian was a bishop occupied with helping his congregation, and facilitating synods is harmonious with the fact that there is no speculative theology in Cyprian's works. His theology is intensely practical and oriented towards the church as community.[417]

After just one year as bishop Cyprian had to go into hiding because of the outbreak of the Decian persecution in 250. The persecution lasted about a year during which Cyprian hid near Carthage and stood in contact with his congregation by letters. In one such letter, *Epistle* 8.3, Cyprian mentions an admonition that he has received from heaven to make his congregation offer continual united prayer. This admonition says a great deal about Cyprian, because it shows how his theological ideal was ecclesiological unity. After the death of the Emperor Decius, a synod was held in 251 to discuss how the church should treat the lapsed Christians. In *De Lapsis* 36, it becomes evident that according to Cyprian, in order for the lapsed to be forgiven and reincorporated into the church, they should confess their sin, mourn, pray and apply themselves to good works, especially to almsgiving. When a new persecution, however, seemed to be on its way already in 252, another synod was summoned, and Cyprian decided to be lenient and reincorporate

---

416 Pontius, *Vita Cypriani* 15 (tr. Deferrari).
417 F. Young et al. (eds.), *The Cambridge History of Early Christian Literature,* Cambridge 2004, 156.

the lapsed Christians from the previous persecution without a full period of penitence. This caused a schism with the Carthaginian deacon Felicissimus and the Roman Bishop Novatian. Eventually, however, Cyprian's more pragmatic approach won the day.

During the persecution of Valerianus in 258, Cyprian was beheaded. That was the capital punishment for a distinguished Roman citizen. According to the *Acta Proconsularis 5*, he kneeled down in prayer just before his persecution, and likewise he received his death sentence with the words "Deo Gratias."

2.4.4.1 A prayer of Cyprian

I have not found extant prayers in the works of Cyprian, but Cyprian frequently makes reference to prayer. It is noticeable that Cyprian's longing for a united church is often related to the act of praying, as we shall also see below in the analysis of *De oratione Dominica*. Cyprian's communal ideal is explicit in an admonition such as:

> "Let each one of us pray God not for himself only, but for all the brethren (*pro omnibus fratribus*), even as the Lord has taught us to pray, when He bids to each one, not private prayer (*non singulis privatam precem*), but enjoined them, when they prayed, to pray for all (*pro omnibus*) in common prayer and concordant supplication (*oratione communi et concordi prece orantes*)."[418]

Also in Cyprian's *Epistle* 7.8, he encourages prayer "in simplicity and unanimity (*unanimes*)." Subsequently, Cyprian poetically expresses which objects a petitionary prayer ought to entail: peace, help in danger, the restoration of the church, salvation, serenity, light and the affectionate aids of paternal love that "the blasphemy of persecutors may be restrained, the repentance of the lapsed renewed, and the steadfast faith of the persevering may glory."

In the same way as in Tertullian's writings, also Cyprian puts emphasis on the use of prayer as formalized penitential satisfaction. If you have sinned, you need to pray for forgiveness from God through Jesus Christ who made satisfaction.[419]

---

418 Cypr. ep. 7.7 (Goldhorn; tr. Donna).
419 Id. 7.5.

2.4.5 Conclusion

It is noticeable that the Christian authors who wrote the euchological treatises made reference to or use of prayer in other works as well. Thus they testify to the general importance and use of prayer in the early church. They all seem to agree that prayers for receiving divine grace were of vital importance to maintain further progress. The Christian authors, however, emphasize different issues in their prayers, and we can observe that their theological emphases are reflected in their prayers. The Alexandrians, Clement and Origen, are predominantly focusing on virtue and knowledge. They express the petition of moving closer to Christ and grow in virtue. Especially Origen uses prayers to understand the Scriptures. On the contrary, the Latin authors have a strong focus on sin and intercessions. Moreover, in the Latin texts, it is obvious that prayer is regarded as a very social thing – prayer is important for unity: the unity of the empire, the unity of the Church; and the unity of the individual with Christ. In general, prayer has many different functions. It expresses belonging, attitude, belief, theology, hopes and anthropology. In short, prayer expresses identity. In the following text analysis, we shall look further into the relation between prayer and Christian identity.

2.5 Four Christian treatises on prayer

Before reaching the content analysis that focuses on relations, self and identity, a few paragraphs follow on the dating, structure, general content, usage and audience of the four texts to be investigated.

2.5.1 The dating, structure and general content of the texts

2.5.1.1 Στρωματεῖς, Book 7

In the following, we shall investigate Clement's understanding of prayer in *Stromateis, Book 7*. It is probable that Clement wrote *Stromateis, Book 6 and 7* immediately after his refuge from Alexandria, about c. 203.[420] A handful of Clement's works has been kept for posterity, amongst them

---

420 Méhat, 1966, 54.

Protrepticus, *Paedagogus* and *Stromateis* which are sometimes understood
to be a trilogy.

The eight books of *Stromateis* fit under their title which means
"Miscellanies" or "Patchwork"; the word στρωματεῖς was used to label a
certain genre of writings of mixed content. The full title of Clement's work
is "Miscellanies of notes of revealed knowledge in accordance with the
true philosophy (ὁ ... τῶν κατὰ τὴν ἀληθῆ φιλοσοφίαν γνωστικῶν ὑπομνημ-
άτων Στρωματεὺς)." The structure of the work does not seem to be guided
by a certain principle; the content is a series of notes on different subjects.
However, Louis Roberts argues that the form is not arbitrary, but belongs
to a sort of *hypomnematic* literature, which is concise.[421] Also, according to
Clement, *Stromateis* is "systematic";[422] he writes that it contains the truth
for those who truly seek it and are worthy of it: "The Stromateis will contain the truth, mixed up with, or hidden in the teaching of the philosophers,
as the kernel in the husk."[423] *Book 7*, the book of primary interest for our
purpose, deals with the true gnostic and prayer.

2.5.1.2 Περὶ Εὐχῆς

The general consensus is that *Perì Euchês* was composed after Origen moved
to Caesarea, but before the beginning of the persecution by Maximinus,
probably in 233 or 234.[424] From Origen's *Commentary on John* 6.1.–12
and from Eusebius' *H.E.* 6.24.36, it is known that Origen fled Alexandria
and moved to Caesarea in Palestine. According to Eusebius this happened
in the tenth year of the reign of Alexander Severus. This places Origen's
move to Caesarea to the period between 232 and 235. Paul Koetschau
points to the fact that there are no references to martyrdom in *Perì Euchês*,
and therefore the treatise was likely composed before the persecution by
Maximinus.[425] Since Origen wrote several texts in Caesarea before the persecution by Maximinus broke out in 235, he must have come to Caesarea

---

421 L. Roberts, *The Literary Form of the Stromateis*, in: SecCen 1 (1981), 212.
422 Clem. Strom. 1.1.14.2 (Hort/Mayor).
423 Id. 1.1.18.
424 Heine, 1993, 14 f.
425 P. Koetschau. *Die Griechischen Christlichen Schriftsteller 1*, ORT 1899,
   LXXV-LXXVII.

in 232 or 233.[426] Because of similarities with his *Commentary on John, Book 6,* which we know was written just after his arrival in Caesarea, we can assume that *Perì Euchês* was written c. 233.[427]

Actually, Origen possibly did not write, but rather dictated the text – this is the theory of Wilhelm Gessel, who explains the stylistic/rhetorical complexity of *Perì Euchês* with reference to its original oral form.[428] However, the complexity of the written text can also be explained by its long transmissions history which we cannot follow in detail, because the text of *Perì Euchês* has come down to us in just one codex.[429]

In *Perì Euchês,* Origen deals with "outer" aspects of prayer, such as times and postures, but his focus is more on the inner demands to the praying person, what Buchinger terms "inneren Formgesetzten christlichen Betens."[430] Origen notes in the introduction of his treatise on prayer that prayer consists of both "words" (οἱ λόγοι) and "disposition" (κατάστασις).[431] A large part of the text centres on the Lord's Prayer (18–30).

2.5.1.3 De Oratione

Tertullian's *De Oratione* can only be dated by relative measures because there is no direct indication in the text concerning its time of origin. *De Oratione* shows no sign of Montanism which makes T.D. Barnes think it was written before 206, in the period between 193 and 203. G.D. Dunn believes it to be dated before 203.[432]

Concerning structure, Tertullian's *De Oratione* firstly entails an exposition of the Lord's Prayer in the form of a commentary phrase by phrase,

---

426 Heine, 1993, 4 ff.

427 Id.

428 L. Perrone, *Zur Edition von Perì Euchês des Origenes. Rückblick und Ausblich,* Berlin 2009.

429 Our *Codex Unicus* of de or. was produced in the 14th or 15th century (Perrone, 2009, 5).

430 Buchinger, 2003, 309.

431 Or. or. 2.2 (Koetschau; tr. Stewart-Sykes).

432 G.D. Dunn, *Tertullian,* London 2004, 5. *De Oratione* is preserved in two manuscripts and one *editio princeps.* The oldest manuscript is *Codex Argobardinus* from the ninth century. None of the versions contain the entire text of the treatise.

and secondly it discusses various subjects connected with conduct and disposition in relation to prayer.

2.5.1.4 De Dominica Oratione

Cyprian's treatise on prayer bears resemblance to his writing *De unitate ecclesiae* from 251 because of the recurrent themes of unity, brotherhood and unanimity among Christians. *De Dominica oratione* is therefore dated to 253.[433] There are no references to contemporary problems that allow us to date it precisely.[434]

It has often been suggested that Cyprian was strongly inspired by Tertullian's treatise *De Oratione*, when he wrote *De Dominica Oratione*.[435] It is very likely when considering the resemblance between the two works in terms of content. As in Tertullian's treatise, also Cyprian's treatise entails a phrase-by-phrase exposition of the Lord's Prayer (9–27) and paragraphs on different issues related to prayer.

2.5.2 The usage and target groups of the four texts

In the four treatises under investigation, there are no direct references to their original use and *Sitz im Leben*. However, Tertullian's and Cyprian's treatises on prayer are frequently taken to have been catechetical texts used in the baptismal education of the early church, and even Origen's treatise, although more complicated, is occasionally referred to as a catechetical text.[436] Tertullian's and Cyprian's treatises are thus understood as manuals

---

433   T.H. Bindley, *St. Cyprian on the Lord's Prayer*, London 1914, 14.

434   Young, 2004, 155. Cyprian's *De Dominica Oratione* has been transmitted in four manuscripts: the oldest is *Codex Seguieranus* from the sixth or seventh century.

435   For a discussion of Cyprian's possible dependence on Tertullian's treatise, see Stewart-Sykes, 2004, 31-33 and Schnurr, 1985, 60-64. There is no clear conclusion, but it is possible.

436   A. Stewart-Sykes finds it "entirely reasonable to see these discourses [i.e. Tertullian's, Cyprian's and Origen's treatises] reflecting the instruction that was given to catechumens" (Stewart-Sykes, 2004, 22-26). M.B. von Stritzky reckons that both Tertullian's and Origen's treatise had the objective of edifying the congregation. Von Stritzky presents Tertullian's treatise as a catechetical text with emphasis on ethical and practical issues and specifies that Origen's treatise

or literary reservoirs for teaching baptismal candidates about prayer. They
fit into the tradition of introducing the Lord's Prayer to baptismal candidates
that is vaguely apparent already in *Didachē* from the second century and
clearly testified from the fourth century onwards.[437] Origen's *Perì Euchês*
and Clement's *Stromateis* 7 do not fit unproblematically into the category
of catechetical text, but I reckon that they are edifying texts, addressing
people who have already come a long way in their Christian "education."

The categorization of the texts as either catechetical instruction or edifying philosophical treatises has several reasons: Firstly, their aim is to
enlighten and instruct Christians in relation to prayer. Their style is instructive and persuasive; *protreptic* and *didactic*.[438] Each of the texts presents
how prayer is to be understood and carried out. The authors dwell on
ethical and behavioural instructions which fit an educational context with
a focus on socializing new members into a particular group with a distinct ethos and behavioural code. Having these elements in common, the
texts vary on other parameters, and they were obviously directed to groups
with differing educational, social and cultural background. Whereas both
Clement and Origen seem to address a learned audience, Tertullian and
Cyprian deal with people of less philosophical sophistication. Clement thus
endorses already educated Christians to become what he calls "true gnostics," W. Webber characterizes "true gnostics" as "mature believers."[439]
Clement writes for Greeks, Ἕλληνες,[440] whom he wants to make into not

---

was a text for the philosophically learned among the Christians (Stritzky, 1989,
49). H. Buchinger does not draw conclusions about the exact *Sitz im Leben*
of the treatises, but he acknowledges that all three texts might have belonged
in a catechetical setting (Buchinger, 2003, 317-318, n. 47).

For Tertullian's and Cyprian's texts, see also Schnurr, 1985, 23; Barnes, 1971,
118. For Origen's text, see McGuckin, 2004, 39.

437 See above n. 295; Hammerling, 2008, Schnurr, 1985.
Some scholars have understood the Lord's Prayer and its literary context in the
Gospel of Matthew (Matt 6:1-18) as being catechetical from the outset, thus
being constructed for educating Christians on prayer, almsgiving and fasting
(Stritzky, 1989, 9).

438 D.I. Rankin, *From Clement to Origen. The Social and Historical Context of
the Church Fathers*, Farnham 2006, 6.

439 Webber, 2010, 66.

440 E.g. Clem. Strom. 7.1.1 (Hort/Mayor).

only regular Christians, but perfect Christians, i.e. gnostics. According to Clement, even the gnostic has to advance, because that is his very nature: "... our gnostic has all good things in potentiality, though not yet in full tale; since he would otherwise have been incapable of change in reference to the inspired progresses and orderings which are still due to him by God's degree."[441] Clement thinks that when the gnostic has reached a certain level, he/she does not need the guidance of an external teacher anymore, but can suffice with his/her own contemplation[442] and Christ, Logos, as teacher. Clement holds that the Logos reaches out and instructs pupils at the level where they are "through discipline, hope for a better life, and through the holy mysteries of the incarnation, resurrection and Eucharistic presence."[443] Clement gets this point across by referring to Hebrews 5:12 and its mentioning of "milk" to babies and "solid food" for the full-grown. According to Clement's interpretation: "milk will be understood to be catechetical instruction - the first food, as it were, of the soul. And solid food is the mystical contemplation..."[444] In *Stromateis*, Clement thus approaches Christians whom he wants to advance, they have reached a certain level and are ready to progress to the next level – from faith to knowledge (ἐκ πίστεως εἰς γνῶσιν).[445] Clement writes in *Stromateis* 7.10 that faith is "a comprehensive knowledge of the essentials; and knowledge is the strong and sure demonstration of what is received by faith, built upon faith by the Lord's teaching (διὰ τῆς κυριακῆς διδασκαλίας)...." Clement might also have the Lord's Prayer in mind when he mentions "the Lord's teaching." Clement sees "the Lord's teachings" as the basis of faith wherefrom the gnostic should progress to higher levels and greater knowledge. Origen sees Jesus Christ as the one who can make incomprehendable things

---

441 Id. 7.7.
442 This resembles Epict. ench. 48: "This is the position and character of a layman: He never looks for either help or harm from himself, but only from externals. This is the position and character of a philosopher: He looks for all his help or harm from himself."
443 M. Havrda/V. Hušek/J. Plátova (eds.), *The Seventh Book of the Stromateis. Proceedings of the Colloquium on Clement of Alexandria*, Olomouc 2010, 295.
444 Clem. Strom. 5.10 (Früchtel /Stählin/Treu; tr. Roberts).
445 Id. 7.10.57.4 (Hort/Mayor).

comprehendable.[446] Origen makes it clear from the outset of the treatise that the subject of prayer would completely elude human beings if they were not granted knowledge through Christ by grace. Origen states that besides the "teaching of the firstborn Word," "illumination of the Father" and "the inner working of the Spirit" are also necessary components in understanding prayer.[447] At the beginning of his edifying treatise, he is thus making his audience aware that there is a limit to one's intellectual comprehension of prayer and ability to pray, and for this reason, he entreats the Spirit to help him write about this subject. This is not the obvious way to open a treatise, but it helps him emphasize his point that humans are dependent on the Spirit to pray.

The Latin authors keep the training simple and dwell on what is necessary for "a simple faith." According to Cyprian, the Lord's Prayer is one such essential element. Cyprian expresses it thus:

> "For when the Word of God, our Savior Jesus Christ, came and gathered the learned along the unlearned and handed over the commands of salvation to every sex and age, he made a sublime summary of his commands so that the memory of his disciples should not be taxed by the holy rule but that they should speedily learn what is necessary for a simple faith."[448]

This focus on a simple faith does not mean that the Latin authors do not have any sense of progression which will become clear in the further analyses of their texts below. Likewise, the attempt to describe a simple faith does not exclude a focus on spirituality and spiritual readings of Scripture.

The differing styles of the texts – from the sophisticated and elusive in Clement over the learned and constructive in Origen to the relatively more simple and practical in Tertullian's and Cyprian's texts – tell us something about how Christian education and catechetical training varied tremendously in form and content in different areas and contexts. While Tertullian was probably dealing with newly converts whom he was "making" from scratch in many senses,[449] Clement's "school" in Alexandria attracted

---

446 Or. or. 1 (Koetschau; tr. Stewart-Sykes).
447 Id.
448 Cypr. Dom. orat. 28 (Réveillaud; tr. Stewart-Sykes).
449 He famously referred to Christians as being "made not born" (Tert. Apol. 18 (Becker; tr. Souter)).

well-educated people, also people like Clement himself who was already Christian by arrival. M.E. Johnson notes that Clement's school "was more of a philosophical and theological academy than it was an institute for prebaptismal or catechumenal instruction."[450] But it *was* a catechumenal "school" in the sense that its aim was to edify Christians. This can be observed when seeing *Stromateis* in relation to Clement's works *Paedagogus* and *Protrepticus*, because in these works held together one sees both the outline of the progression that Clement expects from his hearers, and the shifting roles that the Logos assumes at different stages in relation to the development of the individual. In the beginning, Logos is a pedagogue dealing with practical concerns (πρακτικὸς), whereas later Logos becomes a teacher dealing with doctrine (ἐν τοῖς δογματικοῖς).[451] The actual teacher, physically present, must be as the Logos and help the individual by taking different roles in the teaching process.

Concerning the addressees of the treatises, in *De Oratione* 1.4, Tertullian addresses his hearers as "blessed ones," *benedicti*. He does the same in his writing *De Baptismo* 20.5 which is also assumed to be a catechetical text, and we can argue that the text is directed at catechumens in a congregation. Cyprian constantly addresses his audience as "dearest brothers," which is typical for him when addressing a congregation.[452] Clement does not directly address his audience, but refers all the way through to an ideal person that he calls "our" or "the (true) gnostic."[453] Origen addresses his treatise to his patron Ambrosius and a female by the name Tatiana. Ambrosius has created the financial opportunity for Origen to write about prayer and seems also to have asked questions about the subject.[454] The content of *Perì Euchês* is, however, of a general character, and like the three other texts, it seems to be directed also to a broader audience.

---

450 M.E. Johnson, *The Rites of Christian Initiation: Their Evolution and Interpretation*, Collegeville 2007, 64.
451 Clem. Paed. 1.1.1.4-2.1 (Marrou).
452 Cypr. Dom. Orat. 1.1, 2.1 etc (Réveillaud; tr. Stewart-Sykes).
453 Clem. Strom. 7.7 (Hort/Mayor).
454 Or. Or. 5.6 (Koetschau; tr. Stewart-Sykes).

2.5.3 Conclusion

It seems to me quite reasonable to assume that the euchological treatises have been used in an edifying or baptismal context at a more or less
advanced state. Regardless of the intellectual levels of the "schools" and
congregations of early Christianity, there is no doubt that they were places
where Christians were shaped and a Christian identity was formed.[455] Since
the texts were probably used to teach lay people, it is reasonable to assume
that the treatises give a historical glimpse of how Christians in a congregational context were instructed regarding prayer. More specifically, all
of the four treatises are "a form of ritual instruction and reflection (cultic
didachēs) aimed at those desiring to worship God properly."[456]

---

455 Cf. below paragraph 5.2.6. Christian prayer as part of Christian paideia and
      catechetical education.
456 M.J. Brown defines Clement's *Stromateis, Book 7* and Tertullian's *On Prayer*
      as examples of cultic *didachēs* (Brown, 2004, 132). Brown has the term from
      Hans Dieter Betz.

Part II: Textual Analysis

3 The relationship established with God in prayer

We shall now focus on the four euchological treatises by Clement, Origen, Tertullian and Cyprian. The following paragraphs focus on the image and idea of God that arises from the reflections on prayer in the four treatises and on the human possibility to approach God in prayer. It was a widespread belief among Christians in late antiquity that it was possible to communicate with God. Christians did not disregard the human-divine relationship; on the contrary, they embraced it and allowed themselves to be defined by it. This chapter investigates how the early Christian authors handled the ambiguity of the Christian God who was believed to be both personal and beyond-personal; furthermore, the human-divine relationship offered in the treatises will be investigated. Such issues are theological in nature. Nevertheless, they are likely to have influenced the historical development of Christian identity, because of the above-mentioned correlation between identity and the symbols with which one associates oneself. For a believer, it is natural to expect that the way one understands God and one's relationship with God has an effect on the way one understands and presents oneself.

The chapter is divided into two main parts: The first main part is an analysis of the Christian understanding of God in the four treatises on prayer by Clement, Origen, Tertullian and Cyprian. The following themes are dealt with in relation to prayer: God's name, the role ascribed to Jesus Christ and the Spirit, Trinitarian ideas, and finally God's will and providence. These themes are dealt with in order to find out who the Christian God is according to the third century theologians.

The second main part of this chapter is an investigation of how Christians believed that they could approach God. This part is divided, firstly, according to four New Testament expressions that are used frequently by the authors about the proper manner of praying which is: "in secret," "in spirit and in truth," "without ceasing" and in mind of the admonition: "Ask for great things"/"Seek First his Kingdom." Subsequently, four paragraphs follow on how Christians concretely were instructed to approach God – by which gestures, in which direction, at which time and in which form.

3.1 Characterizing the addressee of prayer: God

3.1.1 The address of prayer: God as Father

Marcel Mauss has noted that: "An invocation, such as the beginning of the Lord's Prayer, is the fruit of the work of centuries. A prayer is not just the effusion of a soul, a cry which expresses a feeling. It is a fragment of a religion."[457] Thereby, Mauss points to the fact that Christian expressions are loaded with meaning that tradition has ascribed to it, and this is also the case with prayer.

When the Christians began to address God as "Father," it was not a complete *novum* in the religious world of late antiquity. The Jews and the Greco-Romans did already occasionally invoke God as "Father,"[458] but seldom as "*Our* Father."[459] The father figure was the dominating social figure in antiquity, and in general "father" did not invoke the association of "daddy," but of *paterfamilias*.[460] The *paterfamilias* was an authority figure around whom social life was structured.[461] For the Christians, God is "Our Father" as it says in the Matthean version of the Lord's Prayer. In this prayer, Christians did not make use of any cognomina as e.g. Odysseus who invoked "Father *Zeus* (Ζεῦ πάτερ)."[462] For the Christians there was

---

457 Pickering, 2003, 31.

458 For several pagan examples of addressing gods as "Father," see e.g. Brown, 2004, 8. For an example from the Hebrew Scriptures, see Isa 63:16.

459 H. Klein/V. Mihoc/K.W. Niebuhr (eds.), *Das Gebet im Neuen Testament. Vierte europäische orthodox-westliche Exegetenkonferenz in Sambata de Sus, 4.-8, August 2007.* Tübingen 2009, 95.

460 J. Barr, '*Abba Isn't 'Daddy*,' in: JThS NS 39 (1988), 28-47.

461 Brown, 2004, 3-10. Brown writes that: "the family was the locus for understanding the structure of society. In a strict sense, it is a legal term referring to those under the the control of a paterfamilias, who was the head of this social unit." (Brown, 2004, 4).

462 Eg. Hom. Il. I.503 (Murray/Wyatt). J.B. Rives has noted a shift among pagans in the third century; they began to address "Panthea" which could indicate a more theological and monotheistic turn of mind (Rives, 1995, 191). Addressing God as Pantheia suggests that the one God encompasses all gods.

only one God, *our* Father, and therefore no sacred epithets were necessary to distinguish him from other gods. Consequently, the Christians expected God the Father to help and provide for his children as a father should do, depending on their behaviour and prayers. Calling God by the familiar name "Father" was believed to be an immense privilege and came with certain obligations.

3.1.1.1 Clement and Origen on the invocation of God

Out of the four authors under investigation only Origen explicitly states that the Christians have to pray to God the Father and *not* to God the Son. Tertullian and Cyprian for their part seem to take that address for granted because they have the Lord's Prayer as their absolute ideal for prayer.[463] Of the four authors, Clement is the only one that does not make it completely clear what the proper address ought to be. He is not specific about the wording and is also not referring to the Lord's Prayer as a "perfect template."

There must have been historical reasons for Origen's explicit statement about the Father as the proper address of prayer. Maybe Origen preached in a context where the Son was not understood as subordinate to the Father, and Origen wanted to emphasize his subordination. Origen's emphasizes on God the Father as address seems to be apologetic. It could seem that someone has charged the Christians with some sort of heresy, and Origen defensively assures that there is only one way to address God: as Father.[464] However, as we have seen above, in his homilies Origen did not live up to his own admonition. Origen also addressed the Son, even "the little child" directly: "Let us pray to Almighty God, and let us pray to Jesus himself, the little child (*oremus omnipotentem Deum, oremus et ipsum parvulum Jesum*)."[465] However, in *Perì Euchês*, Origen stands firmly on the proper

---

463 Tert. Or. 1 (Schleyer; tr. Stewart-Sykes); Cypr. Dom. Orat. 1-2 (Réveillaud; tr. Stewart-Sykes).

464 Similar in Or. Cels. 8,56,21-22 (Borret).

465 Or. Hom. I-39 in Lc. 15.5 (Migne; tr. Lienhard).
    W. Gessel refers to E.G. Jay's explanation: it could be the case that Origen deliberately approaches the subject of invocation differently when he writes a theological treatise compared to a personal and pious homily (W. Gessel, *Die Theologie des Gebetes nach „De Oratione" von Origenes*. Paderborn 1975, 97).

address being God the Father. As argument for his own claim about the address, Origen writes that it is universally agreed: "That prayer to the Son and not to the Father is absurd, and contrary to obvious evidence."[466] Furthermore, Origen defends his admonition with ontological reasoning. He states that everything has been created except from the Father; because even the Son was generated, although "eternally." God the Father is true "being,"[467] and he so utterly transcends the creation that even the heavenly bodies also address God in prayer.[468]

In *Stromateis* 7, Clement does not mention the address to the Father from the Lord's Prayer, although he designates God as Father on several occasions in the text. Clement even calls Jesus Christ "the true Father and Teacher (πατέρα καὶ διδάσκαλον τῆς ἀληθείας)."[469] Thereby it is indicated that Clement not always distinguishes sharply between the divine persons. Most often in *Stromateis* 7, Clement refers to God by writing ὁ θεός, thus avoiding constraining metaphors. But Clement does occasionally liken God to a father and expresses that Christians owe God virtue like a son owes his father virtue and a subject owes his king.[470] Clement also refers to Romans 8:26 and thereby mentions how Christians need the Spirit to call upon the Father on their behalf "in groanings which cannot be uttered."[471] Thereby Clement acknowledges that it is a fatherly God who is approached in prayer although it is not stated explicitly in *Stromateis* 7.[472] However, in *Paedagogos* 1.8, Clement comments specifically on "Our Father, who is in heaven." Here Clement points to the fact that the heavens belong

---

For commentaries on the different invocations in the writings of Origen, see Sheerin, 1988, 201 n. 4.

466 Or. Or. 15.1 (Koetschau; tr. Stewart-Sykes).
467 Or. Jo. 2. 96 (Blanc; tr. Heine).
468 L. Perrone, *Prayer in Origen's Contra Celsum. The Knowledge of God and the Truth of Christianity*, in: VigChr, 55/1 (2001), 18.
469 Clem. Strom. 7.16.93 (Hort/Mayor).
470 Id. 7.3.16.
471 Id. 7.7.49.
472 Clem. Q.d.s. 37.2: "God in his very self is love, and for love's sake he becomes visible to us. And while the unspeakable part is father, the part that has sympathy for us is mother." (quoted from E. Osborn, *Clement of Alexandria*, Cambridge 2005, 147).

to God, since he created them, and "the Lord is the Son of the Creator." Consequently Clement comes to the conclusion that God is the Father, and the Son reveals the character of the Father: "So that it is veritably clear that the God of all is only one good, just Creator, and the Son in the Father." In *Paedagogos*, Clement thus describes complete unity between Father and Son, whereas in *Stromateis* 7, the relationship between the two is described as nearness: "the Son, which approaches most closely (προσεχεστάτη) to the one Almighty Being."[473]

In *Eclogae propheticae* 19.1, Clement also comments upon the invocation of God as Father. Here, it becomes evident that according to Clement, each Christian is in a progress that ideally moves the individual from faith in and fear of God into knowledge and love of God. To begin with a Christian needs to remind himself to be a child of God, eventually he will be so naturally, and the Spirit will testify to this as it will work within him, and "bears witness when we cry, Abba, Father" (cf. Romans 8:15). However, although in *Paedagogus*, Clement presents the Holy Spirit as acting from within the individual, this is not the case in *Stromateis* 7, where the Spirit is understood as an external agent that persuades from outside and cannot directly influence the will of human beings.[474]

When holding more of Clement's works together like this, it becomes obvious that it is not alien to Clement to invoke God as "Our Father," but in *Stromateis* 7, he does not mention this address. Henny Fiskå Hägg has pointed out that Clement "seems to emphasize the mystical, supra-natural aspect in man's relationship with God."[475] This mystical emphasis must be seen in relation with Clement's general apophatic approach to theology. Clement believes that humans cannot know God as he is, since he is essentially unknown. It might be the case that Clement felt that "Father" could become a constraining metaphor for the unknown God if he used it regularly. However, Clement also believed that man can only know God through

---

473 Clem. Strom. 7.2.5 (Hort/Mayor).

474 Id. 7.2.9.

475 H.F. Hägg, *Prayer and Knowledge in Clement of Alexandria*, in: M. Havrda/V. Hušek/J. Plátova (eds.), *The Seventh Book of the Stromateis. Proceedings of the Colloquium on Clement of Alexandria*, Leiden 2012, 137.

the incarnate Christ,[476] and through Christ, God is known as Father. Father is thus a valid address to God, but does not capture the entire idea of God.[477]

3.1.1.2 Tertullian and Cyprian on the invocation of God

In *De Oratione*, Tertullian deals with the question of invocation when he interprets the address of the Lord's Prayer, *Pater qui in caelis es*. Tertullian seems to take it for granted that prayers should be directed to God the Father, although when taking other of his texts into consideration, he occasionally seems to accept prayers addressed to Christ as well.[478] However, Tertullian begins his exposition of the Lord's Prayer by stating that this prayer bears witness to God;[479] "For we are praying to God and professing the faith (*fidem commendamus*) of which this mode of address is an indication (*cuius meritum est haec appellatio*)."[480] Hereby Tertullian specifies that prayer is a kind of confession to God, and he indicates that praying to God presupposes a certain belief in God, namely that God is the Father.

---

476 Id.
477 According to M. J. Brown the lack of references to the Lord's Prayer in Strom. 7 has the specific reason that the Lord's Prayer stood in direct conflict with Clement's theology of prayer. Brown writes in his analysis that the Lord's Prayer is petitionary and seems to express a lack on the part of God which Clement could not accept (Brown, 2004, 153 ff.). According to Brown, this does not suit Clement's theology because Clement is solely focused on spiritual issues (id.). Brown shows how Clement puts emphasis on the hiddenness of God. Brown's theory is to some degree corroborated, when we look at Strom. 7. However, two things must be added to Brown's conclusion: (1) God remains a personal God, even in *Stromateis* which is the most abstract and "gnostic" text of Clement. Clement portrays God slightly interchangeably in different texts, dependent on the readers and his accents in the particular context, but he never disregards the idea that God is fatherly. (2) None of the ante-Nicene treatises on prayer disregards the spiritual character of prayer and of God. For these two reasons, Brown's conclusion is not exact. Also Lorenzo Perrone criticises Brown's conclusion in a footnote in Perrone, *preghiera*, 2011, 544 n. 1746).
478 B.A. Paschkel points to two instances: Tert. Spect. 25.5. and Apol. 2.6. (B.A. Paschkel, *Tertullian on Liturgical Prayer to Christ. New Insights from De Spect. 25.5 and Apol. 2.6*, in: VigChr (2012), 20-29.).
479 Tert. Or. 2 (Schleyer; tr. Stewart-Sykes).
480 Id.

Furthermore, Tertullian adds that addressing God as Father is a privilege merited because of faith (*merito fidei*).[481] Faith in the name of the Father is thus a major issue from the outset of Tertullian's treatise – the relationship with God is a reality because of faith.

Furthermore, Tertullian mentions that the invocation of the Father entails that one is to free oneself from the ties to one's earthly father (cf. Matt 23:9).[482] When having the almighty God as Father, one is to offer one's devotion to him alone.[483] This makes the address, "Our Father," very exclusive because not only does this address entail a positive dedication of oneself to God, it also entails a withdrawal from one's biological family. However, Tertullian does not linger on this point which might be because Tertullian in this particular context did not want to transform Roman family values radically.[484] The individual believer is, however, expected to change drastically because of his new belonging. He/she is supposed to change his/her being into spiritual being, because God is a Spirit with certain characteristics and can only be approached by a similar spirit.[485] We shall get back to this spiritual assimilation below.

In *De Oratione* 2, Tertullian stresses the point that the Son is also invoked when the Father is addressed: *Item in Patre Filius invocatur*. This is the case because of the close relationship between the Father and the Son.[486] Furthermore, Tertullian combines the Father-invocation with a mentioning of the Church as "Mother" (*mater*).[487] In fact, all four authors under investigation at some point in their works make use of the term "Mother" about the church, but only Tertullian mentions "the Mother" in connection with the invocation of the Father.[488] Tertullian holds that *Pater* is also an invocation of the Son and Mother, i.e. the Church.[489] Thereby, Tertullian

---

481 Id.
482 Id.
483 Id. 1.
484 Sandnes, 2014, 214.
485 Tert. Or. 28 and 12 (Schleyer; tr. Stewart-Sykes).
486 John 10:30; Tert Or. 2 (Schleyer; tr. Stewart-Sykes).
487 Id.
488 J.C. Plumpe, *Mater Ecclesia. An Inquiry into the Concept of the Church as Mother in Early Christianity*, Washington 1943.
489 Tert. Or. 2.

establishes a kind of trinity, consisting of Father, Son and Mother – a *familia Dei*. [490] It is – so to speak – in relation to this *familia Dei* that the individual is to form his/her identity. Tertullian thus expresses a strong ecclesiological interest. This is also seen in the spiritual interpretation of the petition for daily bread in the Lord's Prayer. Tertullian believes the bread to be both literal bread and, more importantly, the body of Christ. Without saying it explicitly, the petition for daily bread thereby becomes a prayer for the unity of the congregation:

> "For Christ is our bread, because Christ is life and bread is life... Therefore, when we ask for our daily bread, we are asking that we should perpetually (*perpetuitatem*) be in Christ (*in Christo*) and that we should not be separated from his body (*et individuitatem a corpore eius*)."[491]

Tertullian also combines prayer with the idea of the church as mother in another of his pre-Montanist texts. In *De Baptismo*, he admonishes the neophytes to pray their first prayer to God as Father, immediately after they have been baptized. Tertullian admonishes:

> "... when you ascend from that most sacred font of your new birth, and spread your hands for the first time in the house of your mother (*apud matrem*), together with your brethren, ask from the Father (*petite patre*), ask from the Lord."[492]

In *De Baptismo*, we see how the Christian identity is related to baptism, to prayer, to the church and to the Christian community. In the following chapter, I shall analyse the kinship language in relation to prayer; here, it suffices to accentuate that Tertullian stresses the connection between prayer and a close relation to both God (the Father) and the Church (the Mother).[493] Tertullian states that those who have God as "Father" are fortunate, *Felices qui patrem*

---

490 Plumpe, 1943, 49 f. J.C. Plumpe hypothesizes that Tertullian's "omission of the Third Person of the Holy Trinity and the mention instead, of the Church with the other two Persons, presupposes Tertullian's later Montanist concept of the Church as a purely spiritual, pneumatic phenomenon, as an *ecclesia spiritus*."

491 Tert. Or. 6 (Schleyer; tr. Stewart-Sykes).

492 Tert. Bapt. 20 (Evans).

493 In his Montanist writings, these issues will be even more defined, thus in Tert. Pud. 5 (Micaelli/Munier; tr. Claesson), he writes that: "... they will cry the same cry, fawn your mercy with the same prayers, on their knees they will call

agnoscunt.[494]

In parallel with Tertullian, also Cyprian has the church and the unity of the church very much at heart when dealing with prayer. This is of course partly due to the fact that in Cyprian's time the congregations of North Africa were threatened by persecutions and schisms. Cyprian's ecclesiological interest becomes evident when he interprets "Our Father." He focuses on the pronoun "our" (*noster*) and interprets it to mean that collective prayer and a collective sentiment are to be prioritized over the individual. God is not "my" Father, but "our Father."[495] The community of Christians is thus in and of itself a condition for addressing God as Father, and just as there is no salvation outside the church, so there can be no effective prayer either.[496] However, there are more conditions for addressing God as father, because you have to deserve this right. If you do not behave as a child of God you cannot address God as "Father."[497] Furthermore, according to Cyprian, you have to believe in God to be his child; God is the "Father of believers (*credentium Pater*)"[498] and "of those who have knowledge and faith (*intellegentium et credentium pater est*)."[499] Cyprian implies that it is dangerous to call God Father if you have not deserved this privileged.[500] Related to this is Cyprian's conviction that remission of sins is also a condition for having God as Father: "but the name of children is ascribed to those to whom the remission of sins is given, and to them eternity promised by God himself…"[501] Since it is the church that holds the keys to remission of sins, either in the form of baptism or penance, the Church as a corporate

---

the same way, and try to relent the same mother (i.e. your church)." The idea behind Tertullian's statement resembles Cyprian idea that: "He cannot have God for father, who has not the Church for mother." (unit.eccl. 6 (tr. Jürgens)).

494 Tert. Orat. 2 (Schleyer; tr. Stewart-Sykes).
495 Cypr. Dom. Orat. 8; 10 (Réveillaud; tr. Stewart-Sykes). This is not a point that he takes over from Tertullian, since Tertullian uses a version of the Lord's Prayer without the pronoun. There thus seems to have been small differences between the versions of the Lord's Prayer in use at the time.
496 Cypr. Ep. 73, 21 (Goldhorn; tr. Donna).
497 Cypr. Dom. Orat. 11 (Réveillaud; tr. Stewart-Sykes).
498 Id. 9.
499 Id. 18.
500 Id. 10.
501 Id.

union under synodal government is, *de facto*, the only agent in establishing relations to God. This is the view point of both Cyprian and Tertullian.

For both Tertullian and Cyprian, the invocation of "Father" in prayer has a creedal character, understood in the sense that one professes one's faith by addressing God as Father. Therefore, prayer to God the Father becomes, in a way, a creed, an "Ausweisgebet."[502] The Latin authors thus show that they are aware of the symbolic importance of the address, and we can safely call the invocation of God as Father an "identity marker."[503] Clement also sees the connection between faith and prayer, but not only in the sense that prayer is a sign of faith, contrary, faith is prayer waiting to happen: "the mere faith that one will receive is itself also a kind of prayer stored up in the gnostic spirit."[504]

3.1.1.3 God as Father and Friend

While Father is by far the most predominant metaphor for God in the treatises, there are also other metaphors for God, such as King, Shepherd and Friend. These other metaphors are presumably not supposed to be used as invocations, but they describe the relationship that the believer can expect to have with God. Besides sonship which occurs in all four treatises, one finds mention of friendship in the two Greek treatises by Clement and Origen.

---

502 K.H. Ostmeyer, *Das Vaterunser: Gründe für seine Durchsetzung als 'Urgebet' der Christenheit*, in: NTS 50/3 (2004), 330-333.

503 For studies that refer to prayer/the Lord's Prayer as "identity marker" or "carrier of identity," see e.g. Webber, 2010, 61; J. Green, *Persevering Together in Prayer. The Significance of Prayer in the Acts of the Apostles*, in: R.N. Longenecker, *Into God's Presence: Prayer in the New Testament*, Grand Rapids 2001, 200 f.; Perrone, 2003, 268. See also Gerhards/Doeker/Ebenbauer, 2003, 13: "standardisierte Gebete... sind nach innen wie nach außen Zeugen ihrer Identität und ihres Selbstverständnisses." In the introduction to the volume, it is emphasized that prayers can be identity markers either because of their content or because of their use. The Amidah is for instance a Jewish identity marker because of its content, but the Lord's Prayer is an identity marker because of its use in the liturgy and catechetical training. One must therefore distinguish between "inhaltlichen Identitätmarkern" and "Performativen Identitätsmarkern" (Gerhards/Doeker/Ebenbauer, 2003, 17).

504 Clem. Strom. 7.7.41 (Hort/Mayor). Also Id. 7.10.55.

Friendship – like sonship – is so well known a phenomenon that it can
be used without further presentation, although the meaning of friendship
varies between different contexts.[505] As the word friendship is used by the
Greek authors under investigation, it has to do with a relation dominated
by choice and sympathy.[506] God has chosen and love the Christians, and
they ought to choose and love him in return. Only the Greek authors use
the word, Friend, φίλος directly about God, and it is especially Clement
who characterizes the relationship with God as a friendship. For instance,
he writes:

> "but he who is already pure in heart, not because of the commandments, but for
> the sake of knowledge by itself, - that man is a friend of God (φίλος οὗτος τοῦ
> θεοῦ)."[507]

Clement uses the terms "son" and "friend of God" interchangeably about
the gnostic, i.e. the perfect Christian. Thus in *Stromateis* 7.11.68:

> "For by [love] the gnostic, owing to his worship of the Best and Highest the
> stamp of which is unity (τῷ ἑνὶ), is made friend and son at once (φίλον ὁμοῦ καὶ
> υἱὸν) a perfect man indeed (τὸν γνωστικὸν ἀπεργάζεται)…"[508]

According to Clement, friendship and sonship are something that the
gnostic has to earn by being perfectly purified, but when he has earned it,
he will receive not only the right to pray to God,[509] but also unity (ἑνὶ) with
God, which means that he is "being now deemed worthy to behold forever
the Almighty, face to face (πρὸς πρόσωπον)."[510] According to Clement, this
unifying "encounter" with God is the climax of the Christian progression
towards God. This climax resembles the philosopher's prayer that was
described above, in which human and divine came close as "the alone
towards the Alone (μονος πρὸς μόνον)."[511]

---

505 D. Konstan, *Friendship in the Classical World*, Cambridge 1997.
506 As Stweart-Sykes notes friendship could refer to the duties of patronage
     (Stewart-Sykes, 2004, 196 n. 77).
507 Clem. Strom. 7.3.19 (Hort/Mayor).
508 It is more or less repeated later in Strom. 7.11.68 (Hort/Mayor): "a truly per-
     fect man and a friend of God, being ranked and reckoned as a son."
509 Clem. Strom. 7.12.79 (Hort/Mayor).
510 Id. 7.11.68, see also 7.10.57: πρόσωπον πρὸς πρόσωπον.
511 Plot. Enn. 5.1.6.9 (Henry/Schwyzer; tr. MacKenna/Page).

Clement believes that Christians must begin as slaves of God and then advance until they become friends of God and is united with him. The unity with God is described by Clement as "that vision (ἐποπτείαν) of God, which is the crowning height attainable by the gnostic soul..."[512] At this supreme stage, the gnostic is finally a perfect man and moreover a friend and son of God. The gnostic is then thoroughly noble, knowledgeable and perfect, and he is furthermore entirely spiritual and thus able to join the "spiritual church" and the relaxation (ἀνάπαυσιν) that characterizes being in God.[513] This relationship with God and the ultimate being in God are understood as the effect of prayer, but not just verbal prayer addressed to God; rather a life addressed to God.

Also, Origen calls the Christian a friend of God. He does so in a passage that is quite tricky and has a lacuna.[514] After the lacuna follows a statement about "the will of the Lord" which is "that he desires to become a friend to those of whom he was formerly a master." This is probably a reference to a biblical passage, John 15:15, which describes the development of the believer from slave to friend. This verse suits the Alexandrians' anthropology very well, because it corresponds with the idea that humans can progress from being slaves to friends in relation to God. Also for Origen, the friendship with God means that God no longer wants to be the Lord of bounded slaves, but the friend of free people.

The two Greek authors thus use the term "friend" to designate an advanced state in the human-divine relationship and a degree of equality between the human being and God that is not comparable to anything in the Latin treatises. In none of the Latin treatises is God referred to as a "friend."[515] When Cyprian writes that Christians should bear in mind that

---

512 Clem. Strom. 711.68 (Hort/Mayor).
513 Id.
514 It has been suggested to make an emendation and put in a reference to Jesus' saying in John 15:15: "No longer do I call you slaves, for the slave does not know what his master is doing; but I have called you friends, for all things that I have heard from My Father I have made known to you." (Stewart-Sykes, 2004, 112).
515 Cypr. Dom. Orat. 3 (Réveillaud; tr. Stewart-Sykes). However, in Dom. orat. 3, Cyprian calls the Lord's Prayer "a friendly and familiar manner of praying (amica et familiaris oratio)."

they are "standing before the face of God" (*sub conspectus Dei stare*), it does not hold the same connotations as Clement's vision of seeing God "face to face" (πρόσωπον πρὸς πρόσωπον)[516] or Origen's "looking upon the glory of the Lord with face unveiled (ἀνακεκαλυμμένῳ προσώπῳ τὴν δόξαν κυρίου)."[517] For Cyprian, standing before the face of God means being scrutinized by God, and therefore one has to act in a certain way and be "restrained by quiet and reserve."[518] Cyprian does not imagine a complete union between humans and God. The closest possible connection to God is made by the martyrs and confessors, who according to Cyprian could come to see God due to their clean hands and lips, and God would hold and kiss them.[519]

Both Clement and Origen deal with a concept of prayer that fits the metaphor of God as a friend. They suggest understanding prayer as a constant dialogue with a wise man. Drawing on social experience, they conclude that a conversation with a wise and virtuous person does make both parts of the dialogue wise and virtuous. Then they rhetorically ask, how much more would this not be the case, if the dialogue partner was God himself? Such a conversation is bound to change you. Clement thus writes:

> "And if the presence of some good man (ἡ παρουσία τινὸς ἀνδρὸς ἀγαθοῦ) always moulds for the better (πρὸς τὸ κρεῖττον ἀεὶ σχηματίζει) one who converses (τὸν ἐντυγχάνοντα) with him, owing to the respect and reverence which he inspires, with much more reason must he, who is always in uninterrupted presence of God (ἀδιαλείπτως τῷ θεῷ) by means of his knowledge and his life and his thankful spirit, be raised above himself on every occasion, both in regards to his actions and his words and his temper."[520]

---

516 Cypr. Dom. Orat. 4.2 (Réveillaud; tr. Stewart-Sykes).
517 Or. Or. 9.2 (Koetschau; tr. Stewart-Sykes). Cf. 2 Cor 3:18.
       The relation between God and human is not a *unio mystica*, according to Gessels' interpretation of Origen: „Die Relation zwischen Gott und dem Hegemonikon kann daher nicht mit dem Begriff einer unio im Sinne der unio mystica beschrieben werden, sondern muß unter dem Begriff der Metoche (participatio), der Anteilhabe bzw. Anteilnahme erfaßt werden. [...] Somit ist gesagt, der Ort der Gottbegegnung im Gebet ist das Hegemonikon." (Gessel, 1975, 208 ff.).
518 Cypr. Dom. orat. 4 (Réveillaud; tr. Stewart-Sykes).
519 Cypr. ep. 80.4 (Goldhorn; tr. Donna).
520 Clem. Strom. 7.7.35 (Hort/Mayor).

Origen has a similar passage, probably inspired by Clement:

> "For if the memory and recollection of a man who is renowned and who has found benefit in wisdom encourages us the more to emulate (αὐτοῦ προκαλεῖται) him and often restrains our impulses to do evil, how much more should the recollection of God who is the father of all, together with prayer to him (πρὸς αὐτὸν εὐχῆς), give advantage to those who believe that they are present to him, and that they are speaking to a God who is present and who hears them."[521]

Not only does this fit extremely well with the modern theories on discursive development of identity, it also shows that Clement and Origen envisioned God as a wise person with whom one can converse.

3.1.1.4 Expectations to the heavenly Father

The expectations that the Christians held to their heavenly Father are not systematically described in the treatises. The reason for the lack of description is probably that most people already knew intuitively the obligations incurred by being a member of a family and a subject of a father, because father is a "natural symbol."[522] Nothing in the euchological treatises indicates that the Christians had a different understanding of what family relations entail than the surrounding Roman society, and here fathers were expected to assure provisions and security.[523] These cultural expectations were transferred to God, who was expected to provide for his children, both literally and spiritually. Thus Cyprian writes:

> "… we ask pardon for our sin, so that the one who is fed by God may live in God, and provision be made (pascitur) not only for this present and transitory life (nec tantum et temporali uitae) but for the eternal life (sed aeternae) to which we might come if our sins are pardoned."[524]

Furthermore, Cyprian mentions God's "protective care (protectione),"[525] and he writes that "your Father knows that you are in need of all these

---

521 Or. or. 8.2 (Koetschau; tr. Stewart-Sykes). For the transformative effect of recollection of God, see S. Brock's interpretation of Aphrahat (S. Brock, *The Prayer of the Heart in Syriac Tradtion*, in: Sob. 4 (1982), 141).
522 Mary Douglas quoted in Buell, 1999, 3. Cf. below, paragraph 4.2.3.
523 Brown, 2004, 4-6.
524 Cypr. Dom. orat. 22 (Réveillaud; tr. Stewart-Sykes).
525 Id. 12.

things."[526] Cyprian expects the Father to show mercy in accordance with prayers and confessions made to him, because he has promised the mercy and pardon of a father (*paternam misericordiam promisit et ueniam secuturam*).[527] Origen notes that when praying to God, one can "plead like with a father (ἐντυγχάνωμεν δὲ ὡς πατρὶ)."[528] The use of ἐντυγχάνω shows that one is allowed to appeal to and bring forth petitions to God. God was expected both to care for his children and have authority over them. This is expressed clearly by Tertullian who describes God as being both pious (*pietas*) and powerful (*potestas*) towards his family.[529] When describing God's character towards humans, Clement uses another, but similar metaphor than father: He likens God to a shepherd and king. Clement describes God's care to be "like the care of the shepherds for the sheep and of the king for his subjects."[530]

3.1.1.5 Conclusions regarding the address "Father"

All the four authors under investigation designate God as Father. Tertullian, Cyprian and Origen agree that prayers should be addressed to the Father alone. Clement stands out because he does not mention any exact address, and although he uses the word "Father" in *Stromateis* 7, he thereby primarily means to characterize God as Creator and not as a close relative.

The writers differ when it comes to more specific questions, for instance the Latin writers present the relationship to God as dependent on the Christian community and Church in a concrete way and sees it as a collective endeavour to pray, whereas the Greek authors hold a less collective

---

526 Cf. Matt 6:31. See Cypr. Dom. orat. 21 (Réveillaud; tr. Stewart-Sykes).
527 Id. 22.
528 Or. or. 16.1 (Koetschau; tr. Stewart-Sykes).
529 Tert. Orat. 2 (Schleyer; tr. Stewart-Sykes); Marc. 1.27.3 (Evans). *Potestas* is exactly the word used to describe the *pater familias* in Roman household discourse. Saller notes that *pietas* comes to mean "well-wishing duty," and that one can discern a move towards more affectionate family relations in antiquity (R.P. Saller *Patriarchy, Property and Death in the Roman Family*, Cambridge 1996, 102 ff.). D. I. Rankin notes that *pietas* meant loyalty to family, class, city and emperor; and this loyalty was "demonstrated by loyalty to the old ways of religious ritual." (Rankin, 2006, 3).
530 Clem. Strom. 7.42.7 (Hort/Mayor).

approach and sees it as a task of the individual to approach God. The Greek authors generally, and Clement in particular, imagine God in a more abstract way that cannot be kept within the boundaries of the father-image.

When it comes to being unified with the divine in prayer, Clement and Origen are less reserved than the Latin authors. Clement and Origen believe that the perfect Christian can be united with God; whereas the Latin authors have a more distanced relationship to their heavenly father whom they cannot see, but believe is watching them. The difference reveals itself in the metaphors of sight: Clement's πρόσωπον πρὸς πρόσωπον is different from Cyprian's *sub conspecto Dei*.

3.1.2 What's in a name? – the Revelation of God's name

In Greek philosophy, since the days of Plato, an increased abstraction of the divine had taken place. Consequently, God had become a very abstract phenomenon from whom the world was estranged. A mediator had to be inserted into the Greek cosmology to make God approachable, therefore the idea of logos entered the world.[531] As we saw in Chapter 2, in Greek philosophy, logos – understood as divine rationality within – became important for the endeavour of praying, because logos served as the point of reference between the individual human being and the abstract God. This is a rough scheme that underlies much Greek philosophy.[532] The same scheme is recognizable in early forms of Christianity, but the Logos of Christianity is different, because the Christian Logos revealed a personal side of God and revealed the name of God that made it possible for humans to have a relationship with God and know his will.[533]

Although Jesus Christ has revealed the name of God and his fatherly character, this "name" is still a conundrum for the four Christian authors. Each author seems to understand God both as a familiar "Father" whose intentions are revealed in Christ and as an unknown "name." There is

---

531 S.P. Bergjan, *Der fürsorgende Gott. Der Begriff der PRONOIA Gottes in der apologetischen Literatur der Alten Kirche*, Berlin 2004, 27.39-43.

532 Though sometimes, daimons and divine powers figure as mediators in pagan philosophical sources, e.g. Apul. apol. 43.2 (Jones).

533 C. Osborne, *Clement of Alexandria*, in: L. Gerson (ed.), *The Cambridge History of Philosophy in Late Antiquity*, Cambridge 2010, 278.

a dichotomy when it comes to God, he is "known" and "unknown"; "Father" and "Name."

Origen deals explicitly with the "name" of God in *Perì Euchês* 14, where he notes that: "a name is a summary designation indicative of the proper quality of the thing named."[534] According to Origen, God has a name, namely the appellation that Moses was told by God himself in Exodus: "He who is" (τὸ „ὁ ὤν"; in Exodus 3:14: "I am who I am," אֶהְיֶה אֲשֶׁר אֶהְיֶה).[535] Origen explains that this is God's name, because God is unchangeable (ἄτρεπτος) and unalterable (ἀναλλοίωτος), God is "He who is" without change. Origen further notes that contrary to God, human beings are changing, and their names can change as well: "Abram" changed, and his name was changed to "Abraham"; "Saul" changed and became "Paul." God is the only being who is not changing, and this is what becomes evident from the name "He who is." Origen admits that it is almost impossible to get a full notion of God.[536] In fact, the individual can only grasp God through God's dealings with humanity, and therefore God is known "as creating, providing, judging, electing, abandoning, welcoming, rejecting, rewarding… and punishing."[537] With these statements, Origen balances between a positive and negative theological approach.[538]

Contrary to Origen, Tertullian does not even recognize the name that Moses was told by God according to Exodus; Tertullian writes that before Christ: "The name of the Father had been revealed to nobody. Even Moses, who had asked it of God himself, heard of a different name (*aliud nomen*)."[539] Tertullian states that it was not until the arrival of Jesus that

---

534 Or. or. 24.2 (Koetschau; tr. Stewart-Sykes). Mortley talks about a "Philonic principle": God is uncreated and therefore he cannot have a name (R. Mortley, *From Word to Silence: The Rise and Fall of Logos*, Bonn 1986, 133).

535 Or. or. 24.2 (Koetschau; tr. Stewart-Sykes).

536 Or. or. 24.2 (Koetschau; tr. Stewart-Sykes; emendation has been made in the text edition).

537 Id.

538 Clement is a proponent for negative theology; see e.g. Strom. 5.11.71 (Früchtel /Stählin/Treu; tr. Roberts): "The First Cause is not then in space, but above both space, and time, and name, and conception."

539 Tert. Or. 3 (Schleyer; tr. Stewart-Sykes).

God's name was revealed to "us," i.e. the Christians: *Nobis revelatum est in Filio.*[540]

Clement had yet another theory regarding God and his revelation. Clement believed that prior to the revelation of Christ, the wisdom of God had been handed over in the form of the commandments of the Jews and in Greek philosophy.[541] In this way, the will of God was partly known already before Jesus Christ was revealed, but only with Christ did a fuller revelation take place and supplemented the earlier incomplete instructions.

Although disagreeing about the degree to which God was known before the revelation of his Son, all four authors agree that something entirely new happened when the Son entered the stage. The three treatises by Origen, Tertullian and Cyprian all open with reflections about the fundamental change that has occurred because of the revelation of the Son – the change has to do with improvement in the knowledge (about God) and relations (to God). Jesus Christ is the person that makes the "old new" and the "unthinkable thinkable." It thus becomes clear that there is no way to God without Christ who facilitates the way to God, both relationally and "cognitively"; in John Behr's wording: "The Son reveals the Father, the one true God, and is the way to him."[542] Humans could neither know God, nor approach him without the revelatory role of Christ, and for this reason, Christ obviously has a fundamental role regarding prayer.

Tertullian writes: "As the Gospel has been introduced as the completion of everything of antiquity (*totius retro*), the new grace of God has renewed all things from fleshly being into spiritual being."[543] According to Tertullian, the new grace (*nova Dei gratia*) of God marks a new paradigm in history, characterized by completion, alteration and fulfilment, revealed by Christ. The word "new" is used several times in Tertullian's prologue to show that things have been transformed and made spiritual, also prayer has become spiritual. This pattern of new versus old marks out the Christians positively and is significant to the question of identity, because it contrasts the

---

540 Id.
541 Clem. Strom., 7.2.11 (Hort/Mayor).
542 Behr, 2001, 186.
543 Tert. Or. 1 (Schleyer; tr. Stewart-Sykes).

Christians to their predecessors, including the Jews.[544] Although it is not mentioned explicitly, the salvation history constitutes the underlying logic. History is divided into a "before" and "after" Christ. Christ is both the catalyst of paradigmatic changes and meanwhile also the key that makes the transformation and salvation known to humans: "In [the Gospel] our Lord Jesus Christ is recognized as the Spirit (*spiritus*) of God and the Word (*sermo*) of God and the reason (*ratio*) of God."[545] Again in the concluding part of his treatise, Tertullian makes use of the scheme of old versus new by contrasting the old prayer with the new and spiritual prayer, introduced by Christ.[546]

Like Tertullian, also Cyprian takes note of the Son's ability to reveal new information. Cyprian writes: "the Son... coming himself, showing us and opening to us the way."[547] On this new way of Christianity, Christ is the leader and guide. Cyprian contrasts the former situation of humanity, before Christ when "we... were wandering, blind, and reckless in the shadow of death," with the new condition which is a journey of life in the light of grace.[548] This new journey is the way of salvation, and a new worship in spirit and truth belongs to this way.[549] Those who are able to be spiritual worshippers are called "true worshippers" (*veri adoratores*).[550]

Also Origen begins his treatise *Perì Euchês* by explaining the revelatory role of Christ, and how Christ and the Spirit has opened for a new reality:

> "Matters which are so immense and so beyond humanity, so surpassing and exceeding our perishable nature (τῆς ἐπικήρου φύσεως ἡμῶν)... have become... comprehensible through Jesus Christ (ἡμᾶς χάριτος ὑπηρέτου Ἰησοῦ Χριστοῦ)... and through the collaborating Spirit (καὶ τοῦ συνεργοῦ πνεύματος)."[551]

Origen dwells on how the impossible has become possible by grace and through Christ, and notes that also true prayer has become possible because

---

544 Hvalvik/Sandnes, 2014.
545 Tert. Or. 1 (Schleyer; tr. Stewart-Sykes).
546 Id. 29.
547 Cypr. Dom. orat. 1 (Réveillaud; tr. Stewart-Sykes).
548 Id.
549 Id. 1-2.
550 Id. 28.
551 Or. or. 1 (Koetschau; tr. Stewart-Sykes).

of Christ's intervention.[552] Likewise he stresses the importance of the Spirit
that is essential for the very endeavour of praying, because without the
Spirit, humans do not know how to pray or begin doing it. He points to
several passages from Scripture that show the work of the Spirit in prayer
and the failing ability of humans to pray (e.g., Rom 8:26–27, Gal 4:6, 1
Cor 14,15).

In *Stromateis* 7, Clement mentions the revelatory purpose of Christ
"who taught the truth concerning God." Moreover, Clement describes
Christ as the "face of the God of Jacob,"[553] as "the power of the Father"[554]
and as the Son "from whom the gnostic believes that he received the knowledge of the ultimate course (τὸ ἐπέκεινα αἴτιον), the Father of the Universe
(τὸν πατέρα τῶν ὅλων)."[555] Thus Christ is also a cause of knowledge in
Clement's opinion. Earlier in *Stromateis, Book 5*, Clement furthermore
points to Christ as the key to any understanding of the fundamentally
transcendent God: "we cast ourselves into the greatness of Christ (εἰς τὸ
μέγεθος τοῦ χριστοῦ), and thence advance into immensity by holiness,
we may reach somehow to the conception of the Almighty, knowing not
what He is, but what He is not (οὐχ ὅ ἐστιν, ὅ δὲ μή ἐστι γνωρίσαντες·)."[556]
Again, Christ is the only way to God, and therefore also important for
prayer.

These passages from the euchological treatises suffice to show that before
entering the concrete instructions on prayer, the listeners/readers were introduced to God as their new Father, mediated through Christ. Jesus Christ
provides a name for the Father; he supplies a name for what is nameless.
Knowing the name marks a close relationship.[557] Eric Osborn describes it
in the following way: "the God beyond is found through the God within
God."[558] However, not only did Jesus Christ reveal the name of the Father,
even more importantly, he revealed the salutary will of the Father. Christ is

---

552 Id. 2.
553 Clem. Strom. 7.10.58 (Hort/Mayor).
554 Id. 7.2.9.
555 Id. 7.1.2.
556 Clem. Strom. 5.11.71 (Früchtel /Stählin/Treu; tr. Roberts).
557 Hvalvik/Sandnes, 2014, 215.
558 Osborn, 2005, 125.

therefore *sine qua non* for Christian prayer: he reveals the Father to whom one should pray; he reveals the things for which it is sensible to pray; and he has a role in the act of prayer. Therefore, prayer is fundamentally changed after the revelation of Christ, and Christian prayer is a "new form" of prayer, *novam orationis formam*.[559] We shall look into the role of Jesus Christ and the Spirit in the following.

3.1.3 The role of Christ and the Holy Spirit in prayer

According to the Christian authors under investigation, the "Lord, Jesus Christ," is highly important in the endeavour of praying. According to the four authors, there are at least three reasons for this:

1) Jesus is the true teacher and role model when it comes to prayer;
2) Jesus Christ plays an active part in prayer – he functions as advocate, intercessor and true high priest for the believers before God;
3) The life and death of Jesus Christ has thrown new light on how Christian prayer ought to be performed namely "in spirit and truth" (cf. John 4:24).

When it comes to prayer, Jesus is a teacher because he prayed himself and taught his disciples how to pray. For Origen, Tertullian and Cyprian alike the Lord's Prayer is the apex of prayer and the rule of prayer (*orandi disciplina; Orationis legem*).[560] For this reason, these authors place special emphasis on the fact that the Lord's Prayer came from the mouth of Jesus himself.[561] According to Cyprian, Jesus came and handed over "the commands of salvation," and these commands are summarized in the Lord's Prayer as well as in a few other simple sentences such as the Great Commandment.[562] Tertullian, Cyprian and Origen share this idea that the Lord's Prayer contains saving knowledge. Cyprian writes that:

---

559 Tert. Or. 1 (Schleyer; tr. Stewart-Sykes).
560 Id. and Cypr. Dom. orat. 8 (Réveillaud; tr. Stewart-Sykes).
561 See Tert. Or. 9 (Schleyer; tr. Stewart-Sykes). Tertullian mentions how the Lord's Prayer goes up to heaven "by its own special right," "commending to the Father the things the Son has taught."
562 Cypr. Dom. orat. 28 (Réveillaud; tr. Stewart-Sykes).

"Among [Christ's] other saving guidance and divine instructions by which he coun-
selled his people in the way of salvation, he himself gave them by which to pray and
directed the purposes of our prayers."[563]

This should not be understood as if the Lord's Prayer is a magical spell that
works in a concrete "do ut des"-fashion, although there are a few instances
that seems to express such a way of thinking.[564] Contrary, the Lord's Prayer is
"a summary of the whole Gospel" (*breviarium totius Evangelii*), and it works
spiritual "results."[565]

Cyprian notes that Jesus taught people how to pray by praying himself
(e.g., Luke 5:16),[566] and that Jesus was praying not for himself, but for "our
sins" (*pro delictis nostris*).[567] According to Cyprian, Jesus pleaded for humans
while he was on earth, and he is continually pleading for humans. He serves as
"our advocate," and this proves to Cyprian how eager God is to save people:

"… so great are the kindness and fidelity alike of God, with regard to our salvation, that he was not only content simply to redeem us with his own flesh and
blood but beyond this that he should plead for us so fully (*pro nobis amplius et
rogaret*)."[568]

That Jesus Christ is understood as "our" advocate, high priest and intercessor is a common feature in the four treatises under investigation, and
so is the expression that prayers should be offered "through the Son."[569]
All of these ideas are derived from the Scriptures.[570] Clement, Origen and

---

563 Id. 2.
564 For instance, Tertullian warns that someone who adds his own desires to the
Lord's Prayers will distance himself from God's ears (Tert. Or. 10 (Schleyer;
tr. Stewart-Sykes)). See also Cypr. Dom. orat. 18.1-2 (Réveillaud; tr. Stewart-
Sykes), cf. Simpson, 1965, 75-79.
565 Tert. Or. 1 (Schleyer; tr. Stewart-Sykes). On the meaning of Christ for the Lord's
Prayer, see also Simpson, 1965, 79-81.
566 Cypr. Dom. orat. 29 (Réveillaud; tr. Stewart-Sykes).
567 Id. 30.
568 Id. 30.
569 Origen writes on prayers "through Christ" in or. 15.2; 33.6; 15.4 (Koetschau;
tr. Stewart-Sykes).
      Cyprian writes on Christ as an advocate in Dom. orat. 3 (Réveillaud; tr.
Stewart-Sykes); see also Chapter 30.
570 Prayer is offered "through" Jesus in, e.g. Rom 1:8 or "in the name of Jesus"
in, e.g. John 16:23-24. Especially in the Pauline corpus, prayer is offered to

Cyprian put a strong emphasis on Jesus' role as a mediator who works both ways – Christ is the one who confers thanksgiving, praise and requests to God, and meanwhile he is the one who mediates knowledge, forgiveness and salvation.[571] Origen emphasizes the role of Christ as mediator, and mentioned that the Word which "mediates (ὑπ' αὐτοῦ μεσιτευομένῳ)" is the "high priest (ἀρχιερεὺς) of our offerings" and "advocate (παράκλητός) with the Father."[572]

Clement also mentions the mediatory role of Christ. He holds that it is through the Son that believers reach the Father (δι' υἱοῦ πρὸς τὸν πατέρα).[573] Clement refers to Christ as "high priest" three times in *Stromateis* 7. One time is in his very definition of how the life of a perfect Christian ought to be:

> "This, therefore, is the life-work of the perfected gnostic, viz. to hold communion (προσομιλεῖν) with God through the great High Priest (διὰ τοῦ μεγάλου ἀρχιερέ ως)."[574]

Therefore, Clement also describes the progress of Christian life and knowledge as "being brought closer to the great High Priest, in the vestibule, so to speak, of the Father."[575] The gnostic himself is likewise likened to a priest, Clement claims that the gnostic is "the holy priest of God (ἱερεὺς ὅσιος τοῦ θεοῦ)."[576] The perfect gnostic is thus placed in a holy hierarchy and is a lower priest (ἱερεὺς) under Logos, the high priest (ἀρχιερεὺς). This is one way of describing the hierarchy that is part of Clement's cosmology. According to Clement, all rational creatures have some rank in the hierarchy and are either approaching God or receding from God by every act.

"the God and Father of our Lord Jesus Christ" (e.g., 2 Cor 1:3; Eph 1:3; Col 1:3) (See Hurtado, 2014). In 1 John 2:1 Jesus is presented as an advocate for the Christians. In, e.g. Rom 8:34 Jesus is understood as intercessor. Jesus as the true high priest is furthermore a characteristic feature of the Letter to the Hebrews (e.g. 2:14-18; 4:14-15).
571 In the case of Origen, see: J. Laporte, *Philonic Models of Eucharistia in the Eucharist of Origen*, in: LTP 41/1 (1986), 81.
572 Or. or. 10.2 (Koetschau; tr. Stewart-Sykes).
573 Clem. Strom. 7.18.109 (Hort/Mayor).
574 Id. 7.3.13.
575 Id. 7.7.45.
576 Id. 7.7.36.

In this order, the angels rank above ordinary human beings, while demons are below. Jesus Christ is close to God the Father, and the perfect gnostic is approaching this divine orbit. Origen's cosmology is similar to that of Clement. They both view creation as divided into a hierarchy, and they hold that the Word of God and prayer are essential elements for the individual's ascension within the hierarchy. The Word of God serves as image and ideal, while prayer or contemplation is a way to approach God. Clement believes that Christ's close proximity to God is due to his eternal contemplation (ἐν ἀιδιότητι θεωρίας) of the Father,[577] and Origen develops theories about human contemplation of God and the possibility of being united to God through contemplation (θεωρία).[578] The Latin authors, however, do not share this speculative and idealistic cosmology, and in relation to the thought of Christ as mediator, Tertullian takes a different approach in *De Oratione*. From the beginning of his treatise, Tertullian points out that addressing the Father means that one is also addressing the Son, because the Father and the Son are one (cf. John 10:3).[579] Tertullian thus effectively closes the speculations on different persons in the immanent Trinity.

3.1.4 The Holy Spirit

All authors acknowledge the role of Jesus Christ in prayer and see the unique and positive character of Christian prayer as closely connected to Christ. It is obvious that the person and symbol of Jesus Christ is a strong identity marker for the *Christ*ians in relation to prayer and everything else for that matter. Origen, however, also includes the Holy Spirit in the act of prayer. In fact, as Lorenzo Perrone has pointed out in his book, *La preghiera secondo Origene: l'impossibilità donate*, it is the Holy Spirit that makes the whole endeavour of prayer possible. Human beings cannot pray on their own accord, they need the Holy Spirit to give them the impetus to pray. In *Perì Euchês* 2.3, Origen mentions that the Spirit intercedes and that it is the Spirit which "in the heart of the blessed, cries out: 'Abba Father' (Gal 4:6)." For Origen, prayer is thus fundamentally an act caused by the Spirit,

---

577 Id. 7.2.10.
578 Paddle on "Contemplation" in McGuckin, 2004, 81-83.
579 Tert. Or. 2 (Schleyer; tr. Stewart-Sykes).

originating from God, moving through the hearts of humans and returning to God: "For our mind cannot pray unless the Spirit prays first."[580] Origen mentions Paul's reservations concerning prayer in Rom 8:26: "We do not know the manner in which we should pray."[581] Origen, however, assumes that humans are able to pray, but only because of the Holy Spirit. In fact, Origen states that "our mind cannot pray unless the Spirit prays first."[582] Not only can Christians pray, their prayers will also be efficient when the Spirit graciously takes part: "For when anyone who is accompanied by the Holy Spirit (τοῦ κεκοσμημένου τῷ ἁγίῳ πνεύματι) calls upon the Lord, God sends thunder from heaven and rain to irrigate the soul."[583] In another passage in *Perì Euchês*, Origen mentions how the human mind in itself is barren, but can "become pregnant from the Holy Spirit through constancy in prayer..."[584]

It seems to be a Platonic anthropology that influences Origen to a pessimistic approach to earthly life where the soul is entrapped in a body, weighing it down and preventing it from reaching God by its own efforts; "we maintain that human nature is in no way able to seek after God, or to attain a clear knowledge of Him without the help of Him whom it seeks."[585] For this reason, humans need God to take the initiative for there to be any contact between humans and God. In a commentary on Psalm 116, Origen formulates it succinctly: "Since we are not able to extend ourselves to God when praying, he must bend down to us (Ἐπεὶ μὴ δυνάμεθα ἑαυτοὺς ἐκτείνειν πρὸς Θεὸν εὐχόμενοι, αὐτὸς τὸ οὖς αὐτοῦ κλίνει πρὸς ἡμᾶς)."[586] Nevertheless, this does not mean that Origen takes all responsibility away from the individual. Although the impetus to pray and approach God must come from the Spirit; the Spirit only helps those who are willing to co-operate: "It would seem that [the Spirit] simply intercedes for those who conquer, and more than intercedes for those who 'more than conquer,' and does not

---

580 Or. or. 2.4 (Koetschau; tr. Stewart-Sykes).
581 Id. 2.4.
582 Id. 2.4.
583 Id. 13.5.
584 Id. 13.3.
585 Or. Cels. 7.42 (Borret; tr. Crombie).
586 Or. sel. in Ps. on Psalm 114/116 (Migne).

intercede at all for those who are conquered."[587] The process of prayer is thus a synergistic process, although God is the one initiating the relationship in the first place.[588] We shall return to this point.

The Trinitarian God is thus very active according to the teachings of Origen who understood prayer as a Trinitarian act during which the individual is incorporated into the divine relations. In the following chapter, we shall take a look at more of these "relations" established in prayer. Here the purpose has been to illustrate that because of the triune character of God, humans can enter into a relationship with God by the help of Jesus Christ and/or the Holy Spirit. Also Clement expects the individual to establish a relationship to God in prayer; the relation in itself is more important than any benefit gained by petitions.[589] Scholars have interpreted Clement's and Origen's views on the relations between the Father, Son and Holy Spirit as existing because of a shared love.[590] The Christian can take part in these relations, if they wish. According to Clement, the participation in the divine relations is a matter of choice. In Clement's treatise, the Holy Spirit is defined as attracting (ἑλκόμενοι) people like a magnet, but the Spirit does not work *in* people, since this would compromise their freedom to choose for themselves whether they want to approach God or not. Clement writes: "For this is the law from the beginning, that he who would have virtue must choose it (αἱρεῖσθαι τὸν βουλόμενον ἀρετήν)."[591]

In the treatises under investigation we see the emergence of Trinitarian ideas of God, although at times it seems to be more correct to call them "binitarian ideas"[592] of God, since the Spirit as Trinitarian person still

---

587   Or. or. 2.4 (Koetschau; tr. Stewart-Sykes).

588   We shall encounter more instances of the term "synergy" below. Lorenzo Perrone utters a reservation towards the term "synergism": "Finally, man's endeavour to know God has a chance to succeed, only if God himself comes to sustain his efforts, in response to a prayer that recognizes such a necessity—that is, Origen establishes anew what is rather incorrectly called a "synergistic" model between man and God, inasmuch as in the last instance only the initiative of God is effective." (Perrone, 2001, 15).

589   Osborn, 2005, 273.

590   Id. 147 ff.

591   Clem. Strom. 7.2.9 (Hort/Mayor).

592   The New Testament scholar Larry Hurtado explains "binitarian" as: "Not simply two figures, but a linkage and, indeed, a clear functional subordination

played a relatively small role in regard to prayer in all but Origen's treatise. Indeed, the role of the Spirit is often confused with the role of the Father or Son – as when Tertullian writes that Jesus Christ is the revelation of "the Spirit of God" (*Dei spiritus*).[593] Eric Osborn writes about Tertullian's understanding of prayer that: "Trinity points to prayer, as the cross points to trinity."[594] There is some truth to this, but the understanding of Trinity seems at times somewhat not sharp. When comparing the Trinitarian ideas in the euchological treatises under investigation with Trinitarian ideas in more systematically oriented treatises, such as Origen's *De Principiis* or Tertullian's *Adversus Praxean*, one sees that the euchological treatises are less detailed and thus more pastoral in character. For this reason, it seems correct to infer that the ideas expressed in the euchological treatises had a bigger influence on lay Christians and are better representations of the predominant Christian idea of God. Although it will of course remain speculative what "Christians" *de facto* believed.

In *De Dominica Oratione*, Cyprian expresses Trinitarian formulas, e.g. in chapter 23: "The greater sacrifice to God is our peace and brotherly agreement, as a people unified in the unity of the Father and the Son and the Holy Spirit." This seems to be an echo of a liturgical formula, maybe used in relation to the Eucharist.[595] According to Cyprian, the Father and the Son is a unity, and people are invited to take part in this unity (cf. John 17:20).[596]

3.1.5 Summary on the role of Son and Spirit

All of the four authors under investigation understand the Son as being subordinate to the Father. This subordination, however, serves the purpose

---

of Jesus to God, a "shaped two-ishness" exhibited in the characteristic expressions of belief and in cultic practices." (L. Hurtado, *The Binitarian Pattern of Earliest Christian Devotion and Early Doctrinal Development*, in: B.D. Spinks (ed.), *The Place of Christ in Liturgical Prayer. Trinity, Christology, and Liturgical Theology*, Collegeville 2008, 23-50, 33).

593 Tert. Or. 1 (Schleyer; tr. Stewart-Sykes).
594 Osborn, 2005, 144. Cf. Perrone, *preghiera*, 2011, 519.
595 Cf. M. Réveillaud (ed.), *L'orasion dominical par saint Cyprien*, Paris 1964, 192-193. Emphasis added.
596 Cypr. Dom. orat. 30 (Réveillaud; tr. Stewart-Sykes).

of making God approachable by way of his revelation and by the aid of intermediaries, primarily his Son, but also to some varying degrees his Spirit. The revelation serves both a cognitive and social purpose: the Son of God reveals a certain knowledge regarding God and makes it possible to step into a human-divine relation with God. Without the revelation and mediator of God, prayer would be an irrelevant phenomenon, because Christians would not know God or know how to pray. The Christian Logos theory and Trinitarian ideas emphasized the "personal" character of the deity, "The act of emanation was a voluntary act on the part of God."[597] All four authors are in accord on this point.

There are, of course, differences between the authors. The Greek authors present the possibility of a close unity between humans and God, whereas the Latin authors do not emphasize this aspect, aside from Cyprian's statement that the Church as such is in unity with God. Hereby the difference between the mystically[598] oriented Greek theology and the ecclesiological theology of the Latin authors comes to the fore; although the distinctions are not sharp – there are also mystical traits in the Latin treatises and ecclesiology in the Greek treatises.

There are also differences internally between the Greek and Latin authors respectively. The two Greek authors are not in complete accord when they describe the role of the Holy Spirit. For Origen, the Holy Spirit penetrates the human mind and heart, and thereby it is the Holy Spirit that makes it possible for humans to approach God. For Clement, the human freedom cannot be compromised, not even by the intervention of the Holy Spirit, and for this reason, the Holy Spirit is only said to be able to attract people to God, like a magnet, not to push them from within. The Latin authors

597 M. Hillar, *From Logos to Trinity. The Evolution of Religious Beliefs from Pythagoras to Tertullian*, Cambridge 2008, 211.
598 "Mysticism" is a debated concept. Here I use it as defined by A. Louth: "… it can be characterized as a search for and experience of immediacy with God. The mystic is not content to know *about* God, he longs for union with God" (A. Louth, *The Origins of the Christian Mystical Tradition*, Oxford 1981, xiii-xiv). In his introduction to Origen's *Peri Euches*, E. Jay distinguishes between different "levels" of mysticism and holds that Origen is not a "real" mystical thinker, despite of what Völker once claimed (E.F. Jay (ed.), *Origen's Treatise On Prayer*, London 1954, 62 ff.).

do not present an elaborate pneumatology. It is noticeable that Tertullian and Cyprian are not in complete accord regarding the role they ascribe to the Son as mediator in prayer. Tertullian stands out as the only author not pointing to Jesus Christ as either advocate or high priest in relation to prayer. As we shall investigate further below, Tertullian envisions a direct meeting between the purified human spirit and God's pure spirit.

3.1.6 On God's will and providence

God's will and God's providence are themes that occur frequently in the four treatises on prayer. One reason for this is that according to the authors, people ought to pray in accordance with God's will which means in accordance with the Word of God. Another reason why the will of God is mentioned frequently in the treatises is that the third petition of the Lord's Prayer is about the will of God: "Your will be done…," and all of the authors refer to this petition in their commentaries on the Lord's Prayer – or, in Clement's case, in *Stromateis* 4.9.[599]

Another reason for the focus on will and providence is that the entire endeavour of prayer is rendered invalid if people do not have a free will, but are subdued to God's will. The two following paragraphs will shortly describe how God's will and God's providence are presented in the treatises on prayer.

3.1.6.1 *The will of God*

According to Cyprian, it is the will of God "that the spiritual and godly should prevail."[600] Cyprian elaborates by stating that: "the will of God is that which Christ both did and taught."[601] The ideal is therefore to follow Jesus Christ, and if one follows his behaviour and teachings, it will in due time lead to "safety and salvation."[602] Tertullian agrees that "the sum total of [God's] will is the salvation of those whom he has adopted."[603] Jesus

---

599 Tertullian, Cyprian and Origen all interpret the third petition of the Lord's Prayer, "Your will be done in heaven and on earth" in a similar manner, namely to mean that it is really about God's will being done in humans.
600 Cypr. Dom. orat. 16 (Réveillaud; tr. Stewart-Sykes).
601 Id. 15.
602 Id. 16.
603 Tert. Or. 4 (Schleyer; tr. Stewart-Sykes).

Christ revealed the will of God "in his proclamation and in his labors and in his suffering."[604] Tertullian therefore, like Cyprian, wants Christians to act as Jesus acted, even unto death if necessary. The Latin authors thus encouraged martyrdom, and they thereby indirectly stated that if the Christian identity could not be upheld, it was better not to have any identity at all on earth.

The Latin authors hold that the will of God is one, and his children is to take God's will upon themselves like Jesus did in the Garden of Gethsemane. Jesus "abandoned himself to the Father's will."[605] It remains somewhat unclear in the Latin euchological treatises if people can decide for themselves regarding their obedience, sometimes it seems that Tertullian expects God to be the ruler also of the will of humans. It is noteworthy that the two Greek authors do not refer to Jesus' prayer in Gethsemane in their euchological treatises, while the Latin authors do. It seems that the Alexandrians do not want to draw attention to the fact that even Jesus momentarily wanted something else than his heavenly Father.[606] Tertullian holds that the "ability to do [what Jesus did] is through the will of God (*Quae ut implore possimus, opus est Dei voluntate*)."[607] In other words, Tertullian wants humans to obey the will of God, and at the same time he believes that the ability to do anything is up to the will of God. In this way, Tertullian's argumentation touches upon fatalism and predestination; although in *Against Marcion* he refutes both.[608] Nevertheless, Tertullian places the responsibility on the believers who are supposed to approach God by praying in every place possible, etc.[609] Tertullian is not very clear about the possibilities of human capability.

The Greek authors, Clement and Origen, are generally more unambiguous when speaking about the free will of humans. They believe that humans possess a free will and can therefore by choice assimilate their will

---

604 Id.
605 Id.
606 Elsewhere Origen comments on Jesus' prayer in Gethsemane, (e.g. Cels. 2,25). Prayers to avoid death is not recognized among philosophers. In hom. in Ier. 17.6, Origen warns against prayers to extend life. See also Perrone, 2001, 6-8.
607 Tert. Or. 4 (Schleyer; tr. Stewart-Sykes).
608 E.g. Tert. Marc. 1.24-25 (Evans).
609 Tert. Or. 24 (Schleyer; tr. Stewart-Sykes).

with God's will. Origen expresses this by writing: "God desires (βούλεται) that people should obtain the good not under compulsion but willingly (ἑ κουσίως)."[610] It is God's will to save people, but God will only save them if they use their own will in a virtuous way. In *Perì Euchês*, Origen expresses this by way of a metaphor. Origen uses the image of a bird and its wings to describe a human being with a free will. The bird's good use of its wings represents the correct, virtuous use of the will. God wants even the smallest bird "to make proper use of its wings, which were given so that it might soar upward."[611] According to this logic, progress and salvation are to a large extent up to the individual, in that the individual must use his/her free will to reach and assimilate to God. Origen finds that the ability of people to be rational and communicate with God spiritually show that humans do have a determining influence on events.[612] Clement's ideas about free will are very similar to Origen's. Clement also emphasizes that the Son is the revelation of the will of God,[613] but whether people follow the will of God is their own choice: "Now we are made to be obedient to the command-ments, if our choice be such as to will salvation (εἰ τὸ βούλεσθαι σῴζεσθαι ἐλοίμεθα)."[614] If a person is able to align his/her own will with the will of God, he/she will always receive what he/she prays for – "he no sooner prays than he receives…"[615] Clement even characterizes a true gnostic as "a partner of the Divine Will."[616] We can thus see how the Greeks believed in a synergism between their own effort and God's grace in regard to having a relationship with God.[617]

---

610 Or. or. 29.15 (Koetschau; tr. Stewart-Sykes).

611 Id. 29.16. The passage alludes to both Luke 12:6 and Plato's myth about the winged soul in Phaedrus.

612 Simpson 1965, 124.

613 Clem. Strom. 7.16.104 (Hort/Mayor).

614 Id. 7.3.20.

615 Id. 7.7.44.

616 Id. 7.12.78.

617 However, it remains a question who is more responsible for the human-divine relationship. In an article on Origen's idea of prayer in *Contra Celsum*, Lorenzo Perrone concludes that "access to God and his truth is provided only by God, in response to prayer" (Perrone, 2001, 6).

For all the authors, it is important to stress God's will to save humans. For Clement and Origen in particular, it is also important to stress human freedom. At the same time, however, they emphasize God's almighty character. This is a paradox, and there is only one solution: "God limits himself to allow [human] freedom, while retaining his long-term providence."[618] There is a will of God to which the Christians are supposed to assimilate, although all four authors believe that God's help is needed in the process of conforming human will to God's will in the endeavour of praying.

3.1.6.2 The providence of God

Providence, *providentia* or πρόνοια, refers to God's ability to foresee events and make due provision. God's alleged providence begged (and still begs) the question why bad things happen when God is good, foresighted and almighty. God's providence also begs questions concerning the relevance of prayer, since one could assume that if God always knows the conditions of his children, would he not give them what they required without needing their petitions. Actually, this last issue was the reason that Origen was asked to write about prayer by his patron Ambrosius. Somebody had criticized prayer and called it superfluous. Origen refutes this claim in *Perì Euchês* 5–7 as we shall see below.

According to Silke-Petra Bergjan, "providence" could mean three different things in late antiquity:[619] (1) ἐκ προνοίας meant an action performed voluntarily or deliberately, while πρόνοια meant either; (2) the fatherly care for his children and subordinates; or (3) the cosmic order (a Stoic concept).[620] In the treatises under investigation, the word "providence" is used by the Greek authors, but almost not at all by the Latin authors. Nevertheless, as we have already seen, all four authors share the belief that God cares for his creation and wants to save humans; as such the idea of

---

618 Osborn, 2005, 100.

619 Bergjan, 2004 15-80.

620 S.P. Bergjan, *Clement of Alexandria on God's Providence and the Gnostic's Life Choice. The Concept of Pronoia in the Stromateis, Book VII*, in: M. Havrda/V. Hušek/J. Plátova (eds.), *The Seventh Book of the Stromateis. Proceedings of the Colloquium on Clement of Alexandria*, Leiden 2012, 63-92, 63.

God's providence is present in all four treatises, although only two reflect on the theme explicitly.

In *De Oratione*, Tertullian describes God's almightiness by a rhetorical question with reference to Proverbs 21:1: "For when is God, in whose hands is the heart of all kings, not the king?" This quotation depicts God's almighty powers. Tertullian, however, does not expand on the question why God does not use his almighty powers to take better care of his children. However, when commenting on the Lord's Prayer it indirectly becomes clear that according to Tertullian, God's will is not easy to entangle. The will of God also entails temptations and meetings with "the evil (one)." Tertullian therefore admonishes the Christians to pray that God will deliver them "from the evil (one) (*a malo*)." Also in Tertullian's work *De Fuga in Persecutione,* Tertullian stresses that everything happens because it is willed by God, even persecutions.[621] God's providence thus remains rather obscure within Tertullian's texts. It is not completely obvious why God provides for his children in the way that he does.[622]

The only extant instance in the Latin texts under investigation where "providence" literally is mentioned is *en passant* in Cyprian's *De Dominica Oratione* 22. It is a passage on the fifth petition of the Lord's Prayer: "Pardon us our debts," and here Cyprian notes "how providently"[623] (*quam prouidenter*) it is that we are reminded of our guilt every day in the Lord's Prayer "so that the mind may be called to a sense of its guilt." Cyprian thus uses the word "providently" to describe what is in accordance with God's will to save people. It is due to the providence of God, then, that human beings repent and pray for forgiveness. Obviously, God's providence is aimed at saving humans more than on physical issues in the current life.

The Greek authors use the word προνοία several times in their treatises on prayer, but they attach a slightly different meaning to the word. As

621 Tert. Fug. 1 (Bulhart).
622 Brown mentions that "The Greco-Roman world held a strong sensibility that placed responsibility for human trials on human beings rather than on God." (Brown, 2004, 26). He refers to Od. 1.32-34: "Oh for shame, how the mortals put the blame upon us Gods, for they say evils come from us, but it is they, rather, who by their own recklessness win sorrow beyond what is given."
623 Stewart-Sykes translates it "properly."

previously mentioned, the incentive for Origen to write *Perì Euchês* was a question about the relevance of prayer. Why are prayers not superfluous if God has perfect foresight and wants to do everything for his children? Origen answers the question by reference to the free will. Humans are rational and free, which is evident from their ability to move by their own will.[624] God knows everything that is going to happen, because God has perfect foreknowledge, but God lets humans decide for themselves. God therefore already knows the prayers that will be made, if they will be wise and consequently if he will respond. In other words, God could decide for his subjects but restrains himself from doing so.[625] Still God responds to the prayers of his people in accord with their faith and "with the will of the giver." Origen is aware that God's responses to prayers might be obscure. Nonetheless, Origen assures his audience that "[God's] will is wise, even if we are unable to give an account of the cause..."[626]

Also Clement is aware of the philosophic reservations towards prayer. According to Clement, *pronoia* is the way in which God works. God educates human beings by the events that occur in their lives. Therefore God's *pronoia* is an education, a *paideia*. In this life humans will experience punishment and chastisement, "which we have to endure as salutary chastening (εἰς παιδείαν ὑπομένομεν σωτήριον)."[627] Silke-Petra Bergjan formulates it thus: "Pronoia beschreibt die Einbindung des einzelnen in den Gesamtzusammenhang, und Clemens interpretiert dies als Erziehung."[628] Clement understands Jesus Christ as steering "the universe" according to the Father's will.[629] Nevertheless, it is up to every individual to move in the right direction, and Clement has a theory that all can be saved by following the teachings of the Word. The gnostic is free to choose, but God has an interest in human salvation, and over time God tries to educate people to use their will in a good way; everything that happens to humans therefore

---

624 Or. or. 6.1-2 (Koetschau; tr. Stewart-Sykes).
625 Id. 6.6.
626 Id. 16.2.
627 Clem. Strom. 7.10.56 (Hort/Mayor).
628 Bergjan, 2004, 173.
629 Clem. Strom. 7.2.5 (Hort/Mayor): "The Son is the highest Pre-eminence, which sets in order all things according to the Father's will, and steers the universe aright."

happens to punish, educate or improve them.[630] In *Stromateis*, Clement writes that: "as children are punished by their teacher, or their father, so are we by providence (πρὸς τῆς προνοίας)."[631] Therefore, "all things in the world are ordered for the best."[632] The individual has no other choice than: "playing irreproachably whatever part in life God may have assigned to him to act, he perceives both what he ought to do and what he ought to endure."[633] Clement is of the opinion that there is no human perfection granted by nature – perfection is an accomplishment of the will.[634] "The gnostic's destiny will not lie in Tyche's hands. It depends on him whether he is happy, blessed, and a kingly friend of God."[635] Becoming virtuous is a matter of free choice, training and persistence.[636] Clement sounds extremely Stoic in these passages where he leaves it up to humans to be virtuous and be in a correct relationship with God. This is also what Clement expresses in a Stoic-sounding passage where he notes that "belief and obedience are in our own power (ἐφ'ἡμῖν)."[637] At the same time, Clement, however, acknowledges that God is the author of the holiness of the gnostic; the gnostic thus owes his holiness to the Divine Providence but receives it "through a voluntary acknowledgement."[638]

According to the Danish scholar Hal Koch's book *Pronoia und Paideusis*, Origen shared the idea of God's *pronoia* as education. Silke-Petra Bergjan has focused on *Contra Celsum* and noted that the ideas of Clement and Origen regarding providence are not completely alike. Origen believed in a harmonic universe, and therefore used the term *pronoia* in a somewhat Stoic fashion which meant that the aim of providence was not primarily

630　Bergjan, 2012, 75.
631　Clem. Strom. 7.16.102 (Hort/Mayor). See also 7.10.56 on "salutary chastening."
632　Id. 7.7.45.
633　Id. 4.11.65 (Früchtel /Stählin/Treu; tr. Roberts).
634　Bergjan, 2012, 76.
635　Clem. Strom. 4.7 (Früchtel /Stählin/Treu; tr. Roberts).
636　Id. See Clem. Strom. 7.3.20 (Hort/Mayor). With an allusion to Pl. r. 10.617E (Emlyn-Jones), Clement states that the conditions laid down by God are equal for all, "but he who is able will choose, and he who will prevails."
637　Clem. Strom. 7.3.16 (Hort/Mayor).
638　Id. 7.7.42.

education of individuals but rather general harmony.[639] Nonetheless, in *Perì Euchês*, Origen confesses: "I do think that God deals with each rational soul in such a way as to lead it to eternal life."[640] According to Clement, God "is the source of Providence both for the individual and the community and for the universe at large."[641] Probably the truth about Origen is that he has both an individual and collective approach regarding providence, and S. Antonova concludes about Origen's view on providence that it "always and necessarily leads to the ultimate goal of enlightenment and perfection of the individual or the collection of individuals."[642]

3.1.7 Preliminary conclusions

While the Christian authors reflected on themes such as God the Father, God as Trinity and God's providence, they created an idealized Christian identity. The ideas developed about the Christian God created a corresponding idea of what it entailed to be Christian. Being Christian meant being a child of God, a privilege that would result in eschatological salvation and already in this life meant that God was nearby. Clement imagined that Christians could come to a kind of unity with God already in the present, although he reckoned that it took a lot of effort and demanded a certain attitude and behaviour. Both Clement and Origen understood God as a friend. The Latin authors did not use mystical terms, such as "unity with God," but they did imagine that their inner thoughts and motives were constantly being scrutinized by God. For this reason, they had to scrutinize themselves as well.

For late antique Christians, God's self-revelation was the main issue that defined them, sat them apart and made them aware that they could be children of God, calling upon God as "Our Father" was a defining moment. Prayer was understood as a response to and an alignment with the will of God. God's saving acts and grace was thus the back drop of every prayer. And as Origen makes explicitly, prayer was first and foremost an

---

639 Bergjan, 2004, 219.
640 Or. or. 29.13 (Koetschau; tr. Stewart-Sykes).
641 Clem. Strom. 7.2.6 (Hort/Mayor).
642 Stamenka Antonova on "Providence" in McGuckin, 2004, 182.

act of grace from God. This leads R.L. Simpson to label prayer as a sacrament, "it seeks what God alone can give."[643] Prayers from humans were not believed to establish the relationship with God, but to respond to the relationship which Christ had revealed. Theological ideas thus placed the Christian in a relationship with God, their Father and Jesus Christ, their brother and advocate. This familial relationship between humans and God is in existence only because of God's initial approach towards his creation, the defining move being Christ.

3.2 Approaching God the Father

In the previous paragraphs, the idea of God was explored on the basis of four treatises on prayer from the third century. These treatises also hold much information about how Christians were admonished to approach God in prayer. Certain formulations from the Holy Scriptures are frequently employed to describe how prayers ought to be conducted: prayer should be done "in secret," "in spirit and truth" and "without ceasing," and furthermore with the admonitions in mind: "Ask for great things" or "Seek First his Kingdom." These sentences are far from being the only New Testament formulations in the discourses on prayer, but they are singled out because they are striking illustrations of the authors' theology of prayer and are found in several of the works studied here. The following paragraphs consist in an analysis of how the authors used these biblical expressions in their euchological treatises.

3.2.1 Pray in secret[644]

Around 250, while the Decian persecution was raging against the Christians, Cyprian composed his treatise on prayer, in which he wrote: "The Lord has bidden us to pray in secret."[645] With these words Cyprian referred to the

---

643 Simpson, 1965, 136.
644 The content of the following paragraphs on "secret prayer" is similar to my article: M.L. Munkholt Christensen. *'The Lord has bidden us to pray in Secret'. Reconciling Personal and Collective Identity through 'Secret Prayer' i" 3rd-Century Christianity*, in: S. Saxkjær/E. Mortensen (eds.), *Secrecy*, Aarhus 2015, 131-44.
645 Cypr. Dom. orat. 4 (Réveillaud; tr. Stewart-Sykes).

Gospel of Matthew 6:6, where Jesus admonishes his followers on prayer by saying: "But you, when you pray, go into your inner room, close your door and pray to your Father who is in secret, and your Father who sees what is done in secret will reward you."[646] This Matthean verse belongs in a passage where Jesus also admonishes his followers not to be like those who make their charity known in order to "have glory from men," and who pray and fast to impress other people.[647] Such behaviour is hypocritical, and Jesus warns against it: "When you pray, you are not to be like the hypocrites; for they love to stand and pray in the synagogues and on the street corners so that they may be seen by men."[648] Instead of such ostentatious behaviour, Jesus stresses that charitable deeds and prayers should be conducted "in your inner room" (εἰς τὸ ταμεῖόν σου) and "in secret" (ἐν τῷ κρυπτῷ): secrecy will annul the possibility of erroneous motives such as the intention of gaining praise and fame. When illustrating this admonition, Jesus goes as far as saying that when doing charitable deeds, the right hand should not even know what the left hand is doing.[649] With such a hyperbole Jesus calls for an extreme level of concealment in charity and prayer.[650] What follows in the biblical passage is that Jesus teaches his followers the Lord's Prayer.

Because Jesus himself was quoted in the Gospel as saying that prayer should be performed "in secret," the first Christian theologians writing on prayer had to deal with this admonition. The theologians therefore faced something of a challenge, since Christian worship, including prayer, was a profoundly congregational and communal matter centred on the Eucharistic celebration.[651] However, the authors themselves did not verbalize this

---

646 Matt 6:6.

647 "σὺ δὲ ὅταν προσεύχῃ, εἴσελθε εἰς τὸ ταμεῖόν σου καὶ κλείσας τὴν θύραν σου πρόσευξαι τῷ Πατρί σου τῷ ἐν τῷ κρυπτῷ· καὶ ὁ Πατήρ σου ὁ βλέπων ἐν τῷ κρυπτῷ ἀποδώσει σοι." (Matt 6:1-18, it is a part of the Sermon on the Mount (Matt 5-7)).

648 Matt 6:5.

649 Matt 6:3.

650 C.S. Keener, *The Gospel of Matthew. A Socio-Rhetorical Commentary*, Grand Rapids 2009, 208. C.S. Keener mentions how also others used such exaggerations, e.g. Marcus Aurelius (Marc Aurel, *Meditationes* 8.9).

651 The importance of collective worship is expressed by several early theologians, for instance in relation to Matt 18:20 where Jesus says: "For where two or

ambiguity, but dauntlessly admonished their congregations to pray three to five times a day – and at best, all the time.[652] The following paragraphs will answer the question: What did the Christians in the 3rd century understand by "secret prayer"?

3.2.1.1 What is secret prayer?

In all four treatises, the authors either directly quote or strongly allude to Matt 6:6, where Jesus recommends secret prayer. All four Christian authors under investigation recommend that Christians should pray in their "inner room" or "in secret."[653] Clement alludes to the Matthean pericope in *Stromateis* 7.7.49, when he writes:

> "Accordingly [the gnostic] will pray in every place, not however publicly (οὐκ ἄντικρυς) or for all to see (οὐδὲ ἐμφανῶς τοῖς πολλοῖς); but in every sort of way his prayer ascends, whether he is walking or in company or at rest or reading or engaged in good works; and though it be only a thought *in the secret chamber of the heart* (ἐν αὐτῷ τῷ ταμιείῳ τῆς ψυχῆς), while he calls on the Father in groanings which cannot be uttered, yet the Father is near at hand, even before he has done speaking."[654]

According to this passage, prayers should not be made for others to see and should not (only) be done at certain times a day. Rather, Clement promotes the idea that prayer is a mental endeavour that should take place all the time

---

three gather in my name, there am I with them." Both Tertullian and Cyprian connect this saying with the existence of the church (Tert. Paen. 10 (Borleffs); Cypr. unit.eccl. 12 (P. Siniscalco et al.).

652 Tert. Or. 24-5; Or. or. 12, 31 (Koetschau; tr. Stewart-Sykes); Cypr. Dom. orat. 34-6 (Réveillaud; tr. Stewart-Sykes).

653 In the Greek New Testament (Nestle-Aland) "in secret" is rendered as ἐν τῷ κρυπτῷ, which bears the connotation of something "hidden," "covered" or "concealed" (G. Liddell/R. Scott/H.S. Jones et al. (eds.), *A Greek-English Lexicon*, Oxford 1950 (LSJ)). Hence, prayer is to be performed secluded and alone. In the third century, when commenting on the biblical passage, Origen stays true to the biblical source and uses its phrase for secret: ἐν τῷ κρυπτῷ, while the Latin authors express "in secret" with *secrete*, an adverb from *secerno*, which refers to what is set apart (C.T. Lewis/C. Short, *A Latin Dictionary*, Oxford 1879).

654 Clem. Strom. 7.7.49 (Hort/Mayor).

"in the chamber of the mind."[655] Prayer is something that happens in one's ψυχή. Ψυχή must here be understood as: "the *conscious self* or *personality* as centre of emotions, desires, and affections."[656] Clement stresses that it is not the words of prayer that matter, but rather the willingness to pray and be near the father. God, for his part, is always close and observant of what humans are doing, like the sun can light up the innermost chambers: "so the Word being shed abroad in all directions observes even the minutest details of our actions."[657] According to Clement, the gnostic is aware that "God knows all things, and hears not only the voice but the thought…"[658] Moreover, Clement notes that the perfect Christian not only prays for what he wants himself, rather he prays for what other people need. However, he keeps this secret: "For so he not only gives his prayer to the needy, but he provides that which comes through prayer in a secret and unostentatious manner."[659] In his treatise, Origen quotes the text from Matthew directly and introduces the quotation with the authoritative formula: "our Saviour says on this matter."[660] When explaining where one ought to pray, Origen writes that:

> "every place is rendered fit for prayer by one who prays aright (ὑπὸ τοῦ καλῶς εὐχομένου)… But to arrange the performance of prayer in quiet, and without distraction, each person should select, if possible, what one might term the appropriate (σεμνότερον) place in his house."[661]

At first, Origen thus says that the admonition to pray in secret should be taken quite concretely. However, it soon becomes evident that what is most important to him is not so much the place of prayer but rather the level of attention reached when praying. After all, according to Origen, a Christian can pray anywhere without any outward indication that he is doing so.[662]

---

655 I am not completely satisfied with Mayor's translation: "in the secret chamber of the heart." Secret is an inference from the Matthean context, and although "heart" might semantically be a correct translation of ψυχή, it is too vague.

656 LSJ, ψυχή, IV.

657 Clem. Strom. 7.3.21 (Hort/Mayor).

658 Id. 7.7.36.

659 Id. 7.13.81.

660 Or. or. 19.1 (Koetschau; tr. Stewart-Sykes).

661 Id. 31.4.

662 Id. 31.2.

The crucial thing is that prayer takes place in a location where it is possible to concentrate on God. Origen therefore presents the ideal Christian worshipper as someone who prays in "his own room," which for Origen means someone who is able to withdraw from the surrounding world and find God present within:

> "He does not recognize the outside world, he pays no attention to anything outside, but shuts up every door of the senses, so that the world of the senses should not distract, nor his mind receive any impression from sense-perception, praying to the Father who neither shuns nor deserts such a secret place but dwells there together with his only-begotten one."[663]

It thus becomes clear that for Origen, secret prayer in its finest form is something purely internal that has to do with paying complete attention to God.[664] Prayer therefore earns its own merit, because God is present with those who pray. "A person exalts God when he has dedicated to him a dwelling place within himself (ἐν ἑαυτῷ)."[665] Here Origen's interpretation and Clement's are very alike: prayer is an internal act or state.

Moving westward to the Latin authors, the comments on secret prayer are to a significant extent like the Alexandrians', although less intimate and mystical in nature. The Latin authors also allude to Matt 6:6 in their treatises on prayer. At the beginning of a passage on Jesus' teaching, Tertullian writes: "Therefore let us consider, blessed ones, his heavenly wisdom, firstly regarding his instruction to pray in secret."[666] Half a century later, Cyprian remarks: "the Lord in his pronouncements commands each of us to pray in secret, in hidden and private places, in our hidden rooms."[667] As in Origen's text, both Tertullian's and Cyprian's opening idea of "secret prayer" is quite concrete: they think that one should pray in a hidden chamber.[668] However,

---

663 Id. 20.2.
664 This is at least one way in which Origen thinks of prayer; he also defines prayer broadly as life itself, e.g. Or. or. 12.2, 22.5 (McGuckin, 2004, 176.).
665 Or. or. 24.4 (Koetschau; tr. Stewart-Sykes).
666 Tert. Or. 1 (Schleyer; tr. Stewart-Sykes).
667 Cypr. Dom. orat. 4 (Réveillaud; tr. Stewart-Sykes).
668 Cf. PS-Clem. Recognitiones 8.1 (tr. Smith): "[We] retired to a certain secret place for prayer". See also, Eus. v.C. 4.22.1 (Winkelmann; tr. Cameron/ Hall): "He himself, like someone participating in sacred mysteries, would shut himself at fixed times each day in secret places within his royal palace

they quickly emphasize that what matters is not so much the place of prayer itself as the confidence in the fact that God can hear even a secret prayer and penetrate even a hidden chamber. Cyprian states that "the plenitude of [God's] majesty penetrates into secluded and hidden places."[669] It is important for the Latin authors to point to the fact that God is very close to the person praying wherever he/she prays, and they furthermore stress the idea that God looks for motives rather than for words and gestures. Therefore, the act of praying does not in itself satisfy God, regardless of where it takes place. On the contrary, the important thing is the underlying motivation for the prayer, as well as the attitude of the one praying. Hence, a wicked person praying for his own worldly good cannot expect his prayers to be answered by God. Tertullian makes this clear by saying that God is a listener "not to the voice but to the heart,"[670] and Cyprian reminds his audience that God is "an examiner of the kidney and heart."[671] The Latin authors understand secret prayer to be not only actual prayers kept secret from other human beings, but also prayers whose underlying motives are correct, although these motives are secret to the world. In summary, all four authors share the conviction that God is present with the one praying, and this divine presence is so close and so pervasive that God knows not only the prayer spoken in secret, but also the underlying motives and everyday behaviour of the one who prays. Motivation and behaviour are therefore understood as a part of prayer. This is expressed directly when Origen explains the meaning of Paul's admonition to the Christians in Thessaloniki that they should "pray without ceasing."[672]

3.2.1.2 The rationale behind secret prayer

According to Origen, Tertullian and Cyprian, the main reason why prayer should be secret is that Christian prayer should not be ostentatious; and in agreement with the above-mentioned Matthean text, Christians should not

---

chambers and would converse with his God alone, and kneeling in suppliant petition would plead for the objects of his prayer…"
669 Cypr. Dom. orat. 4 (Réveillaud; tr. Stewart-Sykes).
670 Tert. Or. 17 (Schleyer; tr. Stewart-Sykes).
671 Cypr. Dom. orat. 4 (Réveillaud; tr. Stewart-Sykes), cf. Rev 2:23 and Ps 7:9.
672 1 Thess 5:17.

pray only for the sake of appearing holy. In his treatise, Origen lingers on the term "appear" (φαίνω). He writes: "We should pay careful attention to the term "appear," for nothing that is merely apparent is worthy, since it seems to exist but does not actually do so, deceiving sense-perception and not giving a true or accurate representation."[673] In continuation of this, Origen attacks the Jews and admonishes the Christians that they should not pray only in order to appear holy like the Jews. Origen sarcastically calls the synagogue a "theatre of the Jews" and writes that in the synagogues, the Jews wear "masks" that do not coincide with their actual character. The ritual prayer in the synagogue is not in itself an expression of a true religious sentiment, and the dissimilarity between appearance and inner sentiment is deceitful and wrong. For Origen, it is imperative that Christians do not perform their worship "as actors."[674] According to Origen, an actor is a prime example of someone who appears to be something that he is not. The Christians should strive not only to appear, but actually to be righteous and faithful.[675] In this passage, Origen is distorting the image of Jewish worship. Although, the Jews might have been praying also in public in the day of Origen, the Rabbis were focused on the right intentions behind prayer. Thus in the tractates of the *Mishnah* there is a keen interest on intention.[676] The Latin authors also agree that prayer should not be performed in order for it to be noticed, and Tertullian ironically asks: "What more reward will there be gained by those who pray too noisily except of distracting those

---

673 Or. or. 20.2 (Koetschau; tr. Stewart-Sykes).

674 Id. In Greek, there is an etymological coincidence because a "hypocrite" and an "actor" are both called ὑποκριτής (LSJ). In the New Testament, the Jewish scribes and Pharisees were accused of being hypocrites (people who only pretended to be righteous, but in fact were not, e.g. Matt 23:23). Origen mentions "actors" as deceitful agents, in contrast to Christians, thus alluding to the Biblical use of the word.

675 However, later on Origen remarks that in the same way as actors have responsibilities towards their audience, the Christians "are under obligation to the whole world, to all the angels as to the human race" (Or. or. 28.3 (Koetschau; tr. Stewart-Sykes)).

676 T. Zahavy, *Kavvanah (Concentration) for Prayer in the Mishnah and Talmud*, in: J. Neuser/R.A. Horsley/E.S. Frerichs/P. Borgen (eds.), *New Perspectives on Ancient Judaism. Religion, Literature, & Society in Ancient Israel, Formative Christianity & Judaism*, University of South Florida 1987, 15.

nearby?"[677] The consensus of the third-century authors is that humility and sincerity should be the attitude among praying Christians. Clement seems to take this for granted, as he does not directly warn against hypocritical behaviour in relation with prayer in *Stromateis* 7. Though, Clement does make a warning about the object of prayer – one should not pray for what merely appear good.[678]

A second reason to pray in secret is that such a prayer proves the faith of the one praying, since the one who prays in secret shows faith in the ability of God to hear a secret prayer, even a silent prayer. Praying in secret is thus a confession of God's omnipresence, a *credo*. In his treatise, Tertullian ironically asks: "Do God's ears listen out for a noise?"[679] The answer is of course: No, God does not need a noise to hear a prayer, God is aware of even the unuttered prayers. This belief in God's transcendence of physical location and acoustic range was something that separated third-century Christians from much of the surrounding society where silent prayer was unusual, though not unheard of.[680] In Roman society, worship most often took place near an altar or holy place, either privately or publicly.[681] According to the Christians, their new Christian prayer had (literally) outranged Pagan prayer, because their prayer was not restricted by sound or space. "Clement's concept of prayer, which is defined as inward contact with God, confirms this impression. To understand prayer on the simple model of verbal contact is insufficient, for the spirit ascends to the νοητὴν οὐσίαν. Prayer denotes a state of being; it is ὁμιλία with God."[682] Origen shares the transcendent understanding of prayer which becomes clear from *Contra Celsum* 7.44. Here Origen first describes the physicality of Pagan worship and thereafter lauds the Christian way of praying:

> "But a Christian, even of the common people, is assured that every place forms part of the universe, and that the whole universe is God's temple. In whatever

---

677 Tert. Or. 17 (Schleyer; tr. Stewart-Sykes).
678 Clem. Strom. 7.7.44 (Hort/Mayor).
679 Tert. Or. 17 (Schleyer; tr. Stewart-Sykes).
680 Bitton-Askelony, 2012; P.W. van der Horst, *Silent Prayer in Antiquity*, in: Numen 41 (1994), 1-25; Versnel, 1981, 29-32; Dover, 1974, 258.
681 See above paragraph 2.1.2.
682 R. Moortley, *The theme of Silence in Clement of Alexandria*, in: JThS 24 (1973), 201 f.

part of the world he is, he prays; but he rises above the universe, "shutting the eyes of sense, and raising upwards the eyes of the soul." And he stops not at the vault of heaven; but passing in thought beyond the heavens, under the guidance of the Spirit of God, and having thus as it were gone beyond the visible universe, he offers prayers to God."[683]

A third reason to pray in secret is that it makes it possible for the one praying to withdraw from the world and become aware of God's presence. Especially Origen, who has since gone down in history as a great mystical theologian,[684] dwells on this point. This awareness of God's presence also necessitates living a life that is worthy of being constantly scrutinized by God who knows all unspoken motives and hears all secret prayers. God is always inspecting the inner sentiment, whether this is said to be located in the mind or heart.[685] Later, we shall return to this theme.

In sum, for all the authors, a secret prayer or a prayer uttered in one's own room is a prayer that has to do with the mind/self/heart of the one who utters it. The words of the prayers are secondary to the attitude and thoughts of the one praying. Moreover a "secret prayer" is a significant creed, because the faith to which it testifies is expressed under no false pretexts.

3.2.2 Pray in spirit and in truth

According to the Gospel of John, "God is spirit, and those who worship Him must worship in spirit and truth (ἐν πνεύματι καὶ ἀληθείᾳ)."[686] This

---

683 Or. Cels. 7.44 (Borret; tr. Crombie).

684 E.g. Louth, 1981, 72.

685 On the use of the concepts mind and heart, see Brock, 1982. Brock distinguishes between two ideas of conceptualizing the inner person in Late Antiquity: In Semitic spirituality, the focus is on the heart, whereas the Hellenistic spirituality focuses on the mind and intellect. In the treatises under investigation, it is not possible to label any of the authors as purely Semitic or purely Hellenistic, and they also use different words interchangeably. For instance, Clement uses both "heart" and "mind," and in Strom. 7, he does not use "mind" frequently (although the translation of Mayor uses "mind" to translate also other formulations).

686 John 4:24: Πνεῦμα ὁ Θεός, καὶ τοὺς προσκυνοῦντας ἐν πνεύματι καὶ ἀληθείᾳ δεῖ προσκυνεῖν.

phrase is said by Jesus to a Samaritan woman at the well of Jacob in Samaria. In the Johannine narrative, Jesus reveals his divine identity to the Samaritan woman and furthermore points out that the time is coming "when the true worshipers will worship the Father in spirit and truth; for such people the Father seeks to be His worshipers."[687] All authors under investigation at some point allude to John 4:23–24 in their works. The following paragraphs will mainly explore the interpretations of the formulation about prayer "in spirit," since the authors in this context do not dwell much on the "truth."[688]

3.2.2.1 Tertullian and Cyprian on praying "in spirit"

In *De Oratione* 28, Tertullian quotes from John 4:23–24 and writes that the Father requires worshippers that pray in spirit and truth (*in spiritu et veritate*). Tertullian furthermore notes that God is spirit, and if humans want to have contact with God, they have to assimilate to his divine spirit: "[Prayer] should be sent forth from the same sort of spirit as that to which it is sent (*de tali spiritu emissa, qualis est spiritus ad quem emittitur*)."[689] A polluted/saddened/shackled spirit cannot communicate with a holy/gladdened/free spirit. Therefore, Christians should strive to obtain a spirit similar to the spirit of God. Also in his writing *On Exhortation to Chastity* 10.3, Tertullian mentions that: "It is the spirit which conducts prayer to God (*Spiritus deducit orationem ad deum*)." Here he also mentions that prayer proceeds from the conscience, and he thus combines the idea of a clean conscience and a clean spirit. Prayers are sent forth and brought to God by the clean human spirit.

In the *De Oratione* 13, Tertullian gives some concrete instructions about how to avoid a "filthy spirit" (*spiritu vero sordente*). Here Tertullian makes it clear that ritual cleanness has been taken care of once and for all in

---

687 John 4:23.

688 According to Aristotle: "Truth is the supreme work of the rational part of the soul" (quoted in Rankin, 2006, 9). If these words are held together with the admonition to pray "in spirit and truth," it would mean that prayer is an act of the "rational" and highest part of the mind. This is not completely unlike the Christian idea of prayer.

689 Tert. Or. 12 (Schleyer; tr. Stewart-Sykes).

baptism. However, people are obliged to remain spiritually clean by living up to a certain moral code. This moral code requires that Christians remain pure of "fraud, murder, violence, sorcery, idolatry and other stains that originate in the spirit (*maculis, quae spiritu conceptae*)..."[690] In the catechetical context, Tertullian says this as a warning and not as a verbal attack. He swiftly follows up his statement with the comforting utterance: "*We are* true worshippers (*Nos sumus veri adoratores*)... praying in the spirit (*qui spiritu orantes*)."[691] According to Tertullian's idea of a human-divine relationship, "spirit" plays a key role as the contact potential between God and human beings. It has the same role as the image of God has in Origen's theology, to which we shall return below.[692] The idea is that by developing a certain moral standard, behaviour and faith, one's ability to communicate with God increases.

Also Cyprian makes direct use of John 4:24 and alludes to it in the beginning of *De Dominica Oratione*. By using the pericope already from the beginning of his text, Cyprian gives "spirit and truth" a prominent position in the correct understanding of prayer. Cyprian writes that:

> "[Jesus] had already said that the hour would come when true worshippers would worship the Father in spirit and in truth (*ueri adoratores adorarent patrem in spiritu et ueritate*), and he fulfilled what he had previously promised so that we who receive spirit and truth through his sanctification may truly and spiritually worship through what he has handed on to us [i.e. the Lord's Prayer]."[693]

Cyprian mentions the pericope, John 4:23–24, in a passage where he reflects on the value of the Lord's Prayer, and he equals the Lord's Prayer with "worship in spirit and truth." Cyprian's interpretation thus becomes more concrete than Tertullian's. However, Cyprian also states that the Lord's Prayer is part of the teachings that will lead people to salvation, and by employing the passage from John, Cyprian is pointing to the spiritual character of the Lord's Prayer.[694] It seems that Cyprian understands spiritual prayer as having to do with a certain faith in Christ and his teachings. In

---

690 Id. 13.
691 Id. 28.
692 Or. or. 9.2 (Koetschau; tr. Stewart-Sykes). See below paragraph 5.2.2.
693 Cypr. Dom. orat. 2 (Réveillaud; tr. Stewart-Sykes).
694 Id. 2.

this way, the creedal character of the Lord's Prayer is further emphasized. Nevertheless, Cyprian also writes that: "It is not the sound of our voice (*non uocis sonus*) but the mind and the heart (*sed animus et sensus*) which should pray to God with sincere intent (*intentione sincera*)."[695] Thereby, Cyprian shows that prayer is more than words and teachings, it also has to do with a certain attitude of mind and heart. Cyprian's interpretation thus resembles Tertullian's point that the human being can and should strive to the appropriate spiritual state. However, Cyprian does not mention Tertullian's idea that one is to assimilate one's own spirit to God.

3.2.2.2 Clement and Origen on praying "in spirit"

In *Stromateis* 7, Clement makes frequent mention of the Spirit and the gnostic's ability to live a spiritual life. For instance, Clement writes about the gnostic: "he is brought close to the Almighty Power and, by his earnest striving after spirituality, is united to the Spirit through the love that knows no bounds."[696] According to Clement, this closeness between the gnostic and the Spirit is affected by the gnostic's independence from worldly authorities and accordance with the Omnipotent Will. This passage in *Stromateis* 7 is but one example of Clement's mentioning of the spiritual life of the gnostic. Nevertheless, Clement does not make direct use of John 4:23–24 in *Stromateis* 7, but he does so in *Stromateis* 1,5. Here Clement alludes to John 4:24 and writes:

> "And if 'thou prayest in the closet,' (ἐν τῷ ταμείῳ) as the Lord taught, 'to worship in spirit,' (πνεύματι προσκυνῶν) thy management will no longer be solely occupied about the house (περὶ τὸν οἶκον), but also about the soul (περὶ τὴν ψυχήν), what must be bestowed on it, and how, and how much; and what must be laid aside and treasured up in it; and when it ought to be produced, and to whom."

In this passage, Clement shows that worship in spirit has to do with the soul and how one takes care of one's soul and cultivates it. Clement contrasts the "management of the house" with "the management of the soul," and thus differentiates between different spheres of life – the concrete and the spiritual. He expresses the importance of taking care of one's soul.[697] Clement

---

695 Id. 31. Réveillaud translates *sensus* as "heart."
696 Clem. Strom. 7.7.43 (Hort/Mayor).
697 Cf. below, Chapter 5.

is thus in accord with the Latin writers that the individual has to take care of his/her soul, and this is part of or precondition for "worship in spirit."

Origen does not use the exact formulations from John 4:23–24 in *Perì Euchês*, but does so several times in *Contra Celsum* and *Commentary on the Gospel of John*.[698] The fact that Origen does not directly quote the pericope in *Perì Euchês* does not mean that Origen disregards the spiritual side of prayer in this work. On the contrary, as also Robert L. Simpson points out, when Origen interprets the Lord's Prayer, he understands its petitions as "different facets of one theme: Prayer for spiritual and great things."[699] In chapter 14, Origen praises the things that are "true and intelligible" (τῶν ἀληθινῶν καὶ νοητῶν), and Origen stresses that the things worth praying for should have this "true and spiritual" character. The word translated "spiritual" in this context is the word νοητῶν which is derived from νοῦς. The word bears the connotation "mental." Origen is thus praising "things" that have to do with the mind and the God-given capacity to think and reason – these are true *spiritual* gifts." "Spiritual" gifts are positive in contrast to what is petty and earthly. This is one way in which Origen emphasizes the spiritual side of prayer.

Moreover, chapter 13 is a reflection on the spiritual character of prayer. Here Origen stresses that people ought to hear the "spiritual law with spiritual ears (ἀκούουσι τοῦ πνευματικοῦ νόμου ὠσὶ πνευματικοῖς)."[700] He contrasts the spiritual with what is "barren and sterile." He furthermore contrasts the "spiritual" and "mystical" with "the flesh" and "the deeds of the body." Origen thus uses "spiritual" to describe a certain state wherein the body is not dominating the mind, and wherein the individual is aware that he/she is dependent on God. When Christians are in this state, God is willing to grant what they might pray for: "Everyone who is genuinely dependent upon God, and has become worthy of being heard, can now, in a *spiritual sense*, perform the mightiest act..."[701]

---

698 Or. Cels. 2.71.10; 6.70.33; 7.27.18 (Borret; tr. Crombie); Also in his Jo. 10.13.68; 10.14.88; 13.18.112; 13.19.117; 13.21.2; 13.25.148 (Blanc; tr. Heine).

699 Simpson, 1965, 136 n. 43.

700 Or. or. 13.5 (Koetschau; tr. Stewart-Sykes).

701 Id.

Furthermore, as we saw in the previous paragraphs, Origen also believes that "the Spirit prays in the hearts of the saints."[702] The prayers coming from the Holy Spirit in this way are: "truly prayers that are spoken in the Spirit."[703] According to Origen, it is in fact the Spirit of God that activates humans to pray spiritually. This stands in contrast to Tertullian's view where human beings must themselves refine their own spirit to communicate with God's spirit. However, Origen and Tertullian are not completely in disagreement, since Origen expects that the individual who prays and contemplates on God will become like to the image of God.[704] In the process of prayer and contemplation, Origen imagines that the human soul is connected to the Spirit. Origen describes it thus:

> "And the soul which is lifted up and which separated from the body, follows the Spirit, which not only follows the Spirit but is actually in the Spirit... is surely putting of its existence as soul and becoming spiritual."[705]

Consequently, all authors under investigation believe that prayer can connect the human spirit to God's spirit/Spirit. The point of disagreement is to which extent human beings are responsible in this process. In Chapter 5, we shall return to the transformative power attributed to prayer, and which role humans are supposed to play in this process. Here we will conclude that "spiritual prayer" or "prayer in spirit" lay at the heart of all authors, although they understood it slightly differently. Nevertheless for all, it meant that prayer was a mental occupation and that the benefits of prayer had to do with mentality and attitude.

3.2.2.3 Prayer as spiritual sacrifice

A recurrent theme in the four treatises is that Christian prayers replace concrete sacrifices; either Christian prayers are understood as spiritual sacrifices or the appropriate attitude and behaviour in relation with prayer make Christian worship a sacrifice. The point is that the sacrifices of the Christians are spiritual and therefore worthy of God unlike sacrifices of

---

702 Id. 2.5.
703 Id. 2.5.
704 Id. 9.2.
705 Id. 9.2. On the soul becoming spiritual by following the spirit, see also princ. 3.4.2 (Koetschau; tr. Butterworth).

material goods that were so common in antiquity. It is notable that although there were no bloody sacrifices in Christianity in late antiquity, sacrificial language was still dominant and used to legitimize prayer.

According to Clement – and the Holy Scriptures to which he alludes – "the unboastful heart" "is a perfect sacrifice to God."[706] In Clement's interpretation, this means that people must put themselves – or rather their old being – to death, in order to rise up as "new men."[707] The Christians are thus themselves sacrifices to God and make no other offerings (οὐ θύομεν εἰκότως). Clement holds that Christians consecrate themselves, because Christ was consecrated for them (σφᾶς, lit. *slaughter* victim for sacrifice). In *Stromateis* 7.6.31–32, Clement is very sarcastic when dealing with the Greek sacrificial institution, and propounds the idea that sacrifices were invented by men as an excuse to eat meat (σαρκοφαγιῶν).[708] Clement contrasts concrete sacrifices with Christian prayers which constitute the "holiest sacrifices when joined with righteousness…" Moreover, Clement describes prayers as "speech rising like incense from holy souls." He likens the congregation who has "one common voice and one mind (μίαν… φωνὴν τὴν κοινὴν καὶ μίαν γνώμην)" to an altar (θυσιαστήριον), and he also likens the righteous soul (τὴν δικαίαν ψυχὴν) to an altar. With such formulations, Clement dissociates the Christians from any form of concrete sacrificial cult, although he reinterprets the sacrificial language to describe how the Christians by being righteous and by being in harmony are themselves a sacrifice to God. The Greek authors probably owe their interpretation of the priesthood of the individual persons to Philo and his understanding of individuals as priests. With this interpretation, Philo had individualized the liturgy of the temple. "In this sense, one is priest, altar and victim when he offers up to God the sacrifice of his thoughts, words and deeds."[709] The smoke from actual sacrifices reaches only some low region far below the densest clouds, Clement ponders.

The same ideas and reinterpretations of the classical sacrifice can be found in the other three treatises under investigation. Origen, for instance,

---

706 Clem. Strom. 7.3.14 (Hort/Mayor).
707 Id. 7.3.14. Cf. Eph 4:24.
708 Id. 7.6.32.
709 Laporte, 1986, 84.

mentions that the Son of God is "high priest of our offerings (ἀρχιερεὺς ... τῶν προσφορῶν ἡμῶν)."[710] By using the image of the high priest, Origen is clearly aware that Jesus' role resembles the role of the high priests in the Temple who had sacrificial duties. However, Origen also mentions that Jesus Christ is a priest "after the order of Melchizedek,"[711] thereby indicating that Christ is not only a priest for the Jews but also for the uncircumcised.[712] Elsewhere Origen specifies that Christ is the only one who is priest of this distinguished order, whereas Christian people can be priests according to the order of Aron.[713] Besides these references, there is not much overt sacrificial language in Origen's treatise, where "sacrifices" are mentioned by Origen they are not used to contrast the Christian prayers from Pagan sacrifices.

Tertullian makes use of sacrificial language when he writes that prayers with responses from the congregation are "an excellent custom, like an opulent offering (opimam hostiam), a prayer fattened (saturatam orationem) with all that tend to dignify and honor God."[714] Moreover, Tertullian mentions how prayer is a "spiritual oblation (hostia spiritalis)" that has wiped out the ancient sacrifices and can be delivered from the altar, devoted, fattened, prepared, spotless, etc.[715] Also Cyprian likens Christian worship with old-school sacrifice.[716] He typically uses sacrifices to contrast the outer performance of worship with the inner attitude of the individual, since "God looks not at the gifts but at the hearts."[717]

All authors make it clear that the best sacrifice is brotherly agreement, and they also assume that prayers can be conceived of as sacrifices. All in all, there is a lot of sacrificial vocabulary in the treatises and in early Christian texts in general. Prayer could be comprehended as sacrifices of

---

710 Or. or. 10.2 (Koetschau; tr. Stewart-Sykes).

711 Id. 15.1.

712 A gnostic treatise on Melchizedek exists, wherein Melchizedek says that he is – and those who follow him are – an offering to God, see in Melchizedek 16,7-11 (Meyer).

713 Or. Jo. 1,3 (Blanc; tr. Heine).

714 Tert. Or. 27 (Schleyer; tr. Stewart-Sykes).

715 Id. 28.

716 E.g. Cypr. Dom. orat. 4 (Réveillaud; tr. Stewart-Sykes).

717 Id. 4; 24.

praise, thanksgiving, worship, of communion and for sin.[718] This is not always explicitly stated in the treatises, but as Francis M. Young has noted these kinds of sacrifices were well known in late antiquity and could readily be understood in a spiritual way. For this reason, G. Stroumsa is correct in mentioning that the way in which Christians understood their religion was not void of sacrificial thinking, the opposite was more likely the case.[719] Guy Stroumsa has shown how religious worship generally was interiorized in late antiquity, and he proposes that the fall of the Jewish Temple in 70 AD is the most important catalyst of this general transformation from external to internal worship, which is characteristic of both Rabbinic Judaism and Christianity.[720] Although, in my view, Stroumsa draws the historical dividing lines too sharply,[721] it seems correct that Christianity and Rabbinic Judaism simultaneously internalized and spiritualized worship. It also seems that the prayers of the Eucharist were understood as an offering in their own right by the early Christians, and thus as if the Eucharist depended on the prayers being offered – "the spiritual oblation that has wiped out the ancient sacrifices," as Tertullian framed it.[722]

3.2.3 Pray without ceasing

Several times in the New Testament one finds admonitions to pray unceasingly.[723] The four authors under investigation all took this admonition seriously, but interpreted it differently. The Latin authors understood the admonition quite concretely as a call for the Christians to pray as often as they could, literally, also during the night.[724] Contrary, the Greek authors interpreted the admonition figuratively and understood it as having to do with manners and attitudes in life. This is expressed directly when Origen

---

718 F. Young, *Sacrifice and the death of Christ*, London 1975, 61-63.
719 Stroumsa, 2009, 63.
720 Id.
721 Already in Qumran the idea that prayers could be spiritual offerings existed, see e.g. Turner et al., 2014, 103 f.
722 Tert. Or. 28 (Schleyer; tr. Stewart-Sykes).
723 Luke 18:1; Eph 6:8; 1 Thess 5:17 and Col 4:2.
724 Tertullian admonishes that people should pray at the coming of the day and of the night (Tert. orat. 25 (Schleyer; tr. Stewart-Sykes); Cypr. Dom. orat. 36 (Réveillaud; tr. Stewart-Sykes)).

explains the meaning of Paul's admonition to the Christians to "pray without ceasing":[725]

> "Since works of virtue and the keeping of the commandments have a part in prayer, the person who prays 'ceaselessly' is the one who integrates prayer with good works and noble actions with prayer. For we can only accept the saying 'Pray ceaselessly' (ἀδιαλείπτως προσεύχεσθε) as realistic if we can say that the whole life of the saint is one mighty, integrated prayer (εἰ πάντα τὸν βίον τοῦ ἁγίου μίαν συναπτομένην μεγάλην εἴποιμεν εὐχήν)."[726]

Origen shows that prayer and Christian life in general are intertwined; "Gebet und Christliches Leben bilden ein Kontinuum."[727] It does not mean that one should not pray concretely, but contrary that prayer and a virtuous life are two sides of the same coin. Unceasing prayer has a further meaning according to Origen, since it points in the direction of salvation. Origen explicitly assures that the one who lives his/her life as if it was a prayer will experience God's Kingdom within and thereby a proleptic salvation. Each Christian has his/her citizenship in heaven;[728] and that is manifest already on earth. Origen places significant emphasis on the point that heaven is "not to be interpreted spatially."[729] Furthermore, he writes: "For our citizenship is in no way upon earth but is in every way in the heavens which are the thrones of God, in that the Kingdom of God is established in all those who bear the image of the heavenly one…"[730] Gessel concludes from this: "Das unablässige Gebet wird somit zum Kriterion der Zugehörigkeit zum Reich Gottes."[731] Maria-Barbara von Stritzky understands Origen's focus on the integration of prayer in life as an expression of the fact that Origen is focused on the whole of creation more than on the individual. Origen has a collective interest both when it comes to prayer, and when it comes to salvation. This means, according to von Stritzky, that Origen does not imagine prayer in the Platonic sense that was outlined above as

---

725 1 Thess 5:17.
726 Or. or. 12.2 (Koetschau; tr. Stewart-Sykes).
727 Gessel, 1975, 245.
728 Or. or. 22.5 (Koetschau; tr. Stewart-Sykes). Cf. Clem. Strom. 7.7.35 (Hort/ Mayor).
729 Stewart-Sykes, 2004, 163 n.3; Or. or. 23.2 (Koetschau; tr. Stewart-Sykes).
730 Or. or. 22.5 (Koetschau; tr. Stewart-Sykes). Cf. Gr.Nyss. or. dom 2 (Oehler).
731 Gessel, 1975, 247.

φυγὴ μόνου πρὸς μόνον. For Origen, prayer always also includes the rest of creation, as does salvation. Neither prayer, nor salvation is solely focused on the individual, but has to do with the whole of creation.[732] Von Stritzky describes Origen's position thus:

> "Die Vollendung des Christen im ununterbrochenen Gebet und dem stets fortschreitenden Aufstieg zu Gott ist niemals im Sinne platonischer Philosophie eine φυγὴ μόνου πρὸς μόνον [Plotin, Enn. VI 9,11,51], sondern hat durch das Erlösungswerk Jesu Christi Anteil am Heil der Schöpfung insgesamt. Christliche Existenz kann sich nur im Hinblick auf das Heil aller vollziehen und ist nicht auf sich selbst beschränkt, womit Origenes den Heilsegoismus philosophischer wie gnostischer Prägung ablehnt."[733]

Von Stritzky is probably correct in this interpretation, although it must be added that there is a little room for Gebets- und Erlösungsegoismus in Origen's works. For instance, he does allow for personal prayers, but there is also an emphasis on the transcendence of the individual within Origen's works, as in the case of continuous prayer. Clement expresses the same perception regarding the close connection between prayer and life. He distinguishes between gnostics and more ordinary Christians, but for both "types" of Christians prayer should surround life: "no occasion for our approach to God must be neglected."[734] And elsewhere:

> "*all our life* is a festival (πάντα τοίνυν τὸν βίον ἑορτὴν ἄγοντες): being persuaded that God is everywhere present on all sides, we praise Him as we till the ground, we sing hymns as we sail the sea, we feel his inspiration in all that we do. And the gnostic enjoys a still closer intimacy with God (προσεχέστερον δὲ ὁ γνωστικὸς οἰκειοῦται θεῷ), being at once serious and cheerful in everything, serious owing to his thoughts being turned towards heaven, and cheerful, as he reckons up the blessings with which God has enriched our human life."[735]

Clement furthermore believes that "undisturbed intercourse and communion with the Lord (ἀπερισπάστως προσομιλῶν τε καὶ συνὼν τῷ κυρίῳ)" can affect a passionless state that is suiting for a gnostic.[736] The word

---

732 Stritzky, 2009.
733 Stritzky, 1989, 124.
734 Clem. Strom. 7.7.42 (Hort/Mayor).
735 Clem. Strom. 7.7.35 (Hort/Mayor). See also Strom. 7.3.14: "undisturbed intercourse and communion with the Lord." and Strom. 7.12.73: "For all his life is prayer and communion with God."
736 Clem. Strom. 7.3.14 (Hort/Mayor).

ἀπερισπάστως bears the meaning not distracted or hindered,[737] so Clement promotes prayer that demands the whole life and also full concentration. As such prayer is a "state," cheerful and free of passion. "Diese das gesamte Leben umgreifende Art des Gebets äußert sich in Dank, Erkenntnis und Lebenswandel, wodurch eine dauernde Verbindung mit Gott hergestellt wird, so dass das Leben des vollkommenen Christen als Gebet im Sinne eines Gesprächs mit Gott angesehen werden kann."[738]

As mentioned Tertullian and Cyprian go about the issue of constant prayer in a more concrete way. Thus Tertullian writes that: "No rule (*nihil omnino praescriptum*) whatever has been laid down concerning the times of prayer, except of course, to pray at every time and place (*omni in tempore et loco orare*)."[739] Nevertheless, Tertullian is pragmatically enough to add that "every place" means "which propriety, or even necessity, suggests ('*Omni... loco*', *quem oportunitas aut etiam necessitas impotarit*)." Cyprian's interpretation is like Tertullian's, literal and less idealistic than the Greek. Cyprian notes that because humans need to have their sins forgiven every day, they need to pray every day.[740] Cyprian also calls for constant and continual worship and for petition and prayer all day long.[741] It does not mean that the Latin authors disregard moral in relation to prayer, but apparently they did not see the continuum between concrete worship and life as the Greek authors did. Consequently, there is less of a holistic approach in the Latin theology of prayer.

3.2.4 "Ask for great things" and "Seek First his Kingdom"

Another aspect of the third-century theology of prayer derived from an apocryphal saying of Jesus which is employed by Origen in *Perì Euchês* 2.2: "Ask for great things, and minor matters will be provided for you" together with the canonical "Ask for heavenly things, and mundane things will be provided for to you." Clement also knew this saying and used it in *Stromateis* 1.24.158 in a shorter version: "Ask for the great things, and

---

737 LSJ, ἀπερίσπαστος.
738 Stritzky, 2009, 229-249.
739 Tert. Or. 24.1 (Schleyer; tr. Stewart-Sykes).
740 Cypr. Dom. orat. 12 (Réveillaud; tr. Stewart-Sykes).
741 Id. 35.

God will add to you what is small." Since the two Alexandrians knew the apocryphal quotation, it must have been in use in Alexandria, but probably not elsewhere. This apocryphal saying is very similar to the Matthean Jesus-saying: "But seek first His kingdom and His righteousness, and all these things will be added to you" (Matt 6:33). The Matthean version is employed by both Tertullian and Cyprian; Tertullian mentions Matt 6:33 in his interpretation of the petition for bread in the Lord's Prayer.[742] Tertullian recognizes that the bread can be understood both as spiritual and literal bread, and he finds that the place of the petition within the Lord's Prayer shows that God has an interest in his children's physical needs. However, Tertullian is hesitant when it comes to making further petitions regarding one's individual needs. He warns that someone who adds his own desires to the Lord's Prayer will distance himself from God's ears.[743] By such a statement, Tertullian is removing himself and his congregation from *Gebetsegoismus*, i.e. egoism in prayers.

Cyprian employs Matt 6:33 in *De Dominica Oratione*, and when he does so, he also gives some examples of people who received something from God, because they had sought his Kingdom; Cyprian for instance mentions Daniel who survived his stay in the lion's den. Cyprian thus provides a very concrete example of the benefits that might come from the correct use of prayer. All these authors stress "the great things" and "the Kingdom of God" as worthy prayer objects. As shown in the previous, especially Origen was very dedicated in pointing out that prayers ought to be aimed at "spiritual," "mental" and "moral" effects. A happy outcome of prayer for Origen would therefore be "that the Lord may walk in us as in a spiritual garden as he alone reigns within us, with his Christ seated at the right hand of that spiritual power which we have prayed to receive."[744] In Chapter 17, Origen deals with the value of different objects of prayer and distinguishes between "principal gifts" and "the matter of the shadows that accompany these principal gifts." Origen here uses a Platonic frame of thought in which "the real" belongs to the world of ideas whereas the

---

742 Tert. Or. 6 (Schleyer; tr. Stewart-Sykes).
743 Id. 10.
744 Or. or. 25.3 (Koetschau; tr. Stewart-Sykes).

concrete things in this world are "matter of the shadows."[745] Humans are ideally supposed to pray for the pure and true things of the world of ideas, then earthly necessities are supposed to follow. The prayer for bread in the Lord's Prayer formed a limit to material requests.[746]

3.2.5 Concretum pro abstracto: On gestures, times and forms of prayer

In the following paragraphs, the more concrete practices and wording of prayer will be dealt with on the basis of the four evaluated treatises. The spiritual, inner relationship with God outlined above, was reflected in acts and words by people praying. As we shall see, it was essential for the theologians to argue theologically for the practices relating to prayer in order to legitimize practices that also were used in pagan and Jewish worship. There are thus several occasions of *interpretatio christiana*. It is noticeable that more of the Christian practices were absorbed from the surrounding religious communities. Consequently, we can assume that theological arguments given by the authors in support for certain gestures and times of prayer most likely are secondary compared to the practices themselves.[747] However, that does not render the prescribed practices invalid for the formation of Christian identity; rather, it shows how overt practices work as physical symbols that demand an interpretation in order to give shape to the community practising them. The treatises give directions concerning gestures, as well as times for prayer and guidelines regarding the wording of prayer. These issues have to some extent been treated in other studies, but will be mentioned here, because they function as concrete symbols forming and upholding Christian identity.[748] It is a general

---

745 Id. 17.2.

746 Simpson, 1965, 111 ff.

747 Wallraff notes that one must differentiate "zwischen dem Brauch einerseits und seiner Deutung andererseits." (M. Wallraff, *Christus verus Sol. Sonnenverehrung und Christentum in der Spätantike*, Münster 2001, 60 ff.).

748 R. Hvalvik, *Praying with Outstretched Hands: Nonverbal Aspects of Early Christian Prayer and the Question of Identity*, in R. Hvalvik/K.O. Sandnes (eds.), *Early Christian Prayer and Identity Formation*, Tübingen 2014, 57-90.

conclusion in identity studies that performance is vital for identity.[749] Of course, it remains an open question whether the prescribed practices were actually performed (and especially if they were performed as frequently as intended). Nonetheless, the demanding ideals show the serious expectations to Christians and thus a clear idea of perfect Christian identity.

3.2.5.1 On gestures when praying

According to Clement, Origen, Tertullian and Cyprian, prayers should be conducted either standing or kneeling, depending on the character of the prayer. When celebrating on the Lord's Day, praise and thanksgiving were said standing, while people generally had to kneel when confessing sins and praying for forgiveness. Tertullian mentions that one should kneel when coming together for prayers on fasting days, on station days[750] and on the Sabbath.[751] Tertullian refers to the kneeling pose as one of the "postures of humility" (*humilitatis more*); just as Origen calls it a "symbol of humility and submission" (σύμβολον ... τοῦ ὑποπεπτωκότος καὶ ὑποτεταγμένου).[752] Peculiarly, Origen also accounts for "rational kneeling" (νοητὴν γονυκλισίαν). He believed that heavenly bodies do not have "corporeal knees" and consequently cannot kneel physically, but that they on the other hand *can* do so rationally.[753]

Furthermore, Tertullian writes that on "the Lord's day of resurrection," i.e. Sunday, and during Pentecost, kneeling should be avoided as well as other attitudes or activities of concern or business.[754] Tertullian also

---

749 Penn refers to several studies in M. Penn, *Performing Family. Ritual Kissing and the Construction of Early Christian Kinship*, in: JECS 10/2 (2002), 152 n. 6.

750 "The so-called 'station days' were fasts of public, though not of obligatory, observance" (E. Evans (ed.), *Tertullian's Tract on The Prayer*, London 1953, xvii–xviii).

751 Or. or. 23 (Koetschau; tr. Stewart-Sykes). Evans notes: "In Africa, in the third century, as in Egypt in the fourth, Saturdays also were liturgical days" (Evans, 1953, xvii).

752 Tert. Or. 23 (Schleyer; tr. Stewart-Sykes) and Or. or. 31.3 (Koetschau; tr. Stewart-Sykes).

753 Or. or. 31.3 (Koetschau; tr. Stewart-Sykes).

754 Tert. Or. 23. Note that by the fourth century, the practice of kneeling when praying was so frequent that the Niceae synod made a canon to the effect of

mentions that one should prostrate (*prosternere*) oneself when praying on ordinary days, at least at morning prayer.[755] Prostration is not mentioned by the other authors in the euchological treatises, and it reflects an extreme limit of physical acts related to prayer. That Tertullian promotes prostration, suits the fact that Tertullian would eventually become the most rigorous moralist of the four authors – his extreme sentiment is reflected in the extremity of the physical gestures that he describes. From the treatises, it becomes evident that prayer was supposed to be a very physical activity, both when carried out individually and collectively. Emotions of either guilt or celebration were thus reflected and probably enhanced by the postures.

As mentioned earlier, the *orans* is a praying pose frequently found on material art from Christian antiquity,[756] and from antiquity in general. When posing in *orans*, the person praying stood erect with the arms and hands stretch out and upwards. This pose is admonished in the treatises on prayer. Tertullian admonishes that one should lift up one's hands,[757] and later on explicates that "we do not simply lift them up, but spread them out in imitation of the passion of the Lord (*Dominica passione modulata*)."[758] With the construction "*not simply* lift them up, *but*" (*non tantum, sed etiam*), Tertullian is lashing out against the Jews who apparently were using a similar, but – according to Tertullian – too simple pose.[759] Tertullian sees it as too simple because it lacks the reference to the passion of Christ. According to Tertullian, the bodily reference to the cross makes every prayer into praise of Christ. Furthermore, Tertullian notes that Christians should not lift up their hands too high in order not to be presumptuous; this could also be a hint to the *orans* pose of the gentiles whom Tertullian probably understood as presumptuous.

---

having people stand while praying: "it seems good to the holy Synod that prayer be made to God standing" (Canon 20).

755   Tert. Or. 23 (Schleyer; tr. Stewart-Sykes).
756   The word *orans* is a medieval loanword.
757   Tert. Or. 13.2 (Schleyer; tr. Stewart-Sykes).
758   Id. 14.
759   It seems to have been Jewish practice to stand while praying. The most important liturgical Jewish prayer is called *Amidah*, העמידה, which literally means "the standing" (U. Ehrlich, *The Nonverbal Language of Prayer. A New Approach of Jewish Liturgy*, Tübingen 2004, 9 ff.).

It seems that the *orans* pose was often interpreted by the Christian authors as signalling the shape of the cross. It would seem that the cross as prayer posture has several meanings although not much is said directly about this point. Standing as a cross could be praise to or confession of Christ, a symbol of one's willingness to sacrifice oneself in prayer, or symbolizing an expectation of taking part in the power or grace coming from Christ. Making the sign of the cross with one's hand in front of oneself is not mentioned in the treatises, but is mentioned elsewhere by Tertullian in *De Corona* 3 in a passage on prayer and other physical forms of piety. Here Tertullian writes that kneeling and fasting are unlawful for Christians on the Lord's Day and in the period between Easter and Pentecost. Thereafter, Tertullian writes that in everyday life all kinds of acts should be followed by a crossing: "we trace upon the forehead the sign," i.e. the sign of the cross. In *Ad uxorem* 2.5, Tertullian also refers to the sign of the cross in a passage where he writes about prayers during the night. According to Tertullian, the physical sign of the cross is thus an important feature that should frame life and prayer.

The upright position *per se* was explained by Clement and Origen without reference to the cross. They saw it as signifying the fact that when praying, the soul stretches towards heaven; thus Clement writes:

> "For this reason also we raise the head and lift the hands towards heaven, and stand on tiptoe as we join in the closing outburst of prayer, following the eager flight of the spirit into the intelligible world: and while we thus endeavor to detach the body from the earth by lifting it upwards along with the uttered words, we spurn the fetters of the flesh and constrain the soul, winged with desire of better things, to ascend into the holy place."[760]

Similarly, Origen sees the erect position as reflecting the willingness and character of the soul. He writes:

> "standing with hands extended and eyes upraised is much to be preferred, in that one thereby wears on the body the image of the characteristics which are becoming to the soul in prayer."[761]

---

760 Clem. Strom. 7.7.40 (Hort/Mayor).
761 Or. or. 31.2 (Koetschau; tr. Stewart-Sykes).

David T. Runia notes that Origen in his *Homilies on Exodus* explains the upright praying position by reference to both the power of Christ's cross,[762] and "also in accordance with the Philonic interpretation of raising one's thoughts and actions away from earth and up towards heavenly and immaterial realities (11.4)."[763] Also Clement, maybe inspired by Philo, passes on the Stoic commonplace that man was given an erect posture in order to contemplate heaven. Likewise, Cyprian in *Ad Demetrianum* refers to the erect posture as made by God in heaven to seek God on high.[764]

In *De Oratione*, Tertullian mentions another physical feature related to prayer: the "kiss of peace (*osculum pacis*)." [765] The other three authors are silent about the kiss in their treatises on prayer, but there are other references to this practice in third-century Christianity.[766] Tertullian gives the kiss a prominent position as he calls it the "seal of prayer (*signaculum orationis*)" [767] The combination of prayer and kiss underlines the social character of Christian prayer, which will be investigated further in the following chapter. Michael Penn has convincingly showed that the kiss underlined the close relations among Christians; the kiss was a means to perform and thereby create the Christian "family."[768] This corresponds with Stefan Heid's conclusion that: "Der Kuss nach dem Gebet besiegelte also, was schon der begrüßende Bruderkuss zum Ausdruck brachte: die Gemeinschaft im Frieden Christi."[769] Stefan Heid also notes that the kiss of peace is known from contexts of intercession,[770] and Heid understands this to mean that the kiss was a mark of fellowship in prayer and life: "Der Kuss drückte demnach die gegenseitige Gebetsunterstützung und den Wunsch aus, die Gebete

---

762 Or. hom. in Ex. 3.3, see D.T. Runia, *Philo in Early Christian Literature. A Survey*, Assen 1993, 166.

763 Runia, 1993, 166.

764 Cypr. Demetr. 16 (tr. Baer).

765 Tert. Or. 18 (Schleyer; tr. Stewart-Sykes).

766 Penn lists many third-century examples: e.g. Tert. praescr. 41; Apostolic Tradition 4, 21, see Penn, 2002, 157 n. 16.

767 Tert. Or. 18 (Schleyer; tr. Stewart-Sykes).

768 Penn, 2002.

769 S. Heid, *Der gebetsabschließende Bruderkuss im frühen Christentum*, in: H. Grieser/A. Merkt (eds.), *Volksglaube im antiken Christentum*, Darmstadt 2009.

770 Apostolic Tradition 18 and in Just. apol. 65, see Heid, 2009, 253.

des anderen mögen erhört werden. Zum anderen verband für Tertullian der Friedenskuss die *oratio pacis* mit der *operatio pacis*," that is: for Tertullian, the kiss combined the prayer of peace and the act of peace.[771] "Auf diese Weise bildeten Gebet und Tat, Gottes- und Nächstenliebe eine Einheit."[772] It might seem contradictory that the authors stress both physical postures and the spiritual nature of prayer. Only Origen tries to explain the combination of physicality and spirituality by pointing to the fact that the postures are meant for the person to fix his/her mind upon the activity of prayer.[773] Origen also points out that if the circumstances do not allow physical gestures to be made, "we may pray without outward indication that we are so doing."[774] Hence, Origen is aware that the gestures of prayer are secondary and meant for enforcing the concentration on the spiritual exercise.

For the fellowship among Christians, the collective movements and postures must have strengthened the feeling of communion and must have functioned as symbols of belonging. As such prayer was a physical symbol with relevance for identity in the sense that identity is also expressed via motion or performance. Assuming a posture of prayer meant performing one's Christian identity and showing it to the world. What Uri Erhlich notes about the body language of the *Amidah* in Jewish liturgy could also be said about the Christian body language: it built "qualitative mutual-interpersonal relationships in prayer."[775] Not only was a relationship with God established by the very act of standing up and spreading one's arms; the person praying would likewise be connected to other Christians.

3.2.5.2 On direction

As mentioned in the paragraph on "secret prayer," the authors under investigation emphasized the ubiquity of God's presence. Logically, this means that prayers could be offered everywhere and in all directions. Tertullian and Cyprian might be of that opinion since they do not explicate any directions

---

771 Heid, 2009, 253.
772 Heid, 2009, 254.
773 Or. or. 8.2 (Koetschau; tr. Stewart-Sykes).
774 Id. 31.2.
775 Ehrlich, 2004, 218 f.

for prayer in their euchological treatises.[776] However, in *Apologeticum* 16, Tertullian mentions that Christians were praying towards the east (*ad orientis regionem*), and here Tertullian also denies that this has anything to do with worship of the sun; if anything, Christ is the sun of the Christians. In relation with prayer, Cyprian mentions that we are in Christ, and he is "the true sun and the true day."[777] Christ is thus regularly referred to as sun, and east occasionally was specified as the right direction of prayers. In their euchological treatises, Clement and Origen prescribe east as the correct direction.

The focus on direction shows that the Christians were influenced by the practice of other religious communities that claimed certain appropriate directions for worship, frequently east. M. Wallraff mentions how the sun was often worshipped among gentiles, and when studying late antiquity, he notes a general "'Solarisierung' der religiösen Kultur der Zeit."[778] Early on, it would seem that Christians began praying towards east, indeed already by the second century, martyr acts mention that martyrs prayed towards east. By the third century, it was apparently commonplace for Christians to pray facing eastwards. This practice might have been taken over from gentile's heliolatry, although Christian authors of course denied any link.[779]

It is probable that Christians took over a pagan practice when praying towards east, but the Christian theologians came up with interpretations that legitimized their actions. Thus Clement approves the eastward direction:

"And since East symbolizes the day of birth, and it is from thence that the light spreads, after it has first shone forth out of darkness, aye, and from thence that the day of the knowledge of the truth dawned like the sun upon those who were

---

776 Cf. Aug. Ev.Jo. 10,1 (ed. Schaff): "You need not direct your eyes towards some mountain; you need not raise your face to the stars, or to the sun, or to the moon; nor must you suppose that you are heard when you pray beside the sea: rather detest such prayers. Only cleanse the chamber of your heart; wheresoever you are, wherever you pray. He that hears is within, within in the secret place..."

777 Cypr. Dom. orat. 35 (Réveillaud; tr. Stewart-Sykes).

778 Wallraff, 2001, 87.

779 Id.; F.J. Dölger, *Sol salutis. Gebet und Gesang im christlichen Altertum mit besonderer Rücksicht auf die Ostung in Gebet und Liturgie*, Münster 1925.

lying in ignorance, therefore our prayers are directed towards the rise of dawn (πρὸς τὴν ἑωθινὴν ἀνατολὴν αἱ εὐχαί)."[780]

Clement here reflects pagan ideas and lets these ideas melt together with Christian practice by simply asserting that this is what Christians do. However, we know that Clement often used a light-metaphor about Christ.[781] Origen is the first Christian author who makes a real *interpretatio christiana* regarding the Christian practice of praying towards east. This is not so much the case in *Perì Euchês*, but in his homilies, e.g. in *Hom. in Lev.* 9.10. Here Origen reminds his audience that the man, who brought reconciliation between humans and God, will come from the east. Origen refers to a quote from Zachariah 7:12: ἀνήρ Ἀνατολὴ ὄνομα αὐτῷ. In this quotation, a man by the name of Ἀνατολὴ is presented. Ἀνατολὴ literally means "sun rise"/"East." Origen identifies this man as Christ and combines him with sunrise and light. Thereafter, he invites Christians to look in this direction. Origen thus gives the eastward prayers a christological interpretation, but not by explicitly referring to the expected *parousia* of Christ from east. Other texts use the explicit *parousia*-motive as argument for praying towards east.[782] In *Perì Euchês* Origen mentions the practice of prayer towards east with reference to Christ, the true light:

> "who would not immediately agree that the direction of sunrise obviously indicates that we should make our prayer facing in that direction, as having the implication that the soul is facing the rising of the true light?"[783]

After having explained that one should pray facing eastwards, Origen closes the passage in *Perì Euchês* by stating: "And that is enough on that subject." However, here we shall take one more point into consideration, inspired by Wallraff. Wallraff ponders that it probably attracted some converts to Christianity that the Christian practice reminded of heliolatric worship which apparently in some form was familiar to most people at this time. As such the practice of praying towards the east might have had an integrative function as a gradual adaptation to a Christian identity. Wallraff concludes

---

780 Clem. Strom. 7.7.43 (Hort/Mayor).
781 E.g. Osborn, 2005, 35 paraphrases Clem. prot. 2,114,4: "The whole universe has woken to unsleeping light, and sunset has turned into sunrise."
782 Wallraff mentions *Didascalia Addai can.* 1 (Wallraff, 2001, 83 ff.).
783 Or. or. 32 (Koetschau; tr. Stewart-Sykes).

that it was an advantage: "Ein Vorteil der Sonnenverehrung bestand ja gerade in ihrem hohen integrativen Potential."[784]

3.2.5.3 On times for prayer

By the third century, Christians seem to have taken over the Jewish practice of praying three times a day.[785] All authors under investigation mention a threefold prayer scheme, and all, except for Clement, use the *Book of Daniel* as their argumentation, because Dan 6:10 tells us: "Three times a day he got down on his knees and prayed, giving thanks to his God, just as he had done before." Tertullian recommends prayers at the third, sixth and ninth hour. He notes that this is in accordance with Daniel and with the "discipline of Israel." He also finds other arguments in Scripture: the Spirit was infused into the disciples at the third hour (Acts 2:1–4), Peter prayed at the sixth hour (Acts 10:9). Peter and John went to the temple at the ninth hour (Acts 3:1).[786] Although partly relying on Jewish tradition, Tertullian breaks definitely with Jewish practice by stating that the reason for the threefold Christian prayer pattern is the three persons of the Trinity. With this statement, Tertullian gives an *interpretatio christiana* of the Jewish practice that, unlike the practice itself, cannot have a non-Christian origin.

Furthermore, Tertullian notes that the prayers of these hours are additional to the statutory prayers at daybreak and at night. In this way, Tertullian ends up recommending five periods of prayer a day. Tertullian is the only author who also admonishes his audience to pray when eating, bathing and having guests.[787] It is unclear which prayers were to be said at the admonished five daily times for prayer; it might be the Lord's Prayer. Likewise, Cyprian recommends a threefold prayer pattern, and also Cyprian seems to expand it with further morning and evening prayers.[788] However, it

---

784 Wallraff, 2001, 203.
785 On the Jewish practice and the Christian tradition, see Bradshaw, 1981 and L.E. Phillips, *Prayer in the first Four Centuries AD*, in: R. Hammerling (ed.), *A History of Prayer. The First to the Fifteenth Century*, Leiden 2008, 32-46.
786 Tert. Or. 25 (Schleyer; tr. Stewart-Sykes).
787 In his later Montanist writing, Tertullian is stricter on the issue of observing prayer hours and fasting (Tert. Ieiun.).
788 Cypr. Dom. orat. 34 (Réveillaud; tr. Stewart-Sykes).

is not completely clear, if he recommends additional prayers in the morning and night, or if these times of prayer are included in the threefold pattern.[789] Indeed Cyprian states that there is no hour, at which Christians should not pray, and urges occasional nocturnal vigils with prayer as well.[790] Like Tertullian, Cyprian refers to the *Book of Daniel* as explanation for three daily times for prayer, and like Tertullian, also Cyprian points to the practice as a "figure... of the Trinity which should be made manifest in more recent times."[791] Thus, like Tertullian, Cyprian christianizes the Jewish practice by way of interpretation. He even refers to the three hours between the third, sixth and ninth hour as symbolizing the Trinity as well (*alteram trinitatem*). Furthermore, Cyprian supports his interpretation with other New Testament passages. Unlike Tertullian, Cyprian uses examples from Mark's passion story and recommends prayer at the sixth and ninth hour, because the Lord was crucified at the sixth hour and died at the ninth – whereby "he washed away our sins by his blood" (Mark 15:33–34). Likewise, Cyprian makes a Christological point about morning prayers when he states that this occasion of prayer should be used to celebrate the resurrection.

Similarly Clement is aware of a threefold prayer scheme, although mainly focusing his attention on the gnostic's life of *constant* prayer:

> "And if there are any who assign fixed hours to prayer, such as the third and the sixth and the ninth, yet the gnostic at all events prays all his life through, striving to be united with God."[792]

Scholars disagree whether Clement follows an already established pattern of prayer, an Alexandrian *horarium*, or if he is expressing his general admonition "pray always" in another way by referring to prayers at morning, noon and night.[793] In any case, the ideal of constant prayer and the many set hours of prayer are expressions of the same ideal of living a pious

---

789 Id. 35.
790 Id. 36.
791 Id. 34.
792 Clem. Strom. 7.7.40 (Hort/Mayor). Clement gives other admonitions in paed. 2,9-10 (Mondésert) where he admonishes people to pray after rising, before retiring, at night, and before, during and after meals.
793 Taft mentions divergent views in R. Taft, *The Liturgy of the Hours in East and West, The Origins and Its Meaning for Today,* Collegeville 1993, 17.

life. Clement also seems to combine the hours of prayer with the Trinity, although the meaning is not completely clear and seemingly more speculative. Clement writes:

> "However, the triple distribution of the hours and their observance by corresponding prayers is also familiar to those who are acquainted with the blessed triad of the holy mansions (τῶν ἁγίων τριάδα μονῶν)."[794]

Origen also admonishes prayers not less than three times a day, because Daniel prayed three times a day (Dan 6:10). Origen supports his idea with more Biblical "evidence": the apostle Peter prayed at noon according to Acts 10:9, Psalm 5:3 mentions prayer in the morning, and Ps. 141:2 mentions an evening sacrifice that Origen interprets as a call for evening prayer. Furthermore Origen interprets Ps 119:62 to mean that Christians should pray at night as well, which Origen finds is supported by the fact that Paul prayed at midnight (Acts 16:26).[795] Origen thus seems to admonish prayers morning, noon, evening and midnight. Nonetheless, he writes in his treatises that it is not about saying the words of the Lord's Prayer at certain times; it is about having one's life praying ceaselessly.[796]

The practice of praying at certain appointed times has the function not only of making Christians persistent in prayer, but also to have them pray at the same time. The latter reason is not explicitly mentioned in the treatises, but more scholars have pointed to the fact that the determined times created a fellowship between Christians although they prayed at different locations. Thomas O'Loughlin mentions that this is also the case with the Old Testament figure Judith who deliberately makes her most intense prayer "at the very time when that evening's incense was being offered in the house of God in Jerusalem (9:2–14)." O'Loughlin comments that:

> "This assumes a belief that one could link one's own prayer with the formal liturgy of the temple far away through using the same moment. This linking in prayer meant that one was not praying alone, but as part of the whole of Israel. Such combined prayer presumably added force to one's own ritual of prayer..., but also established a notion of spiritual identity: the temple may be far away, but I too am involved in its liturgy."

---

794 Clem. Strom. 7.7.40 (Hort/Mayor).
795 Or. or. 12.2 (Koetschau; tr. Stewart-Sykes) and Cels. 6.41 (Borret; tr. Crombie).
796 Or. or. 22 (Koetschau; tr. Stewart-Sykes). Cf. Taft, 1993, 17.

O'Loughlin uses the example of Judith's prayer to shed light on the Christian church order *Didache*. In this text he sees that the same sense of "sacred time" is used to join people into a communion. Therefore, he believes that one must see the instructions on common fasting in *Didache* not simply as reflecting an external church order and a group with a clear organizational identity. Rather, it gives an insight into the Christian ecclesiology: "the Christians are bound together for they participate in a single liturgy, not just as a community, but as a body made up of geographically dispersed communities."[797] O'Loughlin assumes that what is done synchronically will contribute to a sense of unification. On the basis of *Didache*, he mentions common prayer, fasting and Eucharist as such practices that can create union among people, even if they are not doing it together at the same place. Also Paul Bradshaw hints at this effect of the office of prayer. Bradshaw notes that Christians in the early church seem to have prayed very frequently, and their prayers were in some sense liturgical. By 'liturgical' Bradshaw refers to the fact that prayer "either was done corporately, or at least involved forms of worship which were also being offered by other Christians and was *associated with the prayer of the rest of the church by being said at the regular hours of the day and night which others were praying.*"[798] Eventually the practice of set times for daily prayers would evolve into the formal practice of the "Liturgy of the hours" or "Divine office." Bradshaw finds that this "liturgical" character of private prayer did not cease until recently.[799]

The physical traits of prayer must not be underestimated. They are a part of the performance of prayer that arguably strengthens the common identity. Also Christian theology as such value the ritual and concrete acts as a link to the spiritual meaning. Sacraments are exactly links and signs that

---

797 O'Loughlin, *The Didache and Early Christian Communities*, in: K.J O'Mahony (ed.), *Christian Origins. Worship, Belief, and Society. The Milltown Institute and the Irish Biblical Association Millennium Conference*, London 2003, 83-112, 103.

798 P. Bradshaw, *What Happened to Daily Prayer?*, in: Worship 64 (1990), 10. Emphasis added.

799 Id.

establish a connection between the physical and the transcendent reality. Lorenzo Perrone concludes:

> "for Origen both the senses and the intellect are required for someone aiming at knowledge of God. It is no accident that he attributes to the body an important role in the human accomplishment of prayer, though physical reality represents only a preliminary level (with Rom. 1, 20), to be subsequently overcome in the mind's journey towards God."[800]

3.2.5.4 On the content and wording of prayer

There is remarkably little information to be found in the treatises regarding the exact wording of prayer. Of course the Lord's Prayer is held in high esteem, and it must have been in use at the recommended hours of prayer. The Lord's Prayer is the perfect form of prayer, and the authors are hesitant to allow for personal petitions to be added. Tertullian leaves a little room for "pleas for additional desires,"[801] and Origen too lets people pose further petitions. In general, prayers of thanksgiving, praise and for forgiveness are taken for granted which is much in accord with the Jewish matrix of Christian prayer.

Origen is the one who gives the most concrete instructions regarding prayer. At the conclusion of his treatise, Origen shows how a prayer ought to be constructed, namely by including four elements: glorification of God, thanksgiving, confession and petition (for what is great and heavenly), accompanied by final "glorification of God through Christ in the Holy Spirit."[802] Origen exemplifies such prayers by showing how Scripture contains suitable passages. One can notice that he gives examples from the Book of Psalms which could indicate the use of Psalms in third-century Christian prayer practice, something which occasionally has been contested.[803]

Cyprian notes that prayers should be ethical, and also Clement notices that the gnostic never prays for anything that could harm other people. What one should pray for according to all the authors is spiritual goods, such as forgiveness of sins, constancy in virtue and eschatological salvation.

---

800 Perrone, 2001, 15.
801 Tert. Or. 10 (Schleyer; tr. Stewart-Sykes).
802 Or. or. 33.1 (Koetschau; tr. Stewart-Sykes).
803 A. de Vogüé, *Psalmodier n'est pas Prier*, in: EO 6 (1989), 8.18.

Clement explicates: "The gnostic... will ask for continuance of the things he possesses and fitness for what is about to happen, and indifference as to what shall be denied, but for the things that are really good, i.e. those pertaining to the soul..."[804]

Of further importance is the commandment that one should pray not only for oneself but for others as well, i.e. intercede for others. Clement thus admonishes: "Yet the petition is not superfluous, even though good things be granted without petition. For instance, both thanksgiving and prayer for the conversion of his neighbours are the duty of the gnostic."[805] Soon we shall return to the obligation of intercession.

3.2.5.5 Silent prayer and contemplation

It should also be mentioned that prayers were not necessarily supposed to be verbal at all; Origen holds Hannah's and Jonah's silent prayers as ideal.[806] Even more or less wordless prayers were approved.[807] It even seems that silent or mental prayer is ideal according to Origen, although he in no way dismisses verbal prayer.[808]

---

804 Clem. Strom. 7.7.44 (Hort/Mayor).

805 Id. 7.7.41.

806 Or. or. 2.5, 4.1–2, 13.2, 16.3 (Koetschau; tr. Stewart-Sykes).

807 In antiquity, silent prayers were generally looked upon with suspicion. First in the imperial period, the Platonic philosophers began to promote silent prayers due to their understanding of the divine world as a noetic, spiritual world (see Horst, 1994). We can recall that Plotinus writes: "... we first invoke God himself not in loud words, but in that way of prayer which is always within our power, leaning in our soul towards him by aspiration, alone towards the alone (μονος πρὸς μόνον)" (Plot. Enn. 5.1.6.9–12 (Henry/Schwyzer; tr. MacKenna/Page)).
B. Bitton-Ashkelony mentions that further new ways of approaching the divine were developed in the ascetic life of the late antique Mediterranean world: pure prayer, unceasing prayer, spiritual prayer, Jesus prayer, remembrance of God, and prayer of the heart (Bitton-Ashkelony, 2012, 304).

808 Genet is quoted in Perrone, preghiera, 2011, 30 n. 76: "À côté des quatre fomes de prièreI...], à côté de la notion de la prière qui se confond avec les actes pieux, il y a chez Origène l'idée d'une prière intérieure suivant laquelle le croyant entre directement en communion avec Dieu, sans avoir besoin de lui exprimer verbalement ses désirs (36)... Les autres prières sont bien au-dessous puisque, au besoin, elles peuvent s'adresser à de simples mortels." (45-46).

The two Alexandrian authors promote contemplation, θεωρία, as the finest form of Christian contact with God. It is an activity for the rational mind, it is thinking about and reflecting on God, and it is perfect prayer. Contemplation is, however, not only presented as an intellectual exercise of reflection, but also as a way to be lead to unification with God. However, it is not an easy endeavour, since it requires knowledge of God, but also a mind worthy of God. For Clement, contemplation is the true and gnostic way to pray, and the true gnostic remains in "uninterrupted contemplation."[809] Clement understands "contemplation" to be a perfection of prayer and life, a way of moving as close to God as possible and thus as proleptic salvation.[810] Soul and mind can communicate with God without use of voice and tongue, and the human thought can pray in a most perfect way.[811] Similarly, Origen understands contemplation as an ideal activity. According to Origen, intellectual beings were made to contemplate God's goodness, but fell away from this activity and now have to find their way back.[812] Origen writes that the greatest benefit of prayer is gained by those who "look beyond what is begotten and contemplate (ἐννοεῖν) God alone, and hold modest and solemn converse with the one who hears them."[813] They will be transformed into God's image (τὴν αὐτὴν εἰκόνα μεταμορφουμένους). Elsewhere in Perì Euchês, Origen is more explicit in that he contrasts those, who are ignorant of God and consequently do not know for what to pray, with those who are contemplating God, and therefore know what is truly good:

> "Anyone who is ignorant of God is ignorant of the things of God, and ignorant of the things that are necessary; what he reckons as necessary are the wrong things. But whoever has contemplated (ὁ τεθεωρηκώς) the better and more divine things, which are necessary to him, will obtain the objects of his contemplation (ὧν τεθεώρηκε), for they are known of God, and are known to the Father even before they are requested."[814]

---

809 Clem. Strom. 7.7.44 (Hort/Mayor).
810 Id. 7.2.10; 7.10.56; 7.11.60.
811 Id. 7.7.43.
812 Or. princ. 2.9.2 (Koetschau; tr. Butterworth).
813 Or. or. 9.2 (Koetschau; tr. Stewart-Sykes).
814 Or. or. 21.2 (Koetschau; tr. Stewart-Sykes).

In his *Commentary on the Song of Songs*, Origen is stating a similar point when he writes that *theoria* is going "beyond things seen and contemplate to a degree things heavenly and divine, beholding them with the mind alone."[815] Contemplation is a mode of piety and is a goal to which "ordinary Christians" can and should strive, since the ability to contemplate God requires a certain practice, mastery of passions, love, faith and knowledge. It is a mode of piety that goes beyond simply praying for earthly goods. As such contemplation is a form of mysticism, because of its focus on heavenly realities and its aim of unification of the soul with God (in a manner like to the union of the souls with God before the fall – a vision mediated by Logos).[816] In other writings Origen makes it clear that contemplation is an advanced form of piety that demands a progress from regular prayer to "moral contemplation" and further to the finest contemplation of nature which in turn will lead to spiritual knowledge of the Trinity.[817] Contemplation will lead to a participation in the divine Logos. However, in my opinion, *Perì Euchês*, does not express such an elitist notion of

---

815 Or. Cant. Prologue 3 (tr. Lawson).
816 In Cant. Prologue 3 (tr. Lawson), Origen interprets the activities of the patri-
     archs allegorically to exemplify the stages of contemplation. The ever-obedient
     Abraham corresponds to the moral contemplation; the activities of Isaac cor-
     responds to "natural contemplation": when he dug wells, he searched out the
     root of things. In the same passage, Jacob's dream of seeing a ladder going to
     heaven is interpreted by Origen as reflecting his contemplation of and striving
     towards heavenly things.
     The debate about whether or not we encounter real mysticism in the works
     of Origen is dealt with in Jay 1954, 62 ff. Völker seems to believe so, but he
     might have misinterpreted Origen by focusing solely on *Perì Euchês* (W. Völker,
     Das Vollkommenheitsideal des Origenes, Tübingen 1931, 197 ff.; Perrone,
     preghiera, 2011, 35).
817 Paddle in McGuckin, 2004, 81-83. Origen uses the examples of Mary and
     Martha and the disciples John and Peter to show that there are different stages
     of contemplation, both practical and theoretical. See also Or. hom. I-28 in
     Num. 10.3. This developmental scheme is elaborated by Evagrius. In *Kephalaia
     Gnostica*, Evagrius explains that the monk must undergo four transforma-
     tions: The first from evil to virtue; the second from freedom of the passions to
     "second natural contemplation"; the third to natural contemplation; and the
     fourth to the knowledge of the Trinity (See D. Brakke, *Demons and the Making
     of the Monk. Spiritual Combat in Early Christianity*, Cambridge 2006, 73).

contemplation. In *Perì Euchês* there is a difference between contemplation and petitionary prayer, but there is a petitionary aspect in contemplation since it represents a striving towards what is really spiritual and good – as such contemplation is the perfect result of prayer. Origen sees the mind as the point of contact between humans and God, and he notes in *De Principiis* that in the same way as the body grows, in particular in the childhood, because of food, so the mind also needs suitable food, "understood to be the contemplation and understanding of God... through purity of heart."[818]

Tertullian and Cyprian do not use the concept of *theoria*, and they are judged as less mystical because of it.[819] However, as McGinn notes, the Latin authors are not completely devoid of mysticism because they have a "sensitivity to introspective experience, a form of subjectivism rare among Greek authors."[820]

The idea of prayer as contemplation is reminiscent of the philosophical concept of prayer that we encountered in the investigation of late antique philosophy,[821] and it was a development in regard to cultic prayer.[822] We thus see how the Christian conceptions of prayer were broad and encompassed more ideas from the surrounding religious groups. Prayer could entail both concrete petitions and abstract contemplation. In all cases, however, Christians were admonished to pray for spiritual gifts, and consequently the expectations to the Christians expressed in the discourses were high. People are inclined to pray because of impulses and personal desires that by a closer theological scrutiny are not worthy. The Christian

---

818 Or. princ. 2.11 (Koetschau; tr. Butterworth).
819 B. McGinn, *The Foundations of Mysticism. Origins to the Fifth Century*, Crossroad 1991, 191.
820 Id.
821 Above Paragraph 2.2. The Christian ideas of contemplation might have been inspired both by Platonism and by Paul who mentions a man taken up in third heaven (2 Cor 2-4).
822 Cf. Brouria Bitton-Ashekonly's article on silent prayer that "drawing on biblical paradigms, Clement of Alexandria and Origen *enhanced* the traditional notion of prayer common in the Greek and Roman religions, which consisted mainly of petitions or requests addressed to the divine, or prayer that accompanied the offering of sacrifices." (Bitton-Ashkelony, 2012, 310. Emphasis added).

leaders wanted to weed out unworthy prayers. By having a strict opinion on worthy purposes for prayer, prayer as such could have a cultivating effect on Christians. Certain prayers were held up as ideal, others were to be avoided. Ideally, when feeling an impulse or desire, the Christian was obliged to consider, if this was worth acting on and praying for. At the same time, Christians were admonished to take the greater fellowship into consideration. In this way, prayer could function as an act of cultivation in the sense that it necessitated a consideration of one's motives and relation to the community. As such I argue prayer took part in shaping selves and identities in late antiquity.[823]

3.2.6 Conclusion: How to approach the divine

All four authors understand prayer as something that brings the individual into contact with the divine, and God will hear his children's pleas as long as they are in accord with his will. God's will – manifested in the person of Jesus Christ – is a measure of how one should pray. God's will towards humanity has been manifested in the revelation of Jesus Christ.

The contact between humans and God is not only spoken out loudly, but can also be silent and even purely mental, described as contact between God and the human mind, heart or soul. Contemplation of God is mentioned by the Alexandrian theologians as a form of advanced prayer since God is the object of contemplation. This might sound mystical, but in fact, all four authors believe in the possibility of spiritual communication with God that goes beyond the verbal and concrete. This kind of spiritual communication anticipates eschatological salvation. Compared to the pagan cult of the Romans with its keen attention to detail regarding words and sacrifices, the Christian manner of approaching God represents a strong spiritualization and interiorizing – and to a certain degree individualization. The Christian idea of prayer is much more comparable to the Stoic and Platonic ideas about prayer, but it is not an exact match. The Christian authors did generally expect God to have personal traits and an interest in helping his children. In contrast the philosophical divinity was unpersonal, and the world view deterministic. Christian prayer, on the other hand, was

---

823 We shall return to this in Chapter 5.

more than expressions of destiny; Christian prayers were believed to really help bring about changes in the world and in the Christians.

According to the Christian authors, prayers entail much more than petitions. Assimilation to the will of God is also part of Christian correspondence with the divine. Prayer was ideally understood to be a matter of attitude, heart, soul and mind. This shows how the Christian identity was supposed to be predominant and salient, because it should be a constant characteristic of the individual Christian. Christianity was supposed to define the entire life, will and attitude of a person. In Chapter 5, we will return to the manner in which prayer functioned as an instrument in transforming the selves and identities of Christians.

Finally, we have seen how Christian identity was overtly performed by the use of prayer postures. These were not exclusive for Christians but were explained with Christian reasoning and became in this process exclusive for the Christians. Furthermore, we saw that prayer was understood a bit differently among the different authors. For all authors, prayer had to do with a verbal performance, but it could also be a silent endeavour as Origen indicates, and prayer could also be combined with contemplation. Prayer is both presented as a concrete practice and verbal activity, and as a mental and behavioural endeavour. The two parts of prayer are interrelated and are prerequisites for one another.

3.3 God, prayer and Christian identity

As noted in the first chapter of this dissertation, religious life is structured around certain symbols some of which are transcendent, as is the case with God. In early Christianity, as it is presented in the four treatises under investigation, the dominant religious symbol is God, but presented via His self-revelation Jesus Christ and – to a varying degree – His Spirit. Because of Christ's role as God's self-revelation, the transcendent symbol of God became "real" and concrete. In this way, God arguably became a more efficient symbol for directing conduct. Within the Christian texts, the Christian narrative is unfolded, depicting how God made everything new by way of his revelation. New versus old is a frequent theme in the treatises and is related to life and prayer. According to the Christian authors, this newness of life is granted to those who are willing to believe in it and allow themselves to be defined by God's revelatory acts.

Faith was one condition for becoming part of the Christian universe, but not the only condition because the Christian narrative is directed towards social obligation and responsibility and towards a reconstitution of life. Christians were supposed to present much more than verbatim creeds and prayers. They were expected to be transformed, or, we could say, gain a new identity, thoroughly defined by Christianity. The authors under investigation proposed prayer as a means to make the Christian (identity) transformation come about. They saw prayer as working in two primary ways: Firstly, one should pray for spiritual gifts and forgiveness that could affect a change within the individual. Secondly, according to Origen and Clement, one should use prayer to assimilate to God and live a prayerful life.[824] Tertullian wanted the believers to assimilate to the divine soul as a prerequisite for praying, and Cyprian wanted the heart of the Christians to pray with sincere intent. For all authors, a prayerful life is a life worthy of constant scrutiny from God. Analysing the texts, we see that prayers could function as catalyst for pondering which thoughts and wishes were worthy to be directed to God.

When the Christians fashioned their narratives and ideas in the first centuries AD, they caused frustration in the surrounding society. The scholar of religion, Philip E. Hammond, has noted that: "Invariably the creation of new sacred forms precipitates conflict because transcendent symbols are used to organize the mundane interactions that constitute the basic fiber of the social order."[825] This quotation from Hammond illustrates how transcendent symbols, such as prayer and the reality to which it points, influence life and human relationships.

---

824 We shall return to this in Chapter 5.
825 P.E. Hammond, *The Sacred in a Secular Age. Toward Revision in the Scientific Study of Religion.* Berkeley 1985, 59.

4 Prayer and the multiaxial relationships of Christians

> *"What we can say is that [prayers] are all multifaceted dialogues - between the speaker and God; the speaker and him or herself; the speaker and any intended or imagined (over)hearer (human beings, angels, and demons) - which are intended to be heard, or overheard, by others."*[826]

4.1 Introduction – the agents of prayer

The following chapter investigates the many relations – besides the relationship with God – that are either encouraged or discouraged in the treatises on prayer. Many of these relations are seen as having an effect on the outcome of prayer. These important relations are with both human and supernatural beings such as angels and the deceased, even the heavenly bodies are mentioned in one instance as agents in relation to prayer. It is for this reason that the title of the chapter mentions "multiaxial relationships." Multiaxial expresses the fact that the person praying is stepping into a relationship not only with God, but with more agents found on both a horizontal and a vertical axis. The praying Christian thus finds himself/herself as centre in a biaxial or even multiaxial "system." Most predominant is the relationship with other Christians. A correct relationship between the individual Christian and his/her fellow-Christians is presented as extremely important for the endeavour of praying and is of positive significance for the effect of prayer. Contrary, pagans, Jews and heretics are agents from whom the "true Christians" to some degree must dissociate themselves, and whose practices represent a risk. Pagans, Jews and heretics thus become a negative contrast in relation to which the Christians are presented positively. All of these human agents are to be found on the horizontal axis, although according to some theologians, Christians potentially move on the vertical axis already in the present. We shall see that human beings can themselves

---

826 C. Harrison, *The Art of Listening in the Early Church*, Oxford 2013, 205.

climb upwards on the vertical axis and find themselves in angelic company and as models for their fellow-Christians. There are more agents in the treatises, and their role will be investigated in this chapter.

Firstly, this chapter deals with the way in which prayer is combined with certain behavioural requirements and relations to fellow-Christians. This theme is dealt with in three stages: firstly, by investigating how the authors perceived the connection between prayer, virtue and behaviour; secondly, by investigating how kinship language was used in relation with prayer; and thirdly, by focusing on admonitions to pray with others and intercede for other Christians. After this, a paragraph follows which investigates how Jews, Pagans and heretics are presented as negative relations in connection with prayer. The last paragraphs of the chapter investigate relations to supernatural agents such as angels and the devil. One hypothesis investigated in this chapter is that prayer, virtue and behaviour were interrelated in the late antique Christian mind-set, at least among theologians. Admittedly, this is speculative since we have no possibility to survey the prayer practice or behaviour of third-century Christians. All paragraphs, however, point in the same direction, namely to the social effects of prayer and the relational emphasis in prayer discourse.

4.2 Prayer and ethics: Relations to other Christians

4.2.1 A theoretical note on ritual, values and behaviour

It is obvious that some behavioural code must exist within a social group; "there can be no community without some degree of coercion."[827] In accordance with this, Christian communities of late antiquity were also working to align the behaviour of Christians. Converted Christians were expected to change their primary reference group and be socialized into the Christian congregation as an alternative community.[828] Virtuous behaviour is therefore stressed as extremely important in the euchological treatises – behaviour is as important as the words of prayer.

---

827 W.A. Meeks, *The Origins of Christian Morality. The First Two Centuries*, New Haven 1993, 216.
828 Meeks, 1993, 26.

As history has shown, "Christians" were good at creating a sense of belonging; better apparently than the philosophical groups around them. W.A. Meeks notes that the Epicurean school was the only philosophical movement that was able to create a sense of real social commitment among its followers. But there are examples of how philosophical schools expected behavioural change from their adherents: The Stoic philosopher Epictetus, for instance, admonished his followers: "Flee your former habits; flee the uninitiated [*idiōtai*], if you want ever to be anyone."[829] And, as noted above, the Neoplatonic Porphyry likewise focused his attention on behaviour and found that legitimate prayer has to do with deeds, because: "It is not the tongue of the wise man that is worthy of honour in God's eyes, but rather his deeds."[830] The Jew Philo also insisted on the religious obligation to offer up to God good deeds as well as prayers. In general, it is a topic of cult criticism in Judaism and pagan philosophies that no cultic actions, like prayer, should be done by an unrighteous person, but it seems that no community was as effective in promoting this view as the early Christian communities were.

According to J.B. Rives, by the third century neither the traditional Greco-Roman religion, including its imperial cult, nor the philosophical associations were believed to have had a strong influence on the behaviour and commitment of the inhabitants of the empire. In other words, by the third century, the empire lacked a unifying religious identity. It is Rives' theory that the religion in the Roman Empire became too heterogeneous, and therefore a crisis arose because of the lack of a common religious identity in the empire.[831] This crisis in turn led to the persecution of Christians and other religious dissidents in an attempt to unify the religious world of the empire. Eventually, Christianity came to fill the void because – amongst other things – it was able to connect the public and private spheres as well as the political and civic aspects of life. One reason for the success of the Christians was arguably their ability to create communities, something which also had to do with their practice of rituals.

829　Epict. diatr. 3.16.16, quoted in Meeks, 1993, 25.
830　Porph. Marc. 16 (Wicker).
831　Rives, 1995, 249.

Studies have shown that ritual is often used in the creation and maintenance of certain norms and forms of identity.[832] Ritual, understood as public
and formal kinds of display, reinforces the values endemic to a given system.
Clifford Geertz says that rituals give religious systems that force of necessity
that is "the air of simple realism."[833] In other words, values embedded in a
certain religion are more likely to be taken over by people if they perform
rituals. By connecting ritual and values closely, Christianity became real for its
followers and probably effected real changes in regard to behaviour. Lorenzo
Perrone has noticed that "it is precisely through worship that both the institutional and fraternal dimensions of Christian communities make their appearance."[834] W.A. Meeks expresses it thus:

> "The ritual provides a dramatic structure within and on which a pattern of moral
> reasoning may be erected and an interpretive dialectic begun between ritual and
> common life experience."[835]

I argue that in order to understand the function of prayer in late antiquity,
we should accept this theory, and hence accept that ritual, values and behaviour are connected. Furthermore, we should consider prayer, even private
prayer, to be a form of (micro-)ritual.[836] I argue that prayer played a role in

---

832 Sandnes' and Thelbe's contributions in Hvalvik/Sandnes, 2014.
833 Clifford Geertz quoted in Meeks, 1993, 40. For further considerations on
     ritual and identity, see G. Rouwhorst, *Identität durch Gebet. Gebetstexte
     als Zeugen eines jahrhundertelangen Ringens um Kontinuität und Differenz
     zwischen Judentum und Christentum*, in: A. Gerhards/A. Doeker/P. Ebenbauer
     (eds.), *Identität durch Gebet. Zur gemeinschaftsbildenden Funktion institu-
     tionalisierten Betens in Judentum und Christentum*, Paderborn 2003, 37-39.
     Rouwhorst also includes Roy Rappaport who has contributed significantly to
     the study of ritual.
834 L. Perrone, *For the Sake of a 'Rational Worship'. The Issue of Prayer and Cult
     in Early Christian Apologetics*, in: A.-C. Jakobsen/J. Ulrich/D. Brakke (eds.),
     Critique and Apologetics. Jews, Christians and Pagans in Antiquity, Frankfurt
     2009, 231-264.
835 Meeks, 1993, 97.
836 As M. Mauss pointed out, even private and spontaneous prayers are affected
     by the way in which prayer is interpreted and practised in a given religious
     community. Most prayers are thus reflecting (even if vaguely) prayers used in
     formalized religious rituals. Because of this resemblance, there is correspon-
     dence between private prayers and liturgical prayers (W.S.F. Pickering (ed.),
     Marcel Mauss. La Prière. 1909, New York 2003, 31).

the establishment and maintenance of certain Christian values. These values were not necessarily expressed clearly in concrete prayers, but they were expressed in discourses *about* prayer and were thus (ideally) presupposed when prayer took place. In the euchological treatises under investigation, we can see which values were part of shaping Christian identity. Another example of how values and ritual were combined is given by W.A. Meeks when he points to the close connection made between baptism and moral life: "In the earliest documents of the Christian movement, baptism is the ritual most often mentioned, and it is mentioned most often in hortatory contexts. That is, the writers remind their audience of baptism when they want to encourage certain kinds of behavior."[837] In the same way as baptism was a symbol that ideally activated certain behaviour and moral considerations, prayer was meant to stimulate certain moral considerations and actions.

4.2.2 Prayer, virtue and behaviour in the euchological treatises

All four authors under investigation, Tertullian, Cyprian, Clement and Origen, reckoned that prayer, virtue and behaviour are interconnected. Virtue and righteous behaviour are either seen as part of the "sacrifice" which Christians ought to offer to God when praying, or as something that ought to characterize the Christian if he/she should be worthy to approach God. That is, virtuous behaviour is recognized both as a part *of* prayer and as a presupposition *for* prayer. Consequently, prayer is regarded as invalid if it is not combined with correct behaviour. Tertullian for instance notes that

---

Furthermore, prayer shares a performative feature with rituals: Prayers do not only describe a situation or human condition or attitude, but has the purpose of changing, transforming or upholding a given situation/condition/ attitude. For further arguments in favour of understanding prayers – even private prayers – as a kind of ritual, see: J.A. Kapaló, *Text, Context and Performance. Gagauz Folk Religion in Discourse and Practice*, Leiden 2006, 287 ff. E.g. 289: "However, as Joel Robbins points out, 'the part of reality that ritual transforms' is very often the participant himself or herself and not the audience necessarily. In this sense, prayer too, much like ritual, can be seen to have its performative effect on the person or persons performing the prayer rather than on any audience or observer."

837 Meeks, 1993, 92 ff.

"prayers said in anger are wasted,"[838] and Cyprian refers to prayers that are not combined with good acts as "sterile prayers" and futile.[839] Clement even notes that those who are worthy will receive what they require even without uttering a petition.[840]

4.2.2.1 The Latin authors

Tertullian admonishes virtuous behaviour by stating "Wrongdoing... we should avoid it entirely,"[841] and – with reference to Matt 5:23–24: "We should not go up to the altar of God before resolving whatever there might be of offense or discord contracted with the brothers."[842] Tertullian thus advocates virtuous behaviour, and as we saw earlier, Tertullian also wants Christians to align their soul with the soul of God and thus to be changed from within. This is evident from admonitions such as: "The intent of prayer (orationis intentio) should be free not from anger alone (Nec ab ira solummodo) but from all manner of perturbation of the soul (omni omnino confusione animi)."[843] "Intention" is a keyword in Tertullian's theology of prayer. Furthermore, Tertullian demands prayers to be conducted with restraint, humility, faith, innocence, chastity, charity and good works.[844] Similarly, Cyprian demands that Christians make their pleas with discipline, restraint, quietness and reserve,[845] peaceable, just, innocent, with fear of God, with simplicity of heart, with peace and reconciliation, and finally with the Old Testament-figure Abel as paradigm.[846] Cyprian furthermore wants the praying Christians to be humble[847] and points out that: "It is not the sound of voice but the mind and the heart (animus et sensus) which should pray to God with sincere intent (intentione sincera Dominum)."[848]

---

838   Tert. Or. 11 (Schleyer; tr. Stewart-Sykes).
839   Cypr. Dom. orat. 32 (Réveillaud; tr. Stewart-Sykes): reference to Tob 12.8.
840   Clem. Strom. 7.7.41 (Hort/Mayor).
841   Tert. Or. 8 (Schleyer; tr. Stewart-Sykes).
842   Id. 11.
843   Id. 12.
844   Id. 17.
845   Cypr. Dom. orat. 4 (Réveillaud; tr. Stewart-Sykes).
846   Id. 24.
847   Id. 6, with a reference to Luke 18:10-14.
848   Cypr. Dom. orat. 31 (Réveillaud; tr. Stewart-Sykes).

Cyprian, like Tertullian, thus points to the intention of the individual as important for the endeavour of praying.

In line with Tertullian, Cyprian sees the spirit as a paradigm for a correct disposition, thus he admonishes: "Let not our conduct fall away from the spirit."[849] Not only the spirit and Abel serve as paradigms of a correct attitude in regard to prayer; also God himself is an ideal for the Christians, and Cyprian refers to the Biblical admonitions: "be holy as I too am holy,"[850] and "honor and carry God in your body."[851] Moreover, Cyprian understands the Lord's Prayer to be a paradigm for Christian disposition/identity, he writes: "[Jesus] teaches us to pray in this manner [the Lord's Prayer] and to know through the terms of the prayer what sort of person he should be (*qualis esse debeat*)."[852] Thus Cyprian expresses that a certain disposition can be deferred from the Lord's Prayer, a disposition which in turn is necessary for prayer to be sensible.

4.2.2.2 The Alexandrian authors

Also Clement combines behaviour and prayer in different ways, and he declares that the ideal sacrifice is: "purity of heart and upright living, grounded in holy actions and righteous prayer."[853] Clement expresses a very idealistic view on human ability to choose virtue voluntarily, and he presents prayer as a test and expression of inner virtue: "Certainly prayer is a test of the attitude of the character (ὁ τρόπος) towards what is fitting."[854] The perfect Christian, whose words, life and thoughts are in harmony,[855] is expected by Clement even to dream righteously: "his dreams are righteous so that he is always purified for prayer."[856] Clement is thus demanding a seemingly unrealistic degree of self-discipline and consciousness from the

---

849 Id. 11.
850 Id. with a reference to Lev 20:7.
851 Id. 11, cf. 6.20.
852 Id. 20.
853 Clem. Strom. 7.6.34 (Hort/Mayor). What is translated as "heart" is actually "mind" (νῷ).
854 Id. 7.7.43.
855 Id. 7.9.53.
856 Id. 7.12.78.

perfect Christian. At several instances, Clement even presents the very life of the gnostic as virtuous prayer.[857]

Furthermore, Clement is aware that petitions are made for that which humans desire; therefore, prayer can only be conducted correctly by those who have their desires under control. Those in control of their desires are the gnostics, and they can pray "for the things that are really good, i.e. those pertaining to the soul."[858] The gnostic is characterized by virtue that has become part of his being: he "joins his own efforts as well, that he may attain to a habit of goodness (εἰς ἕξιν ἀγαθότητος); so that he no longer has his good things attached to him like ornaments, but may himself be good."[859] Knowing how to conduct oneself and how to pray has to do with special knowledge, *gnosis*, which Clement emphasizes all the way through *Stromateis* 7. For instance, Clement writes: "Hence to pray is most fitting for those who have a right knowledge of the Divinity (τοῖς εἰδόσι τε τὸ θεῖον) and that excellence of character (ἀρετὴν) which is agreeable to Him…"[860]

In fact, according to Clement, it takes a gnostic to pray correctly, and we shall therefore make a little excurse to investigate the concept "gnosis," although the concept of "gnosis" in Clement's work is not easily explained. According to Clement, "gnosis" (γνῶσις) is knowledge about the Word of God, but it is more than faith – it is faith made perfect.[861] Gnosis expresses itself in the gnostic who is perfect in regard to disposition (τὸν τρόπον), manner of life (τὸν βίον) and speech (τὸν λόγον). The gnostic is perfected because of the science of divine things (διὰ τῆς τῶν θείων ἐπιστήμης), i.e. gnosis is attained through contemplation and study. According to Clement, *gnosis* is graciously transferred by tradition, but is more than what can be taught, because it is also faith and love.[862] As mentioned in Chapter 2, Clement was active in Alexandria where he was surrounded by different forms of heterodox "Gnosticism." In *Stromata* 7, Clement notes that his form of Gnosticism is the right one, because his gnostic is "gnostic according

---

857 Id. 7.3.13.
858 Id. 7.7.44.
859 Id. 7.7.38.
860 Id. 7.7.39.
861 Id. 7.10.55 with a reference to Jas 2:22.
862 Id. 7.10.55.

to the rule of the Church (κατὰ τὸν ἐκκλησιαστικὸν κανόνα γνωστικόν)"; and this gnosis is not to be mistaken with "the impious knowledge of these falsely called gnostics."[863] Thereby Clement distinguishes himself and his teaching from the wealth of "Gnosticism" around him. A number of scholars hold that Clement's type of Gnosticism actually can be distinguished from the Gnosticism of Valentinus that thrived in the Alexandrian context, because Clement "domesticated gnosis." Clement kept his "Gnosticism" within the boundaries of the "official church institution" (as ill-defined as it may have been at the time), and Clement constrained gnosis by Scripture.[864] In *Stromateis* 7, we see how Clement makes heavy use of the concept of "gnostic," but he is confining it within the boundaries of the rule/teachings of the Church and the teachings of Christ. The gnostic who has this extraordinary knowledge can pray correctly, i.e. spiritually. In fact only the gnostic can pray in a way that is pleasing to God, and since the gnostic because of his acquired *gnosis* only wants what is good and spiritual, all his petitions will be granted.[865] The gnostic also knows that God can be honoured just as well by acts of kindness between humans as by words: "...the master and saviour accepts as a favour and honour to Himself all that is done for the help and improvement of men..."[866] Among the Christians, not all have this *gnosis*, some are still merely "slaves" who are behaving virtuously out of fear for punishment. The gnostic has a big responsibility towards these Christians, because he has to educate them, treat them with kindness and pray for them. In fact, the gnostic has a responsibility towards everyone, also towards non-Christians, seeing that all were created by God.

Also Origen's treatise on prayer is filled with admonitions to behave well and be virtuous in order to be worthy to approach God in prayer. Origen writes outright that "the works of virtue and the keeping of the commandments have a part in prayer (καὶ τῶν ἔργων τῆς ἀρετῆς ἢ τῶν ἐντολῶν τῶν ἐπιτελουμένων εἰς εὐχῆς ἀναλαμβανομένων μέρος)."[867] In the opening of his treatise, he writes that prayer is about both words (οἱ λόγοι) and disposition

---

863 Id. 7.7.41 with a reference to 1 Tim 6:20.
864 Itter, 2009, 15.
865 Clem. Strom. 7.7.44 (Hort/Mayor).
866 Id. 7.3.21.
867 Or. or. 12.2 (Koetschau; tr. Stewart-Sykes).

(ἡ κατάστασις); thus pointing to the importance of a certain character, dominated by modesty, discretion and good works.[868] In *Perì Euchês* 8.1, Origen uses a comparison to underline the importance of virtue for prayer. He writes that in the same way as there will be no children if there are no women, there will be no benefit of praying if prayer is not accompanied by a virtuous disposition. Having a correct disposition is a matter of the soul[869] and of banishing the passion of anger from the soul.[870] Origen notes that if one by preparing oneself to pray acquires a soul pleasing to God, this might in itself be the greatest benefit of prayer.[871]

In order to obtain the necessary disposition to approach God, humans are dependent on the intermediary role of the Spirit who sees that humans are humbled and "enclosed in the body of ... humiliation."[872] The Spirit is presented as working together with those humans who are willing to approach God. Hence, a synergy between the human and the Spirit is presented; "for when we have done all that is in our power, God will make up whatever is lacking through our human weakness as he works together (συνεργῶν) with those who love him..."[873] According to Origen, a certain disposition and faith are necessary prior to prayer; and prayer should be avoided all together in case of confusion or anger – "without purity it is not possible."[874] Only if a person praying is genuinely turned to God and is in the process of gaining knowledge and virtue, through the Spirit, the prayers

---

868 Id. 2.2 and 19.1.
869 Id. 31.1.
870 Id. 9.1.
871 Id. 8.2.
872 Id. 2.3.
873 Id. 29.19. See also 30.1: "the cooperation (συνεργίᾳ) and presence of the encouraging and saving word of God in the time of misfortune..." Also Clement presupposes a cooperation between God and his creation, see e.g. Strom. 7.2.12 (Hort/Mayor): "[God] made all things to be helpful for virtue (συνεργὰ πρὸς ἀρετὴν)"; Id. 7.7.46: "he will pray too that he may never fall away from virtue, cooperating (συνεργῶν) to the best of his power that he may end his life without a fall"; Id. 7.7.48: "... God provides eternal salvation for those who cooperate (συνεργοῦσι) with him for knowledge and right action"; Id. 7.11.66: the devil can be the agent as well, with whom the ignorant operates "or rather cooperation (μᾶλλον δὲ συνέργειαν)."
874 Or. or. 8.1 (Koetschau; tr. Stewart-Sykes).

will be heard.[875] But in this state, accompanied by the Holy Spirit, prayers are able to work wonders, especially on the soul. Origen notes explicitly that even the sinner, "drought-striken through sin," receives "rain for the soul" through prayer.[876]

4.2.2.3 Preliminary conclusion: Prayer and virtue

All the Christian authors are idealistic in their presentation of the moral character that they expect from Christians. It is obvious that we are dealing with edifying texts that are trying to build up towards perfection. Sin takes up comparatively little space, in contrast to the emphasis on virtue. I see this as a pedagogical strategy – instead of taking up much room warning about sin and encouraging prayers for forgiveness (they are strongly encouraged), most space is used to encourage high ethical standards. The euchological treatises give us a glimpse of how Christians were expected to be disposed. The ideals were sky-high, fitting for people who belonged to a heavenly Kingdom. The discourses on prayer emphasized not only verbal prayer, but just as much the disposition that was fitting in relation with prayer. In this way, prayer pointed away from the ritual context in which it was embedded (whether private or public) and into everyday life. Prayer was thus expected to effect changes in the individual not only as outcome but also as precondition. This means that prayer might have had a social effect. Accordingly, Alan Kreider has noted that Christian worship was not designated to attract non-Christians, but worship might indirectly have had an appeal to outsiders "by shaping the lives and character of individual Christians and their communities so that they would be intriguing."[877] We shall return to the subject of prayer as catalyst for behavioural change in the following.

4.2.3 Prayer and brotherly relations: On kinship language in the euchological treatises

Words that have to do with kinship are "natural symbols,"[878] and they therefore potentially hold a power when they are uttered – a naturalizing

---

875 Id. 13.5; 25.2.
876 Id. 13.5.
877 Kreider quoted in Johnston, 2013, 22.
878 Douglas quoted in Buell, 1999, 3.

power.[879] In other words, concepts such as "father" and "brother" can affect people intuitively because they have a certain natural meaning. D.K. Buell deals with such "natural symbols" in early Christianity in her book *Making Christians*. In her book, Buell notes that: "Procreative and kinship metaphors function polemically in early Christian discourse of self-identity and self-authorization."[880] Buell propounds that the use of natural symbols like calling God Father and calling oneself a child of God is an effective method for creating a feeling of adherence to a certain group, and meanwhile such metaphors can also exclude others from belonging. It was, however, not only among the Christians that familial language was in use in the attempt to create metaphorical families. More likely, when Christians began to refer to each other as brothers, they were mirroring associations within the broader society that were already using these natural symbols from the family sphere.[881]

There is a high frequency of kinship language in the euchological discourses. The following paragraphs will illustrate how kinship language was presented in prayer discourse, and show how prayer was part of establishing new close relations.[882] One can get an immediate impression of the family terminology that one finds in these treatises by the following small collection of examples: As we have already seen prayers were to be directed to "Our Father," thus *Pater noster* or Πάτερ ἡμῶν are frequent in the treatises. Furthermore, the perfect prayer was ideally said, not alone, but together

---

879 Buell, 1999.

880 Id. 4.

881 Harland, 2009, 82.

882 P. A. Harland mentions in his book *Dynamics of Identity in the World of Early Christians* that it was quite frequent in antiquity to express belonging by the use of familial language within associations and organizations of various kinds. Such metaphors cannot be disregarded as less demanding than the Christian metaphors; when family language was used in associations, it was used with serious intent and with an expectation that the intimate language would be followed up with due behaviour. Plutarch, for instance, shows his expectations about correspondence between the word "brother" and behaviour when he asks: "what man is he who in his familiar greetings and salutations, or in his letters, will call his friend and companion brother, and cannot find in his heart so much as to go with his brother in the same way?" (Plut. De frat. amor. 479D; Harland, 2009, 74).

"*with* the brothers," "*for* the brothers," and "*in* brotherly agreement."
Therefore, words from the root *frater* or "ἀδελφοὶ" are numerous, e.g.
fraterna concordia.[883] Moreover, the ideal prayer was to be said near the
"mother," *mater*, that is the Church,[884] where the one praying was said to
be wrapped in "ancestral immortality," that is τὴν πατρικὴν ἀθανασίαν.[885]
As new-born children of God, the first thing Christians had to do after baptism was to address the Father in a "friendly and familiar prayer" (*amica et
familiaris oratio*).[886] And when praying in such a manner, Christians were
rightfully a part of the "kinfolk in devotion," γνησιώτατοι ἐν θεοσεβείᾳ
ἀδελφοὶ .[887]

What it precisely entails to be a child of God and a brother to other
Christians are not elaborately described in the Christian treatises on prayer.
Nothing in the euchological treatises indicates that the Christians have a
different understanding of what family relations entail than the surrounding
Roman society. Thus, becoming a child of God meant being incorporated
into the metaphorical family of Christians and from then on owing to the
other Christians, what previously had been owed only to the next of kin.
Within an antique context, being someone's child came with great demands
of conduct and loyalty, expressed poignantly in for instance Cicero's admonition "piety towards parents," *Pietas erga parentes.*[888] The power of the
kinship language is its intuitive meaning and its inherent obligations.[889]

---

883 Cypr. Dom. orat. 23 (Réveillaud; tr. Stewart-Sykes).
884 Tert. Or. 2 (Schleyer; tr. Stewart-Sykes).
885 Or. or. 25.3 (Koetschau; tr. Stewart-Sykes).
886 Cypr. Dom. orat. 3 (Réveillaud; tr. Stewart-Sykes).
887 Or. or. 34.1 (Koetschau; tr. Stewart-Sykes).
888 See Cic. inv. II.22.66: "*pietatem, quae erga patriam aut parentes aut alios san-
    guine coniunctos officum conservare moneat,*" in G. Emilie, *Cicero and the
    Roman Pietas*, in: CJ 39/9 (1944), 540.
889 With a high probability, where members of a group refer to each other by use
    of kinship language, there is a strong degree of belonging and homogeneity in
    place. This, however, might also be experienced as a provocation for some –
    indeed within a modern, individualistic context. In an article on the symbolic
    interpretive perspective, "family metaphors" are mentioned as examples of
    language that can create homogeneity, but also provoke people to distance
    themselves from one another, see L.R. Frey/Sunwolf, *The Symbolic-Interpretive
    Perspective on Group Dynamics*, in: Small Group Research 35 (2004), 290.

In the euchological treatises, we can observe how third-century Christian communities used familial language to present themselves: They affirmed that they were "God's children" and "brothers."[890] In *Stromateis* 7, Clement does not use kinship-metaphors as bluntly as the other three authors under investigation. He focuses on the unity of the Church by presenting Christians as a cooperation in which people are responsible for one another.[891] However, also Clement characterizes Christians as brothers when they have developed a similar disposition: "And brethren indeed they are according to the elect creation and the similarity of disposition and the character of their actions..."[892] Actually, according to Clement, the perfect Christian prays for his fellow-Christians as if they were his kinsfolk and wishes to take on their sins. He does this:

> "with a view to the repentance and conversion of his kinsfolk (τῶν συγγενῶν), and eager to impart his own good things to those whom he holds dearest (αὐτῷ οἱ φίλοι)."[893]

As we saw in Chapter 3, Clement also describes the gnostic as a son of God, so he does make use of kinship language to propound the special status of Christians. A concrete and telling example of how the other three authors use familial language to affirm their own "identity" as relatives of God can be found in Cyprian's treatise on prayer, when he says: "Anybody who is renewed, reborn and restored to God by grace, first of all say, 'Father,' because *he is now a son (quia filius esse iam coepit)*."[894]

Furthermore, all the authors mention how God has regenerated and recreated Christians. Such recreation-metaphors point in the same direction as the kinship metaphors, namely to the understanding of Christians as a family and unity, descending from the same source. Clement for instance writes that God "regenerates and re-creates and nourishes the

---

890 Examples are: Tert. Or. 2 (Schleyer; tr. Stewart-Sykes), cf. John 1:12; Or. or. 22.3 (Koetschau; tr. Stewart-Sykes); Cypr. Dom. orat. 9 (Réveillaud; tr. Stewart-Sykes).
891 Clem. Strom. 7.17.107 (Hort/Mayor).
892 Id. 7.12.77.
893 Clem. Strom. 7.12.80 (Hort/Mayor).
894 Cypr. Dom. orat. 9 (Réveillaud; tr. Stewart-Sykes).

elect soul (τὸν ἀναγεννῶντα καὶ ἀνακτίζοντα καὶ τιθηνούμενον τὴν ψυχὴν τὴν ἐξειλεγμένην)."[895] And also Cyprian uses the recreation-metaphor:

> "Through the mercy of God we have been spiritually remade and so, when we are reborn, let us imitate what we are destined to become (*Per Dei indulgentiam recreate spiritaliter et renati imitemur quod future sumus*)."[896]

Being a child of God is a privilege that the individual Christian is granted not only because of his/her faith – which is one prerequisite, but also because of the sacramental incorporation into the community of Christians. Although the father–child relationship is a private matter, it is therefore also very explicitly a congregational matter, because the sacraments are where the individual is "reborn" as a Christian with God as Father. But what do these metaphorical family ties have to do with prayer? A great deal according to the treatises on prayer, because it is as God's children that the Christians have the right to ask anything from God. Both the awareness of and the fulfilling of the obligations of brotherhood are a presupposition for approaching God in prayer.

In the treatises, we also encounter instances where the familial language is used to enhance the spiritual family to the detriment of the biological one, or at least to prioritize the spiritual family over the biological one. In these cases, the authors draw on material from the New Testament where the followers of Jesus are admonished to break with their families. In the treatises, the authors refer to Jesus' own words and admonish Christians to "call nobody 'Father' on earth,"[897] to remove themselves from their "original birth and begin to be heavenly, now that they have been born of water and the Spirit,"[898] and Clement furthermore notes that "he that loveth father and mother more than Me... is not worthy of Me, worthy, that is to be a son of God and at once to be a disciple and friend and kin to God (υἱὸς θεοῦ καὶ μαθητὴς θεοῦ ὁμοῦ καὶ φίλος καὶ συγγενής)."[899]

---

895 Clem. Strom. 7.16.93 (Hort/Mayor).
896 Cypr. Dom. orat. 36 (Réveillaud; tr. Stewart-Sykes).
897 Tert. Or. 2 (Schleyer; tr. Stewart-Sykes); Cypr. Dom. orat. 9 (Réveillaud; tr. Stewart-Sykes).
898 John 3:5; Cypr. Dom. orat. 17 (Réveillaud; tr. Stewart-Sykes).
899 Clem. Strom. 7.16.93 (Hort/Mayor).

There is, however, ambivalence in the understanding of the biological family, and, for instance, Origen does not categorize the biological family negatively. Instead, he seems to think that a Christian has both a biological and a metaphorical family. He mentions two kinds of family: "those who are regenerate with us in Christ" and "those who share the same father and mother with us."[900] This passage in Origen's text shows that Origen was not only interested in the relations between Christians, but also between Christians and non-Christians. This is actually a theme that all authors touch upon, since they admonish Christians to pray for all people.[901] When commenting on whom one ought to pray for, Clement thus stresses that Christians must pray for both their enemies and for their brothers – "not only to those who are brethren by faith, but to those also who are newcomers (προσηλύτους) among you."[902] Thereby, Clement broadens the brother-category. He notes that not all are brothers, but should nonetheless be treated as if they were – that is, also the uninitiated catechumens are to be treated with brotherly love before they are baptized.[903] Clement stretched the categories even further, when he suggests that all people in a way belong together, because they are all created. All people are, after all, the creation of one God, and therefore they are clothed (περιβεβλημένους) in one likeness (μίαν εἰκόνα) and one nature (μίαν οὐσίαν) – although, as Clement formulates it, "in some the likeness may be more confused than in others."[904]

4.2.3.1 "Behavioural output" of kinship language and prayer

Thus far, I have tried to show how metaphorical kinship language was used in prayer discourse, and how it functioned as an important component in the integration of people into the Christian world. Now, I will mention the "behavioural outputs" of metaphorical kinship language that are presented in the prayer discourse. With "behavioural outputs" I refer to the actions that ideally were to follow prayer.

---

900 Or. or. 28.2. Cf. Clem. strom. 7.12.69 (Hort/Mayor).
901 Cf. below, paragraph 4.3.3.
902 Clem. Strom. 7.14.85 (Hort/Mayor). Mayor translates προσηλύτους with strangers.
903 Id. 7.14.86.
904 Id. (loosely translated from κἂν τεθολωμένοι τύχωσιν ἄλλοι ἄλλων μᾶλλον).

"Behavioural output" is a word derived from "symbolic interactionism," where it is a theoretical insight that how you act depends on who you think you are. This correspondence between self-definition and behaviour is also reflected in the treatises on prayer, where Christians were told that they were children of God, and were then admonished to live accordingly. This is, for instance, evident when Cyprian writes: "Whoever therefore believes in his name [i.e. the name of the Son] *is made a child of God*, and hence should begin to give thanks and *show himself a child of God* (*profiteatur se Dei filium*) as he names his Father as God in heaven (*dum nominat patrem sibi esse in caelis Deum*)..."[905]

Obviously, from the source material, it is not possible to conclude whether or not the third-century Christians succeeded in living in brotherly agreement, but this does not change the fact that there is a potential correspondence between family metaphors and affectionate behaviour; and Christianity did obviously succeed in integrating new members into the Christian congregations. When thinking prayer into this equation, it is reasonable to argue that prayer was actually understood as an act that helped realize the behaviour implied in kinship metaphors. An important point to recapitulate here is that, in a third-century Christian context, prayer was not only understood as a matter of words, prayer was also understood as an incitement to action and thus as a means of change. Origen, Tertullian and Cyprian all agreed with the New Testament admonition that: "If you are offering your gift [that is prayer] at the altar, and there recall that your brother has something against you, leave the gift there before the altar and go straight away to be reconciled with your brother..."[906] Origen specifies:"... [it is not possible] to obtain anything in prayer unless one has forgiven from the heart one's brother..."[907] The three authors thus share the thought that prayer is ineffective when the praying person is not in agreement with his/her Christian brothers; disagreement equals sin. Also Clement shares this idea and expresses the expectation that for the gnostic

---

905 Cypr. Dom. orat. 9 (Réveillaud; tr. Stewart-Sykes).
906 Reference to Matt 5:25-24 in Or. or. 2.2 (Koetschau; tr. Stewart-Sykes).
907 Or. or. 8.1 (Koetschau; tr. Stewart-Sykes).

Christian "all his life is prayer and communion with God, and if he is free from sins he will assuredly receive what he desires."[908]

A certain ethos and behaviour is thus expected from the praying children of God. The same is the case in Greek philosophical prayer discourse. Praying is not only seen as the utterance of *a* prayer, but is envisioned as a process in which the praying person tends to his/her social relations. This understanding of prayer is taken to an extreme by Origen who at one point presents correct behaviour as prayer *per se*. He says that whenever we act properly towards other people – as if they were our brothers, then we indirectly address God as "Our Father," and: ."... may our entire life pray unceasingly by saying 'our Father' (ὁ βίος ἀδιαλείπτως προσευχομένων λεγέτω τό· πάτερ ἡμῶν)."[909] According to Origen, it therefore makes sense that one benefit of prayer is the forgiving attitude that is presupposed when praying. He writes that: "it is plain that those who stand to pray in this state [i.e. the state of having forgiven one's enemies] have already received the best there is (τὰ κάλλιστα ἤδη κεκτήμεθα)."[910] We can also recall Origen's theatre-metaphor, explored in Chapter 3, which was employed by Origen to warn against dissimilarity between the inner and the outer world of the Christians – their intentions and behaviour should coincide. This should also be the case with prayer; prayer should represent the inner world and intent of the individual.

Prayer thus presupposed relations of a familial character within the Christian community, and thereby prayer ideally gave rise to ethical considerations and affectionate behaviour. However, prayer was also in itself a sign of affection. In Tertullian's treatise, there are examples of this. For instance, Tertullian admonishes his audience that whenever a visitor has stopped by, you have to pray with him before he leaves, because: "Have you seen a brother, you have seen the Lord."[911] In other words, one has to treat and treasure the "brother" as one would have treated and treasured the Lord himself. Apparently one way of showing hospitality and kindness is to pray with someone. Furthermore, Tertullian calls the "kiss of peace

---

908 Clem. Strom. 7.12.73 (Hort/Mayor).
909 Or. or. 22.5 (Koetschau; tr. Stewart-Sykes).
910 Id. 9.3.
911 Tert. Or. 26,1 ff. (Schleyer; tr. Stewart-Sykes).

(*osculum pacis*)" which was a part of the Christian service as the "seal of prayer (*signaculum orationis*)"; thus, he draws a parallel between the physical sign of affection, which is the kiss, and the spiritual sign of affection which prayer apparently was.[912]

4.2.4 Detectable consequences of prayer discourse?

From the treatises on prayer, the following logic of prayer can be reconstructed: When being a part of a Christian community, each Christian is a child of God, and as a child of God, the individual is expected to behave and pray in a certain way. The certain mode of prayer, which is expected from a Christian, is that prayer is always uttered in awareness of the duties owed to the metaphorical family. Prayer is thus more than sheer petition and thanksgiving; it is also the act of moving oneself into and preserving oneself in an appropriate relation with "Our Father" and "our brothers." Prayer is thus presented by the early Christian authors as also having a social orientation. Therefore, their discourse is an argument for the hypothesis of this dissertation: prayer was an activity that helped establish social relations. Since certain relations were presupposed in prayer, prayer was also a catalyst for establishing such relations. And wherever there are social relations, there is, according to "symbolic interactionism," identity formation going on, because wherever there are social relations, interaction occurs, and self-understanding is influenced. We cannot know to which extent the "behavioural output" actually followed the metaphors that are put forward in the prayer discourses, but I argue that we can expect that conversion to Christianity included some degree of change in behaviour and attitude. Furthermore, conversion to Christianity led to the establishment of new relations, primarily to fellow-Christians.

Ilka Ißermann argues in her article "Did Christian Ethics have any Influence on the Conversion to Christianity?," that the "Christian transformation" was more than a literary motive.[913] In her article, Ißermann

---

912 Id. 18. On the function of the kiss in the establishment of Christian relations, see Penn, 2002.

913 I. Ißermann, *Did Christian Ethics have any Influence on the Conversion to Christianity?*, ZAC 16/1 (2012), 99–112. The assumption that the philanthropy of the Christians were more than mere rhetoric is expressed also by other scholars: Already E. Gibbon gives as the fourth cause of the appeal of

deals with conversion stories, and she mentions stories from antiquity about people that changed for the better when becoming Christians: "previously erratic and worthless, evil people are suddenly delivered from their mistakes after their conversions. The converted wife is diligent and modest all at once, and the son honours his father from now on."[914] Ißermann goes on by saying that: "There were similar 'moral' conversion stories among philosophers, and they had a proselytizing function as well. But even if this argument was a literary motif, it could only be useful to Christian argumentation if it was plausible to non-believers."[915] In other words, these stories about the positive social effects of Christianity and philosophy could not have flourished as apologetic texts, had they not contained some grain of truth. Therefore, one can expect that the literature reflects some kind of reality. The same argument could (to some degree) be used in relation with edifying Christian texts such as the euchological treatises. E.R. Dodds agrees with this point and has written that:

> "A Christian congregation was from the first a community in a much fuller sense than any corresponding group of Isiac or Mithraist devotees. Its members were bound together *not only by common rites but by a common way of life*... Love of one's neighbour is not an exclusively Christian virtue, but in [this] period Christians appear to have practiced it much more effectively than any other group... But even more important, I suspect, than these material benefits were the sense of belonging which the Christian community could give."[916]

Here Dodds notes that both common rites and a common way of life distinguished the Christians from the rest of society. I argue that the two, ritual – including prayer – and life, are not independent of one another, but rather that ritual and everyday life have a mutual effect on one another.

Christianity "the virtues of the first Christians" (E. Gibbon, *The History of the Decline and Fall of the Roman Empire, vol. 2*, London 1787, 250). Also Rodney Stark finds that *the ultimate factor* in the rise of Christianity must have been that "Central doctrines of Christianity prompted and sustained attractive, liberating, and effective social relations and organizations." (R. Stark, *The Rise of Christianity. A Sociologist Reconsiders History*, Princeton 1996, 211). See also Fox, 1988.

914 Ißermann, 2012, 103.
915 Id.
916 E.R. Dodds, *Pagan and Christian in an Age of Anxiety*, New York 1970, 136 f. Emphasis added.

This was expressed in Dirkie Smit's rephrasing of the ancient saying *lex orandi, lex credendi, lex convivendi.*[917] Also Maria-Barbara von Stritzky has directed the attention towards the Christian combination of prayer and life and has noted that this was a new thing in comparison with the rest of society: "Gerade hinsichtlich der Forderung nach der Übereinstimmung von Gebet und Tat als Kennzeichen christlichen Lebens... betreten die in ihrem Umfeld weitgehen Neuland."[918]

In other words, the conversion to Christianity and life as a Christian meant transformation for the individual on a practical/behavioural level. We cannot know, if these practical consequences of Christian life to the majority of Christians were among the most appealing elements of the conversion, but from the treatises on prayer we can see that prayer, and thus relations to God, ideally influenced life and relations to other people. Prayer was as such a catalyst for reflections on one's standing among the fellow-Christians.

4.2.5 Preliminary conclusions on prayer and behaviour

In conclusion, we can observe that in the prayer discourse, the positive self-definition of the Christian authors is described by employing metaphorical family language. For Christians, these family boundaries were important because the efficacy of prayer depended on the prayer being uttered within the metaphorical Christian family.

The Christian "brothers" are immensely important for the effect of prayer for two reasons: one reason is that there must exist peace and harmony between Christians before they pray; otherwise, prayer is rendered invalid. Thus, a certain ethical behaviour is presupposed in order for prayer to be relevant. This can be seen in the way that family metaphors, prayer and behaviour are treated together in the treatises. This treatment resembles the philosophical discourse on prayer because both among Stoic and Middle Platonic philosophers and also among Christian thinkers, ethical behaviour and virtue were believed to be the presupposition for any contact with the divine. According to the philosophers, however, not everyone had the ability

---

917 Smit, 2011, 256.
918 Stritzky, 2009, 230.

to come into contact with God. For Christians, on the other hand, this was something that everyone could and should strive for.

The other reason why the Christian "family" is essential for prayer is that all authors see a special benefit in collective prayer, i.e. prayers uttered with one's brothers. We shall now take a look at the idea of collective prayer.

4.3 Praying with and for others

4.3.1 Admonitions to pray together in the congregation

In the foregoing sections, we investigated the content of the euchological treatises with regard to virtue, behaviour and metaphorical family relations. These themes were all seen by the authors as important and as having a direct impact on prayer. However, the treatises also deal with how prayers could be social in other ways – namely, when prayers were common prayers and intercessory prayers. We will now take a look at these overt social dimensions of prayer. In the following couple of paragraphs, we shall look at how the treatises encourage collective prayer, which role prayer had in relation to the clergy and the sacraments, and finally how the early Christians were admonished concerning intercession.

As previously shown, all of the four authors stress the rightfulness and benefit of secret prayer and prayer understood as an inner and (more or less) constant conversation with God. At the same time, the authors also find that common prayer is of great importance and should be performed regularly. One of the most striking recommendations for common prayer is to be found in Cyprian's treatise, when he writes:

> "Before all else, the teacher of peace and master of unity desires that we should not make our prayer individually and alone, as whoever prays by himself prays only for himself. We do not say: "My Father who are in the heavens," ... Our prayer is common and collective (*publica est nobis et communis oratione*), and when we pray we pray not for one but for all people, because we are all one people together."[919]

In this context, Cyprian also mentions the three youths in the fiery furnace from the *Book of Daniel* who had their prayers heard, because they prayed "together in harmony of prayer and agreement of spirit (*consonantes in*

---

919 Cypr. Dom. orat. 8 (Réveillaud; tr. Stewart-Sykes).

prece, et spiritus consensione concordes."[920] And furthermore, Cyprian notes three times in a row that prayers said by people "of one mind" (*unanimus*) are particularly pleasing to God. With these exhortations and examples, Cyprian leaves no doubt that unity is particularly beneficial in relation to prayers.

Tertullian recommends responsory prayer, which is collective prayer with one person leading the prayer and the rest answering with a response such as "hallelujah" or the like.[921] According to Tertullian, such responsory prayer is an excellent practice, and something that is obviously part of communal prayer.

Origen is equally certain concerning the benefits of collective prayer; and he even imagines that when Christians pray together, they are not only praying with each other, but also with Christ, with already deceased Christians and with angels. He thus envisions a cosmic gathering that is called forth by Christians praying in a group – a gathering that makes the prayer as efficient as possible. Origen writes:

> "A place of prayer that has a particular blessing and benefit (ἔχει δέ τι ἐπίχαρι εἰς ὠφέλειαν τόπος εὐχῆς) is the place where believers gather (τῶν πιστευόντων σ υνελεύσεως). It seems probable that angelic powers (ἀγγελικῶν δυνάμεων) are in attendance at the assemblies of the faithful, as well as the power of the Lord and Saviour himself (αὐτοῦ τοῦ κυρίου καὶ σωτῆρος ἡμῶν δυνάμεως), and indeed holy spirits (πνευμάτων ἁγίων) – I think of those who have gone to their rest before us (οἶμαι δὲ ὅτι καὶ προκεκοιμημένων). It is clear that they are around us who continue in life, even if it is difficult to say precisely how."[922]

Note, how Origen in a few lines places the Christian in a *synaxis*, where prayer relates the individual Christian to "angels," "the assembly of the faithful," "the Lord and Savior" and "holy spirits." This kind of *synaxis*

---

920 Id.
921 Tert. Or. 27 (Schleyer; tr. Stewart-Sykes).
922 Or. or. 31.5 (Koetschau; tr. Stewart-Sykes). The way in which Origen presents also the deceased as intercessors in prayer recalls his ideas of the "heavenly priesthood." (Bright in McGuckin, 2004, 180).
    In the early church order Apostolic Tradition 41, another reason for collective prayer is given, namely that the Spirit is present where Christians pray collectively: "For having prayed in the assembly, they will be able to avoid all the evils of the day... Therefore, let each one be certain to go to the assembly, to the place where the Holy Spirit flourishes."

is known from other prayer texts, e.g. the potentially very old: *Anaphora of Addai and Mari*, which B.D. Spinks comments upon with these words: "behind the words of the prayer there seems to be a vision of a cosmic act of praise and thanksgiving in which all creation shares – angels, mankind and those who have died."[923] Below we shall return to the role of supernatural prayer-companions, while here we shall take it *ad notam* that the efficacy of prayer was assumed to grow where believers are assembled and pray together. One can also speculate whether the praying Christians understood themselves as bound together "not just as a community, but as a body made up of geographically dispersed communities."[924] Indeed in collective prayer, ordinary boundaries of time and space were broken down to the benefit of the participants. Praying Christians found themselves sharing a spiritual character with saints in the past and present.

Also Clement, who believes in individual religious progression, is nevertheless interested in the community of Christians and their prayers. Clement notes that it is dangerous to pray with evil men, but recommendable to pray with good – although ordinary – Christians:

> "he who holds intercourse with God (τὸν προσομιλοῦντα τῷ θεῷ) must have his soul (τὴν ψυχὴν) undefiled and absolutely pure... more-over it is fitting that he should offer all his prayers in a good spirit and in concert with good men (τὰς εὐχὰς ἁπάσας ἐπιεικῶς ἅμα)... The gnostic will therefore share his prayers of ordinary believers (συνεύξεται τοῖς κοινότερον πεπιστευκόσι) in those cases in which it is right for him to share their activity also."[925]

In *Stromateis* 7, there are several instances of the word liturgy, λειτουργία – one of its meanings at this time was "ritual," and Clement uses the word to describe the Christian rituals. The rituals of the church serve a purpose on the way towards salvation. One can reach salvation because of Christ, "by public worship (κατά ... τὴν λειτουργίαν) and by teaching and active kindness."[926] Clement thus points to "public worship" as a step towards salvation, and I defer from the context that prayer was part of this λειτουργία.

923 Spinks is quoted in M.L. Munkholt Christensen, *En syrisk kilde til den ældste kritstne nadverforståelse*, in: DTT 73 (2010), 115.
924 This approach is emphasized by O'Loughlin, 2003, 103.
925 Clem. Strom. 7.7.49 (Hort/Mayor).
926 Id. 7.3.13. Also 7.10.56.

Communal worship is thus important, and those standing outside of the congregation cannot reach salvation. Praying with a congregation is a token that one is an insider and on the right path towards salvation. In the treatises from the second and third century investigated here, it would seem that the important boundary is the one between the congregation and the outsiders, and between the saints and the sinners. In Tertullian's *De praescriptione haereticorum* 41, Tertullian writes about a certain group of heretics that they pose a danger because they fail to distinguish between, e.g. heathens and Christians: "To begin with, it is doubtful who is a catechumen, and who a believer; they have all access alike, they hear alike, they pray alike— even heathens, if any such happen to come among them." Tertullian thereby points to the danger of mixing categories that ought to be kept apart – also in prayer. In *Didascalia Apostolorum*, prayer is prohibited with those who have been excommunicated,[927] and the *Apostolic Constitutions* demands penitents to pray separately from the rest of the church.[928] Prayer has thus been used as boundary marker in different contexts.

With such prohibitions and encouragements, the authors make it clear that prayer has a great benefit when said together with other Christians. Cyprian explains that this is the will of God, who is the father of all and therefore wants his people to pray united. He writes that: "Our prayer is common and collective, and when we pray we pray not for one, but for all people, because we are all one people together."[929] A further rationale for common prayer is that the form of prayer then matches the ideal content of prayer – the content of prayer should always be concerned with the common good – which is why the fourth petition of the Lord's Prayer is not: "Give *me* today *my* daily bread," but "Give *us* today *our* daily bread."[930] This is Cyprian's reasoning, and it seems that he is the author who is most explicit in relation to the necessity of common prayer. This might have to do with his function as bishop and thus his responsibility to keep the church united. In general, the encouragements for common prayer show the strong

---

927 Didasc. 15.
928 Const.ap. 8.8-9. For more examples of separation in relation with prayer, see Phillips, 2008, 53-55.
929 Cypr. Dom. orat. 8 (Réveillaud; tr. Stewart-Sykes).
930 Id. Emphasis added.

ecclesiastical and ecclesiological interest of the authors: they all had an interest in forming and maintaining their particular Christian community in a time of distress and persecution. Therefore, it is only natural that the third-century authors call for collective prayer in order to strengthen their congregations and to create an idea of coherence and union. The fact that Cyprian and Origen make the most explicit encouragement to pray together probably have to do with their particular circumstances and audience, but probably also with their eschatological perspectives which are oriented towards the collective. Cyprian ends his treatise on prayer with mentioning that in the Kingdom "we shall pray constantly and give thanks to God."[931] He uses this eschatological perspective to encourage Christians to keep nocturnal vigil and continue to pray. In contrast to this collective scenario of the eschatological situation, Clement presents salvation as "eternal contemplation of God," which although taking place in a "spiritual church" seems as a more individual endeavour.[932]

4.3.2 Formalized elements: Liturgical prayer, sacraments and clergy

There is not much direct information in the treatises on the role of prayer in the liturgy of the sacraments, nor is there much information on the clergy's role in offering prayers. There are, however, indirect references to liturgical and clerical acts of prayer. For instance, in *De Oratione* 19, Tertullian takes up a problem within his congregation, namely that some people do not take part in the Eucharist on station days, i.e. days of fasting, because they see it as breaking the fasting required on those days; "A number think that they should not participate in the prayers of the sacrifices (*non putant plerique sacrificiorum orationibus intervenendum*), because the station would be breached by receiving the body of the Lord."[933] Tertullian warns against this practice of avoiding Eucharist, since it is the duty of the Christians to take part in the Eucharistic prayers which he refers to as "the sacrifice." The way in which Tertullian writes about the "prayers of the sacrifices" indicates that he understands the prayers themselves as a vital part of the

---

931 Cypr. Dom. orat. 36 (Réveillaud; tr. Stewart-Sykes).
932 Clem. Strom. 7.11.68 (Hort/Mayor).
933 Tert. Or. 19 (Schleyer; tr. Stewart-Sykes).

Eucharistic celebration. He might have understood the prayers as sacrifices in their own right – "the spiritual oblation that has wiped out the ancient sacrifices," as Tertullian frames it elsewhere in the treatise.[934] Cyprian has a similar passage in which he indirectly admonishes Christians to take part in the Eucharist. He writes:

> "when, together with our brothers (*in unum cum fratribus*), we gather to celebrate the divine sacrifices (*sacrificial diuina*) with the priest of God (*cum Dei sacerdote*), we should be mindful of reverence and order, not forever tossing ill-judged phrases into the air, nor seeking to commend our requests by bombarding God with a tumultuous verbosity..."[935]

Cyprian here deals with the Eucharistic prayers that are supposed to be said with a disposition of reverence and order. *En passant* Cyprian also mentions a priest being present, but here he does not specify the role of the priest in the Eucharistic. It almost seems as if more people than a single priest are allowed to pray during the Eucharist if they do it with "reverence and order."[936] Elsewhere in *De Dominica Oratione*, it would seem that the liturgical prayers were responsive prayers like those recommended by Tertullian. In Chapter 31, Cyprian writes that "the priest prepares the minds of the brothers by uttering a preface as he says: 'Hearts on high!' (*sursum corda*) The people reply: 'We have them on the Lord (*habemus ad Dominum*).' "[937] Interestingly enough, these words correspond to the

---

934 Id. 28. See also: Young 1975, 61-63, c.f. above 3.2.2.3: "Prayer as spiritual sacrifice."

935 Cypr. Dom. orat. 4 (Réveillaud; tr. Stewart-Sykes).

936 This would fit with the content of the *Apostolic Tradition* 9 (tr. Dix/ Chadwick): "And the bishop shall give thanks according to the aforesaid <models>. It is not altogether necessary for him to recite the very same words which we gave before as though studying to say them by heart in his thanksgiving to God; but let each one pray according to his own ability. If indeed he is able to pray suitably with a grand and elevated prayer, this is a good thing. But if on the other hand he should pray and recite a prayer according to a brief form, no one shall prevemt him. Only let his prayer be correct and right [in doctrine] (ὀρθόδοξος)." And 10: "But ordination is for the clergy on account of their ministry. But the widow is appointed for prayer, and this is a function of all Christians."

937 Cypr. Dom. orat. 31 (Réveillaud; tr. Stewart-Sykes).

praefatio in later Eucharistic liturgy, and this particular formulation thus has a long history in Christian worship.[938]

Clement does not mention the clergy in *Stromateis* 7, but he presents the gnostic Christian as having an elevated position. The gnostic, who takes upon himself to teach others, becomes a mediator between God and humans: "he becomes a mediator (δι' ἧς) to bring about a close union and fellowship with God."[939] Clement also refers to the "exalted office of a teacher,"[940] whereby he could refer to a more or less official teaching position. This gnostic teacher is said by Clement to bring people to faith, "the disciples whom he has himself begotten in faith," and in *Stromateis* 7, this job is lauded more than the job of clergy. But whether this teaching position might have been clerical is difficult to judge. Later Origen could define priests as the "few, extremely rare, souls who devote themselves to knowledge and wisdom. These light up the path for the more simple brethren."[941] As such Origen's priest and Clement's gnostic teacher share the position of being a role model. Pamela Bright notes that Origen clearly saw himself as a "priest" in terms of his office as teacher and exegete. It is the spiritual capacity that validates the real Christian priesthood.[942] Origen can also be found to say that there are different kinds of priesthood, and Christians are a "priestly people."[943]

---

938 Cf. the Anaphora rendered in *The Apostolic Tradition*, Chapter 4 (Botte): "*Su<r>sum corda.*" Also the liturgy of the Eucharist in the Church of Denmark includes: "Opløft jeres hjerter til Herren." (Højmesseordningen à 1992, *Ritualbog*. København 1992).
     See K. Demura, '*Sursum Cor' in the Sermons of St. Augustine*, in: B. Neil/G.D. Dunn/L. Cross (eds.), *Prayer and Spirituality in the Early Church. Liturgy and Life* 3, Sydney 2003, 75-82: "'Sursum Cor' in the Sermons of St. Augustine." Demura notes how Augustine uses "sursum cor(da)" so it refers to ethical life and self-understanding. Lifting one's heart to God means having a certain attitude and behaviour. The liturgical formulations thus corresponded with the discourses on prayer.
939 Clem. Strom. 7.9.52 (Hort/Mayor).
940 Id. 7.9.53.
941 Or. hom. in Jos. 17.2, quoted by Bright in McGuckin, 2004, 181.
942 Bright in McGuckin, 2004, 181.
943 Pamela Bright points out that this idea of a people of priests that pray developed into the Syrio-Byzantine tradition of Christian mysticism (Bright in McGuckin, 1994, 180).

Origen is rather quiet about the role of liturgy and clergy in relation to prayer in *Perì Euchês*. This might be because Origen's piety in general is more scriptural than sacramental. In other words, Origen is more interested in the inner, spiritual meaning of Christianity which is hidden in the Scripture than in institutional traits such as rituals. Nevertheless, Origen does speak negatively about those, probably gnostics, who have done away with baptism and Eucharist.[944] Furthermore, Origen notes that Christians owe particular debts to widows, deacons, presbyters and the bishop. It would thus seem that the church of his time was in charge of some redistribution of goods, and that the clergy was on the pay roll. Soon after making this statement, Origen notes that none other than the right clergy can forgive the so-called sins "which lead to death."[945] This means that Origen does not recognize "those who have taken to themselves authority beyond the priestly dignity..."[946] Moreover in other writings, Origen expresses a great faith in the sacraments and the liturgical prayers. To give an example, Origen in *Contra Celsum* writes that "this bread becomes by prayer a sacred body,"[947] thus ascribing a sacramental effect to prayer. Thereby, Origen also shows that an epiclesis must have taken place during the Eucharist, a prayer for the coming of Christ to transform bread and wine.[948]

The sacraments also function as a prerequisite for prayer in the sense that baptism and Eucharist are parts of the process through which the Christians must go in order to become pure and ready to communicate with God. Clement thus presents "purification and ritual" as part of the positive process that ends with everlasting contemplation of God.[949] The everlasting contemplation of God is eternal salvation, according to Clement, and in this world people can only begin to pray to and contemplate God – that is, *after* "purification and ritual" which are necessary elements on the way. Likewise, Tertullian makes it clear that baptism purify humans so

---

944 Or. or. 5.1 (Koetschau; tr. Stewart-Sykes).
945 Id. 28.10.
946 Id. In this statement, we see the struggle about church authority reflected. We know especially from the writings of Cyprian that there were struggles going on about the authority to forgive sins.
947 Or. Cels. 8.33 (Borret; tr. Crombie).
948 Johnson, 2013, 40 ff.
949 Clem. Strom. 7.10.56 (Hort/Mayor). The same point is expressed in 7.10.57.

that they can stand before God and pray. Therefore Christians do not need further purification rituals after baptism: "the hands that, along with the whole body, have been washed in Christ once for all, are clean enough."[950] Also Cyprian sees the connection between prayer and baptism and writes that: "We ask and beseech that we who are made holy in baptism should have the ability to persist in the way we have begun."[951] In general, as other studies have shown, prayer – especially the Lord's Prayer – and baptism were presented as closely connected in early Christianity.[952] This fits the observation made above that the Lord's Prayer and prayers addressed to "God the Father through Christ" functioned as "marks of identity" for Christians.

4.3.2.1 Hierarchizing prayers

It seems that the authors were more interested in urging "constant prayer" than specific liturgical prayers – although both modes of piety were strongly recommended. It seems that it was expected from Christians that they took part in communal worship and collective prayers in the Eucharist. It also seems to be presupposed that Christians understood that it was by way of baptism that they had any right to approach God in the first place. Furthermore, the authors seem to have been more interested in placing Christians in a direct relationship with God, via Christ, than to present the clergy as intermediates (cf. Chapter 3). Great spiritual authority is placed in the congregation and with its members. Christians are occasionally referred to as priests,[953] and the prayers most pleasing to God are those said by a united congregation.[954] Therefore, if there are earthly intermediaries, it is rather the church as cooperation than any specific person. Thus, the

---

950 Tert. Or. 13. Contrary *Apostolic Tradition* 41 (Botte) admonishes Christians to wash their hands when getting up to pray. It was a well-established Jewish practice, Clement of Alexandria also testifies to it (Philips, 2008, 51).

951 Cypr. Dom. orat. 12 (Réveillaud; tr. Stewart-Sykes).

952 Sandnes traces instances where the Lord's Prayer is used as a "first prayer" after baptism. He points to Tert. Bapt. 21.5; *Apostolic Tradition* 21,25; Just. apol. 1.61-66: Did. 7-8. There might also be traces in the New Testament, but these examples are more speculative (Hvalvik/Sandnes, 2014, 209-232).

953 Tert. Or. 28 (Schleyer; tr. Stewart-Sykes). Except from in Cyprian's treatise.

954 Cf. above, especially Cyprian's point.

bishops had not yet completely assumed the role of "worldly brokers of church goods."[955] There are, however, human mediators, thus for Clement, Christian teachers are intermediaries, but not in the sense that they are needed to pass on prayers to God. The gnostic teacher is the one through whom the saving knowledge is revealed to humans who then in turn must use this knowledge to find their own way to God.

However, there were authorities among the Christians of the third century. The treatises themselves testify to the fact that there were ecclesiastical authorities, viz. Clement, Origen, Tertullian and Cyprian, who with their texts vindicated a certain form and content of prayer, and thus took part in constructing the Christian identity.[956] Bishops and presbyters must have presided during liturgical prayer, but we cannot confirm the century-old judgement by Paul Gottfried Drews that: "It was the bishops who were responsible for the form of liturgical worship in pre-Constantinian times."[957] Furthermore, judged from the treatises on prayer, it would seem that W.H.C. Frend is too categorical when he concluded that in the third century "the role of the laity was restricted in the service to making the

---

955 E. Muehlberger, *Angels in Late Ancient Christianity*, Oxford 2013, 11.
     This of course does not mean that there were no clerical offices in the third century, they were under development as we know from studies by, for instance, von Campenhausen who concludes that: "In the course of the third century the exclusive authority of office attains its full stature. It is true that the right to co-operate and share in decisions is nowhere absolutely denied to the congregation, and that in practice their influence shrank only gradually and step by step before the growing might of the clergy. But everywhere in governing circles we can see the effort to make the effectiveness of clerical authority as unrestricted, unqualified and exclusive as possible." (H. F. von Campenhausen, *Ecclesiastical Authority and Spiritual Power in the Church of the First Three Centuries*, Stanford, CA, 1969, 299). The treatises on prayer do not reflect the authority of the bishops, although claims of church authority were made from above and "the drift towards hierarchical government in the church... was irresistible" (W.H.C. Frend, *The Rise of Christianity*. Minneapolis 1984, 412).
956 Perrone 2003, 266.
957 Drews is quoted in U. Volp, *Liturgical Authority Reconsidered: Remarks on the Bishops Role in Pre-Constantinian Worship*, in: B. Neil/G.D. Dunn/L. Cross (eds.), *Prayer and Spirituality in the Early Church. Liturgy and Life 3*, Strathfield 2003, 189.

responses. Extempore activity as envisioned by Tertullian had no place."[958] Although Tertullian in another text gives testimony to the fact that the bishops had a special authority and had the right to baptise, and Cyprian believes that the church is present where the bishop is, when it came to liturgical prayers the role of neither bishop nor presbyter was emphasized in the treatises on prayer.[959] However, elsewhere in a description of the ritual of baptism, Cyprian indicates that the Holy Spirit is given to the baptized by way of the bishops' prayer.[960]

We are led to assume that many Christian congregations held a rather flexible approach to congregational prayers well into the third century and maybe even beyond. W.H.C. Frend is thus right in mentioning that within the congregation, there was still a partnership in prayer and reception of the Spirit between the clergy and the laity. However, Frend is most likely also right in adding that the partnership was "an increasingly unequal one."[961] During the third century, the role of the clergy changed radically; according to Tertullian, the authority of the clergy was grounded in "the collective faith of the members" or certain charismatic persons, whereas Cyprian saw the clergy and bishop as holding authority in their own right.[962] By distinguishing between prayers said by the clergy or the gnostic Christians and prayers said by the laity, prayer was used to create and uphold different identities within the congregations as well. It would culminate some centuries later, as Peter Brown has shown in his works on the development of the idea of the "holy man," whose "prayers alone could open the gates of heaven to the timorous believer."[963]

---

958 Frend, 1984, 408.
959 Tert. Bapt. 17.1-2 (Evans). See also Tert. Praescr. 41 (Refoulé; tr. Bindley).
960 "This is also now our practice that those who are baptized within the Church are brought before those in authority over the Church, and they acquire the Holy Spirit through the prayer we offer, and the laying on of our hands, and they are made complete with this seal of the Lord." (Cypr. ep. 73.9.2.151-5 (Goldhorn; tr. Donna)).
961 Frend, 1984, 408.
962 Rives, 1995, 283.
963 P. Brown, *The Rise and Function of the Holy Man in Late Antiquity*, in: JRS 61 (1971), 81.

4.3.3 Intercession

When dealing with the role of prayer in the establishment of social relations, intercessory prayers must also be mentioned. Intercession is petition made to God in favour of another and on behalf of another; not all of the authors under investigation have a special name for this type of prayer, but the idea that prayers should be made for others is a common and important feature. Cyprian for instance has no exact word for "intercession" but admonishes prayers for all, "*precem pro omnium.*"[964] Origen takes over the category "intercession," ἐντεύξεις, from 1 Tim 2:1 wherein the following types of prayer are mentioned: δεήσεις, προσευχὰς, ἐντεύξεις, and εὐχαριστίας. All of these types of prayer are to be said "for all," ὑπὲρ πάντων ἀνθρώπων.[965]

4.3.3.1 Intercession for the conversion of non-Christians

The main reason why Christians are to pray for each other and for non-Christians is to imbue faith and secure their salvation. As we saw earlier, Christ/the Logos is the most important intercessor for humans, but humans are also responsible for praying for one another and even for those that persecute them. This admonition to pray for persecutors is mentioned by all four authors under investigation and is taken over from Matt 5:44 where Jesus says: "But I tell you, love your enemies and pray for those who persecute you." Tertullian and Cyprian both combine the admonition to make intercessory prayers with their interpretation of the first petition of the Lord's Prayer "hallowed be thy name." Both of the Latin authors agree that God does not need people to hallow his name – it is hallowed beforehand. Therefore, the petition in the Lord's Prayer must refer not to the hallowing of God's name *per se*, but to the name of God being hallowed in people, i.e. by their faith in God's name. Tertullian and Cyprian thus combine the admonition to pray for persecutors with the idea that God's name should be hallowed in all people. Thereby, intercessory prayers become prayers for the conversion of those who are opposed to Christianity. As such intercessory prayers have the missionary aim of turning people to God,[966] but they

---

964 Cypr. Dom. orat. 8.
965 Or. or. 14.2. Here I do not follow the translation of Stewart-Sykes who translates προσευχὰς as "intercession" and ἐντεύξεις as "pleas."
966 Tert. Or. 3. Cypr. Dom. orat. 17.

are also prayers for Christians to remain steadfast in their faith. Tertullian writes:

> "we ask that [God's name] be hallowed among us who are in him and, at the same time, in others whom the grace of God still awaits."[967]

Cyprian explicitly states that intercession should be made "for the salvation of all (*pro omnium salute*),"[968] so that "those who are earthly from their original birth should begin to be heavenly (*incipiant esse caelestes*), being born of water and the Spirit (*ex aqua et spiritu nati*)."[969] Cyprian thus urges intercessory prayers in order for people to have faith and be baptized.[970]

Clement and Origen also refer to Matt 5:44 and its prayers for persecutors.[971] Consequently, Clement writes that the gnostic does not even allow himself to pray against his enemies because the Lord gave a plain command that we should pray *for* our enemies.[972] Furthermore, Clement notes that the gnostic does not call down vengeance on his persecutors, but instead prays for their conversion,[973] and:

> "[the gnostic] never bears a grudge, is never angry with anyone, even though he should deserve hatred for his conduct: for he worships the Creator and loves his fellow man, pitying him and *praying for him* on account of his ignorance (οἰκτείρων καὶ ὑπερευχόμενος αὐτοῦ διὰ τὴν ἄγνοιαν αὐτοῦ)."[974]

This might be an idealized picture of how Christians prayed, but also in other texts, like in Tertullian's *Apologeticum*, we find comments about Christian intercessory prayers for the emperor and the empire.[975] This could indicate that such prayers were in use in the collective worship. And also in Cyprian's letters, he admonishes Christians to pray for each other, both

---

967 Tert. Or. 3.
968 Cypr. Dom. orat. 17.
969 Cypr. Dom. orat. 17. Also 29.
970 See similar idea in m.Polyc. 12.3 (Musurillo): "Pray for all the saints. Pray also for kings and powers and princes and for them that persecute and hate you and for the enemies of the cross, that your fruit may be manifest among all men, that ye may be perfect in Him."
971 Or. or. 2.2. Clem. Strom. 7.14.84.
972 Clem. Strom. 7.14.84.
973 Id.
974 Id. 7.11.62.
975 Tert. Apol. 30 and 39 (Becker); Acta Cypriani 1 (Musurillo).

in this life and the afterlife, and this tells us that it was very important for Cyprian to emphasize the continual need for intercessions.[976] Indeed, as it is evident from the treatises, due to the supposed efficacy of Christian prayer, the Christian congregations held the belief that they had a responsibility for the whole world and for their pagan neighbours.[977] In the Christian communities, praying for the outsiders was therefore a characteristic of the insiders.[978]

According to the biblical logic, the passage in Matthew that commends intercessory prayers for persecutors demands more from Christians than "mere" prayers – Christians should concurrently show love both to in- and outsiders, because Christians ought to live up to the example of God who distributes good and bad equally to Christians as well as non-Christians (Matt 5:45). However, the authors under investigation are less emphatic concerning this love- and action-oriented conclusion from the Gospel. Tertullian does not mention it at all in his treatise on prayer, and Cyprian seems to suggest that intercessory prayers are the limit of what Christians owe non-Christians.[979] Origen and Clement are more demanding. Origen asks of the Christians to be in accordance with the Creator. Subsequently, this leads Origen to talk about the image of God, and how Christians ought to let themselves be transformed according to the image of God.[980] Also Clement mentions that Christians are not only supposed to pray for non-Christians but also to treat them with kindness. However, it seems that Clement only expects the most perfect Christians to be capable of this: "The

---

976 Cypr. ep. 60.5 (Goldhorn; tr. Donna).
977 Judith Lieu notes: "In a world of many such extravagant claims to a global identity, the Apologists out-claimed them all—according to Aristides the inhabited world is sustained by the prayers of Christians alone (Arist. apol. 16.6.). We should not read this merely as a self-deluding assumption of numerical superiority, nor as predicated on divine omnipresence alone: in an imagined geography the world belongs to the Christians—and so, polemically, not to the Jewish diaspora communities, despite their probable numerical and social superiority (Just. dial. 117), and not even to Roman imperial might." (J. Lieu, *Christian Identity in the Jewish and Greco-Roman World*, Oxford 2004, 235).
978 Judith Lieu comes to the exact same conclusion (Lieu, 2004, 295).
979 Cypr. Dom. orat. 17 (Réveillaud; tr. Stewart-Sykes).
980 Or. or. 22.4 (Koetschau; tr. Stewart-Sykes).

gnostic will attain this result either by his own greatness of mind, or by imitation of one who is better than himself."[981] The gnostic is even supposed to show "kindness to everyone, even though some continue to ill-treat the gnostic all the time of their life here in the flesh."[982]

4.3.3.2 Intercession for fellow-Christians

Intercessory prayers also seem to have played an important role for the internal relations in the church. Christians were supposed to pray for each other, and prayers were believed to have more impact when they were uttered by the people of God unanimously. If all agreed on intercession being made, this form of prayer would be exceptionally pleasing to God, and collective intercession was therefore the most efficient means to secure salvation. As the penitential system evolved, intercessory prayers of the congregation became a vital part of the process of the penitents to earn forgiveness. Tertullian is explicit about this in some of his writings: In order for sinners to repent, Tertullian demanded that the sinner should: "bow before the feet of the presbyters, and kneel to God's dear ones (*caris Dei*[983]); to enjoin on all the brethren to be ambassadors (*legationes*) to bear his deprecatory supplication (before God)."[984] "God's dear ones" could well be interpreted as the congregation, and indeed the brothers are presented as important ambassadors. Nevertheless, in *De Oratione*, Tertullian is not very explicit about collective prayers or intercessions. In general, as already mentioned, the treatises under investigation seem to downplay sin and penitence – probably because of the edifying character of the texts. There are, however, passages that indicate that intercessory prayers were believed to be important in relation with forgiveness of sins. For instance, Origen refers to 1 Samuel 2:25 when he writes: "if a person sins against another person the congregation can pray for him. But should he sin against the Lord, who will pray for him? (τίς προσεύξεται περὶ αὐτοῦ;)."[985] In comparison with the Hebrew

---

981 Clem. Strom. 7.14.86 (Hort/Mayor).
982 Id. 7.14.85.
983 *Caris Dei* according to the edition of Pierre de Lariolle 1906, but *aris dei*, "God's altar," according to J.W. P. Borleffs 1954.
984 Or. paen. 9.4 (Borleffs).
985 Or. or. 28.3 (Koetschau; tr. Stewart-Sykes).

Old Testament source, 1 Sam 2:25, the subject of prayer has been replaced. In the Hebrew text, God is said to mediate before himself (וּפִלְלוֹ אֱלֹהִים).[986] However, in LXX, there is an implicit "they" who will "pray for him [the sinner] to God" (προσεύξονται ὑπὲρ αὐτοῦ πρὸς κύριον). Origen's version in *Perì Euchês* takes over the idea from LXX, so that it is the congregation who is to make intercession on behalf of the sinner. Slowly the idea developed that martyrs, saints, angels and Christ in his role as high priest also joined in when the earthly congregations made intercessions. We already saw how such a "communion of saints" was imagined by Origen in *Perì Euchês* 31.5. This universal communion of saints was believed to make prayers even more efficient, and Origen seems to have held the opinion that the prayers of the congregation as well as the presbyters were needed for forgiveness.[987] A little later, Cyprian struggled and succeeded in allocating the spiritual power to mediate between God and the repentant to the bishop.[988] Cyprian strongly urged Christians to pray for each other, since prayers otherwise could not be beneficial. It seems that he imagined individual prayers as no good. According to Cyprian, Christ wanted unity – he wanted collective prayers for collective benefits.[989]

By studying these three authors, Origen, Tertullian and Cyprian, we can thus clearly see the development of formal hierarchy in the church to the detriment of the laity. Concretely, we see it in the devaluation of the efficacy of lay prayers to obtain forgiveness. This might have been for the best for the "church," since W.H.C. Frend notes that when lay people were in charge of repentance, it tended to be either too severe or too lax.[990] Nonetheless, the development removed responsibility and power from the congregation to the clergy.

As always, Clement's gnostic is taking every virtue a step further than the average norm. In regard to intercession, the gnostic is supposed not only to

---

986 "If a person sins against another, God will mediate for him, but if a person sins against the Lord, who can intercede for him?"
987 Cf. the previous paragraph 4.3.2.
988 See Frend, 1984, 409.
989 Cypr. Dom. orat. 8 (Réveillaud; tr. Stewart-Sykes).
990 Frend, 1986, 409.

pray for sinners, but to take the sins of others upon himself and take part in prayers for forgiveness:

> "When he has once formed the habit of doing good, the gnostic loses no time in benefiting others also, praying that he be reckoned as sharing in the sins of his brethren with a view to the repentance and conversion of his kinsfolk, and eager to impart his own good things to those whom he holds dearest. And his friends for their part feel the same for him."[991]

Clement seems to imagine that the gnostic has a surplus of goodwill and understanding in relation to God whereby the gnostic can afford to take on other people's sins and still be forgiven. Christians are considered to be kinsfolk who should all be willing to share each other's sins. A further degree of collectivism can hardly be imagined, and even if the sharing of sins can only be an ideal, it expressed Clement's high expectations to the close relations among (perfect) Christians.

In early Christian literature, one finds several idealized examples of such intercessory prayer in different martyr acts: About Polycarp it is said: "Day and night he did little else but pray for everyone and for all the churches scattered throughout the world, as he was accustomed to do."[992] In relation with Polycarp's prayer, Judith Lieu draws the attention to another function of intercessory prayers – their ability to transcend a certain locality and bind communities together. Lieu writes that:

> "any local allegiance is sharply qualified by the community itself becoming one among many temporary resting places, whose true identity is found in their totality ('all') and universality ('in every place'). In the same way, the local events — and, specifically, Polycarp's death — are located in that broader sphere by the prayers he offers for 'the churches throughout the world'..."[993]

All authors under investigation recommend intercession for Christians and for others. Intercessory prayers must have had a social effect – either because the individual needed the prayers of the others whose prayers served as penitence, or because someone else needed the prayers of the individual. This would then create a unity in the congregation where all the members were mutually dependent on each other's prayers of intercession.

---

991 Clem. Strom. 7.12.80 (Hort/Mayor).
992 M.Polyc. 5 (Musurillo).
993 Lieu, 2004, 233.

1121723222122122222

4.3.4 Considerations on the overt social aspects of prayer

Christian authors promoted collective prayer and intercessions for the salvation of all. It is difficult to say to which degree these admonitions were carried into effect, but surely they were important for the prevailing idea of what constituted Christian prayer and identity. We can find a lot of examples of collective prayer and intercessions in early Christian texts. Regarding collective prayer, we can note how more texts explain how the Eucharist and common prayer follow directly after baptism, thus emphasizing the social character of the Christian life given in baptism and gaining reality in collective prayer.[994] Regarding intercessions, we likewise find more examples in Christian texts where intercessions are mentioned.[995] We also saw that prayers were inherently part of the Eucharist and liturgy, but apparently so free and/or familiar that there was no need to further describe these prayers in the treatises on prayer. Only the wording and content of the Lord's Prayer was explained in much detail. None of the Christian authors under investigation, not even the individual-oriented Clement, dismiss participation in collective prayer, and no one focus their attention on the clergy in relation to prayer but contrary on the congregation. The focus on collectivity is so emphatic that P. Bradshaw correctly has pointed to the fact that even private prayers was not individual prayers because the individual ideally was so integrated in the Christian congregation that even private expressions of piety were thought of as expressions of a communal sentiment:

> "It is important not to assume from this, however, that what was done [in private] was thought of as a private prayer. Christians understood themselves to be members of the body of Christ, and their prayers to be united with one another whether they happened to be praying alone or with others."[996]

As mentioned in Chapter 1, in his essay, "Giving for a Return: Jewish Votive Offerings in late antiquity,"[997] Michael L. Satlow points to the social manifestation made by the Jews when they offered votive offerings to God. It was

---

994 Just. apol. 1.65 (Minns/Parvis); Tert. Bapt. 20 (Evans).
995 Tert. Apol. 45 (Becker, tr. Souter); m.Polyc. 5 (Musurillo) etc.
996 P. Bradshaw (ed.), *A companion to common worship* 2, London 2006, 2.
997 Satlow, 2005, 91-108.

not only God they wanted to impress, but also the members of the congregation. The inscriptions made about votive offering were not made to remind God of anything, but for other people to see. Every collective manifestation of religion has several motives, also collective prayer. It might take place, not primarily to communicate with God, but for the effect of belonging in the praying community. Participation in collective prayer must have been done both for God and in order to belong to the Christian congregation and share the identity of one's Christian brothers, but these motives do not exclude each other – the horizontal and vertical lines of communication emphasizes one another. We can conclude with K. H. Ostmeyer: "Ein spezifisches Gebet wird zum gemeinschaftsstiftenden Band und zum Signal der Zugehörigkeit."[998]

4.4 Marking boundaries by way of prayer

With the words of Philip A. Harland, we can recapture certain points about identity formation that was already touched upon in Chapter 1:

> "Identity formation and negotiation take place primarily through social interaction... Many social identity theorists stress the importance of language not only in the communication of identities but also in the construction and negotiation of identities, both in terms of internal self-definition and external categorizations."[999]

These "external categorizations" that Harland mentions will be the subject of the following paragraphs, because also the Christian authors made such categorizations in the texts under investigation. That people make categorizations is a sociological and a common sensical fact, but what are these categorizations more precisely? Two processes are part of categorization: (1) the specification of similarities, and (2) the specification of differences.[1000] In other words, in social interaction, one can either identify with the similarities between oneself and others, or categorize these "others" as different because of the dissimilarities between oneself and the others. Furthermore, scholars propose that there are two ideal-typical

---

998   Ostmeyer, 2004, 327.
999   Harland, 2009, 63.
1000 R. Jenkins, *Categorization: Identity, Social Process and Epistemology*, *Current Sociology* 48(3): 7-25, 2000.

modes of identification: self- or group identification (internally oriented) and the categorization of others (externally oriented).[1001] Hence, people will tend to define their own selves by identifying with other members in the groups to which they belong, but will meanwhile categorize non-group members as "others" and often categorize them in a negative way. "The process of definition demands that 'they' should be contrasted with 'us'."[1002] Furthermore, sociological theory holds that identity is formed by creating a boundary between oneself and others: "At the boundary we discover what we are in what we are not and *vice versa*."[1003] People need such boundaries to manoeuvre in the world.

Also the Christian authors under investigation had ideas about certain "others" who were different from them in a negative way and whose practices should be avoided. These "others" were primarily Jews, pagans and heretics. However, these categories are far from clear; "terms such as paganism, Judaism and Christianity must... be used with a certain degree of care. Individual pagans, Jews and Christians could hold widely varying interpretations of their proclaimed religion, and collective labels can easily conceal deep differences."[1004]

The systematic theologian Kathryn Tanner states that: "Christian practices are always the practices of others made odd."[1005] Thereby she means that Christianity works within the boundaries of culture, but makes radical changes in relation to this culture. Tanner explains how the Christian concept of a "second birth" "means in part the renunciation of prior practices, one's prior life is not simply cast aside but given back to one in a radically new form."[1006] Therefore, on the one hand, the early Christians were busy distancing themselves from the world, as Clement's gnostic who ideally

---

1001 Id. 8 ff.

1002 R. Jenkins, Rethinking Ethnicity London 2008, 59.

1003 Jenkins, 2008, 103. See also: Jacobsen in M. Kahlos, *The Faces of the Other. Religious Rivalry and Encounters in the Later Roman World*, Turnhout 2011, 106.

1004 D.M. Gwyn/S. Bangert, *Religious Diversity in Late Antiquity*, 2010, 6.

1005 K. Tanner, *Theories of Culture. A New Agenda for Theology*, Minneapolis 1997, 113.

1006 Id.

"leaves this world behind him, just as the Jews did Egypt."[1007] On the other hand, the early Christians were in fact caught up in the world and changed it by changing themselves within it. This change in turn occurred when they interacted with certain others.

The focus will now be on the way in which the Christian authors for their own advantage presented non-Christians in a certain negative way. We shall thus deal with the Christian process of "othering" Jews, pagans and heretics in the treatises under investigation.[1008]

4.4.1 Anti-Judaism and Christian prayer

None of the authors under investigation took such a radical stance towards Judaism as did, e.g. the Marcionites who denounced the Old Testament altogether. Instead the mainstream authors took a *via media* and saw the Hebrew Scriptures and certain Jewish traditions as authoritative; meanwhile, they understood the Jewish people and their insistence on the Law as misguided. Some scholars have seen this opposition to Judaism as a constitutive feature of Christianity. Also in the treatises under investigation, the Jews (referred to as Jews/Judeans or Israel) are identifiable as the certain "others" in a negative categorization, and some degree of parting of the ways between Jews and Christians have definitely taken place.

1007 Clem. Strom. 7.7.40 (Hort/Mayor).
　　　The discussion about the proper relationship between Christianity and culture is an everlasting one. Willis Jenkins believes that: "The Christian difference from culture is not a boundary that falls along internal narratives or language games, but a boundary made by participating in culture in odd ways. All the interesting theological production happens not safely inside some boundary, as if Christianity was a territory, but in an ironic reproduction of culture that happens at the boundary it makes." (W. Jenkins, *The Future of Ethics. Sustainability, Social Justice, and Religious Creativity*, Georgetown 2013, 93).
1008 On the general theme of "othering" in Late Antiquity as such, see e.g. Kahlos, 2011; M.S. Tayler, *Anti-Judaism and Early Christian Identity. A Critique of the Scholarly Consensus*, Leiden 1995; Iricinschi/Zellentin, 2008; Harland, 2009. In studies of ethnic identity in antiquity, the process of categorization is also emphasized, e.g. J. Neuser/E.S. Frerichs (eds.), *"To See Ourselves as Others See Us." Christians, Jews, "Others" in Late Antiquity*, Decatur, GA 1985.

The privileged role of the Christians as God's children comes at the expense of the Jews. Prayer is presented as the communication between God the Father and his rightful children, i.e. the Christians. According to the logic of the Christian authors, Christians have the opportunity to pray in the right way because they can justly address God as their Father. The Jews, on the other hand, have lost the right to address God as Father, as they did not appreciate the Father when they had their chance. Tertullian believes that the Jews, which he only refers to as "Israel," have reproached themselves by not believing in the Christian God, and to substantiate the argument he follows up with Isaiah 1:2: "I have begotten sons and they have not acknowledged me." Likewise, Cyprian thinks that the word "Father" in itself "accuses the Jews (*Iudaeos... percutit*),"[1009] because of their lack of faith in the name. Cyprian states:

> "previously the Jews were the sons of the Kingdom (*ante filii regni Iudaei*), as long as they continued to be children of God (*filii Dei esse perseuerabant*). But when the name of the Father (*nomen paternum*) was abandoned among them, the Kingdom was abandoned as well (*cessauit et regnum*). And thus we Christians, who in prayer have begun to call on God as the Father (*christiani qui in oratione appellare patrem Deum coepimus nos*), pray that the Kingdom of God might likewise come to us."[1010]

Note here, how Cyprian distinguishes between "them (*illos*)" and "we Christians (*Christiani... nos*)." They are all agents, but whereas the Jews have used their ability to act in a negative way because they have failed to embrace the true faith, the Christians are the rightful children that have begun to call God Father. Prayer is mentioned as the means by which the fatherhood of God gains reality by being articulated (*in oratione appellare patrem Deum coepimus*). Prayer and fatherhood point towards the Kingdom of God, i.e. salvation. The Kingdom, which is subject of the sentence, will "come to us" (*nobis ueniat*) because of prayer. Contrary, the perspective for the Jews is bleak, since they have been excluded from the heavenly realm (*exidamus de regno caelesti, sicut Iudaei*).[1011] Also in other instances in *De Dominca Oratione*, Cyprian rigorously distances

---

1009 Cypr. Dom. orat. 10 (Réveillaud; tr. Stewart-Sykes).
1010 Id. 13.
1011 Id.

the Christians from the Jews. In the commentary of the invocation of the Lord's Prayer, Cyprian notes that: "We Christians hold them guilty when we say: 'Our Father', because he has now begun to be ours (*noster esse iam coepit*) and ceased to be the Father of the Jews who abandoned him (*Iudaeorum qui eum dereliquerunt esse desiuit*)."[1012] Cyprian here combines the fatherhood of God with the remission of sins and eternal salvation. Consequently, only God's true children will be saved, and those who are God's children are marked by prayer.

Origen proposes the same scheme where the Christians are the new sons of God. Origen notes that never before in history, did such a Father–child relationship with God exist as the Christians now experience. Origen writes that: "… a firm and abiding sonship is not to be discerned among the ancient people (τὸ ἀμετάπτω τον τῆς υἱότητος οὐκ ἔστιν ἰδεῖν παρὰ τοῖς ἀρχαίοις)."[1013] Obviously, Christ is the missing link among the Jews, and since Christ is the only mediator between humans and God, the Jews are no longer in contact with God. In the prayer discourses, we encounter these negative categorizations primarily in relation to the Jews, and in the texts of Tertullian and Cyprian these anti-Judaistic passages are to be found near the beginning of the treatises, thus holding a prominent position.

Clement is at the first glance a little different in his approach to the Jews. He is the only one of the four authors under investigation who does not hold up the Lord's Prayer as the ideal Christian prayer. He is also the one who is the least fixated on the Father-metaphor as the proper way to name God. It seems Clement is a little less prone to present sharp distinctions. Clement believes that before Christ's coming, some divine knowledge was given to Jews and Greeks in the form of the Jewish commandments and the philosophy of the Greeks. It was given to pave the way for true gnosis – that is the Word: "For He leads <different> men by a different progress (ἐξ ἑκατέρας προκοπῆς), whether Greek (Ἑλληνικῆς) or barbarian (βαρβάρου), to the perfection which is through faith (ἐπὶ τὴν διὰ πίστεως τελείωσιν)."[1014] Jesus even became a Jew himself to appeal to the Jews; "accommodating himself to the Jews, he became a Jew that he might gain

---

1012 Id. 10.
1013 Or. or. 22.2 (Koetschau; tr. Stewart-Sykes).
1014 Clem. Strom. 7.2.11 (Hort/Mayor).

all (Ἰουδαίοις Ἰουδαῖος ἐγένετο, ἵνα πάντας κερδήσῃ (cf. 1 Cor 19:19)).ᵗ[1015] However, also for Clement, faith in Christ is the ultimate goal, and the only road to "perfection, viz. that of salvation through faith."[1016] Furthermore, Clement believes that meaningful prayers can only arise from faith and via the teachings of Christ. In the end therefore, Clement is equally exclusive when it comes to incorporating Jewish elements into Christian identity, although he is patient with people as long as they begin to seek God via the teachings of his Word: "But the generation of them that seek Him is the chosen race (τὸ γένος ἐστὶ τὸ ἐκλεκτόν) which seeks with a view to knowledge."[1017] What "signify the Jews generally (τοὺς Ἰουδαίους αἰνίσσεται τοὺς πολλούς)," according to Clement, is that they "have the oracles of God in their mouth, but have not the firm footing of faith stayed upon truth, which carries them to the Father through the Son (δι' υἱοῦ πρὸς τὸν πατέρα)."[1018] Thus, also Clement ends up using kinship language in a way that specifically excludes the Jews.

Concerning the actual practice of prayer, Tertullian is also very reserved when it comes to Jewish traditions: For instance, he deals with the Jewish custom of washing hands before praying:[1019] "Though Israel wash in all its members every day, yet is he never clean. His hands are always undeniably unclean, ever encrusted with the blood of the prophets and of the Lord himself."[1020] Now, Tertullian rejects the Jewish custom with an emphatic "*immo et adversari*" - literally meaning "on the contrary and opposite": "It is better that we should not wash hands and so to show ourselves to be the reverse of this pattern (*immo et adversari debemus deditoris exemplo nec propterea manus abluere*)."[1021] Tertullian's idea is that the Jews are ritually clean, but morally dirty, and Tertullian wants the opposite to characterize Christians. The picture painted is of course distorted, but easily fitting the dichotomies generally used to characterize Jews and Christians at the time.

1015 Id. 7.9.53.
1016 Id. 7.2.11.
1017 Id. 7.10.58, cf. 1 Pet 2,9.
1018 Clem. Strom. 7. 18.109 (Hort/Mayor).
1019 To wash one's hands before prayer is also recommended in the *Apostolic Tradition* 41 (Botte).
1020 Tert. Or. 14 (Schleyer; tr. Stewart-Sykes).
1021 Id. 13.

Also in chapter 22 of *De Oratione*, Tertullian mentions Jewish practice. The chapter admonishes the covering of the head of virgins, and Tertullian notes that "this is Israel's practice" as if he thereby legitimates the custom. Then he goes on to say that even if it had not been the practice of Israel, Christians could have rightly taken this practice into use because Christians have an "expanded and completed law (*nostra lex ampliata atque suppleta*)."[1022] Here, Tertullian thus acknowledges the law of the Jews, but prioritizes the Christian law. Tertullian's rationale is not completely stringent, but is nevertheless grounded in Scripture and Christian customs.[1023] Likewise in chapter 25 of *De Oratione*, Tertullian acknowledges that praying three times a day is a practice that arises from "the discipline of Israel (*ex Israelis disciplina*)." Tertullian, however, continues by stating that Christians pray three times a day because they "are debtors of three, the Father and the Son and the Holy Spirit." Thus Tertullian immediately gives the Jewish tradition a distinct Christian interpretation to legitimize it. Concerning practice, Origen also mentions the Jewish practice of praying in the synagogues and on the street corners. Whether Origen thereby was thinking about contemporary Jewish prayers is uncertain, since he could be writing with the Matthean admonition in mind not to pray like the hypocrites (Matt 6:2). However, we did see in Chapter 2.1.3, an example of a rabbi who in addition to the regular services in the Synagogue approached a man in the street to make him pray to God.[1024] Thus it apparently was a Jewish practice in third-century Caesarea to take the worship into the streets in times of crisis.

It is noticeable that the contemporary early-Rabbinic Judaism is not directly mentioned in the treatises. That raises the question about whom the Christians were writing against when mentioning Israel and the Jews. Are the Jews pure straw men and literary constructions, built on the accounts from the Bible? Or is the discursive fight that we are witnessing in the texts the reflection of a real fight in the social world of late antiquity, in which the Christians tried to diminish the influence of the Jews? Miriam S. Taylor has come to the conclusion that the church fathers' references to the Jews make more sense if seen as expressions of an anti-Judaism rooted

---

1022 Id. 22.
1023 Cf. paragraph 2.1.3 in this thesis.
1024 Lieberman, 1942, 30.

in theological ideas than as responses to contemporary Jews in the context of an on-going conflict.[1025] Furthermore, she concludes that the Christian authors used the Jews as "symbolic figures who play an essential role in the communication and development of the church's own distinctive conception of God's plans for His chosen people, and in the formation of the church's cultural identity."[1026] Also in the case of the euchological treatises, it is correct that the Jews are cast in the role of "predecessors," who represent the old life from which Christians have vigorously parted. The treatises on prayer cannot tell us, if the antipathy towards the Jews rose also because of concrete social and political issues between Christians and Jews. It seems hard to imagine that the Christian authors did not have the Jews in their immediate surroundings in mind when writing against Jews and Israel. After all, we saw in Chapter 2 that Jewish communities existed in Carthage and Caesarea simultaneously with the Christian authors under investigation. And when Tertullian, for instance, writes that when it comes to purification rituals, "a majority is superstitiously concerned,"[1027] it would seem that he talks about contemporary living people, i.e. Jews, whom his audience are supposed to recognize.

When studying the presentation of the Jews in the early Christian texts we see that in the same way as kinship language can function as unifying metaphor – as in the case of Christians calling each other family – so it can be used to exclude other people who are not family. In the treatises on the Lord's Prayer, kinship language is consequently used to bind the Christians together and simultaneously to separate the Christians from the Jews. Kinship language is thus as D.K. Buell has rightly observed border discourse.[1028] Binyamin Katzoff convincingly argues that the later prevailing Jewish way of addressing God, "God of our Fathers," developed exactly to counteract the Christian claim that God was a Christian God.[1029] It was an internal statement which use was stimulated by an external, Christian challenge.[1030] The Jews held that God was theirs and had been so for

1025 Tayler, 1995, 127.
1026 Tayler, 1995, 4 ff.
1027 Tert. Or. 13 (Schleyer; tr. Stewart-Sykes).
1028 Buell, 1999, 83.
1029 Katzoff, 2009, 317 ff.
1030 Id. 318.

generations, thus linking God with the Jewish family. Furthermore, some scholars believe that other features entered the Jewish prayers and liturgy in late antiquity in order to be polemic against Christians. For instance, some scholars believe that the *Birkat Ha-minim*, בִּרְכַּת הַמִּינִים, "benediction concerning heretics," which at least in a later period was interpreted as a prayer/curse against Christians, was taken into use already in the second century.[1031] In other words, it would seem that Jews were also forming their religious identity in contrast to Christians. In his article "The Other in Us: Liturgica, Poetica, Polemica," I. J. Yuwal concludes that the Jewish answer to external threats was "a deep process of turning inwards."[1032] Yuwal sees prayer as a "transcript of Jewish culture" and by interpreting liturgical prayers, he sees "a glimpse into the mechanisms of denial and suppression which enabled the Jews to build their own identity as if nobody threatened them at all."[1033] Maybe, however, the Christian authors had a particular need to distance themselves from the Jews in their meta-reflections on prayer, because the actual prayer-tradition and liturgy of the Christians were remarkably "Jewish," e.g. because of the Lord's Prayer.[1034]

4.4.2 Pagan ideas and customs

As mentioned above, Cyprian distinguishes the "enlightened Christians" from, on the one hand, Jews and, on the other hand, "the pagans who are

---

1031 Id. 317. R. Kimelman disagrees; he has written an article that argues against an anti-Christian understanding of *birkat ha-minim* in late antiquity. Kimelman believes that the prayer/curse was directed against Jewish sectarians (R. Kimelman, *Birkat Ha-Minim and the Lack of Evidence for an Anti-Christian Jewish Prayer in Late Antiquity*, in: E.P. Sanders et al. (eds.), *Jewish and Christian Self-definition. Volume Two. Aspects of Judaism in the Graeco-Roman Period*, Philadelphia 1981, 226-244).

1032 I. J. Yuval: *The Other in Us. Liturgica, Poetica, Polemica*, in E. Iricinschi/ H.M. Zellentin, *Heresy and Identity in Late Antiquity*, Tübingen 2008, 364-385, 385.

1033 Id.

1034 P. Sigal claims to show how "Judaic worship materials were acculturated to Christian needs and through the traditional methods of midrash expressed in *piyyutim* the early church christianized older Jewish prayers." (P. Sigal, *Early Christian and Rabbinic Liturgical Affinities. Exploring Liturgical Acculturation*, in: NTS 30/1 (1984), 63-90, 83).

still unenlightened."[1035] In this paragraph, we shall look further into the Christian treatment of the pagan philosophy and pagan rituals. People who are neither Christians nor Jews are referred to in various ways in these texts which can be translated as "gentiles," "nations," "Greeks," "heathens," "superstitious," or "atheists."[1036] There are also instances where it must simply be deferred from the context that the authors are dealing with what we nowadays have come to label "pagans." When we are dealing with the broad category of late antique "paganism," we must remember that it was always "by nature diverse, for paganism as a religious 'system' is primarily a Christian construct, uniting all the widely varied classical cults and practices which Christianity rejected within a single polemical collective."[1037] Nowadays one issue in the scholarly debate on paganism in late antiquity is the question whether or not "paganism" was in decline when Christianity arose.[1038] This cannot be deduced from the treatises on prayer, wherein pagan ideas and customs are only mentioned in passing and as phenomena that should be avoided by the Christians. However, the very fact that the Christian authors mention pagans of course means that they were aware of the pagans as "others." As we saw earlier, even the Christian vocabulary on prayer was apparently formed in opposition to the pagan

---

1035 Cypr. Dom. orat. 36 (Réveillaud; tr. Stewart-Sykes).
1036 Examples of how people who are neither Jews nor Christians are referred to (the list does not account for all instances in the texts):
- *Gentiles*: Tert. Or. 15; Cypr. Dom. orat. 34; 36;
- *nationes*: Tert. Or. 5; 6; 15; 16;
- *superstitiose*: Tert. Or. 13 (used about Jews);
- ἔθνος: Or. or. 21.1; 27.12;
- δεισιδαίμων: Clem. Strom. 7.1.4.
- Ἕλληνες: Clem. Strom. 7.4.22,
- βάρβαρος: Clem. Strom. 7.2.6;
- ἄθεος: Clem. Strom. 7.1.4. etc; Or. or. 5.1.
1037 Gwyn/Bangert, 2010, 5.
1038 Robin Lane Fox believes that paganism was not in decline (Fox, 1988). E. Glenn Hinson holds the opposite view. He believes that the religions from the Orient had already paved the way and met some of the needs that the ancient Roman cults failed to satisfy. The Roman cults lacked something which grabbed people and made them stay (E.G. Hinson, *The Evangelization of the Roman Empire. Identity and Adaptability*, Macon 1981).

vocabulary;[1039] Lorenzo Perrone calls this "a new semantics of prayer, albeit with the important premise of Septuagint Greek."[1040] Before embarking on the text analyses, it might be appropriate to note that at the level of popular religion, the differences between Christians and pagans might not have been as pronounced, as it is described in the treatises; on the contrary, the admonitions not to do as the pagans or gentiles only show that someone probably did so.

4.4.2.1 The Latin authors

In Tertullian's *De Oratione*, several passages, including chapters 15–17, are devoted to the attack on certain practices that Christians have taken over from Jews and pagans. Before going into detail with these practices, Tertullian mentions that exterior practices are not of great importance – they are matters of empty expression (*attigimus vacuae*),[1041] and such issues have nothing to do with religion but with superstition (*non religioni, sed superstitioni*). However, wrong practices should be avoided, because "they put us on the level of the gentiles (*quod gentilibus adaequent*)."[1042] The first practice that Tertullian condemns is the habit of taking off one's coat when praying: "It is thus that the gentiles attend their idols (*sic enim adeunt ad idola nationes*)."[1043] Tertullian ridicules this idea and reminds his audience that nothing can be found in the Christian tradition that defends this practice. Contrary, God even paid attention to the three young men in the fiery furnace (Dan 3:21), and Tertullian sarcastically asks: "Perhaps God might not hear those with their coats on, God who listened to the saints in the furnace of the Babylonian king, when they pray in their pantaloons and their hats!" In chapter 16, Tertullian continues his campaign against pagan practices by diminishing the custom of sitting down while praying. He refutes the idea and uses the argument that exactly because the gentiles do it, it should be avoided by Christians:

1039 See above: 2.3.2.
1040 Perrone, 2003, 277.
1041 Tert. Or. 15 (Schleyer; tr. Stewart-Sykes).
1042 Id.
1043 Id.

"Moreover, since the gentiles likewise, when they have worshipped their little idols, sit down again, all the more should this practice, used in idol worship be reprimanded among us (*Porro cum proinde faciant nationes vel adoratis sigillaribus suis residendo, vel propterea in nobis reprehendi meretur, quod apud idola celebratur*)."

The strategy appears to be quite clear here: simply to reverse a pagan practice and thereby make it acceptable. Clement uses a similar reasoning in *Stromateis* 7.7.43, when he writes that the pagan worship was directed in the complete opposite direction than what is right and true: "It was for this reason that the most ancient temples looked toward the west in order that they who stood facing the images might be taught to turn (τρέπεσθαι) eastwards." Clement thus sees the radical shift that conversion to Christianity represents as something that demands a physical turn. Clement expresses this by the use of a sort of logical *passivum divinum* in that God seems to be the strategist who ordered it thus that the pagan temples were built in one way in order for the Christians to reverse this practice and pray in a completely different direction.

In chapter 17, Tertullian lashes out against those who pray too loudly. By this he could be referring either to the Jews or to the pagans, since the prejudice about the Jews was that they were hypocrites who prayed in order for their piety to be noticed, and the prejudice against pagans often was that they were overly concrete and thought that their gods were manifest in statues and temples and could be approached by addressing these concrete sanctuaries. The reason why Tertullian attacks certain pagan practices must be that they were still observed by someone in his congregation, and that the general attitude to the practice is still ambivalent among his audience.

Cyprian, who was a convert to Christianity and thus must have known pagan practices from within, is quiet concerning pagans in *De Dominica oratione*. He only mentions pagans once, namely in the passage quoted above where he distinguishes Christians from Jews and pagans. In other writings, Cyprian is, however, not silent on the issue, but treats especially pagan sacrifices with contempt.[1044] Although arguments *ex silentio* should

---

1044 In Cypr. laps. 25 (tr. Wallis), Cyprian explains how awful effects pagan sacrifice can have on people. Regarding philosophy, Cyprian is almost entirely silent, though he rejects it in a quote in a letter: "Quite otherwise is the reasoning of the philosophers and the Stoics, dearly beloved Brother, who say

be avoided, at least two reasons for Cyprian's silence on the matter in *De Dominica Oratione* could be considered: Firstly, Cyprian wrote *De Dominica Oratione* in a heated situation. The text is written about 251, after the pagan emperor Decius in January 249 had promulgated a Roman imperial edict that ordered all citizens to make sacrifice to the Roman gods. The enforcement of this edict caused a lot of Christians to sacrifice to the pagan gods, whilst Cyprian went into hiding in order to direct his flocks from a safe distance. During this tumultuous time, Cyprian wrote his treatise on prayer, and although he could have taken the opportunity to harshly reject pagan religion, Cyprian apparently chose another strategy and kept silent on pagan religion, but urged Christian unity and collective prayer. He thus chose to focus on the internal cohesion instead of the external treats. It makes sense, seen from a pastoral perspective. Another reason for the lack of rejection of the pagan practices could be that Cyprian found himself in a milieu with a great extent of religious syncretism. If Cyprian were to begin to reproach pagans, he would soon have to defend Christian practice, which in many ways resembled pagan practice.[1045] Cyprian, when writing *De Dominica Oratione*, might have simply accepted that this was not the time nor the audience to present with critique of others, what his audience needed was internal self-formation.

4.4.2.2 *The Greek authors*

In the Greek treatises, Clement and Origen both use and reject ideas from contemporary Greco-Roman philosophy. For instance, Origen alludes to philosophical ideas such as Plato's analogy of the sun.[1046] The parable seems to be the background on which Origen explains which objects are worthy of petitionary prayer; the ideal and the perfect should be distinguished from

---

that all sins are equal and that a serious man ought not easily to be influenced. But there is a very great difference between Christians and philosophers." (ep. 55.16 (Goldhorn; tr. Donna)).

1045 In his book *Cyprian and Roman Carthage*, Allan Brent shows how syncretistic the religious culture was at the time; this is also seen in the archaeological evidence, for instance Christian epitaphs have been found in the form of pagan altars (Brent, 2010, 237).

1046 Or. or. 17.1 (Koetschau; tr. Stewart-Sykes).

the shadows.[1047] Also in *Perì Euchês* 31.3, Origen follows the teachings of e.g. Plato concerning the spherical nature of heavenly beings.[1048] Without explicitly stating it, Origen thus to a large degree shows himself to be in accord with contemporary philosophy. However, in 23.3 Origen writes against those who claim that God is "in a material space" and "corporeal." This must be a critique of the Stoics and the Stoic idea that God is material, consisting of fire or aether. Clement for his part rejects any anthropomorphic or sense-oriented ideas of God:

> "There is... no need for God to be in human shape (ἀνθρωποειδὴς) in order that He may hear, nor does He need senses (αἰσθήσεων), as <the Epicureans held>, especially hearing and sight, dependent <as the Stoics held> on the sensitiveness of the air..."[1049]

Despite of confusing Epicureanism and Stoicism in the just-quoted passage (which has been emended by the editor); it seems that Clement had a great knowledge about Pagan cult and religion and Greco-Roman education.[1050] Clement was a convert to Christianity, and he was also a critical thinker. In one passage of *Stromateis* 7, he considers how different people create gods that suit them and their character. He thus proposes that the pagan gods are constructions of the mind, something he of course does not believe to be the case with his own Christian God:

> "But the Greeks assume their gods to be human (ἀνθρωπομόρφους) in passion as they are human in shape; and, as each nation paints their shape after its own likeness..., so each represents them as like itself in soul (τὰς ψυχὰς). For instance, the barbarians make them brutal and savage, the Greeks milder, but subject to passion."[1051]

1047 Cf. Pl. r. 5.517 (Emlyn-Jones); Or. or. 27.9 (Koetschau; tr. Stewart-Sykes).

1048 Pl. Tim. 33B (Bury).

1049 Clem. Strom. 7.7.37 (Hort/Mayor). Note that the translator has inserted "the Epicureans." In the Greek text, both ideas are attributed to the Stoics "Στωϊκοῖς." A scribe probably made a mistake in the text. (see F.J.A. Hort/J.B. Mayor (eds.), *Clement of Alexandria, Miscellanies, Book VII. The Greek text with introduction, translation and notes*, London 1902, 255).

1050 See a list of philosophical terms used by Clement in Strom. 7 in Hort/Mayor, 1902, xlvii-xlix.

1051 Clem. Strom. 7.4.22 (Hort/Mayor).

According to Clement, the construction of pagan gods inevitably leads to misguided worship because the nature of the God being worshiped and the worship are obviously closely related:

> "where there is an unworthy conception of God passing into base and unseemly thoughts and significations, it is impossible to preserve any sort of devoutness either in hymns or discourses or even in writings of doctrine."[1052]

Consequently, according to Clement, the invented pagan gods can never give rise to true worship or to true prayer. As long as the gods worshipped are not honourable or true, the prayers to them cannot be so either. Prayers to unworthy gods would – according to Clement – arise from desires and impulses. For this reason, the created gods are dangerous, and therefore both the pagan ideas about the gods and the pagan gods must be reproached. Clement gives a concrete example of an unfitting custom practised by pagans, namely the worship of concrete objects:

> "and the same people worship every stock and every shining stone, as the phrase is, and are in awe of red wool and grains of salt and torches and squills and brimstone, being bewitched by the sorcerers according to certain impure purifications... But the true God regards nothing as holy but the character of the just man..."[1053]

Clement contrasts the pagan focus on the holiness of concrete objects with the Christian focus on the holiness of the virtuous character. Clement is probably distorting pagan cult by pointing only to its interest in the concrete materials, but also internally among "pagans" and pagan philosophers, the concreteness of the cult was a debated issue. The materiality of pagan religion is explained by the Neoplatonic philosopher Porphyry as a means of remembering: "For images of living creatures and temples were built for the sake of remembrance in order that those who frequent those places meditate when they arrive there."[1054] Nonetheless, by way of the negative categorization of the pagans, Clement builds up Christian religious identity by idealizing its virtuous character. The exact same strategy is used in another passage:

1052 Id. 7.7.38.
1053 Id. 7.4.26.
1054 Porph. Chr. frag. 76, quoted in R.M. Berchman (ed.), *Porphyry. Against the Christians*, Leiden 2005.

"And as they that worship earthly things pray to the images as though they heard them...; so the true majesty of the word is received from the trustworthy teacher in the presence of men, the living images (κατ'εἰκόνα)..., and the benefit done to them is referred to the Lord Himself, after whose likeness the man creates and molds (δημιουργεῖ καὶ μεταρρυθμίζει) the character of the man under instruction (τὸν κατηχούμενον ἄνθρωπον), renewing him to salvation (εἰς σωτηρίαν)."[1055]

It is striking how Clement describes Christian life as something dynamic and processuel – Christians are living images that are being created, moulded, renewed and are under instruction. This is contrasted with the pagan stiffness and their orientation towards dead images. Clement is not the only Christian author who emphasized the dynamic character of Christian life. In the following chapter, we shall see that all of the Christian authors emphasized Christian life as life under positive development. D.K. Buell has argued that by demonstrating that Christian identity is a fluid identity, in contrast to the fixed rival identities, Christianity seems the better alternative for converts.[1056]

Both Clement and Origen mention and reject certain ideas from philosophy that render prayer irrelevant, i.e. the so-called "problem of prayer." Origen distinguishes between such ideas, and mentions that the worst ideas are held by "those who are entirely atheistic and who deny the existence of God or who admit the name of God but deny his providence."[1057] Those who altogether deny God and God's providence are beyond reach, and Origen declares that he will not deal with those. The others, however, are, according to Origen's stance misguided Christians: "the opposing power, desiring to dress the name of Christ and the teachings of the Son of God with the most impious of teachings (τὰ ἀσεβέστατα τῶν δογμάτων)..."[1058] We will get back to the "heretical" Christians in the following paragraph, but note here that also Clement wrote against "philosophers." From Clement's text, it becomes evident that Christians were accused of being atheists. Clement defends Christians against this accusation and insistently writes that: "the Christian therefore is no atheist – this is what we proposed to

---

1055 Clem. Strom. 7.9.52 (Hort/Mayor).
1056 D.K. Buell is referred to in Iricinschi/Zellentin, 2008, 10.
1057 Or. or. 5.1 (Koetschau; tr. Stewart-Sykes).
1058 Id.

prove to the philosophers."[1059] Holding this rejection of atheism together
with Origen's labelling others as "atheists," it is obvious that "atheist" was
a strong pejorative and a forceful way to outflank an opponent in the days
of late antiquity. "Atheist" was a "perfect" negative categorization.[1060]

4.4.3 Prayer and heretical "others"

In the period under investigation, i.e. the decades around the year 200,
Christianity was still a very varied phenomenon. This is reflected in the
treatises on prayer in the way that the authors are struggling with contemporary "heretical" opinions and schisms. Averil Cameron has noted
that "Christian discourse presents a paradox: sprung from a situation of
openness and multiplicity, its spread produced a world with no room for
dissenting opinions."[1061] In the presently considered treatises, the authors
are trying to delimit multiplicity and point to uniformity by reference to
the Scriptures, the teachings of Christ, including the Lord's Prayer, and the
apostles. Still, the authors are not unambiguously "proto-orthodox." We
can note that of the four authors on whom we are focusing, only the latest
one, Cyprian, was "orthodox" in the eyes of the later Catholic Church.[1062]

1059 Clem. Strom. 7.9.54 (Hort/Mayor). Also Strom. 7.1.1. For other accusations
      that the Christians were atheists, see Just. apol. 1.6 (Minns/Parvis).
1060 J.G. Cook, *Roman Attitudes Towards the Christians*, Tübingen 2011, 4. Cook
      mentions how the early Roman reaction against Christians was to label them
      as "atheists." W.H.C. Frend also notices that converting to Christianity meant
      that one would be looked upon as an "atheotes," which meant that one
      was "putting oneself outside the ambit of Roman religion." In other words,
      being called an atheist meant being looked upon as having a negative identity
      (Frend, 1986, 148). See also Gibbon, 1787, 67. He notes that Christians were
      represented "as a society of atheists."
1061 A. Cameron quoted in Buell, 1999, 181. Averil Cameron subscribes to the
      widespread view on Christian development that Christianity evolved from a
      multiple phenomenon to the more uniform.
1062 Hilary of Poitiers, a Catholic Bishop from the fourth century, testified to
      the positive reception of Cyprian's treatise on prayer, when he wrote in his
      Commentary on Matthew: "Concerning the sacrament of prayer, Cyprian, the
      man of blessed memory, has freed us from the necessity of making comment
      [because he wrote De Dominica Oratione]. And although Tertullian wrote a
      most competent volume on this matter, the subsequent error of the man has
      detracted from the authority of his commendable writings" (Commentary on

Nonetheless, in the third century, they all took part in the discursive fight about orthodoxy, and they held views on prayer that they wanted to defend against differing ideas of prayer existing in their surroundings. This takes up some space, but not the predominant part of the treatises.

When taking into account that the treatises under investigation were meant for edifying purposes, it is understandable that there is not much information on heretical practices and opinions. On the contrary, Cyprian emphasizes unity of mind and unity of prayer several times in *De Dominica Oratione*. Thereby, he positively affirms the need for Christians to stick together. Unity is even presented as a necessity for salvation, when Cyprian notes that "sectarianism" (*haereses*) is one of the things that cannot get into the Kingdom of God.[1063] Likewise Cyprian warns that not even martyrdom will save the one who is not in harmony with his brothers in the church.[1064] This is a severe statement against any kind of schism, bearing in mind that this was a period where martyrdom was equalled with baptism as a road to salvation. Apparently, to break unity is a grievous sin. Unanimous prayer is a sign of the necessary unity.

As mentioned, the Greek authors, whose orthodoxy was later looked upon with great suspicion, addressed an audience that was more advanced in studying Christianity. It therefore makes sense that the tricky issues of heresy and the "problem of prayer" are given greater attention in the Greek treatises. Clement thus, on his own accord, mentions the charge made against Christians by "Jews and Greeks" that Christianity cannot hold one truth due to the many sects:

> "The first charge they allege is this very point, that the diversity of sects (διὰ τὴν διαφωνίαν τῶν αἱρέσεων) shows belief to be wrong... To whom we reply that, both among you Jews and among the most approved of the Greek philosophers, there have been multitudes of sects (πάμπολλαι γεγόνασιν αἱρέσεις), yet of course you do

---

Matthew 5.1 (tr. Williams)). We can infer that already in the fourth century, Cyprian was held in high esteem, wheras Tertullian was looked upon with some suspicion. Clement was written out of the martyrology in the sixteenth century, and Origen's teachings was condemned at a Church council in 553.

1063 Cypr. Dom. orat. 16 (Réveillaud; tr. Stewart-Sykes).
1064 Id. 24.

not say that one should hesitate to be a philosopher or a follower of the Jews on account of the internal discord of your sects."[1065]

Who, then, were the heretics? Origen mentions that there was in his time an "opposing power (ἡ ἀντικειμένη ἐνέργεια)" that tried to "persuade some people that they should not pray."[1066] Furthermore, he tells us about this opposition: "These people also accuse the Scriptures of not intending prayer (συκοφαντοῦντες τὰς γραφάς, ὡς καὶ τὸ εὔχεσθαι τοῦτο οὐ βουλομένας)."[1067] There were apparently groups that used the "Christian" Scriptures but downplayed the role of prayer. These were probably gnostics; indeed, we know that some so-called gnostic sources from the second-third century present prayer as secondary or overtly discourage prayer.[1068] Nonetheless, we know that there also exist "gnostic" prayers, as we saw above by the example of the *Prayer of the Apostle Paul* in Chapter 2.1.2.[1069] Clement also knew a group who disavowed prayer, and he writes:

"certain heterodox persons belonging to the heresy of Prodicus, [are] against the use of prayer (μὴ δεῖν εὔχεσθαι πρός τινων ἑτεροδόξων, τουτέστιν τῶν ἀμφὶ τὴν Προδίκου αἵρεσιν παρεισαγομένων δογμάτων)."[1070]

Earlier in *Stromateis*, Clement has already mentioned this Prodicus as an antinomian as well as his followers. They are by Clement categorized as "falsely calling themselves gnostics."[1071] As we know, Clement wanted to preserve the title "gnostic" as a distinction for the perfect Christian; therefore, he refuses to call Prodicus' followers gnostics since he sees them as

---

1065 Clem. Strom. 7.15.89 (Hort/Mayor). Buell notices that Clement uses much kinship-language towards the end of strom. 7, which is exactly dealing with heresy (Buell, 1999, 11).
1066 Or. or. 5.1 (Koetschau; tr. Stewart-Sykes).
1067 Id.
1068 E.g. The Gospel of Thomas 142: "And if you pray you will be condemned"; 104:1 and the Gospel of Philip 52:25-33 (See N. Dorian, *The Gospel of Thomas. Introduction and Commentary*, Leiden 2014).
1069 In Tert. Val. 10 (Riley), Tertullian refers to gnostic mythology and mentions that prayer takes place.
1070 Clem. Strom. 7.7.41 (Hort/Mayor). Note the use of the word heterodox – a Greek word for the act of mistaking one thing for another.
1071 Clem. Strom. 2.209.30 (Hort/Mayor); cf. 3.31.2 ff. Also mentioned in Strom. 7.16.105.

nothing but sectarians. Prodicus is, it might be added, assumed to be the gnostic thinker who is mentioned twice also by Tertullian.[1072] Furthermore, without mentioning it explicitly, the Christian authors and their limited acceptance of petitionary prayers and prayers for earthly gifts can be seen as an indirect rejection of the flourishing gnostic rejection of prayer in general and especially of petitions for earthly or physical necessities. The Christian authors are, as we have seen not very prone to this kind of prayer, but nor do they reject them entirely. There is some room for everyday requests and petitions for things regarding this present life.

In *Perì Euchês* 29, Origen refers to the Marcionites by allegations such as: "we should confront those who divide the divinity, who consider the good Father of our Lord to be distinct from the God of the Law."[1073] He continues: "They have fashioned another God apart from the one that made heaven and earth."[1074] Because of this division of Father- and Creator-God, Origen assumes that the Marcionites cannot come to terms with the petition from the Lord's Prayer "Do not lead us into temptation." The Marcionites could not believe that "Our Father," i.e. the good God, could lead people into testing, and according to Origen, their heretical doctrines would lead them to misinterpret the Lord's Prayer. Whether or not Origin is correct, this reminds us that not only can a certain tradition of prayer affect and influence the identity of individual and groups, the interpretation of prayer is also highly dependent on the context. Concrete prayer texts or practices of prayer can easily be modelled to express doctrinal orthodoxy, or set prayers can be interpreted in ways that make them orthodox.[1075]

1072 Tert. Prax. 3.6. (Evans) and Scorp. 15 (tr. Thelwall).
1073 Or. or. 29.12 (Koetschau; tr. Stewart-Sykes). Clement also lashes out against Marcion in Clem. Strom. 7.16.103 (Hort/Mayor).
1074 Or. or. 29.13 (Koetschau; tr. Stewart-Sykes).
1075 It is not seldom that prayer texts or hymns must be altered in order to fit doctrinal matters. Later, for instance, it would be more fine-drawn Christological distinctions that caused Christians to mark their different identities through prayer. Thus Sozomen describes how "heterodox" ("Arian") and "orthodox" Christians sang hymns with slightly different wordings at services (Soz. EH III,20,8 (Bidez et al.).

4.4.4 Considerations on prayer, identity and "othering"

The preceding paragraphs have shown that prayer was used by Christians in late antiquity not only as a unifying act and symbol. The correct use of prayer and the right to address God in prayer were obviously believed to be something that positively contrasted Christians from others; this includes contrasting "orthodox" Christians from "heterodox" Christians – although none of the "Christian" communities yet had the power to effectuate their claim of orthodoxy. As it has already been discussed in the previous chapter, prayer was an identity marker, and a convenient one since prayer is an overt gesture for supposed inner sentiments and beliefs. As such prayer was expected to reveal the inner character of the one praying, and common prayer was prayer not only confessing God but also belonging to the community with which one was praying. In order to gain internal cohesion, prayer was also used as a paradigm for orthodoxy, in other words: according to the authors, a correct understanding and practice of prayer existed, and those who did not pray aright could not be part of the community. This becomes evident in the treatises on prayer where non-Christians are reproached because of their inefficient prayer practice and their lack of faith in Christ. The lack of faith in Christ made their prayers irrelevant, since God had to be approached through Christ.

J. Lieu has noted that "The creation of otherness is a literary enterprise, reproduced no doubt in worship and homily."[1076] This is in agreement with what we see in the discourses on prayer. It is reasonable to expect that "the others" mentioned in the treatises correspond to a reality outside of literature. Nonetheless, these "others" only take shape as they are described in literature. The categorizations spontaneously and not necessarily consistently made in the social world are outlined and fixed in literature, and thereby they gain reality. When outlined the categorizations are supposed to have consequences for life and worship. E. Iricinschi and H.M. Zellentin points to this "performative" character of writing about "others" – heretics are "created" when they are being named as such.[1077]

1076 Lieu, 2004, 297.
1077 Iricinschi/Zellentin, 2008, 20.

Christian communities imposed a strong sense of religious identity on their adherents; this was done in part by separating themselves from other religious viewpoints and interpretations of prayer.[1078] Other ways of understanding and performing prayer were not only seen as irrelevant for Christians, but as harmful and signs of rejection of the Kingdom of God. Christianity was presented as the radical new alternative also when it came to prayer, although Christian prayers and practice in some ways *de facto* were similar to those of the surrounding society.[1079]

4.5 Relations to supernatural beings

In the article "Prayer in Origen's Contra Celsum: the Knowledge of God and the Truth of Christianity," Lorenzo Perrone describes a pattern prevalent in Origen's *Contra Celsum* regarding prayer. The pattern is that prayer journeys from the individual to God through Christ, by way of the Spirit. Perrone then notes:

> "We find traces here of the 'trinitarian' context which accompanies even the most intimate expression of prayer in *PE,* where the act of praying is never held to be merely a moment of self-isolation, just an accomplishment of interiority, but is rather seen as the realization of a larger communion. Such an act of communion not only involves the persons of the Trinity, but implies also the active assistance of the angels and the saints, with the whole 'cosmic theatre' as the proper scene of this most personal act."[1080]

Perrone thereby depicts the large social situation in which the praying person is located because of his/her prayer. A larger communion surrounds the praying individual whether he/she is alone or in the midst of people. For a modern mind, this wealth of beings might seem odd, but the third-century

---

1078 Gwyn/Bangert, 2010, 5 f.
1079 Prayer did function as an identity marker that distinguished communities from one another, if not because of the practices themselves, then because of the gods addressed. From late antique historiography, we hold a peculiar example of how prayer was used in power struggles between religious groups, i.e. "The story of the Thundering Legion." Christian authors wrote that Christian prayer had been effective in a certain battle against the Quadi in 174, whereas pagans held that pagan prayer had saved the day (M. Ott, *Thundering Legion*, in: CE 14, New York 1912).
1080 Perrone, 2001, 16.

treatises suggest that the idea of spiritual beings was such an integrated part of the antique world view that the authors could employ it without further explanation. Thus the authors portray angels as agents in the world; in some instances, heavenly bodies and evil powers are also expected to be around, as it will be outlined below. These beings are mentioned here because they have an effect on prayer. As we shall see, prayers are understood to be witnessed and influenced, both positively and negatively, by rational beings in the cosmos.

4.5.1 Angels[1081]

Although in modern times, Karl Barth has characterized angels as "essentially marginal figures,"[1082] this was not the prevailing view in late antiquity. In all four treatises dealt with here, there are frequent references to angels as agents with important roles for prayer and worship. The authors understood the role of angels in varied ways. Hence, there does not seem to have been a unified concept of angels in the late antique period.[1083]

Ellen Muehlberger has studied the Christian ideas about angels in late antiquity with a focus especially on the fourth and fifth centuries. Muehlberger points to a distinction between two discourses about angels that were more prevalent than others. I shall briefly describe these two discourses, which Muehlberger characterizes as "cultivation" and "contestation" discourses, respectively.[1084] Furthermore, Muehlberger points to the

---

1081 The content of the following paragraphs is similar to my article "Witnessed by Angels: The Role of Angels in Relation to Prayer in Four Ante-Nicene Euchological Treatises" in: *Studia Patristica. Papers presented at the Seventeenth International Conference on Patristic Studies held in Oxford 2015*, vol. LXXV, Leuven 2017, 49–56.
1082 Barth, *Church Dogmatics*, 1960, 371.
1083 In her book *Angels in Late Ancient Christianity*, Ellen Muehlberger shows that the ideas and beliefs about angels were varying among Christinians also in the following centuries (Muehlberger, 2013), cf. M. Recinová, *Clement's Angelological doctrines: Between Jewish Models and Philosophic-Religious Streams of Late Antiquity*, in: M. Havrda/V. Hušek/J. Plátova (eds.), *The Seventh Book of the Stromateis. Proceedings of the Colloquium on Clement of Alexandria*, Leiden 2012, 93-112.
1084 Muehlberger, 2013, 212.

fact that these two discourses were used in two different social contexts. The "cultivation discourse" was dominating in the context of Egyptian monks and ascetics. In the ascetic milieus, the discourse about angels presented angels as guardians and guides for human souls on their way back to God. Muehlberger mentions how Origen and later on Evagrius proposed that angels were rational beings who were in the process of returning to union with God. Humans found themselves in the same situation and had to find their way back to God. Angels were believed to help people in their individual return to God, which was made possible through studies and prayer. One way in which the angels could help was by being witnesses to prayer and help to purify and educate the praying individual.[1085] In this way, angels were connected to a certain "cultivation" of the individual.

In another context, angels were understood differently, namely in the urban congregations where the bishops presided. The prevailing discourse in these urban milieus was the "contestation discourse." Here angels were used in theological debates not to cultivate individuals, but to form communities and justify the rituals of the community.[1086] Angels were thus used with the aim of assembling congregations through persuasive rhetoric. "Cultivation" and "contestation" are different "modes of piety." I shall argue that both "discourses" and "modes of piety" are present already in the third-century treatises on prayer, although conflated and in less developed form.

4.5.1.1 Contestation and cultivation discourses in the euchological treatises

The contestation discourse is reflected in the euchological treatises where angels are used in theological arguments about the life of the church. This is, for example, the case when angels are said to take part in the worship of the entire congregation. The four authors under investigation share one belief concerning angels, namely that eschatological salvation involve collective worship with angels, and already here on earth this eschatological state of worship was anticipated by the Christians. Worship here on earth

---

1085 Ead. e.g. 38.
1086 Muehlberger, 2013, 210.

was seen as a foreshadowing of the heavenly liturgy in which angels were already engaged.

Tertullian believes that angels are worshipping in heaven, and he refers to Isaiah 6:3 as his argument: "the attendant angels do not cease to say: 'holy, holy, holy (*Santus, sanctus, sanctus*).'"[1087] These three exclamations "holy, holy, holy," known as *trishagion* or *Sanctus* in liturgical studies,[1088] could indicate that this expression was also used in Tertullian's congregation, exactly with the aim of creating a link between the angelic worship in heaven and the concrete worship below. Moreover, Tertullian is even more direct when he mentions that Christians "are here already learning that heavenly song to God and that task of future glory (*iam hinc caelestem illam in Deum vocem et officium future claritatis ediscimus*)."[1089] There is a correspondence between current worship and future glorification. Tertullian understood salvation as connected to the heavenly worship. He returns to the eschatological prayer again in the last paragraph of *De Oratione*, where he expresses the idea that a cosmic act of prayer is taking place at the moment, i.e. when the congregation prays: "Indeed, every angel prays, every creature."[1090] Tertullian writes as if the future salvation and the present worship are conflated right here and now. Prayer is thus breaking boundaries of time and space, and allows the whole of creation – past and present, heavenly and earthly – to be united in prayer. In this last passage, Tertullian changes his focus and instead of explaining issues related to prayer, he depicts how prayer sways the entire creation: "And even now (*nunc*[1091]), the birds arise, lifting themselves to heaven,

---

1087 Tert. Or. 3 (Schleyer; tr. Stewart-Sykes). See also Or. 5.
1088 For liturgical studies on this theme, see Taft, 1993; B.D. Spinks, *The Place of Christ in Liturgical Prayer. Trinity, Christology, and Liturgical Theology*, Collegeville 2008; G. Winkler. See references in G. Winkler, *The Sanctus. Some Observations with Regard to its Origins and Theological Significance*, in: B. Neil/G.D. Dunn/L. Cross (eds.), *Prayer and Spirituality in the Early Church. Liturgy and Life 3*, Strathfield 2003 and Munkholt Christensen, 2010.
1089 Tert. Or. 3 (Schleyer; tr. Stewart-Sykes).
1090 Id. 29.
1091 Here I follow the editions of Evans and Diercks (Evans, 1953; G.F. Diercks: *Tertullianus De Oratione*. Bussum 1947), since Schleyer has *tunc*,

spreading out their wings like a cross whilst uttering what appears to be prayer."[1092]

The fact that Tertullian lets animals join in on worship – even if it is only a poetical expression – is a rather peculiar element in comparison with the Greek theologians. The Alexandrian theologians had "rational worship" as the ideal.[1093] To them, an important point of prayer and contemplation was that it consists in union between the rational mind, *nous*, of the individual and God. From the perspective of the Greeks, it is therefore only rational beings that can pray and be united with God, i.e. human beings and angels. On the contrary, Tertullian is convinced that the entire creation is turned towards the Creator, at least in a poetical way, and in this respect, rationality is downplayed as a point of departure for worship. In Tertullian's vision, the entire creation can approach God in prayer, and the flying bird has the shape of the cross, it is meant to fly and confess the sign of the cross. According to Tertullian, prayer is to some extent an integrated part of the created world as it should function. However, this does not mean that Tertullian disregarded "rationality." On the contrary, also Tertullian saw rationality as a divine characteristic given to Christians by God.[1094]

Also Clement envisioned the heavenly liturgy as taking place in parallel to human worship. He notes that the angels are praying and are doing so in a better way than the ordinary Christians, because the angels only pray for continuance of blessings and not for anything new.[1095] The most perfect Christians, however, can take part in the worship of the angels already here on earth:

"[The gnostic] prays also with angels (μετ' ἀγγέλων εὔχεται), as being already equal to angels (ὡς ἂν ἤδη καὶ ἰσάγγελος), and never passes out of the holy

---

i. e. "then" (D. Schleyer (ed.), *Tertullian. De baptismo, De oratione/Von der Taufe, vom Gebet*, Turnhout 2006).
1092 Tert. Or. 29 (Schleyer; tr. Stewart-Sykes).
1093 L. Perrone, For the Sake of a 'Rational Worship', 2009.
     Note e.g. Origen's reference to the "governing faculty," ἡγεμονικόν (or. 25.1 (Koetschau; tr. Stewart-Sykes)) and to the "rational worship" (λογικὴν ἱερουργίαν) offered to God by the angel Raphael (or. 11.1(Koetschau; tr. Stewart-Sykes)).
1094 See e.g. Tert. An. 16 (Waszink; tr. Holms).
1095 Clem. Strom. 7.7.39 (Hort/Mayor).

keeping: even if he prays alone (κἂν μόνος εὔχηται) he has the chorus of saints (τὸν τῶν ἁγίων χορὸν) banded with him."[1096]

According to Origen, the angels pray with the Church.[1097] Origen believes that where a church is in place, it will in fact be a twofold church, both human and angelic.[1098] Clement hints at the same when he mentions that "the earthly church is the image of the heavenly."[1099] Cyprian for his part does not mention angelic worship in *De Dominica Oratione,* but he envisions future salvation as worship. We see this in the last passage of his treatise on prayer, where he writes that Christians should pray now because in the Kingdom of God "we shall pray constantly and give thanks to God."[1100] There are thus slight differences between the Christian authors' view on celebrating angels. Whereas, Tertullian and Origen hold that angels are actively praying with Christians on earth, Clement seems to believe that angels are praying on their own, distanced from humans. According to Clement, only perfect Christians have reached a level where they pray with the angels. A benefit of being a perfect Christian is thus the added empowerment of one's prayers by angels. These examples show that angels were definitely understood as having a positive influence, and angels were frequently employed to create a positive image of congregational worship. The congregation as such stood in connection with the heavens and the heavenly worship.

Ellen Muehlberger mentions a passage in which Cyprian expounds the idea that angels are involved in the "baptism" of martyrs. He believes that martyrs are baptized in heaven by angels. Ellen Muehlberger then concludes that:

> "[in] situations when the legitimacy of ritual and ritual celebrants were challenged, the suggestion that an angel might somehow be involved, lending its power to the baptism, whether actual or figurative, allowed Christian leaders to invoke both authority for themselves and authenticity for their ritual communities, whether large or small."[1101]

1096 Id. 7.12.78.
1097 Or. or. 31.5 (Koetschau; tr. Stewart-Sykes).
1098 Id.
1099 Clem. Strom. 4.8.66 (Hort/Mayor).
1100 Cypr. Dom. orat. 36 (Réveillaud; tr. Stewart-Sykes).
1101 Muehlberger, 2013, 183.

Angels were thus occasionally used to lend authority to a ritual or to an authority figure, e.g. a bishop. However, there is a noticeable absence of empowerment of authority figures in the euchological treatises. Ellen Muehlberger has argued that this comes later in church history. In her book, she examines how the understanding of angels and the liturgy changed from the earliest paradigm, in which the earthly liturgy was imagined to be an imitation of the angelic worship in heaven. Muehlberger sees a transformation taking place in the late-fourth century because from about that time, the angels were rather understood as being present in the earthly liturgy and responding directly to priestly performance. This latter conception was not a rejection of the heavenly liturgy, but it prioritized the earthly liturgy and the priest's role and thus authorized the priest in a way that the third-century authors did not.[1102] Angels and their prayers were thus eventually used in order to empower the ecclesial hierarchy, but in the texts under investigation this shift had not yet occurred.

As previously mentioned, also the "cultivation discourse" regarding angels can be found in the treatises on prayer dealt with in this study. This is especially the case in the texts by the Alexandrian authors, Clement and Origen. Muhlberger also acknowledges Origen as a predecessor for this sort of discourse (she sees it developed further by Evagrius Ponticus, Gregory of Nazianzus, etc.). However, here I want to begin by showing that Clement presented angels in "cultivation discourses" as well. He presents angels both as ideal figures, representing the highest level of being (except from the divine persons) and as guides that help the individual in his/her progress towards God. As such angels had a "cultivating effect" both as ideals and as assumed helpers. Angels were, according to Clement:

> "at the extreme end of the visible world there is the blessed ordinance of angels; and so, even down to ourselves, ranks below ranks are appointed, all saving and being saved by the initiation and through the instrumentality of One."[1103]

These angels are themselves in need of salvation, and therefore their progression is an ideal for human beings. The true gnostic is therefore admonished to:

1102 Id.
1103 Clem. Strom. 7.2.9 (Hort/Mayor).

[fix] his eyes on noble images, on the many patriarchs who have fought their fight
before him, on a still greater multitude of prophets, on angels beyond our power
to number, on the Lord who is over all, who taught him, and made it possible for
him to attain that crowning life.[1104]

The role of angels, however, goes beyond being ideals. Clement also believes
that angels actually work in the world for the benefit of human beings; the
process towards salvation is for instance furthered by the chastening act
of angels.[1105] But at some point, the individual Christian reaches a point
at which angels cannot help any further, because the gnostic has reached
"equality with the angels."[1106] When having been thus perfected, prayer
becomes a confession and response to the promise of salvation:

"the gnostic should no longer need the help given through the angels, but being
made worthy should receive it from himself, and have his protection from himself
by means of his obedience. The prayer of such an one is the claiming of a promise
from the Lord."[1107]

In *Perì Euchês*, Origen presents similar ideas. For instance, he notes that
to the person who prays perfectly, God will give more than what is prayed
for, namely also the guidance of an angel (cf. Eph 3:20). Origen writes that
God will send an angel: "To this other person who will be of a particular
character, I shall send this angel to assist (τὸν ἄγγελον λειτουργὸν) him,
to work with him for a certain time for his salvation…"[1108] According to
Origen, angels are "superior co-workers" (τὸν κρείττονα συνεργόν) of God,
i.e. superior in comparison with human beings and other "inferior powers"
(χείρων … ἡ δύναμις). Origen also believes that angels pray with humans
and work to fulfil prayers. He summarizes:

"But more than this, the angel of each of us (ὁ ἑκάστου ἄγγελος), even of "little
ones" in the church, who for ever look upon the face of the Father in heaven and
on the divinity of the one who formed us, prays alongside us and acts together

---

1104 Id. 7.11.63.
1105 Id. 7.2.11. On the role of angels in Clement's work, see also Bergjan,
      2012, 78 ff.
1106 Clem. Strom. 7.10.57 (Hort/Mayor). The gnostic also prays with the angels
      and saints whenever he prays (Clem. Strom. 7.12.78).
1107 Id. 7.13.81.
1108 Or. or. 6.4 (Koetschau; tr. Stewart-Sykes).

with us, as much as is possible, with regard to the matters concerning which we pray."[1109]

Origen presented the idea that the world is "a theater of angels and humans (ἐν θεάτρῳ ἐσμὲν κόσμου καὶ ἀγγέλων)," and that every human has an individual angel who is in contact, face to face, with the Father in heaven (τίς ὁ ἑκάστου ἡμῶν ἄγγελος βλέπων "τοῦ ἐν οὐρανοῖς" "πατρὸς" τὸ πρόσωπον).[1110] Angels are thus mediators between humans and God.

The Latin authors do not in the same way understand angels to play a role in the development of human beings, although Tertullian admonishes Christians to be "angelic" (*angelorum candidati*)."[1111] That admonition has positive connotations and is related to the anticipated salvation. Cyprian refers to angels mentioned in the Scriptures and makes the point that angels are witnesses before God; angels testify to the prayers and good deeds that people have done. Cyprian mentions the angel coming to Cornelius in Acts 10:3–4 to testify to the efficiency of Cornelius' prayers and almsgiving.[1112] Cyprian also refers to the angel Raphael as a witness to prayer. It is the angel who bears the "recollection of your prayers into the presence of the holiness of God."[1113] Angels are thus part of the monitoring of Christians that Cyprian mentions at several instances but also helpers in the communication with God. Cyprian is the only author, who, in his writing on prayer, does not combine the liturgy of the church with the worship of angels in heaven.

We cannot point to one specific function of angels in relation to prayer in the four treatises studied here. Angels are role models, witnesses, mediators and helpers in the act of praying. According to the Alexandrian mind-set, angels are dynamic and act on their own accord for the benefit of individual Christians who pray; they exercise *pronoia* on behalf of God.[1114] On the contrary, according to the Latin authors, angels are more passive in relation to human prayers, they observe and witness. It has been suggested that

---

1109 Id. 11.5. Matt 18:10.
1110 Or. or. 28.3 (Koetschau; tr. Stewart-Sykes).
1111 Tert. Or. 3 (Schleyer; tr. Stewart-Sykes).
1112 Cypr. Dom. orat. 32 (Réveillaud; tr. Stewart-Sykes).
1113 Tob 8:12; Tert. Or. 33 (Schleyer; tr. Stewart-Sykes).
1114 Bergjan, 2012, 78 ff.

Christ was understood as a superior angel among some Christians in early Christianity, hence the so-called angelic and angleomorphic Christology, and somewhere Clement proposes such an idea.[1115] However, there is nothing pointing in that direction in the euchological treatises; they place Christ on a higher ontological level than angels. However, angels and Christ share the role as mediators between humans and God regarding prayer.

4.5.1.2 Planets and stars

Angels were not imagined in just one specific form in antiquity; this becomes obvious from the fact that there were serious considerations about the angelic nature of heavenly bodies such as planets and stars. Also Clement and Origen, who were well aware of philosophical ideas of their day, considered the question whether the heavenly bodies were angels.[1116] The idea arose from the fact that the heavenly bodies moved, and were therefore believed to be rational beings with a will to set themselves in perfect motion. Attributing rationality to stars and planets was a widespread idea in antiquity, and Clement and Origen took it over from Platonic philosophy and astrology. Within pagan Platonism planets were occasionally presented as high-ranking beings in the ontological hierarchy, and there were speculations as to whether the planets might serve as intermediate dwelling places for the souls after death.[1117] As mentioned above, Stoics held that a rational soul permeated the universe and thus also the heavenly bodies.[1118] The regularity of movement in the heavenly bodies was recognized as beautiful and as more perfect than human movements which are so often led astray by passions. The harmonious movements of the planets were understood as a result of perfect providence, and it was believed that the will of the heavenly bodies were harmonized with God's will.

The Christian authors were inspired by philosophy and by the Jewish thinker Philo. Philo condemned astrology and worship of heavenly bodies,

---

1115 D.D. Hannah, *Michael and Christ. Michael Traditions and Angel Christology in Early Christianity*, Tübingen 1999, 212 f.; Recinová 2012, 105 ff.
1116 See e.g. above paragraph 2.2.1. and A. Scott, *Origen and the Life of the Stars. A History of an Idea*, Oxford 1994.
1117 Scott, 1994, 108.
1118 Cf. above, paragraph 2.2.1.

but still he admonished his readers: "Just like the heavens and the choir of the stars, the human mind has received a vocation of praise of God in the universe."[1119] Philo thus expected the stars to worship God.

Out of the four authors, only Origen directly mentions "heavenly bodies" in his treatise on prayer. That happens in a context in which Origen says that one cannot affect the free will of perfect souls by prayer. The stars and the planets are as rational beings believed to have a free will, and they use it for the well-being of all when they move. No prayer can change their course, because they are more perfect than human beings who are easily affected and change their mind (for the worse).[1120] Origen asks:

"But what sense-impressions might interpose, and oust or derange heavenly beings from a course that is of benefit to the whole world, since each is in possession of a soul that is fashioned by reason and is entirely self-motivated, and since they employ bodies so ethereal and supremely good?"

Origen uses the heavenly bodies both as an example of the perfect use of free will, and to demonstrate that beings exist whose will is perfect and cannot be changed. Origen did not agree with the contemporary philosophy that the heavenly bodies were gods in their own right. On the contrary, Origen argued that since sun, moon and stars pray to God, it does not make sense to pray to them.[1121]

In Clement's treatise, *Stromateis* 7, there is not a similar direct mentioning of heavenly bodies. However, the editors of the text Mort and Mayor consider if there is an indirect reference to the stars as angels in *Stromateis* 7.2.9. In this passage, Clement mentions the hierarchy of visible beings which begins "at the extreme end of the visible world." Clement writes that at this extreme end "is the blessed ordinance of angels."[1122] This

---

1119 Phil. Som. 1.35; Q.E. II, 73; Laporte, 1986, 81 and Scott, 1994, 110.
1120 Or. or. 7 (Koetschau; tr. Stewart-Sykes).
1121 Scott, 1994, 132 f.; for instances where Origen mentions the ontological character of the heavenly bodies: Cels. 5.11 (2.12.11–16.) and Mart. 7. Also Clem. Strom. 6.148.1 (Früchtel /Stählin/Treu; tr. Roberts): "But most people, together with the philosophers, ascribe growth and change primarily to the stars and rob, as far as it is up to them, the father of the universe of his inexhaustible power."
1122 Clem. Strom. 7.2.9 (Hort/Mayor).

could well be a reference to the heavenly bodies as angels, since we know that Clement was familiar with this idea.[1123]

As mentioned earlier, the Latin authors do not make use of similar speculative ontology and cosmology. None of them combines prayer with heavenly bodies, and such speculations also seem to have been beyond their interest. In another text, Tertullian makes an ironic remark about astrology by mentioning the pre-Socratic philosopher Thales of Miletus who fell into a well because he was looking at the sky and not paying attention to what was right in front of him: "Such, however, is the enormous preoccupation of the philosophic mind, that it is generally unable to see straight before it. (Hence the story of Thales falling into the well)."[1124]

4.5.2 Evil powers

In the treatises on prayer, angels are presented positively as beings that pray correctly and can have a beneficial role in effectuating requests. Contrary to the angels that hold a high rank in the hierarchy of beings, there are evil spirits and "the evil one," i.e. the devil. The evil powers are presented as being able to tempt and influence Christians, and therefore the evil powers indirectly have a negative effect on prayer.[1125] The evil powers can affect individuals in a negative and unvirtuous way which in turn will have a negative influence on their prayers. The negative beings receive relatively little attention in the treatises, although demons were to become the " 'stars' of the religious drama of late antiquity."[1126] Again, this probably has to do

---

1123 Hort/Mayor, 1902, 212.
1124 Tert. An. 6.8 (Waszink; tr. Holms): "*Sed enormis intentio philosophiae solet plerumque nec prospicere pro pedibus (sic Thales in puteum).*"
1125 Brakke, 2006, 70 ff., for a treatment of negative influence of demons on prayer in the monastic milieu of late antiquity. Brakke points out that since monks were so good at controlling the passions of their "desiring part," the demons attacked the irascible part, i.e. tried to make them angry. Anger would ruin their "pure prayers." For instance, Evagrius insists that anger "darkens the ruling faculty of the one who prays and leaves his prayers in obscurity." As such demons were believed to have the opposite of a cultivating effect on the monks who could not hold sway.
1126 Brown, 1971, 54. Bitton-Ashkelony sees a link between the developing anxiety towards demons and the development of private prayer as a spiritual exercise (B. Bitton-Ashkelony, *Demons and Prayers. Spiritual Exercises in*

with the edifying genre of the texts under investigation, but in the case of Clement, it also has to do with his theology and soteriology according to which there in general is not much room for "evil powers." Everything that happens to people happens for their own good according to Clement. God's providence is perfect, and what appears as an evil occurrence in a human's life is part of God's plan for the salvation of this person. Human beings can of course be evil towards one another, but this is due to the mal-practice of their wills. Clement ascribes evil behaviour to ignorance and weakness; seeking knowledge and abiding to it willfully can thus extinguish evil. There is only one instance in *Stromateis* 7 in which Clement mentions the devil, i.e.:

> "For it does not follow that, if an action has its rise in folly and the operation, or rather co-operation, of the devil (διαβόλου ἐνέργειαν), it is to be at once identified with folly or the devil (διάβολος)."[1127]

Here, even though Clement acknowledges a possible influence from the devil, there is no weakening of the human responsibility. Clement interposes the correction "the co-operation of the devil," thereby making it clear that humans have a say in relation to evil.

Origen refers to "evil spirits and cruel people (πονηροῖς πνεύμασι καὶ ἀνθρώποις)" whom Christians can and should hold at a distance by way of prayer.[1128] According to Origen, God responds to prayers for help against evil powers. This "agonistic" aspect of prayer is a constitutive element, ac-cording to Origen. One of God's measures to protect his people is letting angels guard them, as we saw above. Origen notes that if the accompanying angel is withdrawn from a person, "the inferior power" finds an oppor-tunity to incite this person to certain sins.[1129] Angels are thus protecting human beings from evil incitements. Humans are a battlefield where good and evil powers fight to win individuals over to their side, and prayers are beneficial in this situation, because God helps those who pray and those who are fighting against evil on their own accord. Origen therefore makes

---

the Monastic Community of Gaza in the Fifth and Sixth Century, in: VigChr 57/2 (2003), 200-221; Bitton-Ashkelony/Kofsky, 2006, 163).
1127 Clem. Strom. 7.11.66 (Hort/Mayor).
1128 Or. or. 13.3 (Koetschau; tr. Stewart-Sykes).
1129 Id. 6.4.

the suggestion: "let us pray that the will of God might be spread out over us for our restoration."[1130] The evil powers attacking humans are, however, not just to be understood as external powers, but are also within the individual where a struggle between spirit and flesh goes on.[1131] It is thus not unambiguous to which extent evil powers are regarded as outward agents or evil impulses from within. Demons were considered as inciting the inner impulses. Clement describes it thus that demons can make "imprents" on the intellect and thereby have distorting effects of demonically inspired passions on the soul. "For Clement and Evagrius, the intellect or soul is like a wax tablet, and incoming impressions can alter its shape."[1132]

Origen shows some realism when he recognizes that here on earth people cannot be completely immune to evil incitements, and humans will be tested – even by the good God.[1133] Therefore people should pray, like in the Lord's Prayer: "do not bring us into testing."[1134] This prayer means, according to Origen, that humans ask to be able to overcome the unavoidable testing in this life. The important task for Christians is to restrain themselves from acting on evil impulses. Rather evil impulses should be mastered and ignored, and prayers for the overcoming of evil emotions are admonished by Origen. He expresses this point with a metaphor from Ephesians 6:16 of a burning arrow: "let us implore [God]… that when we are assaulted by the fiery darts of the evil one (τοῦ πονηροῦ) we be not set on fire by them."[1135] Thus Origen indicates that people will experience evils and evil desires, but they have to overcome them and not allow them to have further effect. Using the metaphor of burning arrows, Origen describes the measures that can put out the fire caused by desire. He mentions "contemplation of the truth" as something that will create a spiritual character: "The flood" of spiritual thought will put out the fire of passion.[1136] The individual holds the responsibility for his/her actions; according to Origen, God rescues

---

1130 Id. 25.6.
1131 Id. 26.1-2; Clem. Strom. 7.3.20 (Hort/Mayor).
1132 Brakke, 2006, 73.
1133 Or. or. 29.9 (Koetschau; tr. Stewart-Sykes).
1134 Id. 29.1.
1135 Or. or. 30.3 (Koetschau; tr. Stewart-Sykes).
1136 Id.

people only "when we make a brave stand against these contingencies, and are victorious."[1137]

The ability not to sin and thus to avoid the evil forces of this world, is a proof of whether or not one belongs to God. By alluding to Scripture, Origen makes clear that if a person is committing a wrongdoing, he cannot be the child of God, but must be "of the Devil."[1138] Therefore, the address "Father" can just as well be an invocation of the devil, if the person praying has not earned the fatherhood of God. Cyprian makes the same combination of fatherhood and belonging in *De Dominica Oratione* 10. He writes about the Jews with a reference to John 8:44: "You are born of your father, the devil."

Whereas the Greek authors are a little hesitant to blame the devil for all kinds of temptations and evils in the world, the Latin authors have a more rigid view on the devil as an evil force acting against God. According to the Latin authors, it is the devil that creates weakness and malice.[1139] The idea of God as a salvific pedagogue that harms people for their own eternal good is not at all a theme in the Latin texts. The Latin authors cannot imagine that God could be the originator of any kind of temptation, and therefore Tertullian understands the two petitions "Do not let us into temptation" and "remove us from the evil one" as one petition, namely for God to keep the devil at a safe distance. Not being let into temptation equals not being near to the devil, according to Tertullian. This exegesis, however, does not offer any solution to the theodicy problem; God is here simply presented as competing with another power for influence on the free will of people.

In his mentioning of the seventh petition of the Lord's Prayer, Tertullian uses the phrase *a malo*, which can be either masculine in ablative "from the evil one" or neuter in ablative, "from evil." According to the interpretation made by Tertullian, he must understand *a malo* as masculine and hence as an evil figure and not as evil in a more abstract sense. It can be noted that Cyprian uses the same phrase, *a malo*, and seems to understand it in a similar manner, as an evil, personal power. It seems that in Tertullian's point of view, humans can only conquer the forces of the devil by praying to God

---

1137 Id. 30.1.
1138 τοῦ διαβόλου, e.g. 1 John 3:10.
1139 Tert. Or. 8 (Schleyer; tr. Stewart-Sykes).

and by remaining in a relationship with God. This is also what Cyprian makes clear: humans must depend on God to fight their battles: "If we pray and beseech he will show us his succor."[1140] And furthermore: "For when we have requested the protection of God against the evil one, and when it is granted, we stand secure and safe against everything that the devil and the world may do against us."[1141] In general, Cyprian, like Tertullian, is concrete when describing the devil. The devil is a force between humans and God. When commenting on the Lord's Prayer, Cyprian argues that humans should pray to God because "we are opposed by the Devil, and our thoughts and deeds are so prevented from complete submission to God."[1142] Contact with the almighty God is the only weapon against the disastrous work of the devil. Consequently, prayer has an indirect function as renunciation.

4.6 Conclusions on prayer and social relations with various others

The preceding chapter has shown the various ways in which prayer was presented as having to do with social relations and relations to beings of various types. The treatises were written from a theological and pastoral perspective, but the ease with which the Christian authors present angels and evil powers etc. could indicate that these were widely regarded as influential characters in life. Christian prayer was emphasized as essential in gaining the best from these beings and keeping evil powers at bay. A person praying finds himself/herself in a *synaxis* whether he/she prays alone or in a congregation. The social responsibility of the individual Christian begins before the actual prayer, since the efficacy of prayer to a large degree has to do with and is identical with harmonious relationships to fellow-Christians.

In the first paragraphs of the chapter, we saw how the treatises on prayer present a form of cult criticism by stressing that virtuous intent and behaviour are crucial elements in relation to prayer. Meanwhile, prayer as ritual and mode of piety was upheld and encouraged. Thereby, the Christian authors created a tension between the concrete prayers and the expectations

---

1140 Cypr. Dom. orat. 27 (Réveillaud; tr. Stewart-Sykes).
1141 Id.
1142 Id. 14.

to the character of the one praying – these two, prayer and character, should ideally always be balanced and affect one another. In fact, according to this logic, praying had a lot to do with one's relations to other people. The late antique interpretations of prayer introduced an element of social stimulus into the concept of prayer.

The preceding paragraphs showed that prayer was used in liturgical and congregational settings, and this was highly recommended. The content of prayer was supposed to be oriented towards the larger society in the form of intercession. The treatises show a noteworthy lack of priests and other clergy or elected intercessors between the congregation and God; only Cyprian, and to a small extent Origen, point forward to the important role that priests and "holy men" would later assume.

Since prayer was ubiquitous in antiquity, Christians had to distance their own prayer culture from that of the surrounding society. The harshest criticism of other types of pious behaviour was directed at the Jews, and this might be due to the fact that Jewish prayer formally resembled Christian prayer to a large extent. Clement, however, also attacked so-called gnostic prayer practice vehemently, which could well have to do with his own gnostic tendencies and context. This suits G. Stroumsa's conclusion that: "For the early Christian theologians, heresies appeared as the closest hence the most immediate and dangerous threat to their, emerging collective identity."[1143] Though, apparently, concerning prayer, the Jews were the most dangerous "others." In general, the negative descriptions of "the others" can be explained by the concept "negative categorization."

Kathryn Tanner has characterized Christian identity as "essentially relational."[1144] According to the outlined social theories above,[1145] identities are always relational; identity is shaped by the involvement with others and by the debt and intimacy of these relations. It is certain that within the Christian congregations the aim was a high degree of intimacy and dependence, and prayer apparently had the effect of establishing intimacy, dependence and belonging. Christians prayed for each other and with each

---

1143 G. Stroumsa, *Caro salutis cardo. Shaping the Person in Early Christian Thought*, in: HR 30 (1990), 25–50, 181 f.
1144 Tanner, 1997, 108.
1145 Paragraph 1.2, esp. 1.2.2. and 1.2.3.

other, but they were also encouraged to pray for everyone, and thus they used their prayers to create positive and exclusive relations. Intercession was a conscious social act, but also in indirect ways, there were relations established in prayer, because the very act of praying together is a form of confession of the community as such. It seems fair to talk about the relations established in prayer as multiaxial, because prayer links people both to heavenly and earthly beings; and according to the prayer theology of the third century, when praying each person should strive both upwards and sideways. William Fitzgerald comes to the same conclusion in a study on prayer as rhetoric and performance:

> "In so far as prayer can be distinguished from rhetoric, it is concerned with the purpose of discourse in relating to others – with beings like ourselves and with beings both like and unlike ourselves. In its essence, prayer positions discourse in a scheme of ethical orientation. In other words, we discover our character through discourse."[1146]

1146 W. Fitzgerald, *Spiritual Modalities. Prayer as Rhetoric and Performance.* University Park 2012, 133.

5 From sinner to saint: Self-relations and prayer

5.1 Introduction – the self as analytical category

We have seen in the previous chapter that collective identity and social relations were formed and upheld by way of a certain interpretation of prayer. This last of the main analytical chapters deals with the influence of prayer on the human self and personal identity. According to modern theoretical studies, the human self is processual, changeable and manifold, and multiple selves constitute the personal identity. As we saw in Chapter 1, George Herbert Mead defined the self as the discourse going on within a human mind. In this inner discourse, the voice of the "I" is in dialogue with the internalized voice of the surrounding world. Consequently, the self is not an entity, but represents the ongoing relationship that humans have with themselves and others. Selves are not fully autonomous; they are shaped and limited by the culture in which they develop. Patricia Cox Miller has noted:

> "*Subjectivity* is a term used in a variety of contemporary critical theories to describe a 'self' not as an autonomous source of meaning but rather as a construct, the product of systems of cultural convention. The discourses of a culture not only set limits to how a self may be understood but also provide models or paradigms that are used to classify or represent that culture's understanding of 'selfhood.' "[1147]

As mentioned already in the survey of secondary literature, the self has become a frequent and important theme in studies on early Christianity, also in the context of prayer and liturgy. Some scholars of late antiquity, such as Brouria Bitton-Ashkelony and Derek Krueger, have pointed to prayer and liturgy as important factors in the formation of ancient Christian selves. These studies focus upon the monastic milieu or the Byzantine liturgy where the theology and ascetic culture are more developed than in

---

1147 P.C. Miller, *Strategies of Representation in Collective Biography: Constructing the Subject as Holy*, in: T.Hägg/P. Rousseau (eds.), *Greek Biography and Panegyrics in Late Antiquity*, Oakland 2000, 221 n. 45.

the earlier church history. However, this thesis will investigate the earlier Christian prayer discourse as a way to Christianize selves.

Derek Krueger has shown how Orthodox liturgy in the Byzantine church had a formative role on the church-goers. Krueger points to the "Orthodox liturgy as a mechanism for the formation of interiority."[1148] Liturgy helped Christians gain access not only to God, but to themselves as well, because in the liturgy and through liturgical texts people were told who they were, and how they ought to be. The liturgy thus shaped each subject. Worth noting is that each subject was thus shaped in a similar way, and liturgy therefore expressed "a common individuality that in its generic force is not quite individual at all."[1149] Christian liturgy thus offers every individual a certain shape determined by the embedded anthropology of the specific theology.

Brouria Bitton-Ashkelony has also worked on the role of prayer for the formation of Christian selves. In a book by Bitton-Ashkelony and A. Kofsky on the monastic school of Gaza in the fourth to seventh century, a chapter is devoted to the effect of individual prayer on the spiritual progress of the monks, i.e. Chapter 8. *Spiritual Exercises: The Continuous Conversation of the Mind with God.*[1150] In this investigation, it is mentioned that the emergence of individual prayer in ascetic culture was a factor of spiritual progress.[1151] Furthermore, it is rightly claimed that the spiritual school of Gaza contributed with an "individual direction and help to each member in constructing his new self through the mechanism of prayer."[1152] However, already before the development of this ascetic culture in the fourth and fifth century, prayer was put forward as a means to cultivate the selves by the Christian authors of the second and third century. This is also mentioned *en passant* in the said contribution by Bitton-Ashkelony and Kofsky where they mention that Clement and Origen interpreted prayer to be

---

1148 Krueger, 2014, 6.
1149 Krueger, 2014, 8.
1150 Bitton-Ashkelony/Kofsky, 2006, 157. Similar with Bitton-Ashkelony, 2003.
1151 Bitton-Ashkelony/Kofsky, 2006, 157. Also Bitton-Ashkelony, 2003. P. Hadot, *Philosophy as a Way of Life. Spiritual Exercises from Socrates to Foucault*, Hoboken 1995.
1152 Bitton-Ashkelony/Kofsky, 2006, 158.

a state of mind and a means for further spiritual progress. We shall look into this below.

5.1.1 Tracing a line of self-orientated studies

Concerning studies of the self in antiquity, Brouria Bitton-Ashkelony mentions a line of inspiration going from the French philosopher and historian, Pierre Hadot, to the French philosopher and cultural historian, Michel Foucault, and further on to recent studies such as her own. It is worthwhile to trace this line: Pierre Hadot understood antique philosophy to have had an existential dimension; the starting point for philosophy in its various forms was to find a way to live good, virtuous lives. Antique philosophy made use of spiritual exercises such as forms of dialogue and theoretical contemplation that fashioned the philosophers' way of being.[1153] For instance, the Platonic dialogues intended "to form more than to inform."[1154] Philosophy was not a purely intellectual enterprise, but an "art of living." As mentioned, Michel Foucault was inspired by Pierre Hadot, and Foucault noted that there were different spiritual exercises in antiquity that formed people of the time, but these exercises changed as Christianity developed. Antique philosophers wished to take care of their selves and focused on rationality and practice, whereas Christian ascetics wanted to know their selves in order to renounce their own will and desires. Foucault thus saw a change in the self-formation that collided with the shift from Pagan philosophy to monastic Christianity. Foucault believed that selves are liable to change by way of certain techniques. He pointed to obedience and penitence as the two techniques being used in early Christian monasticism to shape the selves of the monks. The early Christian procedures of *exomologesis* (a penitential practice) and *exagoreusis* (a monastic practice) were emphasized by Foucault as techniques by which Christian selves were formed. According to Foucault, in the *exomolegesis*, the individual Christian was revealing his/her self in order to destroy it, and in the *exagoreusis*, the individual accepted

---

1153 For both appraisal and critique of Foucault's idea, see M.C. Nussbaum, *The Therapy of Desire. Theory and Desire in Hellenistic Ethics*, Princeton 1994, 5.353. Nussbaum critizises Foucault for not recognizing the value of reason in antique philosophy.

1154 Hadot quoting Victor Goldschmidt (Hadot, 1995, 20).

to be obedient at the expense of his/her own will. Foucault called such exercises *techniques de soi*. Neither Hadot, nor Foucault looked closely at prayer as a technique in itself,[1155] but in the following, we shall see that prayer was used for "cultivation" of Christian selves. Because prayer here will be understood as formative, it also makes sense to think of prayer discourse as a part of Christian *paideia* in the sense of formation.[1156]

In his studies, Foucault focused some attention on the antique bon mot: "Know thyself" from the Temple of Apollo at Delphi. According to Foucault, in antique philosophy, this principle was closely linked to another principle, namely the Socratic: "take care of yourself."[1157] According to Foucault, it was not until the arrival of Christian asceticism that "know thyself" came to be interpreted as "know your inner thoughts and desires in order to abolish them." In the ascetic milieus, self-renunciation was the condition for salvation.[1158] Foucault's thesis was that the ancient Greek self was formed by self-mastery, whereas the Christian self was a product of self-renunciation.

The Christian ascetics that Foucault studied represent a radical stance in the development of the Christian self, and Foucault interpreted the ascetic milieu one-sidedly. Still, there is a point in Foucault's study that is recognizable also in the texts under investigation, namely the focus on the will and desires of humans as something that should eventually be renounced in order for the Christian self to be obedient to the Christian teachings. In the ante-Nicene tradition under investigation, there is a tendency to focus attention on the transformation of the personal will, but not to the degree that Foucault saw in the later ascetic material.

Also in Christian sources, there was a reception and interpretation of the Delfic Oracle, and a deliberate consideration as to what it means to a

---

1155 Though Foucault did mention prayer: he used Philo's mentioning of the Therapeutae and their different practices, including collective prayer (Foucault 1988, 21) to describe technologies of the self. He also mentions prayer as part of the Senecan style of self-examination (Foucault 1988, 44).

1156 For a similar idea, see J.D. Dawson, "Christian Teaching," in F. Young et al. (eds.), *The Cambridge History of Early Christian Literature*, Cambridge 2004, 222-238, 237.

1157 Foucault, 1988, 20.

1158 Id. 22.

Christian to know oneself.[1159] In his text *On the flesh of Christ*, Tertullian seems to allude to and rejects the Delfic Oracle with the words:

> "For this cause did the Son of God come down and submit to having a soul, that soul might obtain knowledge, not of itself in Christ (*non ut ipsa se anima cognosceret in Christo*) but of Christ in itself. For it was through ignorance, not of itself (*non enim se ignorando*) but of the Word of God, that it was in peril of its salvation."[1160]

Using terminology from identity theories, we can conclude that Tertullian here expresses what the individual is lacking, and what potentially blocks the individual from salvation is not a knowledge of the self, but rather the awareness of the self or selves that prevent a *Christ-like self* to become the prevailing manifestation of that person's identity. According to the authors of the prayer discourses, the effect of prayer on the strengthening of the Christ-like self, which allows God to act through the individual, is of the utmost importance. This likeness to God, via a likeness to Christ, is a reoccurring theme in the discourses that we shall revisit throughout this chapter. Clement also combines salvation and self-knowledge, and being firmly rooted in Greek philosophy, he made use of the Delphic maxim in *Stromateis* 7:

> "we have received reason in order to know what to do. And the maxim *Know thyself* (γνῶθι σαυτὸν) means in this case, to know for what purpose we are made. Now we are made to be obedient (πειθήνιοι) to the commandments, if our choice be made such as to will salvation. This, I find, is the real Adrasteia [i.e. personification of the inescapable], owing to which we cannot escape from God."[1161]

In accordance with Foucault's interpretation of early Christianity, also Tertullian and Clement removes the focus from the individual's self to Christ and the Christian teachings. A Christian has to know himself/herself

---

1159 I deal with this topic more explicitly in a Danish article: M.L. Munkholt Christensen: *Om at bede og kende sig selv. Et studium af fire før-nikænske skrifter om bøn*, in: *Patristica Nordica Annuaria* 32 (2018) 91–116.

1160 Tert. Carn. 12 (Evans). For a direct reference by Tertullian to the Pythian Oracle, see Apol. 48 (Becker, tr. Souter): "Thou, O man, a name of such might, if thou wouldst understand thyself, learning even from the inscription of the Pythian priestess, thou who art lord of all that die and rise again, wilt thou die to this end, so as to perish for ever?"

1161 Clem. Strom. 7.3.20 (Hort/Mayor).

by knowing his/her relation to God, and it is in this process that prayer becomes a technique to establish a self with a relationship to God. The individual is asked to reflect on himself/herself in the light of the ideal set forward by the Christian teachings. Corresponding to this interpretation, the theologian Stephen Sykes has noted: "It is undeniable, from even a cursory knowledge of the Christian tradition, that 'inwardness' has played an important role in the development of Christian identity."[1162]

In the following, we shall investigate how prayer was presented as having an effect on Christian lives and selves. There will be an outline of how Christian anthropology and the personal effects of Christian prayer were presented in the treatises under investigation. I do not suggest that all Christians in antiquity were fashioned only by way of prayer, but I suggest that prayer was playing a part in the formation of Christians. Obviously, prayer was understood as having a formative potential, and this idea of prayer seems to have had an effect on the social world. In the following, we shall see how.

5.2 Transformation as effect of prayer

All authors under investigation expected prayer to make a difference. They also expected Christian life to be a progression, a life striving towards perfection and salvation. Christian life was initiated with baptism, wherefrom it was to continue in a positive manner. This is expressed clearly in a quote from Cyprian's *De Dominica Oratione*: "Through the mercy of God we have been spiritually remade (*recreate spiritaliter*) and so, when we are reborn (*renati*), let us imitate what we are destined to become (*imitemur quod future sumus*)."[1163] Baptism alone, however, was not believed to secure salvation; people could act so carelessly that they would fall away from grace. The early Christian authors therefore called attention to virtue and pointed to prayer as a safeguarding practice both to uphold virtue and secure salvation. As such prayer had the function of creating awareness of sin and meanwhile guide towards virtue and a certain way of life. In the

---

1162 Quoted from C.C.H. Cook, *The Philokalia and the Inner Life. On Passions and Prayer*, Eugene 2012, 229.
1163 Cypr. Dom. orat. 36 (Réveillaud; tr. Stewart-Sykes).

following, we shall investigate how prayer and its effects corresponded to Christian anthropology. We shall first take a look at the Christian ideas of progression and thereafter see how prayer was thought to be involved in the progress.

5.2.1 Christian anthropology and progression

In order to judge the believed effect of prayer on the individual, we need to know how individuals were perceived in the time under investigation. That is, however, not so clear, since different anthropologies seem to be caught up, and different concepts are mixed in the treatises. Generally speaking, earthly versus heavenly is a predominant scheme in all treatises, and it is used to describe the composition of humans as fundamentally bipartite. Earth and physicality are regularly linked with desire and sin and seen in opposition to what is heavenly, pure and virtuous. Christian life is thus regularly presented as a fight against desire. This was also the dominating idea of humans in the intellectual life of antiquity in general. The philosophical elite strove towards apathy, understood as a state free of passions and with a "final serenity of purpose."[1164] Clement likewise had apathy as ideal.[1165] To secure salvation, people were urged to keep their desires under control, a state called *metriopatheia*. At best people could completely negate their desires and be in a state of *apatheia*. Desire was "the many-headed beast" to be avoided.[1166] Origen describes the dichotomy and its effect on prayer in his *Commentary on the Epistle to the Romans*:

> "But what our weakness is the Lord himself teaches when he says: 'The spirit is ready but the flesh is weak.' So then our weakness is a consequence of the weakness of our flesh. For it is the [flesh] that lusts against the spirit; and as long as the [flesh] pours forth its lusts, it impedes the purity of the spirit and it clouds the sincerity of prayer."[1167]

The treatises on prayer present a warfare-discourse about the struggle of spirit, soul and mind versus bodily desires and sin. The treatises present

---

1164 Brown quoted in McGinn, 1991, 105.
1165 McGinn, 1991, 105.
1166 Pl. r. 9.588b-589a (Emlyn-Jones).
1167 Or. Comm. in Rom. 7.6.4 (tr. Scheck).

humans as consisting of primarily two parts which correspond to the opposites of earthly and heavenly, desire and virtue, flesh and spirit. This anthropological scheme is frequently mingled with a tripartite anthropology according to which humans are seen as consisting of body, soul and spirit.

The reason and will of humans are located in their heart, mind or "governing faculty."[1168] Human reason was supposed to tackle the struggle between desire and virtue.[1169] This anthropology resembles the Platonic one, illustrated in *Phaedrus* 253d-e where the human soul is presented as a charioteer who drives two winged horses, one horse is "a friend of honor joined with temperance and modesty, and a follower of true glory," the other "the friend of insolence and pride." As charioteer we find the reason of the human mind. This part of the soul resembles the mind or heart of the Christian authors; it is the ruler of each human. This is where decisions are made, and this part of a human is thought to be scrutinized by God at all times. According to the Alexandrian authors, this is the part of humans that can be unified with God already in the present by the mind's ascent (*anabasis*) to God. This reasonable part of a human needs to, figuratively, steer its winged horses wisely, and not be "carried away by things which has nothing to do with the true self."[1170]

The Latin authors also saw humans as caught in the struggle between flesh and spirit, body and soul.[1171] According to the Latin treatises on prayer, humans are earthly beings that need God's grace to live good and virtuous lives since they are tainted by original sin.[1172] By the time of Cyprian, the idea of original sin was becoming increasingly dominant which made the anthropology less optimistic. Nonetheless, although humans find themselves in a primordial sinful state, they can develop as we see in the tracts

---

1168 That these concepts could be used interchangeably, at least when being translated, can be seen in the fact that Rufinus and Jerome translated Origen's ἡγεμονικόν with *principale cordis* or *animae* (W. Gessel, "Der origeneische Gebetslogos und die Theologie der Mystik des Gebetes" i *Münchner Theologische Zeitschrift*, 28, 1977, 397-407, 402).

1169 Or. or. 32 (Koetschau; tr. Stewart-Sykes).

1170 Clem. Strom. 7.11.62 (Hort/Mayor).

1171 M.C. Steenberg, *Impatience and Humanity's Sinful State in Tertullian of Carthage*, in: VigChr 62/2 (2008), 107-132.

1172 Tert. An. 40 (Waszink; tr. Holms).

of Tertullian – in fact, humans are intended to undergo a maturational development in the course of their individual life.[1173] In their respective treatises on prayer, both Tertullian and Cyprian draw attention to the idea that humans "are in possession of a body from the earth and a spirit from heaven." – hence, "we are ourselves (*ipse*) both earth and heaven."[1174] Tertullian frames it: "by a figurative interpretation of flesh and spirit, the heaven and the earth indicate ourselves (*nos sumus*)."[1175] The two can only be reconciled by the grace of God which helps individuals follow the will of God both in the spirit and in the flesh. By following the will of God, "the soul (*anima*) which is reborn through him may be saved."[1176] Therefore, it makes sense that Cyprian admonishes daily prayer for God's intervention in the life of the individual: "And so we pray daily, or rather unceasingly, the prayer that the will of God be done around us both in heaven and on earth."[1177] Cyprian gives the same explanation for intercessory prayers, since these prayers are supposed to help others to salvation – others who were earthly from their original birth, but "should begin to be heavenly, being born of water and Spirit."[1178]

According to Cyprian, a Christian ought to be reminded of his/her sinfulness every day, and therefore Christians should steadily pray "forgive us our debts." Thereby the mind (*animus*) is daily "recalled to a sense of guilt,"[1179] and can subsequently be forgiven and avoid condemnation.[1180] We thus see that the Latin authors dealt with an idea of human life where baptism constituted the major shift, and from this point onwards, the individual Christians had to take responsibility for their own progression.

The Alexandrian authors are even more focused on human progression than the Latin authors. Where the Latin authors reckon two overall phases in the life of Christians: a pre- and post-baptismal phase, the Alexandrian authors understand Christian life as a constant development

---

1173 Steenberg, 2008, 109.
1174 Cypr. Dom. orat. 16 (Réveillaud; tr. Stewart-Sykes).
1175 Tert. Or. 4 (Schleyer; tr. Stewart-Sykes).
1176 Cypr. Dom. orat. 16 (Réveillaud; tr. Stewart-Sykes).
1177 Id.
1178 Id.
1179 Id. 22.
1180 Id. 23.

with many degrees of perfection, a constant hierarchical progress. The Latin authors talk about Christian adoption by way of baptism, a Christian is perfected when baptized and must strive to remain this way. In contrast, the Alexandrian authors see more levels of progression in perfection.[1181] Clement at one point enumerates some of these levels: people are to progress from heathenism to faith, from faith to knowledge, then develop knowledge into love and thereby gain "equality with angels" (ἰσάγγελος).[1182] Walter Völker argues that ἰσάγγελος is a synonym for becoming similar to God.[1183] This state is reached by way of prayer, apathy and knowledge. Humans with knowledge of God are thus capable of making a change (μεταβολήν) towards the better.[1184] Thereby knowledge "transplants a man to that divine and holy state which is akin to the soul (τῆς ψυχῆς)."[1185] Having reached the perfect state, the Christian is as close to God as possible, "in immediate subordination to Him (προσεχῶς ὑποτεταγμένη)."[1186] The process of becoming like to God is a matter of being changed from within. Clement mentions how habits can be changed into nature (φυσιοῦται ἡ ἕξις), thereby indicating that an ontological change takes place within the Christian. In a similar manner, Origen expects humans to experience spiritual growth. He mentions how the petition for bread in the Lord's Prayer is not only a prayer

---

1181 Behr, 2000, 214 f. When studying Clement and Irenaeus, Behr distinguishes between two patterns of narratives in which man was inscribed in early Christianity. Irenaeus' narrative is one of the economy of salvation as unfolded in Scripture: "creation and animation by a breath, apostasy, preparation, adoption, and finally life through death" (214). Clement's narrative is paideia, "which, through progressive training and instruction leads, beyond salvation, to the height of Gnostic perfection." (215). When describing the ascetism and anthropology in Clement's work, Behr has to mention Clement's use of unceasing prayer, since this happens to be a fundamental category for Clement. The difference between the narratives of economy and paideia can be used to describe the overall difference that we encounter between, on the one hand, Tertullian and Cyprian with their salvation economy, and, on the other hand, Clement and Origen with their idea of paideia.
1182 Clem. Strom. 7.10.57 (Hort/Mayor).
1183 Völker, 1931, 604.
1184 Clem. Strom. 7.10.56 (Hort/Mayor).
1185 Id. 7.10.57.
1186 Id.

for concrete bread, but also for reason (λόγου) that will make humans grow into the likeness of God.[1187] Concretely, what is nourished by God is the human mind (νοῦς), soul (ψυχή) and "rational nature" (ἡ λογικὴ φύσις).

We have seen how the authors admonish their listeners to strive for Christ-like selves rather than for selves devoted to unworthy desires. Virtuous selves should be prevailing, ideally exclusively, and ideally these selves should be manifested in the identity of the individual Christian. Especially in the texts of the Alexandrian writers, the human progress is seen as assimilation to God. It is expressed in the idea of the Christian becoming an image of God. The Latin authors are less idealistic concerning this change, but they do expect Christians to become like to God as far as possible. We already saw how Tertullian admonishes Christians to change their spirit in accordance with the spirit of God. In any case, God is a positive pole towards which the Christian should strive: "Man therefore finds himself caught between the goodness of God on the one hand and the danger of his inner temptation on the other, a situation in which he must consciously seek out the countenance of God. His longing for God is the driving force here, as his inclination towards temptation compels him to do so. This causes tension in his life of prayer, tension from which he cannot escape, however much progress he may make towards recovery during his earthly existence."[1188]

5.2.2 An image of (an image of) God and likeness with God

In their treatises on prayer, the two Alexandrian authors use the idea of human beings as images of God. The Alexandrian authors think that humans can be an "image of an image" of God since Christ/the Logos is always intermediary between God and humanity, and in the same way as humans are created by way of Logos, Logos is the image by which humans can achieve a likeness to God.[1189] For our purpose, it is interesting to note that Clement holds that the process of attaining a likeness to God has to do

---

1187 Or. or. 27.2 (Koetschau; tr. Stewart-Sykes).
1188 Lefeber quoted in Perrone, *preghiera*, 2011, 47 n. 133.
1189 See A.C. Jacobsen, *Christ. The Teacher of Salvation. A Study on Origen's Christology and Soteriology.* Münster 2015, 316 et al.

with communion with God. According to Clement, it is by being in contact with God that Christ can be imitated and a Christ-like self established:

> "This… is the life-work of the perfect gnostic, viz. to hold communion with God through the great High Priest, being made like the Lord (ἐξομοιούμενον), as far as may be, by means of all his service towards God … by public worship and by teaching and by active kindness. Aye, and in being thus assimilated to God, the gnostic is making and fashioning himself (ἑαυτὸν κτίζει καὶ δημιουργεῖ) and also forming (κοσμεῖ) those who hear him… and this he effects by undisturbed communion with the Lord."[1190]

Clement calls this transformation "gnostic assimilation" (γνωστικῆς ἐξο μοιώσεως) and characterizes the gnostic by the traits gentleness, kindness and noble devoutness and by being in a passionless state.[1191] By changing himself, the gnostic is simultaneously changing those who are influenced by him, and thus the gnostic is a catalyst for change. Clement describes the gnostic transformation by referring to wax being softened and copper refined so that a stamp can be impressed upon it.[1192] In the same way as in relation to these formable materials, the human mind is changed in order to receive the imprint of God. This metaphor of an imprint points to divine assimilation/deification, *theosis*, as a two-way process where the individual Christian as well as God takes part in perfecting the gnostic.

> "the soul of the just man is an image divine, made like to God Himself… the one Saviour… He is in true the only-begotten, the express image of the glory of the universal King and almighty Father, stamping (ἐναποσφραγιζόμενος) on the mind of the gnostic the perfect vision after his own image (κατ' εἰκόνα τὴν ἑαυτοῦ); so that the divine image (τὴν θείαν εἰκόνα) is now beheld in a third embodiment (τρίτην), assimilated as far as possible to the Second Cause (δεύτερον αἴτιον)… copying (ἀπογράφοντες) the image (τύπον) of Him…"[1193]

As we see here, becoming like to the image of God can only take place by the intermediate role of Christ. Origen has the exact same idea, and he believes that:

> "the saints are therefore an image of an image (εἰκὼν οὖν εἰκόνος), that of the Son (τῆς εἰκόνος οὔσης υἱοῦ). They are stamped with sonship (ἀπομάττονται υἱότητα)

1190 Clem. Strom. 7.3.13 (Hort/Mayor).
1191 Id.
1192 Id. 7.12.10.
1193 Id. 7.3.16.

and are conformed (σύμμορφοι) not only to the glorified body of Christ, but to the one who is in that body." [1194]

Origen refers to the image of God in *Perì Euchês* in a passage on the address "Our Father." Origen admonishes that when praying to God as "Our Father," behaviour, words and thoughts should all be formed according to the only begotten Word. Gaining likeness with God is thus a precondition and an effect of contact with God.

In the euchological treatises by Clement and Origen, it seems that being an image of God and approaching a likeness to God are results of a progress. Since Irenaeus, however, theologians have presented the image of God, *imago*, as something that is God-given from creation, whereas the likeness of God, *similitudo*, is attained in life. This is also how Origen presents the idea of image and likeness of God in *De Principiis*. Here Origen presents humans as having the image of God from creation in the form of the intellect (cf. 1 Gen 1:26–28).[1195] The image is, however, an image in potency, and humans have to acquire likeness with God by their own honest effort.[1196] For both Clement and Origen, the image is the starting point for human development and return to God; the image is given in creation, but does not in itself lead to salvation. The perfection of the individual takes place in this life – it is a divinization, a *theosis*, in which prayer, love and faith play a role. Likeness to God is not a state, but a process.

The Latin authors do not use the idea of God's image actively in their treatment of prayer. We can note, however, that when Tertullian uses this idea in another part of his work, he does not linger on the divinization of humans as much as on the inherent divine breath given to humans in creation. Tertullian distinguishes between the breath (*afflatus*) of God and the spirit of God. The Spirit of God is the divine essence, whereas the *afflatus* is the breath. According to the creation narrative in Genesis, God breathed into the first human to give him life. That, however, did not mean that the first human was made divine; rather, he received divine gifts from his divine

---

1194 Id. See also Or. or. 22.4 (Koetschau; tr. Stewart-Sykes): ... ἀπομάττονται υἱότητα, οὐ μόνῳ „τῷ σώματι τῆς δόξης" τοῦ Χριστοῦ γινόμενοι σύμμορφοι ἀλλὰ καὶ ὄντι ἐν „τῷ σώματι."

1195 Or. princ. 3.1.13 (Koetschau; tr. Butterworth).

1196 Id. 3.6.1 (Koetschau; tr. Stewart-Sykes).

creator, such as rationality. As R.E. Roberts interprets Tertullian: "The soul
of man possesses the true lineaments of divinity, immortality (in a sense),
freedom of will, foreknowledge (to a degree), reasonableness, capacity of
understanding, and knowledge. But it is not on that account blessed with
the actual power of deity, nor is it free from fault."[1197]

All four authors mention the necessity of similarity between humans
and God in order for there to be a relation between the two in prayer. The
Alexandrian authors use the word "likeness" to describe the ideal relation to
God, namely a relation where the individual has achieved a likeness to God.
Buell notes, when commenting on Clement's theology, that: "In theory, likeness is a defining feature of the relation between father and son."[1198] Tertullian
makes the same point. He does not call for likeness directly, but for a spirit that
is of the same sort as the spirit of God.[1199] Furthermore, Tertullian mentions
that no one wants to receive someone who is an adversary to oneself (*nemo
adversarium recipit*); therefore, a human who is unlike God cannot expect
God to receive him/her. This is used as an argument in favour of striving for
a likeness to God. Cyprian mentions the need for humans to be like and similar to God in regard to certain acts, such as to care for all alike and to be
forgiving.[1200] Cyprian does not seem to believe that humans ontologically can
be like God, but can in certain acts be God-like.

The human anthropology embedded in the ideas of God's image and
likeness can be interpreted differently. All four authors under investigation
use this language to activate humans. For the authors, Christian life is strife
and a dynamic process from one state to another. Christianity thus entails
a constant refinement and reorientation of the self. E. von der Goltz has
also pointed to transformation as a desired goal of prayer: "Die Absicht
der großen Gelehrten, auch den Gebildeten das christliche Gebet nahezu-
bringen und es ihnen zu einem heiligen und geschätzten Mittel zu machen,
gottähnlicher zu werden und Gott näher zu kommen."[1201] We shall look
further at prayer and its personal effects in the following.

1197 E.R. Roberts, *The Theology of Tertullian*, London 1924, 162 f.
1198 Buell, 1999, 92.
1199 Tert. Or. 12 (Schleyer; tr. Stewart-Sykes).
1200 Cypr. Dom. orat. 17 (Réveillaud; tr. Stewart-Sykes).
1201 Goltz, 1901, 278.

5.2.3 Effects of prayer according to the Latin authors

Robert L. Simpson states that it is "virtually impossible to separate the fathers' confidence in prayer's efficacy from the relationship with God which is presupposed."[1202] As Simpson makes clear, the idea of God is deciding for the effects God is believed to grant in response to prayer. The four Christian authors do not expect God to be primarily engaged in changing concrete affairs in the world, since only spiritual requests are really worthy.

Tertullian ends his 29-chapter long treatise on prayer with a chapter on the effects of prayer. The chapter forms a conclusion and is a kind of manifesto:

> "For what will God, who so demands, deny to a prayer that derives from the spirit and the truth (Jn. 4.24). We read and we hear and we believe in the greatness of the witnesses to its efficacy (*efficaciae*). Indeed, the old prayer (*vetus oratio*) brought deliverance from fire and from wild beasts and from starvation, even though it had not been given shape by Christ. How much more effective, then, is the Christian prayer (*oratio Christiana*)."

Twice Tertullian elaborately specifies what prayer does not do by making recourse to the Old Testament. Tertullian contrasts "old prayer" with Christian prayer, and as example of old prayer he mentions for instance Daniel's prayer in the Lion's den; it saved him from being eaten by the lions. In the time before Christ, there was a paradigm of "old prayer," but it changed with the coming of Christ. We met this same contrast of before and after Christ in the beginning of Tertullian's treatise. Tertullian notes that whereas "old prayer" was able to hinder misery quite directly, Christian prayer has now changed and works spiritual benefits. About the Christian prayer, Tertullian writes:

> "... *but* it arms with endurance those who are suffering and knowing pain and grieving. It increases grace (*gratiam*) with bravery (*virtute*) so that faith might know what it obtains from the Lord, understanding what it is suffering for the sake of the name of the Lord...
>
> *But now* the prayer of justice turns away the entire anger of God (*nunc vero oratio iustitiae omnem iram dei avertit*)... makes supplication for persecutors (*pro persequentibus supplicat*)... Prayer alone conquers God (*sola est oratio quae deum vincit*)..."[1203]

1202 Simpson, 1965, 115.
1203 Tert. Or. 29 (Schleyer; tr. Stewart-Sykes).

According to Tertullian, the effect of prayer is primarily that it strengthens
the one praying by arming with endurance, adding bravery and giving awareness of God's grace. Christian prayer is thus envisioned to have an effect on
the sentiment and perspectives of the individual – the person praying is being
changed from within; it is not the surrounding world that is changed. E.G. Jay
notes: "Tertullian regarded the psychological effect of prayer as one of its most
valuable results… the subjective result of inward strengthening is assured to
Christian prayer."[1204] Tertullian also points to other effects of Christian prayer
that are more miraculous – such as prayer that "call[s] back the departed
from the journey of death itself," "strengthens the weak," "restores the sick,"
"cleanses the possessed," "opens the doors of the prison," "puts down persecution" and "feeds the poor." However, there still is a stress on the spiritual
benefits of Christian prayer – for instance, prayer is said to "absolve sins,"
"strengthen the weakhearted," "lift up the fallen," "support the unsteady"
and "hold firm those who stand" and, not least important, strengthen faith.
It should be noted that Tertullian was sure that the misery of the world will
soon come to an end with judgment day, and this could explain his relative
disregard of earthly matters in prayers. But still, Tertullian here, in a quite
poetic tone, is being realistic as to which effects of prayer are certain.

Cyprian was probably influenced by Tertullian when he wrote about
the effects of prayer. If a conclusion is a fitting place to put a manifesto,
as Tertullian did, so is the very beginning of a text. In the beginning of his
text, Cyprian echoes Tertullian by writing that the Lord's Prayer as part of
the divine instructions effectuates spiritual benefits – by praying you gain
hope, faith and salvation:

> "The instruction of the Gospel, dearest brothers, are nothing other than divine
> commands (*magisteria diuina*), foundations on which hope is built (*fundamenta
> aedificandae spei*), buttresses by which faith is strengthened (*firmamenta conrob-
> orandae fidei*), food by which the heart is fed (*nutrimenta fouendi cordis*), direc-
> tions by which our journey is guided (*gubernacula dirigendi itineris*), bulwarks
> by which salvation is attained (*praesidia obtinendae salutis*). … Among his other
> saving guidance and divine instructions…, he [the Lord] himself gave the form by
> which to pray, and himself guided and directed the purpose of our prayer (*orandi
> ipse formam dedit, ipse quid precaremur monuit et instruxit*)."[1205]

1204 Referred to by Simpson, 1965, 132.
1205 Cypr. Dom. orat. 1-2 (Réveillaud; tr. Stewart-Sykes).

Cyprian emphasizes that Jesus himself gave the Lord's Prayer its authority. Cyprian expected the individual to contemplate the words of the Lord's Prayer in order to be changed by them. Furthermore, Cyprian writes that Christians are taught the Lord's Prayer so that by the words of the prayer they know how to be and thus how to act: "So that each of us is able to prepare himself, he teaches us to pray in this manner and to know through the terms of prayer what sort of person he should be (*qualis esse debeat noscere*)."[1206] According to Cyprian, prayer is an integral part of Christian life and a vital part in order to remain on the road towards eschatological salvation. The individual needs to pray to be able to live a Christian life with all that it entails of politeness and sinlessness. Cyprian has written that Christians should never waste an opportunity to pray because it is a way to progress. Cyprian is aware that the first transformation in Christian life takes place in baptism, but afterwards, the Christian person must continually pray in order to stay "reborn" and transformed by God's grace:

> "We ask and beseech that we who are made holy in baptism should have the ability to persist in the way that we have begun (*petimus et rogamus, ut qui in baptismo sanctificati sumus in eo quod esse coepimus perseueremus*). And we request this every day.... We make this plea (*hanc precem facimus*) in continuous prayer (*continuis orationibus*); we ask day and night that the hallowing and revival (*sanctificatione et uiuificatio*) which has been received from the grace of God (*de Dei gratia*) should be preserved by his protecting care."[1207]

5.2.4 Effects of prayer according to the Alexandrian authors

Out of the four authors that we are dealing with here, Clement is the most idealistic when it comes to what people ought to pray for, at least when it comes to the so-called perfect Christians, he expects nothing but worthy, i.e. spiritual prayers. That is reflected in his admonitions concerning petitionary prayers. According to Clement, the perfection of the gnostic is reflected in the fact that he does not pray that good things should be attached to him like ornaments, but rather that he may himself be good.[1208] It is thus up

---

1206 Id. 20.
1207 Cypr. Dom. orat. 12 (Réveillaud; tr. Stewart-Sykes). (Cf. Aug. *Sermon to the Catechumens. On the Creed* 7.15 (tr. Wilcox): "We are cleansed but once by baptism, daily we are cleansed by prayer.").
1208 Clem. Strom. 7.7.38 (Hort/Mayor).

to the individual to pray for what is worthy, and here we see the transformative element in Clement's anthropology and theology of prayer, because as a person develops in his/her knowledge of God, prayers should change character:

> "he that turns to God from among the heathen will ask for faith, but he that aspires to knowledge will ask for the perfection of love. And when he has now reached the summit, the gnostic prays that <the power of> contemplation (θεωρίαν) may grow and abide with him, just as the common man (ὁ κοινὸς ἄνθρωπος) prays for a continuance of health."[1209]

Here it becomes obvious that for the gnostic, a worthy object of prayer is the ability to contemplate, whereas prayers for health are not. Most people, the so-called common men, have not come to this insight. Throughout Clement's work, he mentions contemplation, also "scientific contemplation"[1210] as a way to be in a correct relationship with God. From creation, the rational beings were supposed to contemplate God, but fell away from contemplation. To contemplate is a way back to salvation; Origen shares this idea of salvation as contemplation.

Clement notices that God works in ways that are not easily discernible for humans. A sinner might have his/her prayers granted, "but that does not mean that God is unjust. It means that the prayer succeeds because it will help someone else."[1211] Clement thus upholds his idea about God's providence and care for his people. However, the gnostic must accept not to have the fullest benefit of his prayers while on earth, rather:

> "[the gnostic] has all good in potentiality, though not yet in full tale (κατὰ τὴν δύναμιν, οὐδέπω δὲ καὶ κατὰ τὸν ἀριθμόν); since he would otherwise have been incapable of change (ἀμετάθετος) in reference to the inspired progresses and orderings which are still due to him by God's degree."[1212]

Also Origen seems completely convinced that prayer affects the individual. In a passage, after having written about the presence of God within the one praying, he proceeds by pointing to the development that follows prayer:

1209 Id. 7.7.46.
1210 Id. 7.11.61.
1211 Id. 7.12.73.
1212 Id. 7.7.47.

"... we must realize that the one who so devoutly disposes himself (τῷ καταστήσαντι αὐτοῦ τὸν λογισμὸν) at the time of prayer receives no ordinary result. When this is undertaken frequently, from how many sins does it keep us, to how many righteous deeds does it lead us! This is known from experience by those who have most constantly given themselves to prayer."[1213]

Like Clement and Cyprian also Origen points to the contemplative aspect of prayer and its effects. When a person thinks about God and His gracious deeds, he/she will be encouraged to act righteously, and God will help him/her to do so. Origen also points to the benefits that befall the one praying simply because the one praying is supposed to be a just and honest person in order to be worthy to pray in the first place. Thus, prayer both presupposes and is in itself a reminder and prompter of righteous behaviour. That is also what Origen refers to when he writes: "we have nonetheless received the best of gains by praying with understanding of the manner in which we should pray and keeping to this."[1214] According to Origen, a certain aspect of praying has to do with life as such, namely with disposition and attitude.

That prayer is part and outcome of a transformation process which takes place in this life is an underlying premise in Perì Euchês, and it is formulated succinctly in Origen's Contra Celsum by way of a metaphor: as a statue is carved from a block of stone, so each individual is forming a statue of his/her own self. The "statue" raised within should be an imitation of Christ, but as we know from concrete works of art, they are not all equally good, and an unsatisfying result is a possibility.[1215] From this inner statue, which is the perfected self, prayers ascend that will be well pleasing to God:

"we regard the spirit (ἡγεμονικόν) of every good man as an altar from which arises an incense which is truly and spiritually sweet-smelling, namely, the prayers (προσευχαὶ) ascending from a pure conscience (ἀπὸ συνειδήσεως καθαρᾶς)... In all those, then, who plant and cultivate within their souls, according to the divine word, temperance, justice, wisdom, piety, and other virtues, these excellences are their statues they raise, in which we are persuaded that it is becoming for us to honour the model and prototype of all statues: 'the image of the invisible God',

---

1213 Or. or. 8 (Koetschau; tr. Stewart-Sykes).
1214 Id. 10.1.
1215 A similar use of the metaphor is found in Plot. Enn. 1.6.9.1.ff (Henry/Schwyzer; tr. MacKenna/Page). Plotinus, however, does not propose any object or divinity with whom one's inner statue should be conformed.

... And every one who imitates Him according to his ability, does by this very endeavour raise a statue according to the image of the Creator, for in the contemplation of God with a pure heart they become imitators of Him."[1216]

In this passage, we see once again how prayer and contemplation are viewed as closely connected with the establishment of a Christ-like self in the individual. Contemplation is a prerequisite for imitating Christ, and prayer is an outcome. It should, however, be noted that Origen also leaves room for prayers for more earthly and concrete goods if the purpose is worthy, such as money to the poor. Origen believes that God also takes an interest in such kinds of petitionary prayers, and God may answer such requests through people – he lets the rich be the answer to the poor man's request for money and the doctor for the sick man's request for a cure etc.[1217]

5.2.5 Prayer and salvation

According to the four authors, prayer continues to cleanse the baptized and is an anticipation of salvation.[1218] Prayer is a symbol of a constant movement towards fulfilment for the individual and the whole. This view of prayer, as something that has to do with disposition and inner sentiment, is also found within antique philosophy where this form of mental endeavour is also occasionally labelled contemplation. However, one difference between the Stoic and Platonic ideas, on the one hand, and the Christian idea of prayer, on the other hand, is the understanding of what motivates the change of attitude and transformation of the individual which in turn is a proleptic salvation. For the philosophers, the change of attitude must come from a connection with the divine within. For the Christians what makes it possible to change and stay transformed comes from the outside, from God. As a Christian, one is dependent on the grace of God, and prayer brings grace – and is at the same time in itself an expression of grace. Prayer and grace are closely connected, and both are crucially important

---

1216 Or. Cels. 8.17-18 (Borret; tr. Crombie).
1217 Or. or. 11.4 (Koetschau; tr. Stewart-Sykes).
1218 Cf. Behr, 2000, 212 f. Behr sums up Clement's theology of asceticism and mentions Clement's idea that the one who is baptized has a new existence in terms of a proleptic eschatology. This proleptic eschatology is related to the prayerful life of the gnostic.

to live a virtuous life. What grace exactly brings about is not completely clear, but for all four authors, prayer brings faith, knowledge of God and a change in behaviour and disposition. In this way, Christian prayer is different from philosophical prayer. As Lorenzo Perrone has noted, "Instead of being merely a spiritual self-accomplishment, prayer emphasizes for Origen the continuous need of divine help for a frail creature like man."[1219] This is also what Cyprian made clear when admonishing frequent prayer for the individual to remain in the state reached in baptism. As we have seen, especially in Cyprian's treatise, prayer was seen as a perpetuation of baptism. Therefore, prayer was also essential for the ultimate salvation of the believer. Wilhelm Gessel can thus write about Origen that for him: "Ein hervorragendes Mittel auf dem Weg zum ewigen Heil ist das Gebet, auch das Bittgebet."[1220] And "Durch sie [die Gnade] wird ihm [dem Menschen] unter Mitwirkung des Geistes die Erlösung zu einem neuen und letztlich ewigen Leben zuteil…"[1221] For the Christian authors, prayer effects progress which in turn secures salvation.

5.2.6 Prayer as part of Christian *Paideia* and catechetical education

None of the four authors under investigation deal explicitly with the concept of *paideia* or *eruditio* in their euchological treatises. Nonetheless, the concepts of education or formation are meaningful in this context, because prayer was seen as playing a vital role in Christian life and Christian formation, so *de facto* prayer was part of Christian *paideia*. The investigated treatises testify to the important role of prayer in Christian education and show how the Lord's Prayer was often singled out as a key to understanding the larger Christian "curriculum" and teachings.[1222]

1219 Perrone, 2001, 17.
1220 Gessel, 1975, 214.
1221 Id. 215.
1222 For considerations about Christian identity formation, also in comparison with pagan education, see P. Gemeinhardt, "Personale Identität in spätantiken (christlichen) Bildungsprozessen" i C. Bouillon, A. Heiser, M. Iff (red.), *Person, Identität und theologische Bildung*, Stuttgart: Kohlhammer, 2007, 43-64, 50-51.

Paideia was an important element of antique Greco-Roman culture; it referred to the moral, physical and intellectual training that young males from higher society received from their youth. It was seen as fitting to regulate the character (*ethe*) of children from the beginning. After basic training, "education, particularly higher education, was directed towards 'the achievement of the fullest and most perfect development of the personality...' "[1223] Already Cicero said that: "A field, though fertile, cannot be productive without cultivation, nor a mind without teaching. The culture of the mind (cultura animi) is the business of philosophy."[1224] This suffices here to show the important role attributed to teaching and formation in antiquity, at least in the highest strata of Greco-Roman society. Also philosophy was regarded as a way of cultivating oneself, which substantiates Pierre Hadot's and Foucault's thesis that philosophy formed selves and was a way of life. It can be argued that Christian formation and education developed as a parallel to the philosophical *paideia* and training.[1225] In Christianity, knowledge and prayer were, in principle, democratized; all initiates were members and strongly encouraged to pray. Prayer was thus a part of Christian *paideia,* both in a formal and soteriological sense.[1226] In the catechumenate, Christians were not only taught how to pray, but also how to understand prayer as a way of living a Christian life in progress. The latter point was particularly made by the Alexandrian authors. Prayer was a method and an outcome of Christian formation.

5.3 Considerations and conclusion: Prayerful selves and identity

In this chapter, we saw that prayer was presented to third-century Christians as a means of strengthening the spirit and being transformed. Christians were admonished to pray for, among other things, grace and forgiveness in order to be as perfect as possible in terms of virtue, self-restraint and faith.

1223 Rankin, 2006, 3.
1224 Id. 4.
1225 Judith Perkins, *Perpetua's vas. Asserting Christian Identity*, in É. Rebillard/J. Rüpke (eds.), *Group Identity and Religious Individuality in Late Antiquity*, Washington 2015, 129-163.
1226 For a similar idea, see Dawson in Young, 2004, 237.

Prayer was thus a mechanism for the incorporation of a certain anthropology and theology since prayer was seen as an aid in achieving a sinless
life and remaining free of sin. Meanwhile, prayer was also lauded as the
right response and sacrifice to God who was believed to have affected the
said changes in the life of the Christians. Prayer and change of the individual
were combined in different ways, and we saw that the understanding of
prayer takes shape in relation to a given anthropology.

Tertullian, Cyprian, Clement and Origen all agreed that Christian prayer
should not primarily consist of petitions for God to "engineer" events in the
external world. On the contrary, these authors agreed that the benefits of
prayer to a significant extent are spiritual and have to do with the building
of inner qualities like faith, bravery, hope and morality. These benefits were
earned in prayer, both in the recollection of God and in the discourse with
God. As such, prayer was believed to work in the existential realm and have
psychological benefits.[1227] The creation of personal identity is also related to
the build-up of such inner qualities and to the crystallization of an awareness of one's own position in the world and of one's own responsibilities
towards the external world. This leads to the conclusion that one of the
benefits that the Christians gained from their prayers and their discourse
on prayer might in fact have been these inner sentiments that contributed
to the formation of Christian identity.

To a large degree, Foucault's theory of techniques of the self is consistent
with an evaluation of the discourses on prayer. Prayer as concrete practice
was linked closely to a paradigm of transformation and virtue. There were
certain expectations to the person praying who was expected to inspect
his/her own will and character; as such prayer was a technique of the self
because it made people look inward to detect sins and errors before praying.
In this way, Christianity arguably democratized the idea of a reflexive self.
For example, Greg Wolf has argued that that in the Roman period, "there
were no real quasi-modern subjectivities centered on self-conscious and
internalized individuality."[1228] Christianity can be seen as departing from
this by placing on each individual the demand for an introspection that

---

1227 Simpson, 1965, 132-135.
1228 Woolf, 2013, 153 f.

had previously only been explored by the philosophical elite. According to the four authors, a "prayerful self" was a self steadily being cultivated to renounce whatever the church expected it to renounce. However, the prayerful Christian self was not self-renouncing from the beginning. As mentioned above, Foucault emphasized renunciation as a characteristic point of Christian self-formation, but the early authors in the Alexandrian tradition and Tertullian as well were not quite as pessimistic. They knew that sin was an everlasting danger for the individual's fragile self, but their anthropology was not altogether pessimistic. The original self was not to be renounced but to be changed and mastered according to Christian teachings. A Christian self was to be formed steadily – it was the image of God and should be developed into likeness with God. Humanity thus represented a positive starting point for these Christian authors who had not yet taken the idea of original sin to its fullest pessimistic consequences. Rather than being self-denunciating, the Christian self was characterized by being an obedient self that knew how and when to be submissive. It was to some degree a self in charge of its own will and direction, and as such the early Christian authors were on the same page with the ancient Greek thinkers. However, in mastering one's self the Christians emphasized their dependence on the grace and teachings of God and the relation with God expressed in prayer. The prayerful self was held as an ideal that should constitute the foundation of Christian identity.

On a theoretical level, the investigation has shown that it is illuminating to understand the self in a Foucaultian sense as a form influenced by practices. In the treatises on prayer, prayer was presented as influential for Christian life, as such it was a technique of the self. However, the treatises are not in complete accord with Foucault's thesis on the issue of self-renunciation to the point of self-annihilation that was emphasized by Foucault. Christians were not to renounce their selves completely.

Part III: Final Conclusion, Considerations and Perspectives

6 Conclusion

Christian instructions on prayer and theology of prayer had an influence on Christian identity in the early church. This conclusion seems highly probable based on the application of modern identity theories in the preceding analysis of early Christian sources. In the analysis, we have seen how treatises on prayer presented normative views, and from these we can to some extent infer the prominence ascribed to prayer, and how prayer was potentially forming Christian identity both on a collective and on a personal level. Instructions about prayer in many ways reflected ideal Christian identity.

When regarding the early Christian texts through the lens of modern identity theories, we encounter several ways in which prayer worked to delimitate, define and empower Christian communities and hence influence Christian collective identity. Firstly, the language used in and about prayer tended to be slightly different among Christians, Jews and pagans. Early on Christian authors favoured προσευχή (instead of εὐχή) about prayer and εὐχαριστῶ (instead of εὐλογῶ) in prayer. Therefore already on the level of semantics, prayer was a defining issue that created different religious identities in late antiquity, although the Christian prayer *par excellence*, the Lord's Prayer, was not particularly Christian in its vocabulary. The investigated treatises testify to an idealization of the Lord's Prayer among Christians – if not as prayer-formula as such, then at least as a core teaching of Christianity and as a main catechetical text. The address "Our Father" and its familial implications functioned in itself as a confession and became a defining mark for Christians and their understanding of themselves. For this reason, the Lord's Prayer can be called an identity marker, an *Ausweisgebet*. Even Clement of Alexandria who in his writings did not render the Lord's Prayer in its entirety quotes it or alludes to it several times in his works. Moreover, we have seen that prayer came to be linked to certain times and postures which held all Christians together by similar practice at similar intervals. Even if it seems that the many prescribed prayer times were impossible to keep, they point to the norm of frequent (even unceasing) contact with God, and as such they meant something symbolically even if not observed concretely. Private and liturgical prayers were not explicitly distinguished as markedly different phenomena in the treatises; on the contrary, private and collective prayer were linked together and constituted a framework of Christian life.

Additionally, we have seen how a certain ethos was connected with prayer and with being a member of a Christian congregation. Praying with someone to the Father of all was only a meaningful task if one lived up to the responsibilities one had within the congregation – and the world. Also regarding the content of prayer, we saw how prayer was used to bind Christians together, not only with one another, but with everyone, with Christ and angels and with the world to come, as well as keeping evil powers at bay. According to the four authors, prayer was an extremely social act, and a person praying was in contact with God, as well as surrounded by both heavenly and earthly creatures.

In all four investigated treatises, intercessory prayers were seen as important, and in general prayers were seen as more beneficial when uttered by a congregation in accord than by an individual alone. None of the authors under investigation neglected this collective side of prayer, but we have seen that Clement paid relatively little attention to Christianity as manifested in a concrete community, whereas Cyprian emphasized the immense value of collective prayer and hence of a Christian collective identity.

Prayer worked as an external marker and symbol of commitment and responsibility within the Christian congregations and in their relations with the outside world. One could say the same of prayers in the Roman cultic context; these prayers were also markers of commitment to the Roman religion and society. The "philosopher's prayer," on the other hand, was not an exhibition of commitment to the empire at large; it rather symbolized the philosopher's desire to master his own feelings and passions. The emphasis in the Stoic and Platonic ideas of prayer on the inner person and his divine core is not completely unlike the ideas expounded by the Christian authors, especially Clement and Origen, although they also paid attention to the collective and more concrete sides of prayer. In different contexts and religions of late antiquity, prayer was used and understood in different ways, and even within Christianity prayer had different functions and meanings.

According to the Christian treatises on prayer studied here, prayer was more than an external marker of belonging and belief. Prayer was also an existential marker that placed the praying individual in a certain set of relations and conveyed an idea of how one ought to dispose oneself, and what one ought to ask for and give thanks for. As such prayer made a claim on the entire person and had to do with will and virtue. All four authors show a keen interest in the inner constitution of Christians which they label interchangeably as the heart (*corda*), spirit (*animus et sensus*), soul (ἡ ψυχή), condition (ἡ κατάστασις), mind (νοῦς), rational nature (ἡ λογικὴ φύσις) and the governing faculty (ἡγεμονικόν). These categories are names for the locus of human will, and according to the anthropology of the early Christian authors, it is here that prayers and actions are formed. Meanwhile this is also the part of humans that can be formed by grace and prayer, and where the Spirit can enter and pray on behalf of the human being. The four investigated authors share the conviction that people are in need of grace, of the work of the Spirit and of Christ in order to pray in a worthy, effective and spiritual manner. Prayer was essentially seen as a christological and pneumatological endeavour. However, their perception of the work of the Spirit is slightly different: According to Clement, the Spirit pulls from the outside like a magnet to move humans; according to Origen, the Spirit prays in the individual; according to Tertullian, one is supposed to align one's own spirit to meet the Spirit of God; and according to Cyprian, the Spirit can be found in the church and in the harmonious prayers of the united congregation.

It has proved rewarding to understand the ideas of the "heart," "mind," "governing faculty," "soul" and "spirit" as somewhat comparable with modern ideas of the self. At any given time, Christian Scriptures, community and church form the voice of God and thereby address the individual Christian. The address from God is guided through social channels, but nonetheless mediates what Christians perceive of as the revelation of God's Word. According to the early Christian logic, humans can respond to the address from God. They can respond with words and actions, and with their "self," all this fall within the category of prayer. The Christian "self" has (limited) free will to move in the direction of virtue and anticipate salvation. Although bound by human predicaments, each Christian is capable of great achievements when set on the right course in response to God's calling. Historically speaking, the treatises on prayer tell us that Christian communities formed a norm of behaviour, an idea of salvation and a certain anthropology, which is reflected in thoughts about prayer. Meanwhile prayer was a means for the individual Christian to align himself/herself with the norms and beliefs of "Christianity" at large, which was being defined at this very time. Prayer is a "place" where the self is formed in manifold dialogues. Prayer had to do with formation and relations. Theologically speaking, prayer is a means of being moved by God towards God and being transformed in the process.

6.1 Christian prayer in Roman society and beyond

In the course of this study, I have made a few references to the historian J.B. Rives who has studied religious identity in the Roman Empire. In his book on religion and authority in Carthage, Rives points to the fact that religion has both an individual and a collective form, and religious identity can therefore bridge between the individual and the group which is beneficial in the creation of a cohesive society. J.B. Rives claims that this was the reason why religion had "such an important place in the history of the Roman empire."[1229] However, Rives also claims that the traditional Roman and Greek cults did not embrace both aspects of human identity in the empirial period. The official cults were not exclusive and thus allowed for divergence between personal and social identities. In the empirial period, a Roman citizen could attend one kind of public cult, while worshipping other gods in private, and this meant that religious identity was weakened as a means of holding the empire together. As Rives points out, it is no coincidence that Christianity within a century went from being a persecuted minority to a favoured religion. Both the persecution and later the embrace of Christianity were attempts from the side of the authorities to homogenize the religious identities of the empire, probably with the honest intention of gaining help from the true God or gods. Christianity had an advantage, because Christianity made a claim on the entire life of a person, and therefore Christian life should be dominated by the same virtues and behaviour wherever a Christian found himself/herself – in public, civic or private circumstances, even in the inner chamber of his/her (mental) house.

1229 Rives, 1995, 3.

As such the church could help create homogeneity not only in a person's life, but also in the social set-up of an empire. According to J.B. Rives:

> "Christianity more than anything else provided the means both to define collective religious identity suitable for an empire and to enforce a very high degree of individual conformity to that collective norm."[1230]

I argue that the Christian theology of prayer and practice of prayer were part of creating and upholding this overarching religious identity.

The Jewish and Greco-Roman religions, although not wholly distinguishable entities, were cultures in which sacrifice and prayer played a significant role. As we have seen cultic prayer, philosophical prayer and magical prayer-like invocations were in widespread use in antiquity, and prayer was used differently in different contexts. Whereas the Greco-Roman cults and the cultic prayers to some degree conferred the inhabitants of the empire with a common collective identity, the cult did not succeed in forming coherence between this collective identity and the personal identity of people in the empire. Common people looked to magicians and to different associations and local cults for help to communicate with the divine in their everyday lives. On the local and civic level, people thus had their identities formed by various cults and associations that differed from the official cults. Meanwhile, the philosophers concentrated on their own mental practice of prayer, but the philosopher's prayer could not create an official collective identity, as it was too elitist and had the aim of shaping the individual, not the community as such.

The empire lacked a common point of reference for personal as well as collective identity, and Christianity gradually came to be this common orientation, not least because of its piety and prayer. Christian prayer had, as we have seen, the role of binding people together in collective worship and liturgy and summon people to do introspection and align themselves with God's will. The main idea behind Christian prayer was that the same fatherly God was approachable by all at all times. Christians were told of God's salvific will towards his children for whom he cares spiritually. As clearly expressed in the treatises on prayer, God wants his children to care for each other, and prayer only makes sense when certain ethical standards

---

1230 Id. 310.

are met. In this way, prayer could bring official, civic and personal levels of life together. Christian prayer had to do with the Christian church
as overarching unity, connecting the whole Christendom with the local
Christian congregation and with the individual Christian and his/her life.
The Christian authors emphasized the exclusive and penetrating character
of Christian identity.

The extended prayers that the authors left behind in their writings were
more or less aligned with the theology of prayer and instruction on prayer
that they promoted in their treatises. The extant prayers of the Christian
authors were, as we saw in Chapter 2, prayers for forgiveness of sins,
petitionary prayers for virtue and knowledge and intercessory prayers for
the whole empire and for all people. Of course, this does not mean that
Christians in general only prayed in this idealistic manner, but it means
that Christians were told that being a child of the Christian God was a
responsibility, and a matter of mind and heart. For this reason, Christians
were told to be aware of their own behaviour, sins and shortcomings. In
return for their orientation towards God, they received faith, strength and
salvation, already while they were praying, but in full effect in eternity. In
this way, prayer came to form Christian self-perception and identity from
the early days of Christianity, when the Greco-Roman and Jewish ideas of
piety and prayer were merged and developed into Christian piety.

6.2 A few perspectives

Although one should be cautious in comparing phenomena across the
span of centuries, there are noticeable parallels in the function of prayer
in "pietist" communities in different historical epochs.[1231] As in the early
church, also later, Christian lay-people have been formed by way of prayer
and introspection in combination. This combination has at more points
in history created salient Christian identities and has influenced people on
an individual level and bound them to their Christian community. Thus

---

1231 Though von Stritzky reminds us that "pietas" in an antique understanding
was not to be confused with Schleiermacher's modern use of the word as "die
Ausrichtung des Gefühlslebens auf Gott." (E. Dassmann/K.S. Frank (eds.),
Pietas. Festschrift für Bernhard Kötting, Münster 1980, 155).

Peter I. Kaufman has made the observation about the Calvinist pietism in Elisabethian England: "the pietists expected prayers to fashion each petitioner's intense inwardness, to conjure up and compose identity, as well as to articulate it."[1232] The same identity-forming role of prayer comes to the fore in the literary work of the English puritan John Bunyan, *The Pilgrims Progress* (1678). Bunyan points to the interrelatedness between prayer and belonging because he notes that when people stop praying in private, they also withdraw from the Christian community:

> "Then they cast off by degrees private Duties, as Closet-prayer, Curbing their Lusts, Watching, Sorrow for Sin, and the like. Then they shun the company of lively and warm Christians."[1233]

We see that Bunyan saw a connection between the neglect of private or "closet-prayer" and peoples' rejection of the Christian community. Likewise, the German pietists of the sixteenth and seventeenth centuries were led by similar ideas. An early Protestant pietist such as August Herman Francke held that the means of a pious life is self-examination, daily repentance, *prayer*, hearing the Word and participation in the sacraments.[1234] These ideals of Protestant pietism replaced, to some extent, the consolation and discipline of the Catholic institution of penance, in which a combination of self-scrutiny and prayer had been in use for centuries to shape Christian selves.[1235]

The Pietists of the reformation times would occasionally criticize Catholic prayer practice for being too rigid and formalized.[1236] Christians in the third century could have criticized Greco-Roman cultic prayer for the same fallacy. As we saw in the contextual analysis, cultic prayers were occasionally

---

1232 P.I. Kaufman, *Prayer, Despair, and Drama. Elisabethian Introspection*, Champaign 1996, 17.

1233 W.R. Owens (ed.), *John Bunyan. The Pilgrim's Progress*, Oxford 2009, 145.

1234 R.E. Olson, *The Story of Christian Theology. Twenty Centuries of Tradition & Reform*, Downers Grove 1999, 488 ff.

1235 Kaufman, 1996, 161. Cf. Tentler's observations about the function of penance: "I have identified for the institutions of forgiveness two social and psychological functions – discipline (or social control) and consolation (or cure of anxiety)" (T.N. Tentler, *Sin and Confession on the Eve of the Reformation*, Princeton 1977, xvi).

1236 Kaufman, 1996, 15–16.

so archaic and formalized in the Roman cult that people did not always understand them. Today, Christian prayer practice in the Evangelical Lutheran Church in Denmark might sometimes fall prey to the same criticism of being overly formalized and thus somewhat hard to decipher for the members of the church who nonetheless define their collective identity as Evangelical Lutheran. However, the theologian N.F.S. Grundtvig, who has heavily influenced the Church of Denmark, emphasized that the Lord's Prayer was not something only to be read and learned, but was a message from God that ideally and by the grace of God should affect the heart and faith of those uttering the first words "Our Father." Inspired by Luther, Grundtvig urged that prayers should not be "read," but "prayed," which meant that prayer was a matter of heart and not only lips.[1237] It could seem that pietistic awakenings – understanding pietism broadly – are often promoting a certain theology of prayer and attempts to make prayers a matter of the heart and mind. Prayer has certainly been a vital part of Christianity since the early church. The Christian theology of prayer that took shape in the third century has had an impact on the life of the church ever since by forming a tradition that emphasizes both the individual and collective aspects of piety.

1237 N.F.S. Grundtvig, *Den Christelige Børnelærdom*, in: H. Begtrup, *Udvalgte Skrifter* 9, København 1906, 377.

Bibliography

Sources

The four euchological treatises under investigation

Tertullian, *De Oratione* (orat.), D. Schleyer (ed.), *De baptismo, De oratione/ Von der Taufe, vom Gebet*, Turnhout 2006; translation in: A. Stewart-Sykes, *Tertullian, Cyprian, and Origen on the Lord's Prayer*, Crestwood, NY 2004.

Cyprian, *De Dominica Oratione* (domin.orat.), M. Réveillaud (ed.), *L'orasion dominical par saint Cyprien*, Paris 1964; translation in: A. Stewart-Sykes, *Tertullian, Cyprian, and Origen on the Lord's Prayer*, Crestwood, NY 2004.

Clement of Alexandria, *Stromateis* 7 (strom.), edition and translation in: F.J.A. Hort/J.B. Mayor (eds.), *Clement of Alexandria, Miscellanies, Book VII. The Greek text with introduction, translation and notes*, London 1902.

Origen, *Perì Euchês* (de or.), P. Koetschau et al. (eds.), *Origenes Werke* (GCS 3), Leipzig 1899; translation in: A. Stewart-Sykes, *Tertullian, Cyprian, and Origen on the Lord's Prayer*, Crestwood, NY 2004.

Additional Classical and Early Christian Literature

Classical works

Apuleius, *Apologia* (apol.), Christopher P. Jones (ed.), *Apuleius Apologia*, LCL 534, Cambridge 2017.

Cassius Dio, *Historia Romana*, E. Cary/H.B. Foster (eds.), *Dio Cassius. Roman History*, LCL 177, Cambridge 1914-27.

Cato the Elder, *De agricultura* (agr.), W. D. Hooper/H.B. Ash (eds.), *Cato, Varro. Agriculture*. LCL 283, Cambridge 1934; translation in: M.C. Kiley (ed.), Prayer from Alexander to Constantine. A Critical Anthology, London 1997.

Dion Chrysostom, *Orationes*, J. W. Cohoon/H. L. Crosby (eds.), *Discourses 31–36* III, LCL 358, Cambridge 1940.

Epictetus, *Dissertationes* (diatr.), J. Henderson (ed.)/W.A. Oldfather (tr.), *Epictetus. Discourses, Books 1–2*, LCL 131. Cambridge, MA 1925.

Epictetus, *Enchiridion* (ench.), H. Schenkl (ed.), *Epicteti Dissertationes ab Arriano digestae*, Leipzig 1916; translation in G. Long, *Enchiridion and Selections from the Discourses*, London 1877.

Homer, *Illiad* (il.), A. T. Murray (ed.), revised by W. F. Wyatt, *Homer. Iliad*, LCL 170. Cambridge 1924.

Iamblicus, *De mysteriis* (de myst.), E. C. Clarke, J.M. Dillon, J.P. Hershbell (eds.), *Iamblicus. On the Mysteries*, Atlanta 2004.

Lucian of Samosata, *Peregrinus* (Peregr.), quoted in: R. E. van Voorst (ed.), *Jesus Outside the New Testament*, Grand Rapids 2000.

Macrobius, *Saturnalia* (sat.), R. A. Kaster (ed.), *Saturnalia*, LCL 510, Cambridge 2011.

Marc Aurel, *Meditationes* (Med.), C.R. Haines (ed.), *Meditationes*, LCL 58, Cambridge 1916; translation in: M. Staniforth, *Meditations*, London 2005.

Maximus of Tyre, *Dissertationes*, M.B. Trapp (ed.), *Maximus Tyrius Dissertationes*, Bibliotheca scriptorum Graecorum et Romanorum Teubneriana, Stuttgart-Leipzig 1994.

Maximus of Tyre, *Fifth Oration on Prayer*, translation in: M. B. Trapp, *Maximus of Tyre: The Philosophical Orations*, Oxford 1997.

Philo, *De sobrietate*, F. H. Colson/G. H. Whitaker (eds.), *Philo Vol. III*, LCL 247, Cambridge 1930.

Plato, *Leges* (lg.), J. Burnet (ed.), *Platonis opera*, vol. 5, Oxford 1907.

Plato, *Phaedrus* (Phdr.), edition and translation in: H. N. Fowler, *Plato in Twelve Volumes*, LCL 36, Cambridge 1925.

Plato, *Republic* (r.), C. Emlyn-Jones (ed.), *Plato. Republic*, LCL 237, Cambridge 2013.

Plato, *Timaeus* (Tim.), R.G. Bury (ed.), *Plato. Timaeus*, LCL 234, London 1929.

Plotinus, *Enneads* (enn.), P. Henry/ H.-R. Schwyzer (eds.), *Plotini opera*, 3 vols., Museum Lessianum. Series philosophica 33–35, Leiden 1951; translation in: S. MacKenna/B. S. Page, *The Enneads. Great Books of The Western World Collection*, London 1962.

Porphyrios, *Ad Marcellam* (Marc.), K. O'Brien Wicker (ed.), *Porphyry the Philosopher. To Marcella*, Atlanta 1987.

Porphyrios, *Philosophy from Oracles*, in: Augustin, *De civitate Dei* 19.23, B. Dombart/A. Kalb (eds.), *De civitate Dei, Corpus Christianorum*, Series Latina, Turnhout 1955.

Porphyrios, *De vita Plotini et de ordine librorum eius* (Plot.), L. Brisson (ed.), *Porphyre: La vie de Plotin*. 2 vols. Histoire des doctrines de l'antiquité classique 16, Paris 1982–92; translation in: S. Mackenna, *Plotinus. The Ethical Treatises* 1, The Library of Philosophical Translations, Boston 1918.

Porhyrios, *Adversus Christianos* (chr.), translation in: R.M. Berchman, *Porphyry. Against the Christians*, Leiden 2005.

Sallustius, *Concerning the Gods and the Universe*, A.D. Nock (ed.), *Sallustius Concerning the Gods and the Universe. Edited with Prolegomena and Translation*, Cambridge 1926.

Sueton, *Nero*, B.H. Warmington (ed.), *Suetonius: Nero*, Bristol 1977.

Jerusalem Talmud (y. Taan. 1.4, 64a), translation in: M. Jacobs, *Theatres and Performances as Reflected in the Talmud Yerushalmi*, P. Schäfer (ed.), *The Talmud Yerushalmi and Graeco-Roman Culture*, Tübingen 1998.

Christian Sources

Acta Cypriani, H. Musurillo (ed.), *The Acts of the Christian Martyrs*, Oxford 1972.

Acta Martyrum Scillitanorum (Acta scill.), H. Musurillo (ed.), *The Acts of the Christian Martyrs*, Oxford 1972.

Acts of Carpus, Papylus, and Agathonice (m.Carp.), H. Musurillo (ed.), *The Acts of the Christian Martyrs*, Oxford 1972.

Acts of Peter (A.Petr.), L. Vouaux (ed.), *Les actes de Pierre*, Paris 1922; translation in: B. D. Ehrman, *Lost Scriptures. Books That Did Not Make It into the New Testament*, Oxford 2005.

Acts of Thomas, translation in: M.R. James, *The Apocryphal New Testament*, Oxford 1924.

Acta SS. Perpetuæ et Felicitatis (m.Perp.), translation in: H. Musurillo, *The Acts of the Christian Martyrs*, Oxford 1992, 109–119.

A Gnostic prayer, Codex Brucianus 333,3–8, translation in: C. Markschies, *Gnosis. An Introduction*, London 2003.

A Prayer from the Apostle, translation in: M.C. Kiley, *Prayer from Alexander to Constantine. A Critical Anthology*, London 1997, 291.

A prayer to Sarapis in P. Oxy. 1070, Greek edition: http://papyri.info/
hgv/31317/ (last visited 27.08.18); translation in: M.C. Kiley, *Prayer
from Alexander to Constantine. A Critical Anthology*, London 1997,
181–184.

Augustine, *Sermon to the Catechumens. On the Creed*, translation
in: C.T. Wilcox, *Saint Augustine. Treatises on Marriage and other
Subjects*, FaCh 27, Washington 1955.

Augustine, *In Johannis evangelium tractatus* (ev. Io.), translation in: P.
Schaff (ed.), *St. Augustine: Gospel of John, First Epistle of John, and
Soliliques*, Nicene and Post-Nicene Fathers 1:7, New York 1886-90.

Canons of Nicaea, translation in: H. Percival, *The Seven Ecumenical
Councils*, Nicene and Post-Nicene Fathers 2:14, New York 1892.

Clement of Alexandria, *Paedagogus* (paed.), M. Harl/ H.-I. Marrou/C.
Matray/C. Mondésert (eds.), *Clément d'Alexandrie. Le pédagogue*,
SC 70, 108, 158, Paris, 1:1960; 2:1965; 3:1970; translation of paed.
3.12.101.4 in M.C. Kiley, *Prayer from Alexander to Constantine.
A Critical Anthology*, London 1997, 296-303; full translation in W.
Wilson, *Paedagogus and Stromata*, ANF 2, Buffalo, NY 1885.

Clement of Alexandria, *Stromateis* 1–6 (strom.), L. Früchtel/O. Stählin/U.
Treu (eds.), *Clemens Alexandrinus*, GCS 52 (15), 17, Berlin 2:1960;
3:1970; translation in: W. Wilson, *Paedagogus and Stromata*, ANF 2,
Buffalo, NY 1885.

Cyprian, *Ad Demetrianum* (Demetr.), translation in: J. Baer, *Des heiligen
Kirchenvaters Caecilius Cyprianus sämtliche Schriften*, BKV 1:34,
München 1918.

Cyprian, *Epistle* (ep.), D.I.H. Goldhorn (ed.), *Th. C. Cypriani opera
genuina ad optimorum librorum fidem expressa, brevique adnotatione
instructa*, Tauchnitz, 1838; translation in: R.B. Donna, *Letters 1–81*,
FaCh 51, Washington, D.C. 1964.

Cyprian, *De lapsis* (laps.), translation in: R.E. Wallis, *Treatise 3*, ANF 5,
Buffalo, NY 1886.

Cyprian, *De Unitate Ecclesia* (unit.eccl.), P. Siniscalco et al. (eds.),
Cyprien de Carthage. L'unité de l'église, SC 500, Paris 2006;
translation in: W.A. Jürgens, *The Faith of the Early Fathers. Pre-
Nicene and Nicene Eras*, Collegeville 1970.

Didachē (Did.), W. Rordorf/A. Tuilier (eds.), *La Doctrine des Douze
Apôtres (Didaché)*, SC 248, Paris 1978.

Epiphanius of Salamis, *Panarion* (panar.), K. Holl (ed.*)*, *Band 1, Ancoratus und Panarion*, GCS 25, Leipzig 1915.

Euseb, *De laudibus Constantini* (l.C.), I.A. Heikel (ed.), *Eusebius Werke*, 1, GCS 7, Leipzig 1902.

Euseb, *De vita Constantini* (v.C.), F. Winkelmann (ed.), *Über das Leben des Kaisers Konstantins*, GCS, Berlin 1975, rev. 1992; translation in: A. Cameron/S.G. Hall, *Eusebius. Life of Constantine*, Oxford 1999.

Euseb, *Historia Ecclesiastica* (h.e.), G. Bardy (ed.), *Eusèbe de Césarée. Histoire ecclésiastique II*, SC 41, Paris 1955.

Evagrius, *Chapters on Prayer*, J.-P. Migne (ed.), *MPG* 79, Paris 1857-1866; translation in: R.E. Sinkewicz, *Evagrius of Pontus: The Greek Ascetic Corpus*, Oxford 2003.

Gregory of Nyssa, *De oratione dominica* (or. dom.), F. Oehler (ed.), *Gregor's Bischof's von Nyssa Abhandlung von der Erschaffung des Menschen und fünf Reden auf das Gebet*, Leipzig 1859.

Hilary of Poitiers, *Commentary on Matthew*, translation in: D.H. Williams, *Commentary on Matthew,* FaCh 125, Washington 2012.

Hippolytus, *Traditio Apostolica* (trad.ap.), B. Botte (ed.), *Hippolyte de Rome. La tradition apostolique d'après les anciennes versions*, SC 11, Paris 1984; translation in: G. Dix/H. Chadwick (ed.), *The Treatise on The Apostolic Tradition of St Hippolytus of Rome*, London 1991.

Jerome, *De viris Illustribus*, C. Barthold (ed.), *De viris illustribus*, Mülheim 2011.

Justin Martyr, *Apologeticum* (I apol.), D. Minns/P. Parvis, (eds.), *Justin, Philosopher and Martyr, Apologies* Oxford 2009.

Martyrdom of Pionius (m.Pion.), H. Musurillo (ed.), *The Acts of the Christian Martyrs*, Oxford 1972.

Martyrium S. Polycarpi (m.Polyc.), H. Musurillo (ed.), *The Acts of the Christian Martyrs*, Oxford 1972.

Melchizedek, in: M. Meyer (ed.), *The Naghammadi Scriptures*, San Francisco 2007.

Michael bar Elias, *Chronicle* 5.3, in: M. Fraser (ed.), *A Syriac Notitia Urbis Alexandrinae*, JEA 37, 1951, 103–108.

Origen, *Commentarii in Cantica canticorum* (Cant.), translation in: R.P. Lawson, *Origen: The Song of Songs: Commentary and Homilies*, ACW 26, New York 1957.

Origen, *Commentarii in evangelium Joannis (Jo.)* C. Blanc (ed.), *Origène. Commentaire sur saint Jean*, SC 120, Paris 1966; translation in: R.E. Heine, *Origen. Commentary on the Gospel according to John Books 1-10*, FaCh 80, Washington 1989.

Origen, *Commentarii in epistulam ad Romanos* (Comm. in Rom.), translation in: T.P. Scheck, *Origen. Commentary on the Epistle to the Romans*, Books 6-10, FaCh 104, Washington 2002.

Origen, *Contra Celsum* (Cels.), M. Borret (ed.), *Origène. Contre Celse*, SC, Paris 1967; translation in: F. Crombie, *Origen Against Celsus*, ANF 4, Buffalo, NY 1885.

Origen, *Epistula ad Gregorium* (ep.), translation in: F. Crombie, *Letter to Gregory*, ANF 4, Buffalo, NY 1896.

Origen, *Homilia in Ieremiam* (hom. Ier.), P. Nautin (ed.), *Origène. Homélies sur Jérémie*, 1-2, SC 232, 238, Paris 1976, 1977; translation in: J.C. Smith: *Origen. Homiles on Jeremiah. Homilies on 1 Kings 28*, FaCh 97, Washington 1998.

Origen, *Homilia in Lucem* (hom. I-39 in Lc.), Migne (ed.), *S. Eusebeii Hieronymi Stridonensis presbyteri translatio Homiliarum XXXIX Origenes in evangelium Lucae*, PL 26; translation in: J. Y. Lienhard, *Origen. Homilies on Luke*, FaCh 94, Washington 1996.

Origen, *De Principiis* (princ.), P. Koetschau (ed.), *De principiis (Peri archon)*, GCS, Leipzig 1913; translation in: G.W. Butterworth, *Origen. On First Principles*, New York 1966.

Origen, *Selecta in Psalmos* (sel. in Ps.), J.-P. Migne (ed.), PG 12, Paris 1857.

The Passion of Saints Perpetua and Felicitas, H.R. Musurillo (ed.), *The Acts of the Christian Martyrs*, Oxford 1972.

Pontius, *Vita Cypriani*, translation in: R. J. Deferrari, *Early Christian biographies*, FaCh 15, Washington 2001.

Pseudo-Clementine Recognitiones, translation in: T. Smith, *Recognitiones*, ANF 8, Buffalo, NY 1886.

Sozomen, *Ecclesiastica Historia* (EH), J. Bidez (ed.)/Festugière (tr.)/G. Sabbah/B. Grillet, *Sozomène. Histoire Ecclésiastique. Livres III-IV*, SC 148, Paris 1996.

Tertullian, *Apologeticum* (apol.), C. Becker (ed.), *Tertullian. Apologeticum*, München, 1952; translation in: A. Souter, *Tertullian. Q. Septimi Florentis Tertvlliani Apologeticvs*, Cambridge 1917.

Tertullian, *Ad Scapulam* (scap.), translation in: S. Thelwall, *To Scapula*, ANF 3, New York1885.

Tertullian, *Adversus Marcionem* (Marc.), E. Evans (ed.), *Tertullian Adversus Marcionem*, Oxford 1972.

Tertullian, *Adversus Praxean* (Prax.), E. Evans (ed.), *Q. S. Fl. Tertullianus, Treatise against Praxeas*, SPCK, London, 1948.

Tertullian, *Adversus Valentinianos* (Val.), M.T. Riley, *Q. S. Fl. Tertulliani Adversus Valentinianos*, Stanford 1971.

Tertullian, *De anima* (an.), J. H. Waszink, *Tertullianus. De anima*, Amsterdam 1947; translation in: P. Holms, *The Ante-Nicene Christian Library*, London 1870.

Tertullian, *De Baptismo* (bapt.), E. Evans (ed.), *Tertullian: De Baptismo Liber*, London 1964.

Tertullian, *De carne Christi* (carn.), E. Evans (ed.), *Tertullian: De carne Christi*, London 1956.

Tertullian, *De Exhortatione Castitatis* (cast.), C. Moreschini/J.-C. Fredouille (eds.), *Tertullien. Exhortation à la chasteté*, SC 319, Paris 1985; translation in: S. Thelwall, *The Ante-Nicene Christian Library*, 18, London 1870.

Tertullian, *De Fuga in Persecutione* (fug.), V. Bulhart (ed.), *De fuga in persecutione*, CSEL 76, Vienna 1957.

Tertullian, *De Ieiunio adversus Psychicos* (ieiun.), translation in: S. Thelwall, *Tertullian. On Fasting. In Opposition to the Psychics*, ANF 4, Buffalo, NY 1885.

Tertullian, *De Paenitentia* (paen.), J.W. P. Borleffs (ed.), *De paenitentia*, CCSL 1, Turnhout 1954; and P. De Labriolle, *De paenitentia, De pudicitia, texte et trad.*, Paris 1906; translation in: S. Thelwall, *On Repentance*, ANF 3, Buffalo, NY 1885.

Tertullian, *De Pallio* (pall.), V. Hunink (ed.), *Tertullian, De Pallio*, Amsterdam 2005.

Tertullian, *De Praescriptione Haereticorum* (praescr.), R. Refoulé (ed.), *Traité de la prescription contre les hérétiques*, SC 46, Paris 1957; translation in: T. H. Bindley, *On the Testimony of the Soul and On the 'Prescription' of Heretics*, SPCK, London/New York 1914.

Tertullian, *De Pudicitia* (pud.), C. Micaelli/C. Munier (eds.), *La pudicité*, SC 394 and 395, Paris 1993; translation in: G. Claesson,

available online: http://www.tertullian.org/articles/claesson_pudicitia_
translation.htm (last visited 28.01.19).

Tertullian, *Scorpiace* (scorp.), translation in: S Thelwall, *Scorpiace*, ANF
3, Buffalo, NY 1885.

Secondary Literature

J. Albrecht et al., *Religion in the Making: The Lived Ancient Religion
Approach*, in: *Religion* 48/4 (2018), 568–593.

K. Algra, "Epictetus and Stoic Theology" in T. Scaltsas and A.S. Mason
(eds.) *The Philosophy of Epictetus*, Oxford 2007, 32–55.

P. Allen/W. Mayer/L. Cross (eds.), *Prayer and Spirituality in the Early
Church II*, Brisbane 1999.

W. Ameling et al. (eds.), *Caesarea and the Middle Coast: 1121–2160*,
Berlin 2011.

A.S. Atiya (ed.), *The Coptic Encyclopedia*, New York 1990.

R.S. Bagnall, *Egypt in Late Antiquity*, Princeton 1993.

G.J. Bahr, *The Use of the Lord's Prayer in the Primitive Church*, in: JBL
85/2 (1965), 153–159.

J.D. Baldwin, *George Herbert Mead. A Unifying Theory for Sociology*,
New York 1986.

T.D. Barnes, *Tertullian. A Historical and Literary Study*, Oxford 1971.

J. Barr, '*Abba Isn't 'Daddy*,' in: JThS NS 39 (1988), 28–47.

K. Barth, *Church Dogmatics Volume 3. The Doctrine of Creation Part 3.
The Creator and His Creature*, New York 1960.

K. Barth, *The Humanity of God*, Louisville 1960.

F. Barth, *Ethnic Groups and Boundaries. The Social Organization of
Cultural Difference*, London 1969.

J. Behr, *Asceticism and Anthropology in Irenaeus and Clement*, Oxford
2000.

J. Behr, *The Way to Nicaea*, New York 2001.

R.M. Berchman (ed.), *Porphyry. Against the Christians*, Leiden 2005.

S.P. Bergjan, *Der fürsorgende Gott. Der Begriff der PRONOIA Gottes in
der apologetischen Literatur der Alten Kirche*, Berlin 2004.

S.P. Bergjan, *Clement of Alexandria on God's Providence and the
Gnostic's Life Choice. The Concept of Pronoia in the Stromateis*,

Book VII, in: M. Havrda/V. Hušek/J. Plátova (eds.), *The Seventh Book of the Stromateis. Proceedings of the Colloquium on Clement of Alexandria*, Leiden 2012, 63–92.

J. Betz, *The Eucharist in the Didache*, in: J.A. Draper (ed.), *The Didache in Modern Research*, Leiden 1996, 244–275.

H. Bietenhard, *Caesarea, Origenes und die Juden*, Stuttgart 1974.

T.H. Bindley, *St. Cyprian on the Lord's Prayer*, London 1914.

S. Birk, *Using Images for Self-Representation on Roman Sarcophagi*, in: S. Birk/T. Myrup Kristensen/B. Poulsen (eds.), *Using Images in Late Antiquity*, Oxford 2014, 33–47.

B. Bitton-Ashkelony, *Demons and Prayers. Spiritual Exercises in the Monastic Community of Gaza in the Fifth and Sixth Century*, in: VigChr 57/2 (2003), 200–221.

B. Bitton-Ashkelony/A. Kofsky, *The Monastic School of Gaza*, Leiden 2006.

B. Bitton-Ashkelony, 'More Interior than the Lips and Tongue'. *John of Apamea and Silent Prayer in Late Antiquity*, in: JECS 20/2 (2012), 303–331.

M.D. Boulet, *Le Notre Père dans la liturgie*, in: La Maison-Dieu 85 (1966), 69–91.

P. Bradshaw, *Daily Prayer in the Early Church. A Study of the Origin and Early Development of the Divine Office*, London 1981.

P. Bradshaw, *What Happened to Daily Prayer?*, in: Worship 64 (1990), 10–23.

P. Bradshaw, *The Search for the Origins of Christian Worship. Sources and Methods for the Study of Early Liturgy*, London 2002.

P. Bradshaw, *Parallels between Early Jewish and Christian Prayers. Some Methodological Issues*, in: A. Gerhards/A. Doeker/P. Ebenbauer (eds.), *Identität durch Gebet. Zur gemeinschaftsbildenden Funktion institutionalisierten Betens in Judentum und Christentum*, Paderborn 2003, 21–36.

P. Bradshaw (ed.), *A Companion to Common Worship 2*, London 2006.

D. Brakke,/M. Satlow/S. Weitzman (eds.), *Religion and the Self in Antiquity*, Bloomington 2005.

D. Brakke, *Demons and the Making of the Monk. Spiritual Combat in Early Christianity*, Cambridge 2006.

A. Brent, *Cyprian and Roman Carthage*, Cambridge 2010.

M.B. Brewer, *The Social Self. On Being the Same and Different at the Same Time*, in: *Personality and Social Psychology Bulletin*. 17/5 (1991), 475–482.

S. Brock, *The Prayer of the Heart in Syriac Tradtion*, in: Sob. 4 (1982), 131–142.

M.J. Brown, *The Lord's Prayer through North African Eyes. A Window into Early Christianity*, New York 2004.

P. Brown, *The Rise and Function of the Holy Man in Late Antiquity*, in: JRS 61 (1971), 80–101.

P. Brown, *The World of Late Antiquity. From Marcus Aurelius to Muhammad*, London 1971.

R. Brubaker/F. Cooper, *Beyond 'Identity'*, in: Theory and Society 29 (2000), 1–47.

H. Buchinger, *Gebet und Identität bei Origenes. Das Vaterunser im Horizont der Auseinandersetzung um Liturgie und Exergese*, in: A. Gerhards/A. Doeker/P. Ebenbauer (eds.), *Identität durch Gebet. Zur gemeinschaftsbildenden Funktion institutionalisierten Betens in Judentum und Christentum*, Paderborn 2003, 307–354.

D.K. Buell, *Making Christians. Clement of Alexandria and the Rhetoric of Legitimacy*, Princeton 1999.

P.J. Burke/J.E. Stets, Identity Theory and Social Identity Theory, *Social Psychology Quarterly* 63/3 (2000), 224–237.

B. Burrell, *'Curse Tablets' from Caesarea*, in: NEA 61/2 (1998), 128.

A. Cameron, *Redrawing the Map. Early Christian Territory after Foucault*, in: JRS 76 (1986), 266–271.

H. F. von Campenhausen, *Ecclesiastical Authority and Spiritual Power in the Church of the First Three Centuries*, Stanford, CA, 1969.

E. Campi/L. Grane/A.M. Ritter, *Oratio. Das Gebet in patristischer und reformatorischer Sicht Festschrift zum 65. Geburtstag von Alfred Schindler*, Göttingen 1999.

J. Černý, Egyptian Oracles in R.A. Parker (ed.), *A Saite Oracle Papyrus from Thebes in the Brooklyn Museum*, Providence 1962, 35–48.

H. Chadwick, *Early Christian Thought and the Classical Tradition. Studies in Justin, Clement and Origen*, Oxford 1966.

J.M. Charon, *Symbolic Interactionism*, London 2007.

M.L. Munkholt Christensen, *En syrisk kilde til den ældste kritstne nadverforståelse*, in: DTT 73 (2010), 105–123.

M.L. Munkholt Christensen, *'The Lord has bidden us to pray in Secret'. Reconciling Personal and Collective Identity through 'Secret Prayer' in 3rd-Century Christianity*, in: S. Saxkjær/E. Mortensen (eds.), *Secrecy*, Aarhus 2015, 131–144.

M.L. Munkholt Christensen, Witnessed by Angels: The Role of Angels in Relation to Prayer in Four Ante-Nicene Euchological Treatises, in: *Studia Patristica. Papers presented at the Seventeenth International Conference on Patristic Studies held in Oxford 2015*, vol. LXXV, Leuven 2017, 49–56.

M.L. Munkholt Christensen, *Om at bede og kende sig selv. Et studium af fire før-nikænske skrifter om bøn*, in: *Patristica Nordica Annuaria 32* (2018) 91–116.

E.A. Clark, *History, Theory, Text. Historians and the Linguistic Turn*, Cambridge 2004.

J. Cohen, *Living Letters of the Law. Ideas of the Jew in Medieval Christianity*, Oakland 1999.

C.C.H. Cook, *The Philokalia and the Inner Life. On Passions and Prayer*, Eugene 2012.

J.G. Cook, *Roman Attitudes towards the Christians*, Tübingen 2011.

J.K. Coyle, *What Was "Prayer" for Early Christians?*, in: P. Allen/W. Mayer/L. Cross (eds.), *Prayer and Spirituality in the Early Church 2*, Sydney 1999, 25–41.

E. Dassmann/K.S. Frank (eds.), *Pietas. Festschrift für Bernhard Kötting*, Münster 1980.

J.D. Dawson, *Christian Teaching*, in F. Young et al. (eds.), *The Cambridge History of Early Christian Literature*, Cambridge 2004, 222–38.

K. Demura, *'Sursum Cor' in the Sermons of St. Augustine*, in: B. Neil/G.D. Dunn/L. Cross (eds.), *Prayer and Spirituality in the Early Church. Liturgy and Life 3*, Sydney 2003.

O. Dibelius, *Das Vaterunser. Umrisse zu einer Geschichte des Gebets in der alten und mittleren Kirche*, Gießen 1903.

G. F. Diercks, *Tertullianus De Oratione. Critische uitgave met prolegomena, vertaling en philologisch-exegetisch-liturgische commentaar.* Bussum 1947.

A. Dihle, *Das Gebet der Philosophen*, in: E. Campi/L. Grane/A.M. Ritter (eds.), *Oratio. Das Gebet in patristischer und reformatorischer Sicht Festschrift zum 65. Geburtstag von Alfred Schindler*, Göttingen 1999, 23–42.

J. Dillon, *The Platonic Philosopher at Prayer*, in: J. Dillon/A. Timotin (eds.), *Platonic Theories of Prayer*, Boston 2016, 7–25.

D. G. Dix, *The Shape of the Liturgy*. London 1945.

E.R. Dodds (ed.), *Plato. Gorgias*, Oxford 1959.

E.R. Dodds, *Pagan and Christian in an Age of Anxiety*, New York 1965.

T.L. Donaldson, *Religious Rivalries and the Struggle for Success in Caesarea Maritima*, Waterloo 2000.

N. Dorian, *The Gospel of Thomas. Introduction and Commentary*, Leiden 2014.

K.J. Dover, *Greek Popular Morality in the Time of Plato and Aristotle*, Oxford 1974.

F.J. Dölger, *Sol salutis. Gebet und Gesang im christlichen Altertum mit besonderer Rücksicht auf die Ostung in Gebet und Liturgie*, Münster 1925.

G.D. Dunn, *Tertullian*, London 2004.

G.D. Dunn, *Tertullian's Aduersus Iudaeos. A Rhetorical Analysis*, Washington 2008.

B.S. Easton, *The Apostolic Tradition of Hippolytus*, Cambridge 1934.

U. Ehrlich, *The Nonverbal Language of Prayer. A New Approach of Jewish Liturgy*, Tübingen 2004.

A. Elliot/P. du Gay (eds.), *Identity in Question*, London 2009.

G. Emery/M. Levering (eds.), *The Oxford Handbook of the Trinity*, Oxford 2011.

G. Emilie, *Cicero and the Roman Pietas*, in: CJ 39/9 (1944), 536–542.

J. Engberg, *Impulsore Chresto. Opposition to Christianity in the Roman Empire c. 50–250*, Frankfurt 2007.

E. Evans (ed.), *Tertullian's Tract on The Prayer*, London 1953.

E. Ferguson (ed.), *Clement of Alexandria. Stromateis, Books 1–3*, The Fathers of the Church, Volume 85, Washington 1991.

W. Fitzgerald, *Spiritual Modalities. Prayer as Rhetoric and Performance*. University Park 2012.

M. Foucault, *Technologies of the Self*, in: L.H. Martin et al. (eds.), *Technologies of the Self. A Seminar with Michel Foucault*, Amherst 1988.

M. Foucault, *The Hermeneutics of the Subject. Lectures at the Collège de France 1981–82*, ed. by Frédéric Gros, New York 2001.

M. Foucault, *Histoire de la sexualité 4. Les aveux de la chair*, Frédéric Gros (ed.), Paris 2018.

R.L. Fox, *Pagans and Christians in the Mediterranean World from the Second Century AD to the Conversion of Constantine*, London 1988.

P.M. Fraser, *A Syriac Notitia Urbis Alexandrinae*, in: JEA 37 (1951), 103–108.

W.H.C. Frend, *The Rise of Christianity*, Minneapolis 1984.

L.R. Frey, *The Symbolic-Interpretive Perspective on Group Dynamics*, in: Small Group Research 35 (2004), 277–306.

G. Freyburger/L. Pernot/F. Chapot/B. Laurot (eds.), *Bibliographie analytique de la prière grecque et romaine. Deuxième édition complétée et augmentée (1898–2003)*, Turnhout 2008.

K. Froehlich, *The Lord's Prayer in Patristic Literature*, in: R. Hammerling, (ed.), *A History of Prayer. The First to the Fiftheenth Century*, Leiden 2008.

A. Fürst (ed.), *Origenes und sein Erbe im Orient und Okzident*, in,: Adamantiana, Texte und Studien zu Origenes in seinem Erbe 1, Münster 2011.

A. Geertz, *Comparing Prayer*, in: W. Braun/R.T. McCutcheon (eds.), *Guide to the Study of Religion*. London 2000.

P. Gemeinhardt, *Personale Identität in spätantiken (christlichen) Bildungsprozessen* in: C. Bouillon, A. Heiser, M. Iff (eds.), *Person, Identität und theologische Bildung*, Stuttgart: Kohlhammer, 2007, 43–64.

A. Gerhards/A. Doeker/P. Ebenbauer (eds.), *Identität durch Gebet. Zur gemeinschaftsbildenden Funktion institutionalisierten Betens in Judentum und Christentum*, Paderborn 2003.

W. Gessel, *Die Theologie des Gebetes nach „De Oratione" von Origenes*, Paderborn 1975.

W. Gessel, „Der origeneische Gebetslogos und die Theologie der Mystik des Gebetes" i *Münchner Theologische Zeitschrift*, 28, 1977, 397–407.

E. Gibbon, *The History of the Decline and Fall of the Roman Empire*, *vol. 2–3*, London 1787.

A. Giddens, *Modernity and Self-Identity. Self and Society in the Late Modern Age*, Stanford 1991.

S. Gill, *Prayer*, in: L. Jones (ed.), *Encyclopedia of Religion*, Detroit 2005, 7367–7372.

P. Gleason, *Identifying Identity. A Semantic History*, in: The Journal of American History, 69/4 (1983), 910–931.

E.F. von der Goltz, *Das Gebet in der ältesten Christenheit. Eine Geschichtliche Untersuchung*, Leipzig 1901.

J. Green, *Persevering Together in Prayer. The Significance of Prayer in the Acts of the Apostles*, in: R.N. Longenecker, *Into God's Presence: Prayer in the New Testament*, Grand Rapids 2001.

H. Greeven, „εὔχομαι" in *TDNT*, 2:775–808, Grand Rapids 1964.

H. Grieser/A. Merkt (eds.), *Volksglaube im antiken Christentum*, Darmstadt 2009.

N.F.S. Grundtvig, *Den Christelige Børnelærdom*, in: H. Begtrup, *Udvalgte Skrifter 9*, Kopenhagen 1906.

D.M. Gwyn/S. Bangert, *Religious Diversity in Late Antiquity*, Leiden 2010.

R. Hammerling (ed.), *A History of Prayer. The First to the Fifteenth Century*, Leiden 2008.

P.E. Hammond, *The Sacred in a Secular Age. Toward Revision in the Scientific Study of Religion*, Berkeley 1985.

D.D. Hannah, *Michael and Christ. Michael Traditions and Angel Christology in Early Christianity*, Tübingen 1999.

R. Hard/C. Gill (eds.), *Discourses, Fragments, Handbook. Epictetus*, Oxford 2014.

C. Haas, *Alexandria in Late Antiquity. Topography and Social Conflict*, Baltimore 1997.

W. Haase, *Aufstieg und Niedergang der römischen Welt. Geschichte und Kultur Roms im Spiegel der neueren Forschung*, Berlin 1980.

D.Y. Hadidian, *The Lord's Prayer and the Sacraments of Baptism and of the Lord's Supper in the Early Church*, in: StLi 15 (1982/83), 132–144.

P. Hadot, *Philosophy as a Way of Life. Spiritual Exercises from Socrates to Foucault*, Hoboken 1995.

H.F. Hägg, *Seeking the Face of God: Prayer and Knowledge in Clement of Alexandria*, in: M. Havrda/V. Hušek/J. Plátova (eds.), *The Seventh Book of the Stromateis. Proceedings of the Colloquium on Clement of Alexandria*, Leiden 2012, 131–42.

A. G. Hamman, *La prière. Les trois premiers siècles*, Tournai 1962.

A. G. Hamman, *La prière chrétienne et prière païenne, formes et différences*, in: W. Haase (ed.), *Aufstieg und Niedergang der römischen Welt: Geschichte und Kultur Roms im Spiegel der neueren Forschung*, Berlin 1980.

A. G. Hamman, *Das Gebet in der Alte Kirche*, Frankfurt a.M. 1989.

P.A. Harland, *Dynamics of Identity in the World of the Early Christians*, London 2009.

C. Harrison, *The Art of Listening in the Early Church*, Oxford 2003.

M. Havrda,/V. Hušek/J. Plátova (eds.), *The Seventh Book of the Stromateis. Proceedings of the Colloquium on Clement of Alexandria*, Leiden 2012.

P. Heather, *The Fall of the Roman Empire. A New History of Rome and the Barbarians*, Oxford 2005.

S. Heid, *Der gebetsabschließende Bruderkuss im frühen Christentum*, in: H. Grieser/A. Merkt (eds.), *Volksglaube im antiken Christentum*, Darmstadt 2009, 249–259.

F. Heiler, *Das Gebet. Eine religionsgeschichtliche und religionspsychologische Untersuchung*, München 1920.

R. Heine, The Alexandrians in F. Young et al. (eds.), *The Cambridge History of Early Christian Literature*, Cambridge 2004, 113–130.

R.E. Heine, *Commentary on the Gospel According to John, Books 13–32*, in: FaCh 89, Washington 1993.

J. Heinemann, *The Fixed and the Fluid in Jewish Prayer*, in: G.H. Cohn/H. Fisch (eds.), *Prayer in Judaism. Continuity and Change*, Lanham, MD 1996, 45–52.

E.G. Hinson, *The Evangelization of the Roman Empire. Identity and Adaptability*, Macon 1981.

M. Hillar, *From Logos to Trinity. The Evolution of Religious Beliefs from Pythagoras to Tertullian*, Cambridge 2008.

O.W. Holmes, *Tertullian on Prayer*, in: TynB 6–5 (1960), 27–32.

S. Hornblower/A. Spawforth (eds.), *The Oxford Companion to Classical Civilization*, Oxford 1998.

P.W. van der Horst, *Silent Prayer in Antiquity*, in: Numen 41 (1994), 1–25.

L. Hurtado, *The Binitarian Pattern of Earliest Christian Devotion and Early Doctrinal Development*, in: B.D. Spinks (ed.), *The Place of Christ in Liturgical Prayer. Trinity, Christology, and Liturgical Theology*, Collegeville 2008, 23–50.

L. Hurtado, *The Place of Jesus in Earliest Christian Prayer and Its Import for Early Christian Identity*, in: R. Hvalvik/K.O. Sandnes (eds.), *Early Christian Prayer and Identity Formation*, Tübingen 2014, 35–56.

R. Hvalvik, *Praying with Outstretched Hands: Nonverbal Aspects of Early Christian Prayer and the Question of Identity*, in R. Hvalvik/K.O. Sandnes (eds.), *Early Christian Prayer and Identity Formation*, Tübingen 2014, 57–90

R. Hvalvik/K.O. Sandnes (eds.), *Early Christian Prayer and Identity Formation*, Tübingen 2014.

J. Hyldahl, *I Guds varetægt. Bønnens betydning for kristen identitet i den tidlige kirke*, in: Kritisk forum for praktisk teologi 116 (2009), 65–74.

E. Iricinschi/H.M. Zellentin (eds.), *Heresy and Identity in Late Antiquity*, TSAJ, Tübingen 2008.

I. Ißermann, *Did Christian Ethics have any Influence on the Conversion to Christianity?*, ZAC 16/1 (2012), 99–112.

A.C. Itter, *Esoteric Teaching in the Stromateis of Clement of Alexandria*, Leiden 2009.

A.C. Jacobsen, *Christ. The Teacher of Salvation. A Study on Origen's Christology and Soteriology*. Münster 2015.

E.F. Jay (ed.), *Origen's Treatise On Prayer*, London 1954.

R. Jenkins, *Rethinking Ethnicity, Arguments and Explorations*. Thousand Oaks 1997.

R. Jenkins, *Categorization: Identity, Social Process and Epistemology* in: Current Sociology 48(3) (2000), 7–25.

R. Jenkins, *Social Identity*, New York 2014.

W. Jenkins, *The Future of Ethics. Sustainability, Social Justice, and Religious Creativity*, Georgetown 2013.

M.E. Johnson, *The Rites of Christian Initiation: Their Evolution and Interpretation*, Collegeville 2007.

M.E. Johnson, *Praying and Believing in Early Christianity. The Interplay between Christian Worship and Doctrine*, Collegeville 2013.

S.I. Johnston (ed.), *Religions of the Ancient World. A Guide*, Cambridge 2004.

M. Kahlos, *Debate and Dialogue. Christian and Pagan Cultures c. 360–430*, Farnham 2007.

M. Kahlos, *The Faces of the Other. Religious Rivalry and Encounters in the Later Roman World*, Turnhout 2011.

J.A. Kapaló, *Text, Context and Performance. Gagauz Folk Religion in Discourse and Practice*, Leiden 2006.

B. Katzoff, *God of Our Fathers. Rabbinic Liturgy and Jewish-Christian Engagement*, in: JQR 99/3 (2009), 303–322.

P.I. Kaufman, *Prayer, Despair, and Drama. Elisabethian Introspection*, Champaign 1996.

C.S. Keener, *The Gospel of Matthew. A Socio-Rhetorical Commentary*, Grand Rapids 2009.

S. Kierkegaard (ed.), *The Sickness unto Death*, Princeton 1849/1943.

M.C. Kiley (ed.), *Prayer from Alexander to Constantine. A Critical Anthology*, London 1997.

R. Kimelman, *Birkat Ha-Minim and the Lack of Evidence for an Anti-Christian Jewish Prayer in Late Antiquity*, in: E.P. Sanders et al. (eds.), *Jewish and Christian Self-definition. Volume Two. Aspects of Judaism in the Graeco-Roman Period*, Philadelphia 1981, 226–244.

K.L. King, *What is Gnosticism?* Cambridge 2005.

S.J. Kistemaker, *The Lord's Prayer in the First Century*, in: JETS 21 (1978), 23–28.

G. Kittel (ed.), *Theological Dictionary of the New Testament*, Grand Rapids 1964.

H. Klein/V. Mihoc/K.W. Niebuhr (eds.), *Das Gebet im Neuen Testament. Vierte europäische orthodox-westliche Exegetenkonferenz in Sambata de Sus, 4.-8, August 2007*, Tübingen 2009.

D. Konstan, *Friendship in the Classical World*, Cambridge 1997.

T.J. Kraus, *Manuscripts with the Lord's Prayer. They Are More than Simply Witnesses to That Text Itself*, in: T.J. Kraus/T. Nicklas (eds.), *New Testament Manuscripts*, Leiden 2006, 227–266.

D. Krueger, *Liturgical Subjects. Christian Ritual, Biblical Narrative, and the Formation of the Self in Byzantium*, Philadelphia 2014.

K.L. Ladd/B. Spilka, *Inward, Outward, and Upward: Cognitive Aspects of Prayer* in: JSSR 41/3 (2002), 475–484.

N. DeLange, *Origen and the Jews*, Cambridge 1976.

R. Langer, *Cursing the Christians. A History of the Birkat HaMinim*, Oxford 2011.

J. Laporte, *Philonic Models of Eucharistia in the Eucharist of Origen*, in: LTP 41/1 (1986), 71–91.

G.W. Lathrop, *Holy People. A Liturgical Ecclesiology*, Minneapolis 2006.

M.R. Leary, *Handbook of Self and Identity*, New York 2003.

J. Leonhardt, *Jewish Worship in Philo of Alexandria*, Tübingen 2001.

I. Levinskaya, *A Jewish or Gentile Prayer House? The meaning of ΠΡΟΣΕΥΧΗ*, in: TynB 41/1 (1990), 154–159.

A. Lewin, *The Archaeology of Ancient Judea and Palestine*, Los Angeles 2005, 33.

C.T. Lewis/C. Short, *A Latin Dictionary*, Oxford 1879.

H.G. Liddell/R. Scott/H.S. Jones et al. (eds.), *Liddell–Scott–Jones. Greek-English Lexicon (LSJ)*, Oxford 1950.

S. Lieberman, *Greek in Jewish Palestine*, New York City 1942.

J. Lieu, *Christian Identity in the Jewish and Greco-Roman World*, Oxford 2004.

R.N. Longenecker, *Into God's Presence. Prayer in the New Testament*, Grand Rapids 2001.

A. Louth, *The Origins of the Christian Mystical Tradition*, Oxford 1981.

H. Luther, "Identität und Fragment," *Religion und Alltag*, Stuttgart 1992, 160–182.

T.J. Marinello/H.H.D. Williams, *My Brother's Keeper. Essays in Honor of Ellis R. Brotzman*, Eugene 2010.

C. Markschies, *Zwischen den Welten wandern. Strukturen des antiken Christentums*, Frankfurt am Main 1997.

C. Markschies, *Gnosis. An Introduction*, London 2003.

C. Markschies, *Hohe Theologie und schlichte Frömmigkeit? Einige Beobachtungen zum Verhältnis von Theologie und Frömmigkeit in der Antike*, in: H. Grieser/A. Merkt (eds.), *Volksglaube im antiken Christentum*, Darmstadt 2009, 456–471.

D.G. Martinez, *The Papyri and Early Christianity*, in: R.S. Bagnall (ed.), *The Oxford Handbook of Papyrology*, Oxford 2009, 590–622.

B. McGinn, *The Foundations of Mysticism. Origins to the Fifth Century*, New York 1991.

J.A. McGuckin, *The Westminster Handbook to Origen*, Louisville 2004.

J. McKenzie, *The Architecture of Alexandria and Egypt. C. 300 B.C. to A.D. 700*, vol. 63, Yale 2007.

G.H. Mead, *Mind, Self & Society. From a Standpoint of a Social Behaviorist*, in C.W. Morris (ed.), Chicago 1967.

A.M. Méhat, *Etude sur les 'Stromates' de Clement d'Alexandrie*, Éditions du Seuil Collection Patristica Sorbonensia, Paris 1966.

A.M. Méhat, *Sur deux définitions de la prière*, in G. Dorival/A. Le Boulluec (eds.), *Origeniana Sexta*, Louvain 1995, 115–120.

W.A. Meeks, *The Origins of Christian Morality. The First Two Centuries*, New Haven 1993.

E. Menn, *Prayer of the Queen: Esther's Religious Self in the Septuagint*, in: D. Brakke/M. Satlow/S. Weitzman (eds.), *Religion and the Self in Antiquity*, Bloomington 2005, 70–90.

K. Michelsen et al., *Filosofisk Leksikon*, København 2008.

P.C. Miller, *Strategies of Representation in Collective Biography: Constructing the Subject as Holy*, in: T. Hägg/P. Rousseau (eds.), *Greek Biography and Panegyrics in Late Antiquity*, Oakland 2000, 209–254.

P.C. Miller, *Shifting Selves in Late Antiquity*, in: D. Brakke/M. Satlow/S. Weitzman (eds.), *Religion and the Self in Antiquity*, Bloomington 2005.

R. Mortley, *The theme of Silence in Clement of Alexandria*, in: JThS 24 (1973), 197–202.

R. Mortley, *From Word to Silence: The Rise and Fall of Logos*, Bonn 1986.

H. Moxnes, *Det kristne menneske. Konstruksjon av ny identitet i antikken*, in: Norsk Teologisk Tidsskrift 1 (2003), 3–7.

E. Muehlberger, *Angels in Late Ancient Christianity*, Oxford 2013.

J. Neuser/E.S. Frerichs (eds.), *"To See Ourselves as Others See Us." Christians, Jews, "Others" in Late Antiquity*, Decatur, GA 1985.

J.H. Neyrey, *Prayer, In Other Words. A Social Science Model for Interpreting Prayers*, in: J.J. Pilch (ed.), *Social Scientific Models for Interpreting the Bible: Essays by the Context Group in Honor of Bruce J. Malina*, Leiden 2001, 349–380.

B. Nongbri, *The Lord's Prayer and ΧΜΓ. Two Christian Papyrus Amulets*, in: Harvard Theological Review 104 (2011), 59–68.

M.C. Nussbaum, *The Therapy of Desire. Theory and Desire in Hellenistic Ethics*, Princeton 1994.

C. O'Brien, *Prayer in Maximus of Tyre*, in: J. Dillon/A. Timotin (eds.), *Platonic Theories of Prayer*, Boston 2016, 58–72.

T. O'Loughlin, *The Didache and Early Christian Communities*, in: K.J O'Mahony (ed.), *Christian Origins. Worship, Belief, and Society. The Milltown Institute and the Irish Biblical Association Millennium Conference*, London 2003, 83–112.

R.E. Olson, *The Story of Christian Theology. Twenty Centuries of Tradition & Reform*, Downers Grove 1999.

E. Osborn, *Clement of Alexandria*, Cambridge 2005.

C. Osborne, *Clement of Alexandria*, in: L. Gerson (ed.), *The Cambridge History of Philosophy in Late Antiquity*, Cambridge 2010, 270–282.

K.H. Ostmeyer, *Das Vaterunser: Gründe für seine Durchsetzung als 'Urgebet' der Christenheit*, in: NTS 50/3 (2004), 320–333.

K.H. Ostmeyer, *Kommunikation mit Gott und Christus: Sprache und Theologie des Gebetes im Neuen Testament*, Tübingen 2006.

M. Ott, *Thundering Legion*, in: CE 14, New York 1912.

W.R. Owens (ed.), *John Bunyan. The Pilgrim's Progress*, Oxford 2009.

B.A. Paschke, *Tertullian on Liturgical Prayer to Christ. New Insights from De Spect. 25.5 and Apol. 2.6*, in: VigChr 66 (2012), 20–29.

M. Patzelt, *The Rhetoric of Roman Prayer. A Proposal for a Lived Religion Approach*, in: RRE 4 (2018), 162–186.

M. Patzelt, *Über das Beten der Römer. Gebete im spätrepublikanischen und frühkaiserzeitlichen Rom als Ausdruck gelebter Religion*, Berlin/ Boston 2018.

B.A. Pearson, *Theurgic Tendencies in Gnosticism and Iamblichus's Conception of Theurgy*, in: R.T. Wallis/J. Bregman, *Neoplatonism and Gnosticism*, Albany 1992, 253–275.

M. Penn, *Performing Family. Ritual Kissing and the Construction of Early Christian Kinship*, in: JECS 10/2 (2002), 151–174.

J. Perkins, *Perpetua's vas. Asserting Christian Identity*, in: É. Rebillard/J. Rüpke (eds.), *Group Identity and Religious Individuality in Late Antiquity*, Washington, D.C. 2015, 129–163.

L. Perrone, *Prayer in Origen's Contra Celsum. The Knowledge of God and the Truth of Christianity*, in: VigChr, 55/1 (2001), 1–19.

L. Perrone, *Prayer and the Construction of Religious Identity in Early Christianity*, in: POC 53 (2003), 260–288.

L. Perrone, *Zur Edition von Perì Euchês des Origenes. Rückblich und Ausblich*, Berlin 2009.

L. Perrone, *For the Sake of a 'Rational Worship'. The Issue of Prayer and Cult in Early Christian Apologetics*, in: A.-C. Jakobsen/J. Ulrich/D. Brakke (eds.), *Critique and Apologetics. Jews, Christians and Pagans in Antiquity*, Frankfurt 2009, 231–264.

L. Perrone, *La preghiera secondo Origene. L'impossibilità donata*, Letteratura Cristiana Antica. Nuova Serie 24, Brescia 2011.

L. Perrone, *Clemens von Alexandrien und Origenes zum Gebet. Versuch eines Paradigmenvergleichs anhand ihrer Schriftstellen*, in: M. Havrda/V. Hušek/J. Plátova (eds.), *The Seventh Book of the Stromateis. Proceedings of the Colloquium on Clement of Alexandria*, Leiden 2011, 143–164.

L. Perrone, *Origenes' Rede vom Gebet zwischen Frömmigkeit und Theologie.: zur Rezeption von Peri euchēs in der modernen Forschung*, in: A. Fürst (ed.), *Origenes und sein Erbe im Orient und Okzident*, Adamantiana: Texte und Studien zu Origenes in seinem Erbe 1, Münster 2011, 101–128.

L. Perrone, *Die Zukunft der Patristik. Überlegungen und Hoffnungen aus Vergangenheit und Gegenwart*, in: FZPhTh 60 (2013), 5–19.

P. Phemister (ed.), *John Locke. An Essay Concerning Human Understanding 1690*, Oxford 2008.

L.E. Phillips, *Prayer in the first Four Centuries AD*, in: R. Hammerling (ed.), *A History of Prayer. The First to the Fifteenth Century*, Leiden 2008, 32–46.

W.S.F. Pickering (ed.), *Marcel Mauss. La Prière. 1909*, New York 2003.

J.C. Plumpe, *Mater Ecclesia. An Inquiry into the Concept of the Church as Mother in Early Christianity*, Washington 1943.

D.I. Rankin, *From Clement to Origen. The Social and Historical Context of the Church Fathers*, Farnham 2006.

C.H. Ratschow *Gebet I. Religionsgeschichtlich*, in: TRE 12 (1984), 31–34.

É. Rebillard, *Christians and Their Many Identities in Late Antiquity, North Africa, 200–450 CE*, New York 2012.

É. Rebillard/J. Rüpke, *Group Identity and Religious Individuality in Late Antiquity*, Washington, D.C. 2015.

M. Recinová, *Clement's Angelological doctrines: Between Jewish Models and Philosophic-Religious Streams of Late Antiquity*, in: M. Havrda/V. Hušek/J. Plátova (eds.), *The Seventh Book of the Stromateis. Proceedings of the Colloquium on Clement of Alexandria*, Leiden 2012, 93–112.

L.T. Reynolds/N.J. Herman-Kinney (eds.), *Handbook of Symbolic Interactionism*, Walnut Creek, CA 2003.

C. Riggs (ed.), *The Oxford Handbook of Roman Egypt*, Oxford 2012.

Ritualbog. København 1992.

J.M. Rist, *Plotinus. Road to Reality*, Cambridge 1967.

J.B. Rives, *Religion and Authority in Roman Carthage from Augustus to Constantine*, Oxford 1995.

J.B. Rives, *Religion in the Roman empire*, in: J. Huskinson (ed.), *Experiencing Rome. Culture, Identity and Power in the Roman Empire*, Oxford 1999, 245–276.

E.R. Roberts, *The Theology of Tertullian*, London 1924.

L. Roberts, *The Literary Form of the Stromateis*, in: SecCen 1 (1981), 211–222.

W. Rordorf, *The Lord's Prayer in the Light of Its Liturgical Use in the Early Church*, in: StLi 14 (1980/81), 1–19.

G. Rouwhorst., *Identität durch Gebet. Gebetstexte als Zeugen eines jahrhundertelangen Ringens um Kontinuität und Differenz zwischen*

Judentum und Christentum, in: A. Gerhards/A. Doeker/P. Ebenbauer (eds.), *Identität durch Gebet. Zur gemeinschaftsbildenden Funktion institutionalisierten Betens in Judentum und Christentum*, Paderborn 2003.

D.T. Runia, *Philo in Early Christian Literature. A Survey*. Assen 1993.

D.T. Runia, *The Pre-Christian Origin of Early Christian Spirituality*, in: P. Allen/W. Mayer/L. Cross (eds.), *Prayer and Spirituality in the Early Church II*, Brisbane 1999.

J.E. Salisbury, *Perpetua's Passion. The Death and Memory of a Young Roman Woman*, Oxford 2013.

J. Rüpke (ed.), *The Individual in the Religions of the Ancient Mediterranean*, Oxford 2013.

R.P. Saller *Patriarchy, Property and Death in the Roman Family*, Cambridge 1996.

K.O. Sandnes, *The First Prayer. Pater Noster in the Early Church*, in: R. Hvalvik/K.O. Sandnes (eds.), *Early Christian Prayer and Identity Formation*, Tübingen 2014, 209–232.

M.L. Satlow, *Giving for a Return. Jewish Votive Offerings in Late Antiquity*, in: D. Brakke/M. Satlow/S. Weitzman (eds.), *Religion and the Self in Antiquity*, Bloomington 2005, 91–108.

P. Schäfer (ed.), *The Talmud Yerushalmi and Graeco-Roman Culture*, Tübingen 1998.

D. Schleyer (ed.), *Tertullian. De baptismo, De oratione/Von der Taufe, vom Gebet*, Turnhout 2006.

K.B. Schnurr, *Hören und Handeln. Lateinische Auslegungen des Vaterunsers in der Alten Kirche bis zum 5. Jahrhundert*, Freiburg 1985.

A. Scott, *Origen and the Life of the Stars. A History of an Idea*, Oxford 1994.

K. Seddon, *Epictetus' Handbook and the Tablet of Cebes. Guides to Stoic Living*, Oxford 2006.

E. Severus, *Gebet I*, in: T. Klauser (ed.), RAC 8. Stuttgart 1972.

D. Sheerin, *The Role of Prayer in Origen's Homilies*, in: C. Kannengiesser/W.L. Petersen (eds.), *Origen of Alexandria. His World and his Legacy*, Notre Dame 1988.

K. Shillington, *Encyclopedia of African History*, Abingdon 2005.

P. Sigal, *Early Christian and Rabbinic Liturgical Affinities. Exploring Liturgical Acculturation*, in: NTS 30/1 (1984), 63–90.

R.I. Simpson, *The Interpretation of Prayer in the Early Church*, London 1965.

D. Smit, *Worship – and civil Society? Perspectives from a Reformed Tradition in South Africa*, in: W.F. Storrar et al. (eds.), *A World for All? Global Civil Society in Political Theory and Trinitarian Theology*, Grand Rapids 2011.

B.D. Spinks, *The Place of Christ in Liturgical Prayer. Trinity, Christology, and Liturgical Theology*, Collegeville 2008.

P. Stachel, *Identität. Genese, Inflation und Probleme eines für die zeitgenössischen Sozial- und Kulturwissenschaften zentralen Begriffs*, in: AKuG 87/2 (2005), 395–425.

R. Stark, *The Rise of Christianity. A Sociologist Reconsiders History*, Princeton 1996.

M.C. Steenberg, *Impatience and Humanity's Sinful State in Tertullian of Carthage*, in: VigChr 62/2 (2008), 107–132.

P. Stengel, *Die griechischen Kultusaltertümer*, München 1898.

K.B. Stern, *Inscribing Devotion and Death. Archaelogical Evidence for Jewish Populations of North Africa*, Leiden 2007.

J.W. Sterrett, *Re-reading Early Modern Prayer as Social Act. Examples from Shakespeare*, in: Literature Compass 10/6 (2013), 496–507.

C. Stewart, *Prayer*, in: S.A. Harvey/D.G. Hunter (eds.), *The Oxford Handbook of Early Christian Studies*, Oxford 2008, 744–763.

A. Stewart-Sykes, *On the Lord's Prayer. Tertullian, Cyprian, Origen*, Yonkers 2004.

M.B. von Stritzky, *Studien zur Überlieferung und Interpretation des Vaterunsers in der frühchristlichen Literatur*, Münster 1989.

M.B. von Stritzky, *Gebet und Tat im christlichen Alltag. Gedanken früher Kirchenväter*, in: H. Grieser/A. Merkt (eds.), *Volksglaube im antiken Christentum*, Darmstadt 2009.

G. Stroumsa, *Caro salutis cardo. Shaping the Person in Early Christian Thought*, in: HR 30 (1990), 25–50.

G. Stroumsa/J. Assmann (eds.), *Transformations of the Inner Self in Ancient Religions*, Leiden 1999.

G. Stroumsa/D. Schulman (eds.), *Self and Self-Transformation in the History of Religions*, Oxford 2002.

G. Stroumsa, *The End of Sacrifice. Religious Transformations in Late Antiquity*, Chicago 2009.

S. Stryker, *From Mead to a Structural Symbolic Interactionism and Beyond*, in: Annual Review of Sociology 34 (2008), 15–31.

R. Taft, *The Liturgy of the Hours in East and West, The Origins and Its Meaning for Today*, Collegeville 1993.

K. Tanner, *Theories of Culture. A New Agenda for Theology*, Minneapolis 1997.

M.S. Tayler, *Anti-Judaism and Early Christian Identity. A Critique of the Scholarly Consensus*, Leiden 1995.

T.N. Tentler, *Sin and Confession on the Eve of the Reformation*, Princeton 1977.

M. Thellbe, *Prayer and Identity*, in: R. Hvalvik/K.O. Sandnes (eds.), *Early Christian Prayer and Identity Formation*, Tübingen 2014, 115–136.

K.J. Torjesen, *Hermeneutical Procedure and Theological Method in Origen's Exegesis*, Berlin 1985.

M. B. Trapp, *Maximus of Tyre. The Philosophical Orations*, Oxford 1997.

J. Turner et al. (eds.), *The Actuality of Sacrifice. Past and Present*, Leiden 2014.

J.H. Turner, *Contemporary Sociological Theory*, Thousand Oakes, CA 2013.

J.C. Turner/P.J. Oakes/S.A. Haslam/C. McGarty, "Self and collective: Cognition and social context." *Personality and Social Psychology Bulletin*, 20/5, 1994, 454–463.

A. Twigg, *Strong Voices: Conversations with Fifty Canadian Authors*, Madeira Park 1988.

H.S. Versnel (ed.), *Faith, Hope and Worship. Aspects of Religious Mentality in the Ancient World*, Leiden 1981.

A. de Vogüé, *Psalmodier n'est pas Prier*, in: EO 6 (1989), 7–32.

F.E. Vokes, *The Lord's Prayer in the First Three Centuries*, StPatr 10 (1970), 255–260.

U. Volp, *Liturgical Authority Reconsidered: Remarks on the Bishops Role in Pre-Constantinian Worship*, in: B. Neil/G.D. Dunn/L. Cross (eds.), *Prayer and Spirituality in the Early Church. Liturgy and Life 3,* Strathfield 2003.

W. Völker, *Das Vollkommenheitsideal des Origenes,* Tübingen 1931.

K.D. Vryan, P.A. Adler/P. Adler, *Identity,* in: L.T. Reynolds/N.J. Herman-Kinney (eds.), *Handbook of Symbolic Interactionism,* Walnut Creek, CA 2003, 367–391

R.T. Wallis/J. Bregman, *Neoplatonism and Gnosticism,* Albany 1992.

M. Wallraff, *Christus verus Sol. Sonnenverehrung und Christentum in der Spätantike,* Münster 2001.

W. Webber, *Early Christian Views of the Lord's Prayer,* in: T.J. Marinello/H.H.D. Williams (eds.), *My Brother's Keeper. Essays in Honor of Ellis R. Brotzman,* Eugene 2010, 61–77.

K. Weitzmann (ed.), *Age of Spirituality. Late Antique and Early Christian Art, Third to Seventh Century,* New York 1980.

C. Westermann, *Lob und Klage in den Psalmen,* Göttingen 1983.

G. Winkler, *The Sanctus. Some Observations with Regard to Its Origins and Theological Significance,* in: B. Neil/G.D. Dunn/L. Cross (eds.), *Prayer and Spirituality in the Early Church. Liturgy and Life 3,* Strathfield 2003.

S. Willert, *George Herbert Mead and Sören Kierkegaard as theorists of the self. Paper presented at SAAP,* Annual Conference (Society for the Advancement of American Philosophy), Spokane 2011.

D.E. Wilhite, *Tertullian the African. An Anthropological Reading of Tertullian's Context and Identities,* Berlin 2007.

H. Wittaker, *The Purpose of Porphyry's Letter to Marcella,* in: SO 76/1 (2010), 150–168.

G.D. Woolf, *Ritual and the Individual in Roman Religion,* in: J. Rüpke (ed.), *The Individual in the Religions of the Ancient Mediterranean,* Oxford 2013, 136–160.

F. Young, *Sacrifice and the death of Christ,* London 1975.

F.M. Young, *From Suspicion and Sociology to Spirituality. On Method, Hermeneutics and Appropriation with Respect to Patristic Material,* in: StPatr 29 (1997), 421–435.

F. Young et al. (eds.), *The Cambridge History of Early Christian Literature,* Cambridge 2004.

I. J. Yuval: *The Other in Us. Liturgica, Poetica, Polemica*, in E. Iricinschi/H.M. Zellentin, *Heresy and Identity in Late Antiquity*, Tübingen 2008, 364–385.

T. Zahavy, *Kavvanah (Concentration) for Prayer in the Mishnah and Talmud*, in: J. Neuser/R.A. Horsley/E.S. Frerichs/P. Borgen (eds.), *New Perspectives on Ancient Judaism. Religion, Literature, & Society in Ancient Israel, Formative Christianity & Judaism*, Lanham, MD 1987.

General Index

Early Christianity in the Context of Antiquity

Edited by Anders-Christian Jacobsen, Christine Shepardson, Jörg Ulrich

The series ECCA (Early Christianity in the Context of Antiquity) seeks to publish monographs and edited volumes that take as their theme early Christianity and its connections with the religion(s) and culture(s) of antiquity and late antiquity. Special attention is given to the interactions between religion and culture, as well as to the influences that diverse religions and cults had on one another. Works published in ECCA extend chronologically from the second century B.C.E. to the fifth century C.E. and geographically across the expanse of the Roman empire and its immediate neighbors.

Die Reihe ECCA (Early Christianity in the Context of Antiquity) zielt auf die Publikation von Monographien und Sammelbänden, die sich thematisch mit dem frühen Christentum und seinen Beziehungen zu Religion(en) und Kultur(en) der Antike und Spätantike befassen. Dabei gilt das besondere Augenmerk den Wechselwirkungen, die Religion und Kultur aufeinander ausüben, sowie den Einflüssen, die die verschiedenen Religionen und Kulte aufeinander hatten. Zeitlich erstrecken sich die in ECCA publizierten Arbeiten auf das 2. Jh. v. Chr. bis zum 5. Jh. n.Chr., geographisch auf den Raum des Imperium Romanum und seiner unmittelbaren Nachbarn.

www.peterlang.com